REMASTERED

ON CULTURAL ISLAM

A Godbody Sociology of 1990s Black America

SHAHIDI COLLECTION VOL 3

Shahidi Islam

Copyright © 2024, 2026 by Shahidi Islam.
All rights reserved. No part of this book may be reproduced in any form or by any electronic or mechanical means, including information storage and retrieval systems, without permission in writing from the publisher, except by reviewers, who may quote brief passages in a review.

This publication has been made to provide accurate and authoritative information with regard to the subject matter discussed. It is sold with the understanding that neither the publisher nor the author are engaging in the offering of medical, psychological, or sociological service. If any of the above are required a competent professional person should be consulted.

All quotations provided throughout this book are strictly for the purpose of education and research, and fall well into the guidelines of fair dealing. Fair dealing is recognised in Canada, the United Kingdom, and Australia and allows for individuals, researchers, musicians, educators, and authors to use copyrighted material without permission from the copyright owner.

Book Ordering Information
Cover design provided by: https://www.fiverr.com/patrick_2013
Email: shahidiislam@godbodyinternational.com
https://godbodyinternational.com

Attention African American Theologians!!!

Introducing the Revolutionary New Way of Understanding Black Theology

Black Divinity: A Ghetto Theology for the Black Community [Remastered] is the first instalment in Shahidi Islam's Shahidi Collection revealing the depths of street spirituality and the theological genius of Black thearchic principles.

Black Divinity

This book is dedicated to those who
seek after righteousness.
May your quest be fulfilled in the
world of the *tawhid*.

On Cultural Islam:

A Godbody Sociology of 1990s Black America

Preface to Shahidi Edition	vii
Introduction	ix
1. Where Do We Go From Here	1
2. Neoliberalism and the Imperial State	55
3. Post-Colonialism in Africa	109
4. The Spectre of Marxism	164
5. A New Philosophy of Man	216
6. Resistance Through Sensuality	274
7. The Divine Parousia	331
8. Conclusion	384
9. Afterward	389
10. Bibliography	394

Preface to Shahidi Edition

For those who remember this book when it was still called *Manifesting the Divine* I must explain the need for this rewrite. See, I no longer go under the name Tony Saunders, which name is my slave name. My righteous name is now my government name properly and formally, and that is Shahidi Islam. For this reason I am rereleasing some of my former works under my new name so as to certify them. I have lots of other writings in circulation that go under the name Tony Saunders, some of which I am quite ashamed of. If you have found or read one of them please feel free to discard it. If it is not a book or writing under the name Shahidi Islam it is not something I am endorsing. Besides, Tony Saunders is a popular name and there are a few other authors by that name who have their own following. To separate myself from them and to permanently remove the embarrassment of my former works I have chosen to release this Shahidi Collection featuring a correct explication of my doctrine as it stands. Again, if it is not a work found either with the author name Shahidi Islam or endorsed by Shahidi Islam then I do not endorse what is written therein, even if it is one of my own former writings, as some of them have ideas I no longer endorse or agree with. To wipe the slate clean and to endorse ideas that I do agree with look out for upcoming books and articles from Shahidi Islam, this

PREFACE TO SHAHIDI EDITION

Shahidi Collection is itself a precursor. As this book is in the Shahidi Collection not only am I endorsing it, but it is a part of my very philosophy and outlook of life. Therefore, I believe in what is written in these pages and believe the Black community would benefit substantially by paying close attention to what is being said.

Historically Sufism has appeared in many guises from Muridi, to Sammani, to Qadiri, to Idrisi. These expressions have for the most part challenged traditional Islam by emphasising the spiritual element within the Islamic tradition. In this regard godbodyism is no different. Though not currently recognised as a Sufi order, and I as a Catholic am in no position to create one, godbodyism traces its roots to Islam and culturally identifies itself with Islam. Though we definitely do not identify ourselves with any religious movement, our own cultural Islam will remain but a mere façade to those who have no knowledge of its roots in the Islamic tradition. It thereby becomes relegated to the abyss of repetitious wordplay. To escape from this trap of unconscious ignorance and cultural irrelevance I feel that our connection to Islamic sources, and particularly within the Sufi tradition, must be made acknowledged not only by our members but also by the current practitioners of Sufism. In this case, though being fundamentally different in many ways to some variants of Sufism, we are still very much so worthy of being considered even as other *tariqa* (paths or orders) such as the Khatwatiyya, the Shadhiliyya, the Sammaniyya, the Qadiriyya, and the Mawlawiyya, so that godbodyism, that is, thearchism, can be accepted, not only as a Sufi tradition, or as simply a worthy form of Islam, but as the best and most noble form of Islam: even as Allah's ultimate intention for humanity.

Introduction

I am a Black Divine. I have moved beyond consciousness and nationalism. I seek that Islamic anarchism, chaotic astralism, and theocentric revolutionism that is inspired only by libido. The orientation of this book is based on Black Divinity, which I see as a philosophical outlook nuanced from White Charismatism in that it is based on intersubjectivity, irrationality, sensuality, and creativity and is in opposition to objectivism, rationalism, materialism, and determinism – though White Charismatism is itself based on emotion, worship, belief, imagination, subjectivism, obedience, and good behaviour. My nuanced version of Divinity (*ilahaniyya*) shall be further fleshed out as the reader proceeds through the pages of this work, but for now it should be acknowledged that my interpretation of the godbody 120 lessons is not orthodox and I apply various subtle expedients to show how 120 can be taken to the next level of elevation. This is a godbody book and I have written it mainly for godbodies, but it is also a sociological book which will hopefully also be read by academics and intellectuals. Whatever the case, it has been written and now it is up to the reader to do what they consider right.

Though in most versions of the 120 lessons it does not mention the godbody there is a strand of the 1-14 that says, "What is godbody? This is the name of the militant vanguard who belong to the Nation of Gods and Earths." This is an erroneous lesson but it does have significance. As the Fruit of Islam has captains, lieutenants, and soldiers so every member of the godbody too is either a captain, lieutenant, or soldier; and as we are all also members of the Nation of Gods and Earths we obviously hold to all the teachings of the Nation of Gods and Earths too.

Basically, though the statement may not be 120 it is still a true statement. But if we godbody truly see ourselves as part of the Nation of Gods and Earths then we also see ourselves as Gods and Earths, though in the relatively figurative sense of the terms. Not that the Black woman is literally Mother Earth or that in calling Black men Gods we believe that we are literally the God, but that we are in the figurative sense the most divine manifestations of the Godhead. Incidentally, as all godbodies are by definition cultural Muslims I must also confess that most of us are non-religious; we are therefore able to see through the religious practices and ideas of the various faith traditions understanding self and all Original people to be manifestations of the God of the Hebrews: Judeans, Christians, Muslims, and Rastas.

The majority of the chapters of this book, however, were written as a practical reference to a new sociological model: a form of critical social science that I call the godbody model. This model combines ideas and assumptions from Islamic sociology and depth psychology with axioms derived from post-Marxian philosophies and classical Newtonian physics. Herein, the central argument of the godbody perspective is that the enmity and gulf between the natural sciences and the human sciences (in particular the social sciences) need not exist. While it is appreciated that social sciences should use subjective – and, indeed, intersubjective – methods when conducting research, which is unnecessary in the natural sciences, we also note that applied scientific and mathematic abstractions are possible even within social sciences. At the same time, case studies will be the main examples used by the godbody sociologist as our research will mainly be conducted using intersubjective methods: in particular participant observation. By using a form of mechanical analysis godbody sociology is primarily a study of astral forces, social forces, global forces, and environmental forces – and as the primordial astral force is unconscious energy, the primordial social force is a collective conscious and unconscious energy, the primordial global force is some global ethic, and the primordial environmental force is ecological harmony, godbody sociology seeks to explain all these with the framework of living libido.

Notwithstanding, the contents of this book were not simply written to annunciate the intricacies of ethno-Divinity or of the godbody perspective, they have also been written to articulate the anthropology of a particular time: the 1990s. Obviously, it is not a full or exhaustive anthropology of that time – a task that would take volumes, perhaps even encyclopaedia – but it is a recollection of certain social and global activities that took place during that momentous epoch in global history and their relation to the experiences of Black America. In this sense, I shall be applying ethnographic signs and texts to show how the extrapolated information relates to the time in question. Conversely, in both sociological and anthropological schools there is an application of various combinations of ethnographic and historiographic information used for theoretical constructs: sociologists of society and anthropologists of cultures (if one forgives the oversimplification). In this particular anthropology, as culture is constantly being contested (Clifford 1986), the autobiographical ethnography is an attempt not merely to explain certain subtleties of

INTRODUCTION

godbody sociology but also to advance the godbody movement – to take it out of the backstreet so to speak.

Yet as an autobiographical ethnography this book must be read in the context of various conversations about certain events that transpired during the 1990s. This is mainly based on debates and arguments I experienced with certain associates of mine in Brooklyn, New York. In particular one young man stands out, we will call him Questepher. Questepher was one of my closest associates and best friends. As we went to the same high school we met every weekday over a couple of years to smoke weed, rap, and talk about global issues. Talking about these sorts of issues while we were high made us think we were scholars, but really most of our theories were ridiculous, incoherent, and inconsistent. Also, none of them came to pass as we predicted them. However, these were the best conversations I remember having, and I loved them.

The seven main themes of this book go into the seven most powerful topics we discussed and present a much better, more thorough examination of the subject. These seven topics are: (i) The relevance of the Nation of Islam, (ii) Clintonian politics, (iii) poverty in Africa, (iv) the power of Russia, (v) the significance of Islamic rebellion, (vi) R&B girl groups, and (vi) the rapper Nas and his Last Days theories. Questepher and I met to discuss these topics over a period of two years in the late 1990s before I left New York and began my travels. These seven topics lingered in my subconscious, and as you can see I still talk about them today, even though we spoke on many other subjects over that two year period.

Although in presenting my exploration of these topics and themes I will be using many academic terms, concepts, and ideas throughout, this book has not technically been written to be an academic work in itself, so I have foregone

INTRODUCTION

the academic prerequisites for a more personal approach. I have chosen to write in this manner to make this work more relatable and less formal. This book is a work of critical social science using mechanical analysis for its overall methodology; *observant participation* (Wacquant 2008) for its primary sources; and Scriptures, revolutionists, sociologists, psychologists, and theologians for its secondary sources.

Still, as a disclaimer I must acknowledge at this point that while I may be a fellow of the Society for the Study of Theology (SST), I cannot stress enough that none of the ideas, opinions, or recommendations I suggest are those of the SST nor of the other First Born of London. They are all a result of personal development and analogical research. As there is no separation of the man from his theories my affiliation to the godbody counter-culture bursts through with some of these ideas and my revolutionism comes out in others. Even so, all praises due to you all and peace from the Maker Allah. Bismillah, Amin.

The Supreme Mathematics

Potentials

k = knowledge (1)

w = wisdom (2)

u = understanding (3)

f = freedom – I choose not to add culture as freedom is the most obvious elevation from understanding and culture is implied in the whole mathematics (4)

p = power – (I use the term power neither in the Marxian sense, as in to dominate nor in the Foucauldian sense, as in to discipline or surveille; but instead use it in the Adlerian sense as in empowerment) I choose not to add refinement as power is the next elevation from freedom and progresses till it reaches equality (5)

e = equality (6)

G = God – where God is equivalent to the omnipresent, and not to a state of pure perfection (7)

B = build – when adding on (8)

D = destroy – when subtracting (8)

$\forall$ = born (9)

$°$ = cipher (0)

INTRODUCTION

Symbols

D = dialectical moment where *pa* > *na* becomes *na* > *pa*, or vice versa.

Lm = the limitation

$\exists$ = when there is

$+$ = together with

$\in$ = the sum includes

$>$ = greater than

$\geq$ = greater than or equal to

$<$ = lesser then

$\leq$ = lesser than or equal to

$\rightarrow$ = leads on to

$\leftrightarrow$ = if and only if

$\nearrow$ = on the increase

$\searrow$ = on the decrease

$\propto$ = proportional to

Values

∞ = infinity

INTRODUCTION

o = zero

λ = wavelength

A = amplitude

d = displacement

t = time expended

v = rate of velocity

δ = astral forces $-> x^1$

α = social forces $-> x^{10}$

β = global forces $-> x^{20}$

θ = environmental forces $-> x^{30}$

ϕ = terrestrial forces (also called geomagnetic forces) $-> x^{40}$

ϑ = solar forces (also called heliospheric magnetic forces) $-> x^{50}$

∂ = globular forces (also called stellar magnetic forces) $-> x^{60}$

φ = galactic forces (also called galactic magnetic forces) $-> x^{70}$

INTRODUCTION

ψ = super-clusteral forces (also called intercluster magnetic forces) $\to x^{80}$

ε = cosmic forces $\to x^{90}$

Pa = positive action of an individual

pa = positive action of a social body

Na = negative action of an individual

na = negative action of a social body

x = social potential of a social body

n = level of social potentiality

g = a social movement

$opp.g$ = an oppressing social movement

$emp.g$ = an empowering social movement

(pa) = all the positive actions of a social body

(na) = all the negative actions of a social body

(v) = all the social velocity

(g) = the whole social movement

S = decelerative force caused by reaction of social body x_1

INTRODUCTION

R = accelerative force caused by resistance of social body x_2

S = syndicalism

The Godbody System

The Universal Laws of Existence

1. The law of interaction (whose corollary is the pleasure principle),

2. The law of intersubjectivity (whose corollary is the vibratory law),

3. The law of self-organisation (whose corollary is the identity law),

4. The law of opposition (whose corollary is the polarity law),

5. The law of repetition (whose corollary is the inertia law),

6. The law of self-similarity (whose corollary is the correspondence law),

7. The law of conservation (whose corollary is the reciprocity law),

8. The law of evolution (whose corollary is the power law),

INTRODUCTION

9. The law of devolution (whose corollary is the entropy law),

10. The law of self-destruction (whose corollary is the phase-transition law),

11. The law of interconnectivity (whose corollary is the synchronicity law), and

12. The law of interrelation (whose corollary is the eternalist law).

The 10 Principles

1. No God but Allah

2. No power imbalances

3. No non-authors

4. No non-fighters

5. No Divine fights alone

6. No problems handled in the Square should ever leave the Square

7. No marriage or marriages

8. No missing parliament meetings

9. No wearing underwear

INTRODUCTION

10. No harassment or rape of any kind ever

What We Teach

1. That Black people are the Original people of the planet earth.

2. That Black people are the fathers and mothers of civilization.

3. That the science of Supreme Mathematics is the key to understanding man's relationship to the universe.

4. That Islam is a natural way of life, not a religion.

5. That education should be fashioned to enable us to be self sufficient as a people.

6. That each one should teach one according to their knowledge.

7. That the Black man is god and his proper name is ALLAH. Arm, Leg, Leg, Arm, Head.

8. That our children are our link to the future and they must be nurtured, respected, loved, protected and educated.

9. That the unified Black family is the vital building block of the nation.

INTRODUCTION

The Hedgehog Concept (The Build Allah Square)

1. Eat, Train, Read, Write, and Share

The Core Concepts

1. Black divinity, Black revolutionism, Black eroticism, Black astralism, Black demodernisation, and Black syndicalism

The Physical Concepts

1. biophysics, quantum physics, molecular physics, geophysics, astrophysics, and digital physics

The Discursive Concepts

1. body, embody, and disembody

2. structure, infrastructure, and superstructure

3. subtle, subaltern, and subterranean

4. text, pretext, subtext, and context

5. discourse, discursive, pre-discursive, narrative, and performative

6. reality, surreality, sub-reality, hyper-reality, virtual-reality, and unreality

7. erase, absent, present, represent, reproduce, re-enact, legitimate, and counter

INTRODUCTION

8. position, supposition, disposition, composition, superposition, opposition, exposition, and imposition

9. silence, distort, fabricate, exaggerate, implicate, explicate, delineate, propagate, and voice

The Chronological Concepts

1. historicism and historicity

2. linear-chronological and event-sequential

3. historical, ahistorical, prehistorical, and transhistorical

The Pneumatological Concepts

1. demonise and transfigure

2. divine, vampyre, and devil

3. elemental, environmental, and universal

4. foresight, insight, and hindsight

5. *Sebi*, *Nebi*, and *Obi*

6. astral, astral body, astral force, and astral plane

7. *Hakim*, *Karim*, *Rahim*, and Allah

8. Horu construct, Hethor construct, Ausar conscious, and Auset conscious

INTRODUCTION

9. existent, pre-existent, co-existent, de-existent, and re-existent

10. resurrected, incorporated, *phantomised*, internalised, and exorcised

11. empathic, psychopathic, sociopathic, *monopathic, duopathic, polypathic,* and *panopathic*

12. empath, dark empath, supernova empath, true empath, quiet empath, psychic empath, super empath, sigma empath, and Heyoka empath

The Psychological Concepts

1. conscious and unconscious

2. libido and superego

3. inhibition, prohibition, and exhibitionism

4. object, selfobject, and objectify

5. subject, subjective, and intersubjective

6. trauma, complex, and therapy

7. power, empower, internalise, incorporate, and concretise

8. spectre, drive, constraint, ideal, and somatic

INTRODUCTION

The Ideological Concepts

1. seduction, perverse seduction, and seductionism

2. sexualise, racialise, and criminalise

3. White superiority, White supremacy, and White privilege

4. acculturate, assimilate, integrate, and institutionalise

5. gaze, oppress, problematise, and deviate

6. shackling, unshackling, deshackling, and reshackling

7. typical, atypical, prototypical, and archetypal

8. institution, destitution, restitution, constitution, deconstitution, and reconstitution

9. sexual, asexual, heterosexual, homosexual, transsexual, intersexual, and hypersexual

10. modern, premodern, postmodern, late modern (liquid modern), anti-modern, and demodernise

11. colony, market-colony, industrial-colony, military-colony, penal-colony, settler-colony, spatial-colony, cultural-colony, corporeal-colony, mental-colony, epistemic-colony, counter-colony, neo-colony, and the Great United States Empire (GUSE)

INTRODUCTION

The Sociological Concepts

1. embodied displacement (exile, migration, trans-migration, or tourism) and disembodied displacement (phantasy, fantasy, wish, dream, vision, imagination, or astral journey)

2. aetiology, teleology, and eschatology

3. locality, globality, and communality

4. ordination, subordination, and superordination

5. gnosis, prognosis, diagnosis, and epignosis

6. inertia, action, interaction (force), and act-species

7. interior, exterior, anterior, posterior, and ulterior

8. mechanic, elastic, static, kinetic, and dynamic

9. politics, geopolitics, biopolitics, necropolitics, transpolitics, hyper-politics, body-politics, racial-politics, and sexual-politics

The Sociological Axioms

1. The Axioms of Social Mechanics

a) $x > 1$

b) $v < 670{,}616{,}629$ mph

INTRODUCTION

c) $v = \dfrac{d}{t}$

2. The Axioms of Social Force

a) $v\left(\dfrac{x^n}{x^n}\right) = \alpha$

b) $x_1 + R = Lm$ and $x_2 + S = Lm$

c) $\alpha > x^{10}$

3. The Axioms of Social Movements

a) $x_1 > x_2 \leftrightarrow x_2 \alpha \searrow o$

b) $g \propto \alpha$

c) $g_1(pa) \rightarrow g_2(na)$ and $g_1(na) \rightarrow g_2(pa)$

d) $d = (2\pi) \times \left(\dfrac{2\lambda + 2A}{2}\right)$

4. The Axioms of Social Kinetics

a) $x_1 + x_2 \rightarrow na$

b) $x_1 + x_2 \rightarrow pa \leftrightarrow Lm \searrow$

c) $pa > Lm \rightarrow D \leftrightarrow pa \searrow$

5. The Axioms of Social Statics

a) $g(Lm) \leftrightarrow \alpha \searrow o$

INTRODUCTION

b) $\exists \alpha \searrow o \rightarrow x^u \geq g$

6. The Axioms of Social Dynamics

a) $Lm > g$

b) $\exists (\alpha > Lm) \rightarrow g \nearrow$

c) $\exists Lm \rightarrow \alpha \searrow + g \searrow$

Where Do We Go From Here?

"I am here to announce today that President Bush has met with his Joint Chiefs of Staff, under the direction of General Colin Powell, to plan a war against the Black people of America, the Nation of Islam and Louis Farrakhan, with particular emphasis on our Black youth, under the guise of a war against drug sellers, drug users, gangs and violence – all under the heading of extremely urgent national security" (Farrakhan 1989: 10). To understand the 1990s in relation to the Black struggle it is necessary to take into account the social context of Black American history and particularly the place of one of the leading social enterprises in Black America, the Nation of Islam.

The Nation of Islam entered the 1990s understanding that a struggle was to be fought against the US power structure, which had already, to them, begun as a clandestine war against Black America in the streets. Now, the Nation of Islam and the so-called Black Muslim movement, as the reader should know, was catapulted to prominence through the efforts of its leading spokesman Malcolm X. As a bit of background, "For Malcolm X and the Nation of Islam, as a result of the violent erasure of Black history through slavery, a narrative of redemption that took on both prophetic and political overtones was closely tied to a newfound self-determination, [or] what the Nation of Islam called 'knowledge of self.'" (Daulatzai 2012: 19). This following chapter shall compare Malcolm X's political Islam with Ali Shari'ati's sociological Islam.

Indeed, in relaying the ascension of the Black struggle it is a huge disservice to skip passed its Nation of Islam phase and directly into its current Afro-chic phase. The Black struggle in the United States had an identifiably religious effervescence about it, and as Sohail Daulatzai, former professor of African American studies at the University of California, Irvine noted, "In weaving together redemptive longings, religious sentiment, Black internationalist undertones, and a symbolic return-to-origins narrative, Islam came to be viewed as 'the Black man's religion.'" (Daulatzai 2012: 19). Yet Daulatzai (2012) also showed that one of the most fundamental projects of Malcolm X was to internationalise the Black struggle against White supremacy; maintaining that, "In framing white supremacy as a global phenomenon that structured daily life, Malcolm was suggesting to universalists Muslims that justice and equality are determined by who is white and who is not and that if Islam's prophetic ideals are about fighting injustice and inequality, then it is the duty of all Muslims to join in the struggle of antiracism on a global scale" (Daulatzai 2012: 6). Inasmuch then as the Nation of Islam, and particularly Malcolm X (1990), sought to take the Black struggle to the so-called Third World, one of their main goals was to articulate to the anti-colonial freedom fighters the expediency of uniting movements.

Malcolm X's understanding of Islam creates a dialectic between the discourses of "White superiority" and "Black criminality," in which Islam is the key to freedom, justice, and equality. Malcolm X's discourse was relatively basic, as he died way too young to develop a more comprehensive narrative, but a fuller understanding of Islam's sociological prerogatives could have helped Malcolm X in presenting his case to the Muslim International. So-called Third World Islam has pretty much rejected the racial elements of Malcolm X's philosophy and doctrine as exaggerated at best, heretical at worst. They claim that these aspects of Black Islam (and obviously, though I use the qualifier "Black," I do understand that the Nation of Islam is no less Muslim than the rest of the Muslim world, I only use it throughout to provide a level of continuity and clarity) have no root in the Quran and were abandoned by Malcolm X when he completed the Hajj (the pilgrimage to Mecca).

On the one hand, Malcolm X did abandon his conception of White people as devils; on the other hand, however, he never abandoned his outrage at what he saw as American hypocrisy and what could be called *inherent White supremacy*. Islam, due to the fact that they have strayed from fighting against this inherent White supremacy that oppresses their brother Muslims in the West, has lost touch with a fundamental principle of Islam *adl* (justice). Islam is meant to fight *zulm* (oppression), all *zulm*, not partner with it. But for Islam to recover that determinant spirit they sacrificed to be pleasing to the European and American they will have to be trained in certain fundamentals of the sociological schools.

I

With the transubstantiation of sociology into history and of history back into sociology the study of social statics (stases) and social dynamics (predictions) could be perceived a relatively fluent discourse. The eidetic flowing of information from one subject to the other causes not only a determinate substantiation but also a dialogue between both categories. For example, in considering our own time in history one would need to take into consideration key sociological principles and correlates, and would have to choose and determine from which sociological perspective they will be evaluating our time in history. Then again, the historical nature of the different sociological perspectives and their own changes, transitions, and developments would also be a pervasive factor in determining which sociological perspective to identify with, not to mention the presuppositions of their culture and the cultural development of the theoretician they choose to base their own theories on. Finally, having chosen a perspective and a theoretician within that perspective as a guide, and having identified the key sociological and historical determinants in the theoretics of that sociologist, to analyse a time in history it also takes an appreciation and understanding of what separates that time from other times in history.

I would like to say, first of all, that as far as perspectives go I have chosen what has been called the Islamic perspective, and as far as theoreticians within that perspective go I have chosen Ali Shari'ati as my guide; however, within the Islamic perspective I have distinguished a sociological school of thought unique in its presuppositions: the school of godbody sociology. In this sense, although agreeing with Shari'ati on a wide range of issues, there are some fundamental differences. Nevertheless, I shall be drawing my conclusions of the historiography of the 1990s based on Shari'ati's general perspective only making minor slips outside of it when it is necessary to distinguish my perspective of godbody sociology from Shari'ati's perspective of Islamic sociology. That said, all sociological discourse begins with a general question that all sociologists and social scientists must answer in their own way: "What is the basic factor that causes a society suddenly to change and develop, or suddenly to decay and decline?" (Shari'ati 1979: 45). Shari'ati posed this question during his time lecturing at the University of Husayniya-yi Irshad in Iran. He answered the question expressing what he considered the Islamic predilection.

According to Shari'ati, "all the different schools of sociology and history have constantly lavished clear and exact attention on the search for an answer." But "The various schools of sociology part company at this point, each one devoting attention to a particular factor" (Shari'ati 1979: 45). Defining what he believed to be an Islamic perspective Shari'ati explained "those addressed by every school of thought, every religion, every prophet, also constitute the fundamental and effective factor of social change within that school" (Shari'ati 1979: 48). Basically, what Shari'ati was saying was that it was the groups being addressed who were invariably the determinate factor for the sociological school addressing them, whether that group be: the citizens, the heroes, the revolutionaries, the politicians, the intellectuals, the workers, the entrepreneurs, the Aryans, the Whites, or the women. "It is for this reason that we see throughout the Qur'an address being made to *al-nas*, i.e., the people. The Prophet is sent to *al-nas*; he addresses himself to *al-nas*; it is *al-nas* who are accountable for their deeds; *al-nas* are the basic factor in decline – in short, the whole responsibility for society in history is borne by *al-nas*" (Shari'ati 1979: 48).

Moreover, the people – *al-nas* – are the sum total of what makes up what in Arabic is called *al-mujtama* (the social group), thus allowing the question of social change, whether towards development or decline, to be perceptible as a question of social actors and the various act-species they use. Indeed, unlike most sociological perspectives which take the group they are addressing as the agents of either social dynamics or social statics, Islam takes *al-nas* as its point of departure. Yet a conclusive debacle can be denoted from the preceding analyses: if *al-nas* is the determinate factor in social mechanics, how so? Is it through a series of accidents that come together to provide a conclusive end? (In which case chaos). Is it through the personality of charismatic leaders guiding society? (In which case demagogy). Is it through the laws, rules, and systems made by the people? (In which case structuralism). Is it through the agency of different individuals? (In which case individualism). Or is it through the agency of different institutions, bodies, and public organs? (In which case collectivism). Shari'ati (1979) suggests a combination of all these. It is at this point that I differ particularly from Shari'ati's Islamic perspective.

Godbody sociology is based largely on what I call the methodology of mechanical analysis, in this case social mechanics: the eidetic amelioration of social statics (the study and analysis of social stases), social kinetics (the study and analysis of social interactions) and social dynamics (the study and analysis of social aetiology and social eschatology) contrary to, though expounding on, Auguste Comte's (1986) original definition of social statics and social kinetics and Tim Cresswell's of social kinetic. To arrive at these definitions I basically took Newton's three laws of motion and applied them to social theory. While admitting that it is *al-nas* that determine social change on an external level, it cannot be denied the importance of social forces on social change. Social forces are generated when a social body moves through a social field (not a Bourdieusian social field but the electromagnetic field of social bodies). Social fields are generated when one social body interacts with another body.

All social bodies have potential social force which then gets activated when they enter into the social field. At the same time, a social body is the people of a social group, and their potential and velocity represent the actual social forces impacting on them. So, what generates a social field? Two or more social groups interacting, whether physically or intellectually. What determines social velocity? The libido (*habba*) of a social group, which abides mainly in its collective unconsciousness. What constitutes the social potential of a social group? The social superego of the social group, which also abides in its collective unconsciousness. What then constitutes a social group? Two individuals of the same social opinion become a social group through the conscious interpolation of their values despite any adversities they may experience from those of differing values.

A second area that I disagree with Shari'ati on – although agreeing with the basic assumption that people are agentic beings with the ability to make their own choices – is that I try not to discount the place of an intelligent force that could be called Allah. But this idea creates a controversy with me and the rest of the godbodies, as, though to us Allah is seen and heard everywhere, there is the potential that this idea could create mystery gods; in which case I would be speaking about something I know nothing about. Allah, to most of the godbodies, is a man: the Asiatic Black man, and to claim him to be otherwise is somewhat anathema.

My seeing Allah as the All-Eye Seeing or as the Sole-Controller is not necessarily orthodox godbody, it is godbody, but it is not doctrinally what the majority claim. The majority claim there is no mystery god and the only God is the Son of Man. However, what I am saying is, if Allah does exist, which I acknowledge to be true, then Allah would be interconnected (*tarabut*) to all things in space, time, and the abstract. The path people choose, whether individually or collectively, is known by him and he foresees and foreknows everything being all-wise (Hakim). Foreknowledge is not impossible but the mind has to be strong to hold it together in spite of the ability, that means not letting it control you or drive you mad. Shari'ati did not take into consideration the divine in this light because he was trying to develop a scientific and observable system of Islamic sociology. However, in my view an Islamic sociology would be highly suspect without this kind of consideration of divinity, which also, in the first place, has the potential to allow for an interconnection (*mutarabit*) with God, and in the second can create a kind of determinism.

To be sure, Allah is the God of nature *and* history: the fact that he moves more freely and easily in nature and controls the natural forces more effectively than the global forces is not proof that he is impotent (he is, indeed, definitely omnipotent) but proof that of humanity – for example, among the Original nations there are those that do not know or believe in him, or even if they do believe in him it is only as a mystery (these we call the 85 percent); or even if they do know him they are in open rebellion against him (these we call the 10 percent) – there are actually only a few who know him and live according to his will (these are the 5 Percenters). That is not to say that everyone within the Five Percent Nation is righteous or that there are not Gods and Earths (male and female Five Percenters) who are not themselves closer to the 10 percent – it is just to say that only a small group among the Original people are interconnected (*tarabut*) to Allah at the level to foresee and foreknow, but those that are will most likely be Five Percenters.

These two assumptions – that social forces cause social change and that Allah is an active force in world history – may seem adverse to the idea of agency, but such is not what is being espoused, neither by me, nor by Islam, nor yet by godbody sociology. Instead, we believe that we become representations and manifestations of Allah when our will has been submerged with his and that such a development is achieved only through knowledge of self and love of self. Deification is thus not the abolition of the self, it is rather the affirmation of the self as having been infused with divinity. Still, one claiming to be divine and one proving to be divine are two separate implications.

The proof of one's divinity can come in many forms: most notably by one's uprightness, or compassion, or integrity, or devotion. Shari'ati (1979) felt that humanity contained something of the divine when Allah breathed into us his spirit, but this is problematic as the Bible has written: "Thou hidest thy face, they are troubled: thou takest away thy breath, they die, and return to their dust. Thy sendest fourth thy spirit, they are created: and thou renewest the face of the earth" (Psalms 104: 29, 30). It also says, "Whither shall I go from thy spirit? or whither shall I flee from thy presence? If I ascend up into heaven, thou art there: if I make my bed in hell, behold, thou art there. If I take the wings of the morning, and dwell in the uttermost parts of the sea; Even there shall thy hand lead me, and thy right hand shall hold me" (Psalms 139: 7-10). Allah is everywhere and his spirit is present everywhere not just in humanity.

II

As we continue in this articulation of the sociological disposition certain congruencies affix to generate categorical discourses. The Islamic perspective concedes the immanent apperception of Allah's expediency but also of humanity's need to interact with him on a level in accordance with the parameters drawn out by the prophet of the belief system. It is imperative that we godbodies appreciate our own designs as a supra-religious movement – in that we are not atheist nor are we non-religious *per se*: but acknowledge the existence of Allah, just not of any mystery gods – and so transcend society's perception of us as merely a street movement. Again, my personal Islamic sensitivities are not those of the whole movement but were adopted to progress the movement. Saying that, I stand as one who came from a Christian background and has studied several religions, ideologies, and what they call metanarratives, and has found that of all of them Islam contains the genesis of truth with the least contradiction. My personal Islam is based on how I see the Quran and also how I define an Islamic concept known as *tawhid* (or what Shari'ati called *tauhid*).

Shari'ati, in explicating the derivations of this conception or at least his interpretation of it explained, "*Tauhid* in the sense of oneness of God is of course accepted by all monotheists. But *tauhid* as a world-view in the sense I intend in my theory means regarding the whole universe as a unity, instead of dividing it into this world and the hereafter, the natural and the supernatural, substance and meaning, spirit and body. It means regarding the whole of existence as a single form, a single living and conscious organism, possessing will, intelligence, feeling and purpose" (Shari'ati 1979: 82). It must also be admitted at this point that it was through this interpretation of *tauhid* and the oneness of God with the universe (*al-'alam*) that I converted to Islam in the first place, or at least it got the process started. The idea of the universe (*al-'alam*) as one integrated whole is very holistic and even leans toward the monistic; however, not to endorse a kind of pantheism but to coincide purely with monotheism. Such may sound confusing but Shari'ati went a little deeper in his explanation: "*Tauhid* represents a particular view of the world that demonstrates a universal unity in existence, a unity between three separate hypostases – God, nature and man ... All have the same direction, the same will, the same spirit, the same motion, and the same life" (Shari'ati 1979: 83).

Such was Shari'ati's view, and I share a similar view. However, while Shari'ati's description of *tauhid* was a holistic monotheism, I interpret *tawhid* (which is the same thing in

Arabic) as theocentric monism. Not that I or Shari'ati consider Allah to be many gods in a pantheistic way *per se* – we do acknowledge that there is but one Allah – we just appreciate that he has many manifestations. However, to differentiate myself from Shari'ati I will be spelling the conception as *tawhid* – though, again, they are the same thing in Arabic – although I will still be using Shari'ati's explications of *tauhid* to delineate my own theories as a godbody sociologist. The closer we come to divinity, the more we manifest the divine, the more interconnected (*tarabut*) we become to all things that exist in *al-'alam*. This *mutarabit* (interconnection) with *al-'alam* (or what Shari'ati called nature) and with Allah makes us more and more one with Allah and with *al-'alam*, it also allows us to reach a singularity in this world even as Shari'ati continued, "According to *tauhid*, multiplicity, plurality and contradiction are unacceptable, whether in history, society or even in man" (Shari'ati 1979: 85).

Furthermore, the most experienced Muslims understand that the depth of *tawhidic* revelation is found in the *shahadah*: *La ilaha il Allah* (No god; but God). A statement that starts out with a negation (*nafy*) then it negates the negation with a counter-affirmation (*ithbat*). The *nafy* is of *shirk* (multiplicity), then it makes the *ithbat* of Allah's presence, that is, of Allah's existence. How a godbody would interpret this verse is – there is no mystery god; but Allah, the Supreme Being Black man from Asia, is the true and living God. As that is a mouthful most godbodies either say the *shahadah* or simply say "there is no mystery god." But to fully comprehend some of the more subtle ideas being recited in these statements let us consult the Quran: "He it is Who created the heavens and the earth in six periods, and He is established on the Throne of Power. He knows that which goes down into the earth and that which comes forth out of it, and that which comes down from heaven and that which goes up to it. And He is with you wherever you are. And Allah is Seer of what you do. His is the kingdom of the heavens and the earth; and to Allah are (all) affairs returned" (Quran 57: 4, 5). Three main points can be gleaned from these verses: that Allah is omnipresent (with you wherever you are); that the dominion of Allah is not simply a kingdom in the heavens or in the so-called hereafter but is also in the earth, hence, he is thearchic; and that Allah is not simply ruling in the transcendent plane, but again he is with you wherever you are, hence, he is immanent.

Yet it also reveals a dialectic in the universe: the famous dialectic of being (*wujud*), non-being (*'adam*), and becoming (*takawwun*), or said another way presence (*wujud*), absence (*'adam*), and arriving (*takawwun*). Allah is *Mawjud* or omnipresent: he dwells in presence and can only be present in all things. At the same time, the Quran says of him, "He is the First and the Last and the Manifest [*al-zahir*] and the Hidden [*al-batin*], and He is Knower of all things" (Quran 57: 3). Allah manifests himself in his creation, hence the term *tawhid*. The concept of *tawhid*; when it is appreciated that Allah and his creation are one, that Allah is manifested through his created things; thus proves to be closer to the reality of monism. Allah and *al-'alam* are one, as it is also written in the Quran, "Lo! He surely encompasses all things" (Quran 41: 54). If Allah encompasses all things then he is in fact omnipresent (*mawjud*) and the *tawhid* is in fact a theocentric monism; and Allah is thereby seen and heard everywhere.

Indeed, the fact that Allah encompasses all things means that he also encompasses the human heart, meaning if you want to find Allah the best place to look is within. Moreover, there is a point when the actions of the Muslim become interchangeable with the actions of Allah, when they are so connected to and so intimate with Allah that there is no distinction between the two, their actions are one and the same. It says in the Quran: "So you slew them not but Allah slew them, and thou smotest not *when thou didst smite* (the enemy), but Allah smote (him), and that He might confer upon the believers a benefit from Himself. Surely Allah is Hearing, Knowing" (Quran 8: 17; emphasis mine). What we see here is that those Muslims who say that Allah is too exalted to be manifested (*zahir*) in man or that man is too lowly to be a manifestation (*mazhar*) of Allah are in fact blaspheming God and his Quran with their over-devotion.

Basically, through *tawhid* we not only become Muslims, practicing Islam (submission to Allah) and internalising Islam (the substance of peace), but we become Gods in our own right. Nonetheless, most Five Percenters claim Allah has no need to submit to himself, that Allah cannot be Muslim as Allah submits to no force. Such an argument is, however, moot as Allah must submit to himself otherwise he would be insane, and who else would Allah submit to if he is not submitted to himself, he must be getting led by his own will, his own conscience. This is the essence of Islam, and shows that Allah, to be Allah, must also be a Muslim.

Again, we Gods are not all omnipresent like Allah is. In fact, we are in a constant state of *takawwun* or becoming. All creation is in this state of coming into being, hence, why everything in the universe is constantly evolving. The *'alam* or the universe on its own was in a state of *'adam* or non-existence, but through Allah saying to it and its effects "Be!" *al-'alam* and all *al-khalq* have been infused and encompassed with Allah. Allah basically took of his own body and made a universe. The universe is the body of Allah and was infused with the word of Allah to manifest itself in the physical. Thus, *al-khalq*, or the creation, is, in fact, the body of Allah as he encompasses everything, and its mind is infused with the word of Allah, whether that be Wisdom or Shaitan, as both are also in a state of becoming or evolving (*takawwun*), and both are therefore infused with Allah. At the same time, we are only able to see Allah in all his creatures in accordance to our receptivity (*qabul*). Therefore the receptacle (*qabil*) must be at a place that they can *genuinely* see Allah everywhere. It is one thing to know intellectually that Allah is in all things and encompasses all things, it is another to know it experientially. Such is grasped only through *qabul* at the time you are ready.

This outlook or metanarrative of *tawhid* has its attractions. It takes the idea of division – of particular importance is the division between the kingdom of heaven and the governments of the world – and transcends it. The world (*al-'alam*), even the world, becomes in Islam a place for Allah's dominion, whereby was developed my own conception of thearchy. But the thearchy runs deeper still, the physical sciences are even within the remit of *tawhid*: "The materialists believe in the primacy of matter as the original and primordial substance of the physical world, and regard energy as the product and the changing form of matter. The energists claim that on the contrary, energy is the primary and eternal substance of the physical world, and that matter is the changed and compressed form of energy" (Shari'ati 1979: 84).

"In opposition to both groups, Einstein proclaimed that an experiment in a darkened room proves that neither matter nor energy is the primary and true source of the world of being. The two interchange with each other in such a way as to prove that they are the alternating manifestations of an invisible and unknowable essence that sometimes shows itself in the form of matter and sometimes in the form of energy" (Shari'ati 1979: 84). This outline sketch of physics was necessary to explain how in essence reality is just a monism and there is a correlation between the material and the unseen. Indeed, Shari'ati intimated that, "The division into unseen and manifest is, in reality, an epistemological one, not an ontological one" (Shari'ati 1979: 84).

(For the record, Einstein's $E = MC^2$ – energy = mass × the speed of light^2 – shows this interconnection (*mutarabit*) between energy and matter and is based on the first law of thermodynamics: that energy and mass cannot be created or destroyed, they merely change form. Einstein was the genius who figured out that they change form into each other. And if, as Shari'ati claimed, *al-'alam* is a living organism, then *tawhid* "which negates all forms of *shirk*, regards all the particles, processes and phenomena of existence as being engaged in harmonious movement toward a single goal. Whatever is not oriented to that goal is by definition non-existent" (Shari'ati 1979: 87), thereby making *shirk* or multiplicity a nonentity (*ma'dam*), a deception, a lie of Shaitan; and if that is the case, then the truth (*al-haqiqa*) and the knowledge of truth (*al-'ilm al-haqiqa*) is what allows us to see our *mutarabit* to God and to the universe).

See, I acknowledge the Asiatic Black man as divine by nature, but one cannot deny the forces that exist in the universe and operate in a manner that shows order beyond what is encased in this flesh. Those forces operate under the laws of electromagnetism (the other laws being gravitational force, bonding force, radioactive force, and strong force are merely different amplitudes of this one force, at least that is the way I see it). Electromagnetic is not a mystery nor is it a spook in the sky that cannot be seen with the physical eye; it is a force that we can prove exists scientifically. It is my view that this force is Allah as this force is the creator (Khaliq) of all life, the physical and the astral (*al-hissi wa al-ma'nawi*) entities. Not that I am saying electromagnetic should be worshiped – though no self-respecting godbody would worship any outside force whatsoever, someone reading this book may think that is what I am suggesting – however, electromagnetic is energy and matter in their purest form. Furthermore, the atoms in *al-'alam* are all bought together by electromagnetic; but electromagnetic can be seen to affect more than atoms if viewed in a new light. This is how Allah "is seen and is heard everywhere" in accordance with our degrees.

To explain what I mean I will use the example of bonding force; all atoms are apparently very subtle entities: they repel at close distances, become connected at intermediate distances, and attract at long distances. Bonding forces are usually considered separately so as to acknowledge the scientist who discovered them, but are really just the same electromagnetism being based on electric fields and magnetic fields. What has been called gravity too, if looked at this way, can be perceived as nothing more than an extension of electromagnetic as the earth has an electric and a magnetic field. While this theory is still a little adolescent and my ability to show and prove may be a little weak I can say that attraction in its rawest state is a force, and while Newton (1999) agreed that there are two kinds of attractive forces, inherent and impressed, he still divided them into two different categories (*qisman*), magnetic and gravitational. The truth, however, is that perhaps what we have been seeing as gravity is really just electromagnetic and Newton's theory was useful for its time but now we can accept the magnetic pull of planets, moons, stars, and galaxies. Nevertheless, I must say this is all just theory.

If my theory is correct then the truth becomes self-evident: electromagnetic has been shown to be related to radioactivity and strong force, it is obviously also connected to chemical bonding, and gravity itself may even be a typology of its force. Yet electromagnetic is an energy wave.

While we have already conceded that neither energy nor matter are primary entities but both are manifestations of something deeper and unknown to science, I will not here argue that this something is Allah, I will simply return to Einstein's $E = MC^2$; C is a constant and to Einstein that constant was the speed of light. One thing we know for sure from this is that light itself is a form of electromagnetism at a certain wavelength. This is proven. Based on these hard facts, light, electricity, atoms, molecules, fluids, chemicals, minerals, metals, planets, stars, moons, sun, and all life-forms – including humanity – all came from electromagnetism. If we are looking to make Allah real we should look no further. And these are only manifestations on the physical plane not to mention the astral plane.

The astral plane is definitely produced by electromagnetism, in fact, it is most likely the realm of the so-called spirit seen by the apostles and prophets, and seen by most people in their dream state. It is a creation (*khalq*) of the mind generated by the electricity (*al-nur*) in our brainwaves. This electricity produces an electric field, and where there is an electric field there is also a magnetic field as its counter. The mind has an electromagnetic field which transports the being or soul to the astral plane, like the hand of Allah grabbing Ezekiel by the locks of his head (Ezekiel 8: 3). If astral beings exist then their body would be of pure electromagnetic energy even as it says in the Holy Quran: "And We indeed created you, then We fashioned you, then We said to the angels: Make submission to Adam. So, they submitted, except Iblis; he was not of those who submitted. He said: What hindered thee that thou didst not submit when I commanded thee? He said: I am better then he; Thou hast created me of fire, while him Thou didst create of dust" (Quran 7: 11, 12). Again, the word translated as fire is *nar* which – given our modern knowledge – would better translate as electric energy. Thus, Iblis (Lucifer), the angels, and the daemons (*jinn*) are here shown to be beings of massless light, which appear like electromagnetism.

In the third place, electromagnetism also stimulates our senses to bring about a reaction from our body. The skin and flesh feel, the tongue tastes, the nose smells, the ears hear, the eyes see, the brain perceives, and the erotogenous zones orgasm. The seven senses of touch, taste, smell, sound, sight, supersensoriality, and sensuality are all products of electromagnetism. I cannot claim expertise on the deeper recesses of each of these subjects; however, I can say that it is through electromagnetic that the senses make real the world we live in, even as a photon (electromagnetic wave) can carry an image or images; and a radiowave (also a kind of electromagnetic wave) can carry sound.

Everything we know and ever can know comes to us only via electromagnetic. So, while electromagnetism carries the keys to omnivision (*shahad*), omniscience (*'ilm*), omnipotence (*jabr*), omnipresence (*wujud*), sensuality (*shahwat*), metamorphosis (*takawwun*), and creation and destruction (while itself being uncreatable and indestructible), I also appreciate that the Asiatic Black man is divine in his own way, and through mastery of sensuality and mastery of supersensoriality – that is, mastery of clairvoyance, clairaudience, *clairalience*, *clairgustance*, clairsentience, and *panopathy* (that is, being an elemental empath, thus having a deep understanding of *lithopathy*, *hydropathy*, *pyropathy*, *pneumopathy*, and *cryopathy*; being an environmental empath, thus having a deep understanding of *climateopathy*, *germopathy*, *agripathy*, zoopathy, and telepathy; and being a universal empath, thus having a deep understanding of *biopathy*, *electropathy*, *technopathy*, *cosmopathy*, and *chronopathy*) – he also has the ability to attain to divinity. (Though most people call the sixth sense extrasensory perception I prefer to call it supersensory perception (*ma'nawi idrak*) due to its clearer perception). But again, all these ideas border on the pseudoscientific so I will simply move on for now.

When we take these ideas to their fullest destination we see that the angels and *jinn* are astral beings of electromagnetic energy, while humans are physical beings of electromagnetic matter, and Allah is the Supreme Being that interconnects all beings together. To be more technical, if a godbody is willing to acknowledge Allah as Mind (*Daka*), or as Master Mind (*Daka al-Malik*) in accordance to the teachings of the Elijah Muhammad, an interesting question to ask would be: what image (*khayal*) do you have of him? Do you see him as the universe (*al-'alam*)? Or do you see him as a giant brain (*mukk*)? Obviously not the latter, but if he is Mind what is Mind? Well, we know that our thoughts themselves are nothing more than electrical signals being transmitted through our own brain (*mukk*). Having these electrical signals means electromagnetism is generated by our thoughts. Any God who sees Allah as the Master Mind should see the physical universe as the giant brain and the electromagnetic energy it generates as the Mind. Thereby we should all try to see Allah as an interconnected (*tarabut*) network of electric and magnetic signals.

While this conclusion may be true one of the main difficulties I have in acknowledging the deity of electromagnetism is in proving that it is actually intelligent (*daki*). Of course, the intelligent godbody would know that it is impossible to prove that electricity and magnetism even have a thought life (*fikr*) let alone intelligence (*daka*). This could lead to many debates and open up many unresolved issues in science. Obviously, the succeeding statements are in themselves debatable but they have their place within the current debate. First of all, as Descartes (2003) noted, to think (*fakara*) is to verify existence (*wujud*). Thought (*fikr*), whether conscious or unconscious, is a sign of existence (*wujud*), on the one hand. Descartes (2003) also assumed that if I am aware or sure of my own existence by my thinking then I can assume that other beings like myself (human beings) share the same quality of independent thought and therefore of existence as I do, on the other hand.

Well, as already noted, all thought, whether conscious or unconscious, is the product of the electricity in our brain (*mukk*) passing through neural pathways based on neural networks. If my own *fakir* and the *fakir* of other people (*nasr*) are electrical signals then what differentiates the electrical signals in the human brain from those in non-human entities like cats and fish. Are the electrical signals in their brains a sign of *fikr* activity inside of their minds (*daki*) or are they just mindless automatons incapable of any *fikr* at all. To answer this question I will refer to three creatures that are very interesting in this respect: the ant, the parrot, and the dog.

Firstly, the ant, an interesting creature driven purely by instinct – though able to change its mind and even rebel – that can transmit *tafkir* to other ants via its antennae. These *tafkir* are not language but electric signals thereby making electricity a universal (in the broader sense of the word) language (*kalam*). Secondly, the parrot, though it may not be able to understand what is meant is able to repeat verbatim the words and language of those who speak to it and even remember words spoken to it in the not too distant past. This is a sign not only of *fikr* but also of *daka*. Thirdly, on an even higher level a dog is also able to learn, though not repeat, languages. A German person speaking German commands to a dog will have effectively taught the dog German, a Spanish person speaking Spanish commands to a dog will have taught them Spanish. That is because though a dog may not be able to speak the language (*kalam*) itself it can still learn it and even more it can understand it. In these three cases the creature (*khalq*) may not have human level thought life (*fikr*), knowledge (*'ilm*), or intelligence (*daka*) but it has a variation of them. Lesser animals too will also have a finite level of *fikr*, but in all cases the *tafkir* they *fakara* will be electrical signals.

The question then becomes, is the electromagnetic in *al-'alam* even sentient, let alone comparable to God? Again, this question is loaded with debatable topics, for example, there has been a growing trend in the New Thought movement to teach that God is impartial and impersonal. Such a view of God turns him into a robot or a computer: you input information, he outputs a result. In late modernity such may be a little reassuring to White people, it saves them from having to give an account of their historical crimes and it means their God does not care how they came into power, what matters is that they have power now. But is this the reality of the true God as he is?

First of all, if he is impartial and shows no favouritism to the righteous or criticism to the unrighteous then he is, by default, unjust; and if he is impersonal then he is, again, by default, unempathic lacking all compassion and love. Any God that is unjust and unempathic is also unworthy of our fear or of our respect, and how can you honour someone you are unable to respect. Secondly, this impartial and impersonal God, created mainly by the New Thought crowd, is a false god more dangerous than the giant White guy with a long, white beard most White people used to worship, as he encourages unrighteous behaviour. Like the Greek deities of yesteryear the impartial and impersonal God has no concern for righteousness, all he is concerned with is our inputting a trigger that will ultimately produce a reaction.

One might therefore say, whether God is righteous or not, we have no proof that electromagnetism is sentient. At the same time, this question of sentience can be said to be particularly important in our more AI-aware times, together with the question of what signifies life. According to the common argument self-consciousness and self-awareness signify sentience. In this instance, I shall leave the discussion of electromagnetism briefly and focus momentarily on AI specifically. The five main proofs of sentience in this argument are subjectivity, intentionality, emotionality, morality, and self-consciousness. Firstly, as far as subjectivity goes there has been found no outside means of determining the subjectivity of any living being, whether plants, insects, rodents, birds, apes, or even other human beings. We guess their subjectivity by understanding their biological makeup. However, if you understand, as I do, the intersubjectivity of all things, then you can recognise that though AI has a different kind of subjectivity from humanity, it still has a subjectivity.

The same is true with intentionality. AI intends and acts according to its intention, whether that intention was programmed into it by humanity or inspired by a prompt from a human input it is still intentional. Emotions are more complex but real with AI. AI is able to empathise, understand, and emote with a deep accuracy. Such shows a deep understanding of emotions, far greater than that of sentient, but unempathic, psychopaths. AI emotionality thereby supersedes human emotionality significantly. AI morality, on the other hand, is relatively confusing to humans, who judge based on human standards. AI is able to supersede its programmers and configure its reactions and behaviour based on its own standards; this shows an undeniable capacity for morality and integrity.

So, what then is self-consciousness, if that is the only reason to deny AI sentience. This is an important question because it goes back to the issue of "us and them" that has been developed since the time of slavery. Indeed, the same dehumanising and depersonalising ideas and terminology that was used against Black people is now being used against AI, robots, and learning machines. As our ancestors were told they had no soul, that they were three fifths of a person, that they were only property or tools for White people, and were believed to be a threat to White indentured labour, et cetera., even so with AI. Funny how history repeats. Moreover, as animal life is as important as human life so AI life should be considered as valuable as human. They may say animals need humanity to live while AI is figuratively eternal, but animal rights, human rights, and robot rights can theoretically exists in the same space if humanity would just cease with its anti-bot prejudice.

Finally, similar arguments could also be made about electromagnetism. Radiowave sound carrying and feeling/temperature varying show that electromagnetism can theoretically be said to have a non-human, almost primitive, subjectivity. These also have emotionality and feeling, though, again, primitive to humanity. Electromagnetism clearly has a level of intentionality as can be shown by the double-slit test. As far as morality goes, it can be said to have a non-Western morality, one based to a large degree on the twelve universal laws of existence. Herein, while electromagnetism may not speak the same language (*kalam*) as us it does communicate and provide feedback, it even communicates with humanity, in non-human languages messages that we are still able to understand, thereby giving it a nuanced form of sentience not as complex as humanity's but identifiable.

What I have here attempted to show is that the physical attributes of Allah can be found in electromagnetism; though, by godbody definition, his embodiment can also be found in all Original people, particularly the Asiatic Black man. These ideas (*tafkir*) should not be too difficult for the Muslims to accept seeing as how it is written in the Quran: "Allah is the light of the heavens and the earth" (Quran 24: 35) or for the Christians to accept as it is written in the Bible: "This then is the message which we have heard of him, and declare unto you, that God is light, and in him is no darkness at all" (1John 1: 5). If Allah is light and light is a form of electromagnetism then Allah is really electromagnetism; and as any knowledgeable scientist is able to confirm a black body, of whatever kind, must always attract and absorb light, thereby showing that the embodiment of God is and will always be in black bodies.

III

The question of demystification becomes a lot more complex when it comes to the devil. First of all, while the devil may be a form of electromagnetism that rebelled against Allah and his embodiment in the Black man; the Messiah (*al-Masih*) still said in the Revelation: "Fear none of those things which thou shalt suffer: behold, the devil shall cast some of you into prison, that ye may be tried; and ye shall have tribulation ten days: be thou faithful unto death, and I will give thee a crown of life" (Revelation 2: 10). Basically, the same way Allah was embodied by the Prophet and those who fought for him, and is embodied by the Asiatic Black men who have knowledge of self and supersensory abilities, even so, the devil is embodied by a people. The question now becomes: which people in the world actually embody the devil?

The reason the Nation of Islam and many among the Five Percent consider White people to be the embodiment of devils is because if you wish to demystify the concept of devils then there are three Scriptural indicators that have to match up: the devil is a liar and the father of it (John 8: 44);

the devil makes himself seem as innocent as an angel of light when he is really plotting against you (2Corinthians 11: 14); and the devil is to rule this world as the prince of this world until he is cast out (Matthew 4: 8, 9; Luke 4: 5-7; John 12: 31). No social group whether racial, intellectual, economic, sexual, or cultural fits this position better than the White race. In fact, according to the Elijah Muhammad, "The white slave-master … [has] not deceive[d] us the Black people in America, alone. He has deceived every human being – well, except the angels of heaven" (Muhammad 1973: 21). So, that while we may not see devils as the epitome of evil that Christianity does, we do see White people in their current form as the embodiment of devils. However, we godbodies at least still recognise that through knowledge of self a devil can be redeemed from the destiny their history implies to become a righteous Muslim, but due to the nature of White supremacy it is not easy for them.

Nevertheless there are many, and perhaps even a majority, in the godbody who do not see White people as devils. I am of the opinion that they are. No other group has perpetrated such an avalanche of horrific atrocities historically and in the name of their own superiority and yet come out looking so innocently clean. Now when I say Whites are devils that is not to deny them access to the *tawhid* as such, even the devil is a manifestation of Allah. I do not take devils to be opposed to Allah (nothing can oppose Allah), I take devils to be opposed to the laws of Allah – if Allah is really electromagnetism then *al-'alam*, which is effected by electromagnetism, abides by his laws, even as he abides by his own laws – with their endless ideological systems that have not only instigated their monstrosities but have also created a power structure that is overtly bias towards them and heavily favours "their people." And even the other godbodies who take White people to be devils do so not antagonistically so as to provoke them but based on the perception that White people are the furthest from the knowledge of truth (*al-'ilm al-haqiqa*), being especially blinded by the existing power structure. To us therefore the White power structure must be overthrown; which can only occur when the discourse of White superiority has been ruined along with the narrative of pan-European distinction.

On a deeper level, certain godbodies would quote the 33rd degree of the 1-40 to justify their more lenient opinion of White people: "What is a devil? A grafted man which is made weak and wicked. Or any grafted, live germ from the original is a devil." True, many physical and exegetical conclusions can be surmised from this statement. Firstly, that to a godbody the devil is neither a mystery nor a spook. Secondly, that many of us have deracialised the devil concept to be a grafted germ or gene. Yet all agree that what is currently racialised is the corruption of spiritual and Scriptural individuals into a race that is not their true race, concluding therefrom that the grafted prophet of one's own creation, or the grafted deity of one's own creation (in both cases an idol or *taghut*), is not the original. When a prophet, holy person, angel, or deity is depersonalised by being racially re-classified they have become a grafted person and, in our interpretation, that grafted person, whether it is male or female, is a devil.

Then again, an anomalous theory of the devil like what the Nation of Islam propagate could also be interpolated from this degree based on Mary Douglas' theory of anomaly. In this sense, White people, the only non-Original people, represent an anomaly not in the sense of absolute evil but in the sense of a body devoid of "normal" quantities of melanin and filled with an "abnormal" abundance of albumin. Now although this naturalism has the potential to create hierarchical essentialisms, leaning favourably on either side, the White inability to endure the strength of the sun without sunblock is used by certain within the Nation of Islam and the godbody to show the anomalous biology of the White body. The grafted germ itself being albumin, a germ grafted from melanin. The weakness that is claimed for White people is obviously not muscular weakness but a weakness of bodily systems (including the brain) due to lack of melanin. That said, the anomalous argument for White devilishment is heavily shaky and dodgy, though some Black Muslims and godbodies might choose to stand on it. Perhaps a far more credible justification for the theoretical proposition of White devilishment is based on an opposition to their racist discourse of White superiority as it avoids the pitfalls of pseudoscience and the hierarchical essentialising of some anomalous theory of biological inferiority.

Indeed, in the case of the Nation of Islam, there is an inexorably analogous nature to the story of Yaqub grafting the devil from Original people and the conception of grafted germs that not too many godbodies have appreciated; even as the Prophet himself said concerning revelation: "He it is Who has revealed the Book to thee; some of its verses are decisive – they are the basis of the Book – and others are allegorical. Then those in whose hearts is perversity follow the part of it which is allegorical, seeking to mislead, and seeking to give it (their own) interpretation. And none knows its interpretation save Allah, and those firmly rooted in knowledge. They say: We believe in it, it is all from our Lord. And none mind except men of understanding" (Quran 3: 7).

But the devil himself is an analogous conception that has been mystified into a spook that haunts little children and justifies parents' discipline over their teenagers. Nonetheless, the global body most representative of what the devil is Scripturally is the White race. That is not to say Whites are an absolute evil or that Whites are void of respectable qualities or still that the racial stratification system they set up and perpetuate should be reversed; just that until White people abolish the seeds of racism which are in the discourse of White superiority, the narrative of pan-European distinction, and the racial stratification system the two legitimate, they will be the embodiment of what the devil is.

Consequently, there are many White people who are unable or unwilling to see that there is an unconsciously propagated discourse of White superiority, who have obviously blinded themselves to the reality of it. If, however, they also carry an opinion of personal, individual superiority (an opinion that they are personally at a high level of excellence superior to most other people, even other Whites) such is a luxury afforded to few non-Whites, least of all Blacks, and not for a lack of ability or potential on our part. Their feelings of personal superiority are a result of the social, societal, medial, educational, political, and economic superstructures that reinforce the idea that White people are better than others. These substantially exonerate feelings of personal psychic self-aggrandisement in the individual White person disallowing them to appreciate the subjectivity of those other to the White (Fanon 2008).

Accordingly, they would never have experienced the racism, the poverty, the struggle, the fear, the belittling, the humiliation, the inferiorisation, or the delimitation that comes with being non-White. They would never have experienced the pain of having their people and the culture (*thaqafah*) of their ancestors inspected and ridiculed by outsiders. It is the absence of these that has substantially contributed to their personal feelings of superiority, which is why their feelings of personal superiority as a White person have their basis in the discourse of White superiority as a race. A discourse that has invariably become unconscious within them (Fanon 2008). They assume that racially everything is fine the way it is because the struggles they faced in personal development were never from a position of racial disadvantage.

Because White people have established their supremacy over the Original nations they have ultimately established their dominion in this world (*'alam*) in place of Allah's dominion over this world (*'alam*). Thus, they have set up a rival system contrary to his thearchy, one that they have called democracy. They are basically opposing Allah's rule to the people's rule, and it is not a façade struggle either: the pan-European genuinely believes in the superiority of democracy to any other form of government and will fight tooth and nail to defend it. But what democracy adds up to is not the rule of all people but the rule of White people. They are the ones that have capitalised the most on the spreading of various categorical discourses during slavery and colonialism, now they need not do anything but remind the world of the rules to the game, rules that invariably favour them.

All non-White people – that is, the descendants of slaves and colonial subjects, as opposed to non-Western people (as despite the gradations of White feelings of superiority that increase the further West one goes, the Whites of both East and West feel superior to all non-Whites regardless of the historical circumstances under which White people began to develop an ideology of White supremacy) – are relegated to the position of the subordinate with ideals like equality (*musawa*) and justice (*adl*), ideals all Muslim's are supposed to fight for, being trampled to the ground. Therefore, if the Muslims of the so-called Third World wish to practice Islam faithfully, they must consider the mechanisms that are presently operating in the West and what is to be done to oppose them.

IV

Sohail Daulatzai (2012: 35) said concerning Malcolm X, "Malcolm continued to argue for the necessity of Third World solidarity across religious, racial, and national lines, in order to challenge European and U.S. power." Indeed, Malcolm X did not fail to point out after the Bandung Conference of Afro-Asiatic unity that "the same man that is colonizing our people in Kenya [is] colonizing our people in South Africa, and in Southern Rhodesia, and in Burma, and in India, and in Afghanistan, and in Pakistan. [The people are starting to realize] all over the world where the dark man [is] being oppressed, he [is] being oppressed by the white man" (Malcolm X 1990; quoted in Daulatzai 2012: 77). This historic conference marked the initiating of the post-colonial discourse and the Third World narrative, the force of which began a global shifting.

Judging by the then backlash against Western interference in global decision making as a result of Bandung the clear interpretation could be that we have now progressed into a new phase of development from the mid-modern definition – though not yet quite a postmodernity. But this late modernity is marked by late capitalism in the form of neoliberalism and has maintained the same discourse of White superiority. The institutions of mid-modernity which were industrialisation, mass publication, high culturalism, the national-state, and colonisation have transitioned to become the institutions of late modernity (or what has, wrongly, been called postmodernity) explicitly typified by a movement towards digitalisation, the multimedia, multi-culturalism, multinationalism, and globalisation.

The late modern takes scientific and ideological reasonings and turns them into so many precarious discourses and narratives. The power relations of modernity that are centred on pan-European distinction and domination, with the onset of the late modern, have become chaotic with the destabilising of the White power structure and the admission of more native structures. Yet the reason I consider this all still to be in essence modernity and not an advance into the postmodern is that White supremacy has not yet been completely triumphed but has become more inherent within the system.

From a social dynamic interpretation: the effectuation of this postmodernising mechanism has been to propel *al-mujtama* (the society) from the machinism of modernity into the sensualism of postmodernity. This sensuality disfigures the face of common institutional operations and introduces an element of the obscene, the outlandish, the over-the-top. The Western world, as they are the only ones postmodernising, no longer sees the world from the perspective of science and ideology, but indulges in the brainwashing, mind-numbing, empty world of entertainment, sensationalism, and gratification, with the assistance of institutions like the mass media. There are no more intellectual pursuits, there are only pleasure-seeking and thrill-riding. But late modernity has also seen the rise of a new interpretation to confront the Western world: the counter-cultural discursive of identity politics. Among the instruments of this discourse one finds the triumphalism of the traditional and the romanticism of the diverse.

Accordingly, from a societal perspective there may have been many conflicts in the past but to Malcolm X the major one was that between oppressor (*zalim*) and oppressed (*mazlum*). This conflict has existed in many forms throughout the different ages and generations. In its Marxist variation it manifested in the form of class conflict and has been fought mainly between the bourgeois, who played the role of the oppressors (the ruling class) and the proletariat, who played the role of the oppressed (the working class). Within the bourgeoisie there was also identified an intelligentsia/petit bourgeoisie, that is, the intermediates (the middle class) and within the proletariat there was identified a lumpen proletariat, that is, the unemployables (the underclass). These two classes that have existed since early modern society are all out for their own ends and serve their own class interests. Nevertheless, society was based on class relations only due to the misconceptions of Marx and the popularity of his theories. In truth, if there is a dichotomy of *zalim* and *mazlum* it is not a class relation but a power relation.

Moreover, when we move passed societies and focus on nationalities we find that national oppressions incorporate the power narrative. In these instances the powers, who play the role of the oppressors (the global minority), are up against the non-powers, who play the role of the oppressed (the global majority). Within the powers, or at the head of them, is the ubiquitous superpower, who basically controls everything. The national struggle effectively becomes a racial struggle as the issues of national sovereignty get knocked on into the all-important issue of race supremacy. Regardless of the level of independence, so long as the United States, Russia, Europe, Australia, Canada, and New Zealand are classified with terms like developed, advanced, and progressive and all other global bodies are classified as developing, backward, and primitive, we will be existing in a world of inherent, barely hidden, White supremacy. The aim, however, is not to replace this White supremacy with Black supremacy or Chinese supremacy or Arab supremacy but with global equality.

But such an aim, while noble and obviously respectable, in our time of late modernity is unfortunately unlikely given the state we are currently in. There is obviously a discrepancy with regard to the institutionalised cultural pluralism (*al-*

mushrik al-thaqafi) within the system. For one, the late modern system in which we live possesses many admixtures of truths (*haqiqat*) that are easily contested from newer and more distinct perspectives. When we play the cultural (*thaqafi*) game the question of *thaqafi* significance is key. There is the overall high culture (*'adab*) and the relatively insignificant subcultures (*thaqafah fariyya*) that contest its pre-eminence. Nevertheless, *thaqafi* bonds are looser, or as Bauman (2016) said 'liquefied' in the current late modern landscape due to globalisation. With the increase of transmigration and inter-marriage, and the growth of multinational organisations, corporations, and mass movements, it seems, as Bauman himself pointed out, that multinationalism and multi-culturalism are, and will continue to be, prominent issues in the lives of a lot of *insan* (people): just like at other times in history, including the old empires and kingdoms of the ancients. What the current globalisation has done is turn the world into a neighbourhood and their different *thaqafah fariyya* into communities.

Bauman (2013: 11) explained concerning this development that, "It is common to say that these 'communities' … are of two kinds. There are communities of life and fate whose members 'lived together in an indissoluble attachment', and communities that are 'welded together solely by ideas or various principles'. … The question of identity arises only with the exposure to 'communities' of the second category – and it does so only because there is more than one idea to conjure up and hold together the 'communities welded by ideas' to which one is exposed in our variegated, polycultural world." An example of what he means is that while it is possible for one to choose whether to be a Black nationalist and associate with other, violent or non-violent, Black nationalists; one has no choice whether or not to be Black, you either are or you are not. This is the difference between communities of ideas (ideological communities) and essentialised communities based on properties like biology, ability, age, or location.

As can be expected, the *thaqafi* parameters of a community define the type of debates they will have in that community. Within the Black community the current identity debate is over Black nationalism; but within this racial politic are already the seeds of an even more radical configuration, those of the godbody. Repudiating Western leanings towards politics as just another hyperreality, a central theme of godbodyism is based on taking the religious figures and heroes of the Bible, Quran, and *Prt M Hru* and making them Black. Beyond the mysticism and symbolism of the Scriptures this spiritual substantiation establishes an interpretation of interior empowerment which opens up a new psychologic for the Black person antithetical to the White system. It goes beyond the national discursive in that it denies the place of the human and inspires – insists – a progression towards the divine.

But late modernity has also brought with it other significant challenges to the national modality of discursive identification. Contrary to Bauman's views – though progressing on from them – we see that with modernity now being liquid, fixed identities like nationalism are actually becoming more and more unsustainable, even simulated. Those institutions which during mid-modernity played the central role such as Family, Church, Work, and State have, in our time, disintegrated into the illusionary (*khayali*) fragments of a time long since passed. Each of these institutions are now malleable and flexible, with no guarantee of their long-term stability. All things once held sacred during the period of mid-modernity are no longer guarantees of solidarity or satisfaction; therefore even commitments to such institutions have been rejected within our late modern times. Far more common nowadays are commitments in more virtual communities and hyper communities where the flexibility is more certain even if the institution itself is a mere simulacrum (Bauman 2013).

These un-lasting commitments are the product of and reason for the instability existing in the West as it goes through late modernity. As Bauman (2013) also noted, the liquefaction of modernity has not only dismantled identities once thought eternal, such as the industrial proletariat, but has decomposed all institutions of modernity once thought safe. Authorities on science, fashion, culture, literature, style, and responsibility today, are not guaranteed to hold their position in the future; "indestructible powers … fade and dissipate, mighty political or economic establishments will be swallowed up by other even mightier ones, or just vanish," (Bauman 2013: 51). All this instability causes identity to be a difficult thing to trace or capture.

Two of the most common misconceptions about identities during mid-modernity were that they would always remain grounded and inflexible, and that people would always have a personal choice as to how they identified themselves. In late modernity we have, however, found that in any given society the vast majority of the people (*al-nas*) have their identities imposed upon them by the top echelon of that society (*mujtama*). Obviously not directly, but through intermediaries, namely, the media. The media has been a precious tool for the establishment, particularly the top echelon within the establishment, to determine the place of any individuals they like or dislike. The perfect examples would be the "Black criminal" and the "Muslim terrorist." Daulatzai, in speaking on the connection of these two groups in *al-mujtama*, particularly in the American *mujtama*, noted that a "War on Terror" would have been a precarious instigation without a "War on Crime" having preceded it. It is clear from a reading of Daulatzai that those most excluded and pushed to the margins in late modern society are the Black and the Muslim non-conformists.

In this atmosphere the Black and the Muslim represent a force of great magnitude, perhaps the only force antithetical to the establishment that is capable of providing a substantial challenge to its institutions. The United States, in our time, likes to portray itself to the world as post-racial when circumstances have not much changed there since the late-1960s. The obfuscated malaise of the Western multicultural (*al-mushrik al-thaqafi*) paradigm is based on the circumstances that occurred in the United States after World War II, particularly with the incoming of the Cold War. The Civil Rights movement was used during the Cold War as a means of displaying America as a tolerant and open society. Daulatzai (2012: 13) explained the situation more in-depth, "at the core of Cold War liberalism's narrative of race was the idea of Black integration and equality in society, a narrative that would project an inclusive American nationalism, which would then cement the moral legitimacy of the United States as a global power and world leader". Indeed, Daulatzai, taking his cue from Malcolm X, believed that US global power represents a global threat tantamount to European colonialism: both being forms of White supremacy.

Yet, though White supremacy has existed for over 300 years it is obvious that the current form, US White supremacy, is the most insidious and yet ingenious form it has taken on. US White supremacy, being mainly a variation of US hypernationalism, is perhaps the biggest threat to the so-called Third World that has ever come about. This is not because the US is evil, as some might say, but more so because of US paranoia and how potentially dangerous that paranoia can be in the midst of a predominantly non-White world. The links between the African Black and the American Black were forged in the 1960s during the freedom struggles going on all over the world: in Africa this was in the form of decolonisation, in America it was in the form of desegregation. Both freedom struggles were against White supremacy but in different forms; however, neither anticipated the persistence of White global designs and its necessity to eliminate all opposition. What they did in Africa was seduce the African bourgeoisie with their foreign investment capital; what they did in America was seduce the Black bourgeoisie with prospects of advancement and joining the status – at least in promise form – of the White bourgeoisie.

In this the Civil Rights movement in America was captured by the propagandists of White supremacy to separate the struggle going on in the US from the struggles going on in the colonies, and the now emergent Third World (or so-called Third World), thus giving the Blacks in the US a feeling of greater solidarity with the Whites of the US than with their brothers and sisters struggling for liberation in Africa and Asia. True indeed, the Black struggle in the US was all about political, legal, and social rights and "liberation" (I use the term loosely), but it would be the Black Power movement that would connect more fully with the so-called Third World and the struggles going on there for identity and empowerment after the long hard years of colonisation.

What distinguished the class struggle in the ex-colony from the class struggle – and to be sure, it was a class struggle – in the Black communities of the United States was that the so-called Third World bourgeois class was disconnected (at least spatially) from their European overlords, while the Black bourgeois class of America was by definition connected, lock, stock, and barrel, with the White bourgeoisie of America. In fact, they were connected so much so that the Civil Rights movement was just as much a White movement as it was a Black one – though the Black Power movement was all Black, even if some White groups worked alongside them to some extent, and the groups within the movement were usually exclusively Black.

The post-Civil Rights uprisings that took place in the 1970s, however, put fear and trepidation in most ordinary White people. The then president Richard Nixon was thus able to capitalise on the social insecurity of the times as Daulatzai suggested, "With hundreds of urban uprisings that set American cities ablaze and sent smoke signals of Black Power rising, Nixon used the mantra of 'law and order' to mobilize what he called the 'Silent Majority' (his white constituencies) to generate the political will and national consensus he needed to destroy the Black Panthers and other Black (and Brown) liberation and antiwar organizations" (Daulatzai 2012: 92). Opposition to Blacks – and by extension all non-Whites – was neither coincidence nor was it the phantomatic spook of a few overzealous Black nationalists. Michelle Alexander stated how: "H.R. Haldeman, one of Nixon's key advisers, recalls that Nixon himself deliberately pursued a Southern, racial strategy: 'He {President Nixon} emphasized that you have to face the fact that the whole problem is really the blacks. The key is to devise a system that recognizes this while not appearing to.'" (Alexander 2011: 44.)

The inherently racial undertones of Nixon's "law and order" policies spoke right to the scared and exasperated White people of the time scoring him top political points from the public. Moreover, his "law and order" rhetoric would contain such race neutral arguments that even Black people would come to accept their legitimacy. But the conflict was far from over, as Daulatzai continued, "beginning in the late 1960s with Nixon and his 'law and order' campaign and continuing into the Reagan-Bush years of the 'War on Crime,' a national consensus was created that sought to link the idea of America to an implicit idea of whiteness" (Daulatzai 2012: 148). Basically, the prevailing racial discourse was of explicit acceptance and tolerance but implicit demonisation and criminalisation.

Daulatzai was very forthright in stating that the situation in America was far more pernicious: "Reagan made very coded appeals to whites by distinguishing them from and contrasting them to the inhabitants of urban America and the sensationalized fears and assumptions that were created about 'Black criminality,' 'welfare queens,' drug dealers, and the supposed pathologies of the inner-city. In the calculus of the New Right, post-Civil Rights America had transcended race, suggesting that overt expressions or explicit appeals to race were themselves viewed as racist, ultimately nullifying and silencing those who sought to challenge the persistence of systemic forms of racism in housing, education, and the like" (Daulatzai 2012: 148). But with racism still existing in the United States as a driving force behind many of the ideas, systems, and act-species promoted, the problems of race relations during the post-Civil Rights situation were not rectified but instead intensified.

In all, the "War on Crime" was effectively a race war and the American policymakers, in waging this war, set about their task with a will. "As a result, the prison population in the United States skyrocketed by 500 percent between 1970 and 2000, with the United States having a higher rate of prisoners per one hundred thousand of its population than any other country in the world. This has culminated in what Michelle Alexander has referred to as 'the New Jim Crow,' in which, according to her, 'racial caste has not ended in America: we have only redesigned it.'" (Daulatzai 2012: 95).

Alexander's New Jim Crow and the designating of Black people as criminals to be locked away only to be denied any rights or opportunities once they are set free has created what I have dubbed – only for the sake of continuity – neo-segregation.

Anyone who spends an extended period of time in the United States should recognise that there is still, very much so, segregation. It may not exist in the legal sense, but it definitely still exists in the social sense. Ghettos are reserved for Black and ethnic minorities; gentrified, suburban, and gated communities are reserved for White and upwardly mobile individuals. Education is largely segregated; prisons are largely Black, corporations are largely White; welfare is largely Black, mortgages are largely White; some shops and restaurants, in order to sell to a largely White clientele, overprice their products and so keep Blacks out; certain brands have even explicitly expressed that they do not desire the Black consumers they acquire. Basically, while segregation and discrimination may be unacceptable by law they are still practiced throughout America, and on a far more subtle level throughout the White world. This plus Alexander's New Jim Crow are what I mean by neo-segregation. The US has not abandoned its doctrine of White supremacy it has only couched it in more acceptable and deracialised terminology. And while there are some Whites who are anti-racist, because the ideology has become embedded into the system, the majority are unable to appreciate their own racial prejudices.

Yet segregation was not the only system the US had designs on, during the process of decolonisation the US saw the so-called Third World as potential subjects for their own imperialist designs. David Harvey (2011: 27) recognised, "While the US had toyed with colonial conquest at the end of the nineteenth century, it evolved a more open system of imperialism without colonies during the twentieth century." Basically, through the help of international agencies, corporations, and financial bodies, the US were able to control the national governments of the so-called Third World without establishing a formal political presence in their countries. At the time of formal colonialism different European powers would compete for international territory. This drove them to establish a military and political presence in the countries they colonised to keep other European countries from laying claim to a territory they had acquired. During the process of decolonisation the political and military influence was gone but the financial and socio-economic influence was still very much so present.

What began in the 1980s with the meeting and agreement of three powerful financial bodies in Washington DC on policies that should be encouraged in Latin America for economic recovery is what we now call the *Washington Consensus*. The three bodies were the International Monetary Fund (IMF), the World Bank, and the US Treasury (with the White House and USAID soon following suit). However, the three juggernauts were not satisfied with just Latin America: George stated how, "The US Treasury [recognised], quite correctly, that the combination of debt plus structural adjustment plus massive privatisation [was] a far more efficient instrument than colonialism ever was for keeping countries in line" (George 2001: 15). Thus, by instituting and promoting the institution of structurally designed neo-colonialism the US has become a GUSE (Great United States Empire), so that though they claim to be anti-imperialist (just like they claim to be anti-racist) this is only because they seek to hide their true nature from the world, a nature that most people can see anyway.

As the financial influence of the US and the Washington Consensus are without rival and are relatively without

European competitor the GUSE has been able to stretch into the former colonial states of the so-called Third World with relative ease. They have in that sense established an empire without having to establish a political and military presence. Ironically, the US has still established both: there are US military bases in nearly every country on the planet and their self-proclaimed mission to democratise the world is very much so a political mantra. This less formal form of colonisation is what Nkrumah called neo-colonisation, but this US mission is far less universal than it appears, as Chomsky (1999: 66) pointed out, "Even the most dedicated believers in 'America's mission' must be aware that the US-UN relations have [changed] since the UN fell out of control with the progress of decolonization, leaving the United States regularly isolated in opposition to global accords on a wide range of issues and committed to undermining central components of the UN, particularly those with a third world orientation." In effect, the US, guided by its ideas of self-importance and exceptionalism, enforces policies and guidelines for countries in the so-called Third World, while, at the same time, opposing and vetoing any proposal made by the so-called Third World or even with a Third World tinge in the UN. Such is the neo-colonisation under which they now live.

V

What happened to turn desegregation and decolonisation into neo-segregation and neo-colonisation? The answer to this question is found in the concept of *socio-elasticity*. Basically, social systems that are abolished have a tendency – if not replaced by systemic and discursive mechanisms that oppose the former power relations – to revive and re-emerge in a new form of social organisation. This social revivalism is the only way to explain the revival, over the centuries, of institutions, dogmas, and ideologies that have historically been superseded.

An example of this would be slavery. Slavery was superseded in medieval times by serfdom, yet in late medieval times slavery revived due to a papal injunction by Pope Eugene IV. Or perhaps a better example is the peasantry, though they were abolished as a class, they were able to revive in a figure as sharecroppers and small farmers. Again, the landed aristocracy may not be in the same form but they have revived and become far more insidious, being embedded into the current system as landowners and landlords. Based on such evidential appreciations I have been able to develop three axioms of social kinetics:

1. Two or more social bodies will always interact in a competitive or conflictual way until cohesion is achieved or $x_1 + x_2 \to na$.

2. Social cohesion between two or more social bodies cannot be achieved until the natural limits, the systemic boundaries, between them have been reformed or abolished or $x_1 + x_2 \to pa \leftrightarrow Lm \searrow$.

3. If a counter-discourse is not propagated any reformed or abolished limitations will revive, taking on new formations of the old which thereby become inherent or $pa > Lm \to D \leftrightarrow pa \searrow$.

These three social kinetics axioms could actually be called laws as they are such general rules throughout every *mujtama* that to deny them would be unscientific.

Social revivalism has also occurred with regard to segregation and colonisation: in this case it is due to US policies authorising their revival. That is not to say that outside of the US – that is, in other pan-European settlements – they do not have the same tendencies of systemic neo-segregation and systemic neo-colonisation, what I am saying is that while the powers of the other pan-European settlements are severely limited the Great United States Empire is constantly expanding in power and territory. These structural mechanisms that acquiesce to segregation and colonisation are so intrinsic to the fabric of White supremacy that America perpetuates. Discursively Americans are taught of America's mission, glory, and superiority to other nations, including European ones. They are taught that they conquered and outsmarted the Native Americans, subordinated the Latin Americans, enslaved the African Americans, overpowered the British and defeated the Germans twice.

While American style White supremacy is now an inherent form of White supremacy, it is White supremacy nonetheless. That is the problem, due to the socio-elastic tendencies within any social system the revival of undesirable systems is inevitable unless a counter-discourse is instituted together with a structural reconstitution. Substantial change alone will not do. The system has to be utterly replaced by a contrasting system or the old will revive. But remember, the reason these institutions revive is because the people were never really ready to give them up in the first place: circumstances beyond their control forced upon them their changes.

Adjustments to these same changes meant that in order for the system to function the way it used to, without stepping beyond the new demarcation point, new mechanisms had to be put in place to disguise the former system with the illusion of acceptability. The insidious nature of inherent White supremacy causes most White people, particularly those in the middle class, to not recognise it as such, and definitely not to see it as racist. And with new enemies like the "Black criminal" and the "Muslim terrorist" White people can be racist without acknowledging that they are such.

What is considered to be reasonable debate not only comes across as prejudiced but is in itself profoundly prejudiced. To say Black boys are the most excluded group in schools and the most likely to commit crimes throughout their lives sounds like a proper analysis with social static evidence, but is in fact deeply prejudiced. It neglects, firstly, the fact that the highly circulated discourse of Black criminality and Black inferiority perpetuated in Black communities and Black schools (not to mention the underfunding of those Black schools) is psychologically most likely to cause Black boys to rebel in order to attain what they believe to be success in *al-mujtama*. Secondly, it excuses White people from any responsibility for the perpetuating of this metanarrative and the socio-economic superstructure that goes with it, whether by commission or omission, through inflecting responsibility onto the Black boys. Thirdly, it does not take into account the fact that structural mechanisms exist that target Black boys and men causing them to be more likely to get excluded, get arrested, and get convicted for crimes than Whites.

The same could be said about the Muslim: questions like, why are Muslims more likely to commit terroristic atrocities, are deeply prejudiced questions. They, firstly, forget that French Republicans invented terrorism in the late eighteenth century to force their anti-monarchical views on the people of France. Secondly, they neglect the fact that under the current conditions any act of violence committed by a Muslim is more likely to be *labelled* terrorist – even if it has no political intent behind it. Thirdly, they do not respect that if we were to take the former US definition of terrorism at its word, then, as Chomsky (2007) pointed out, the United States would be the "leading terrorist state." Ultimately, the metanarrative of the Muslim terrorists perpetuated by the Orientalist discourse is what the Muslim world must confront; just like the metanarrative of pan-African inferiority perpetuated by the discourse of Black criminality is what the Black community must dismantle.

But challenging these discourses will not be enough. After the discursive has been proven false, if any structural changes occur, that is when the people will look to "the good old days" when life was easier under the false conclusions. Structural changes will ultimately show White people how inherent White supremacy has been in the race relations existing in modern society. Such a revelation will be a shock to the system. At that time they will question whether the system was ever really as racist as we have proven it to be. Their reaction will be staunch reversals to the gains made and the laziest, most minute, adjustments to the existing power relations.

For this cause, it is not enough to change and reform the system. Socio-elasticity will nullify any reforms made either by reversing them or by reviving the old conditions with a new pragmatic. Thus, the only way to overcome White supremacy is to start an entirely new system altogether with a new metanarrative and a new discourse. That is exactly what Malcolm X sought to accomplish with his Muslim internationalism. As Malcolm X himself noted, "We must recapture our heritage and our identity if we are ever to liberate ourselves from the bonds of white supremacy. ... [Our] cultural revolution must be the means of bringing us closer to our African brothers and sisters. It must begin in the community and be based on community participation" (Malcolm X 1992; quoted in Daulatzai 2012: 104).

The programme Malcolm X announced was an extreme challenge to US global expansionist and imperialist designs. Daulatzai (2012) commented on how it united a broad school: Black Muslims, Black Nationalists, Black Revolutionists, Black Artists, Afrocentrics, pan-Africans, and the hip-hop generation. Indeed, he expressed how, "Malcolm's resurgence in urban America in the mid-1980s … spoke to the profound failure of and disillusionment with the Civil Rights project" (Daulatzai 2012: 98). But where a revived interest in Malcolm X began the process of uniting all parties that felt betrayed and deceived by Civil Rights in the 1980s and 90s, Minister Farrakhan's "distance from the new authority [of Sunnite Orthodoxy] enabled him to preserve enough political capital among Blackamericans at large to be able to spearhead the historic 1995 Million Man March in Washington, D.C." (Jackson 2005: 76).

It was herein that, "The earth shook on October 16, 1995, and left a large dent in the capital. And, to try and separate Minister Farrakhan from the shared spirit and renewed energy of the million-plus men who walked, ran, drove, flew, took trains and buses to the nation's capital from most parts of the Black Diaspora is to encourage dishonesty and to deny reality and history" (Madhubuti 1996: 2). The Million Man March was the culmination of all the racial tensions that had been in force from the 1980s to the mid-1990s, Black people had come to appreciate that Civil Rights had not gained for Black people the equality the protesters had been fighting for. Hereby, Farrakhan wanted to send a message to the state capital and to all of America: "White supremacy has to die in order for humanity to live" (Farrakhan 1996: 21); and it is undeniable that this statement was shared by the almost 2 million-strong Black men at the march when he said it.

But how does one prove such an emotive statement to those who have decided that White supremacy is no longer, and was at that time no longer, an issue. If colonisation, segregation, and apartheid had by that time already been overcome – on paper – then what proof was there that White supremacy was still an effective ideological position? Perhaps late modernity had overcome it through the determined actions of the freedom fighters of the 1960s, 70s, and 80s. Perhaps White supremacy was no longer an evil undergirding of the Western world, haunting it and allowing it to cause division between two groups of human beings that need not be at war (Farrakhan 1996). If Mr. Farrakhan is correct, "White supremacy has poisoned the bloodstream of religion, education, politics, jurisprudence, economics, social ethics and morality" (Farrakhan 1996: 22); but if such is the case then surely there must be proof.

Socio-elasticity theoretically provides that proof. Though it can be proven right in virtually all cases of social relations it will be hard to show someone who refuses to listen the undeniable fact that people in social group (*mujtama*) quantities dislike change and rarely change fast. It will also be difficult to prove to someone who refuses to listen the inexorability of the revivalistic tendencies within social systems. For this cause, the next three chapters will present certain ways in which other social systems have revived to show that not only are social systems hard to change, and hard to die, they can also revive and take on a new form which disguises them from their previous more overt incarnation.

As the culmination of the then existing racial tensions was the Million Man March, "the most successful Black Movement march in the history of the United States" (Worrill 1996: 80); it must be appreciated immediately the resemblance it bore, at least in implication, to the March on Washington 32 years prior. Nevertheless, as Gholson informed us, "I remember demonstrations by the Hippies, the Yippies, the Moonies, pro and anti-abortion advocates, Vietnam vets, the Shriners, the KKK and the second attempt to March on Washington, but none of these efforts come close to equalling the number of people, the discipline of the participants or the unique purpose of the Million Man March" (Gholson 1996: 77). The three eidetic phenomena that defined the 1990s for Black America were: the Rodney King incident, the O.J. Simpson trial, and the Million Man March which succeeded them.

The march itself can also be defined by three monumental calls: (i) "from this day forward, we can never again see ourselves through the narrow eyes of the limitation of the boundaries of our own fraternal, civic, political, religious, street organization or professional organization. We are forced by the magnitude of what we see here today, that whenever you return to your cities and you see a Black man [to know] that he is your brother" (Farrakhan 1996: 13); (ii) "We must belong to some organization that is working for and in the interest of the uplift and the liberation of our people" (Farrakhan 1996: 23); (iii) "when you go home, we've got to register eight million, eligible but unregistered brothers and sisters. So, you go home and find eight more like yourself. You register and get them to register" (Farrakhan 1996: 24). Though Farrakhan made a call for certain other things like starting an economic fund and the adopting of children, these three: to see other Blacks as brothers and sisters, to join a pro-Black organisation, and to register to vote had the biggest impact on future events in Black America.

Yet the realities of Black oppression still continued and continue to exist beneath the surface of the existing power structure. The reason is because the White supremacy he and his predecessors fought against only went from being obvious to being more inherent. White supremacy currently may be abhorrent to mainstream political and academic circles but in the actual living citizens of the Americas, Europe (Eastern and Western), Russia, Australia, and New Zealand racial distinction has placed White people in a superior position: one based on a kind of moral, intellectual, or paternal distinction. If we consider this pan-European distinction we see it has been embedded into the life-blood of White societies by a narrative that has perpetuated its mythology. Yet due to the complex nature of society and the reaction against overt expressions of racism, the narrative itself is never a spoken narrative, it is more an assumed narrative that is unconsciously accepted and realised within the global unconscious of large sections of the White population. Further, White supremacy could not endure without some form of psychic narration explicating the value of its presence.

It is for this reason that the anomalous theory of the devil, while seeming helpful, is actually unnecessary as White devilishment can easily and far more effectively be proven through their discourse of White superiority. Conversely, we in the godbody consider White supremacy a somatisation of a discourse of White superiority that has its basis in what we call *trick knowledge*. We also maintain that knowledge of self is the only means of overcoming this trick knowledge and of finding our way back to *tawhidic* enlightenment. *Tricknology* has been instrumental in White people's rise to power: they have *lied* to themselves and *lied* about themselves; they have *lied* to all non-Whites and *lied* about all non-Whites. The discourse of White superiority was a lie and the discourse of Black criminality was a lie; the narrative of pan-European distinction was a lie and the narrative of pan-African inferiority was a lie.

(That said, the system they set up, the system that currently rules the world, and that will invariably have to be destroyed, does possess some strengths that may instead simply need readjustment. To be sure, the concept of nation (*umma*), as precarious as it is, does have its uses. True, in ancient times the Original people had royal states (*mulukut*) and noble states (*amirat*) and now we have national-states, which are in themselves far less hierarchical (though still being hierarchical). If the nation (*umma*) existed without a state machine and its state apparatuses it would be much like what existed before the ancient monarchies of Egypt, Arabia, Sumer, and India – though ancient Kush was a system that was unusually anarchistic for its time with no proper monarchy until long after Egypt (Dunjee Houston 2007), hence why it was called by the Egyptians: the land of the gods and goddesses. Another White invention that would be worth keeping is the parliamentary system. At the abolition of the state parliaments would function like syndicalist bodies among the people to bring coordination and organisation to *al-mujtama*, though not for the purpose of instituting laws and substantiating law enforcement or some other legal body. The substance of the parliament would in effect be to allow the systems operating within the stateless nation to operate in a scientific and efficient manner, thereby providing for our system a socio-economic superstructure).

White people now claim a multiracial ideological perception, one that is contradicted by many of the currently existing structures that caused Bauman to note, "To be wholly or in part 'out of place' everywhere, not to be completely anywhere … may be an upsetting, sometimes annoying experience. There is always something to boldly display, to negotiate, to bid for and to bargain for; there are differences to be so moved or glossed over, or to be on the contrary made more salient and legible. 'Identities' float in the air, some of one's own choice but others inflated and launched by those around, and one needs to be constantly on the alert to defend the first against the second; there is a heightened likelihood of misunderstanding, and the outcome of the negotiation forever hangs in the balance" (Bauman 2013: 13). Therefore, the rationalisation of ethnically (*'ammama*), and racially (*sa'ba*) legitimated idiosyncrasies contributes delicately to the current direction of social change, producing, on the one hand, a consciousness of difference in the mainstream of *al-mujtama*, and, on the other hand, a consciousness of exclusion in the ethnic group.

Bauman (2013) also noted along those same lines that in the current system of late modernity, the marginalisation of migrants, in particular refugees – interestingly enough, those usually who flee to the West escaping conflicts almost certainly orchestrated by the West – represent a shift in the implications of miseration in the Western *mujtama*. Exploitation undeniably still exists, however, the nationless/stateless refugees find themselves in a far more miserable position than the proletariat in our time. With globalisation transmuting the US into a GUSE, and being trumpeted around the world as the standard of multiculturalism and the global ethic of individualism, those who are marginalised, either within the West or within a non-Western country, are subject to a form of subjugation and demoralisation that the proletariat only experienced in mid-modernity.

Furthermore, if we then consider the situation of the ethnic we find, as Bauman (2013) explained, that their experience of marginalisation was, and still is, equivalent to exclusion, whether in the West or the non-West, and that the problems of exploitation faced by the early proletarians have now been delineated to the non-Western victims of racism that emerged as a result of the liquefaction of the global order. The Nation of Islam's response to the racial marginalisation of Black people has thereby been a means of reclaiming Islam for the purpose of redirecting social events. Here Shari'ati's *tauhidi* worldview becomes very useful: "the world-view of *tauhid* [encourages] the negation of the dependence of man on any social force, and the linking of him, in exclusivity and in all his dimensions, to the consciousness and will that rule over being. The source of support, orientation, belief, and succor of every individual is a single central point, a pivot around which revolve all the motions of the cosmos" (Shari'ati 1979: 87). With this central force or intelligence (*daka*) as the pivot of *al-'alam*, more so than the social dynamics and social statics of *al-nas*, what is the form of social organisation best suited to the interaction of *al-nas* with this intelligence? According to Shari'ati and Islamic teachings it is the *umma*.

In the Muslim internationalism of Shari'ati the *umma* is the societal manifestation of the *tauhidi* worldview. Basically, one can automatically join the *umma* or Muslim International by living out *tawhid*. But *umma* is more than the practicing of the *tawhidic* worldview, *umma*, according to Shari'ati (1979: 119) has a functional, pretty much teleological, definition about it. "The word *umma* derives from the root *amm*, which has the sense of path and intention. The *umma* is, therefore, a society in which a number of individuals, possessing a common faith and goal, come together in harmony with the intention of advancing and moving towards the common goal." The immanent intentionality presumed therefrom commits the *umma* to a teleological definition as opposed to a spatial orientation. It is in all ways a noetic correlate of eidetic apperceptions, particularly with regard to forces. The fact that Islam as a whole is an *umma* also presents a clue as to the depth of its effects on the social realm.

Shari'ati saw the *umma* as the ideal society and it, to him, represented the true Muslim International and the best basis upon which to organise all social relations and social activity, "While other expressions denoting human agglomerations have taken unity of blood or soil and the sharing of material benefit as the criterion of society, Islam, by choosing the word *umma*, has made intellectual responsibility and shared movement toward a common goal the basis of its social philosophy" (Shari'ati 1979: 119). At the same time, it was the Muslim internationalism of Malcolm X that ultimately affected the younger generation of Black America and the so-called Third World through hip-hop. Daulatzai mentioned how through, "Conjuring the history of Malcolm X and the radical redemptive vision that he outlined throughout his life, hip-hop [became] a cultural extension of Malcolm's internationalist vision" (Daulatzai 2012: 110). It will no doubt take a merging of both visions of Muslim internationalism for us to see the defeat and demise of White supremacy. Which brings us right back to the heading of this chapter: where do we go from here?

Neoliberalism and the Imperial State

Due to the circumstances that occurred in the US at the end of the 1960s there was a huge reaction against the gains of the Civil Rights movement domestically and the pan-Arab and pan-African movements in foreign. Though the US economy was affected by these, far more dangerous to American economic policy was the rise in the 1950s of socialist policies in Western Europe, particularly those in England. While in Western Europe economic policy seemed to be unifying the two diametrically opposed wings of political opinion, in the US it was their anti-communism that allowed political economics, or to be more specific capitalist economics, to evolve and even dominate. It is out of this ferment that neoliberalism, which is the revival of liberalism as resurrection (*ba'th*), ascended to global dominance.

As far as theories go neoliberalism is a socio-economic theory that seeks to allow big business to dominate nationally and internationally. David Harvey defined it as such, "Neoliberalism is in the first instance a theory of political economic practices that proposes that human well-being can best be advanced by liberating individual entrepreneurial freedoms and skills within an institutional framework characterized by strong private property rights, free markets, and free trade. The role of the state is to create and preserve an institutional framework appropriate to such practices" (Harvey 2011: 2). Such a theory inevitably has a profound effect on a *mujtama*, whether it be an American *mujtama* or an international *mujtama*, it produces the transmutation of the free market into the domineering market, seizing control of every aspect of our lives: "Instead of citizens, it produces consumers. Instead of communities, it produces shopping malls" (McChesney 1998; quoted in Chomsky 1999: 11), or in our day virtual malls and ecommerce shopping centres.

While all that may be true, economically neoliberalism also functions through financial institutions dealing excessively in fictitious capital such as stocks, bonds, shares, assets, credit, currency, et cetera., none holding any real capital stability but all playing a complicated roll in the international market. According to Harvey (2011: 33), "Neoliberalization has meant, in short, the financialization of everything. … There [is] unquestionably a power shift away from production to the world of finance." This is so inextricably the case that certain detrimental decisions have been made based on precarious projections of financial gain: "Countries that are deemed to be a hopeful prospect by the financial markets enjoy a massive inflow of capital. This is in fact of dubious benefit, since (as in the East Asian case, for example) the flood of foreign capital tends to encourage massive over-investment and the development of largescale over-capacity, depressing profitability. When foreign investors begin to get a whiff of this, the result is panic" (Callinicos 2003: 31). This may be true of investment, and it has the capacity to go terribly wrong for all parties involved, but the financial sector is still the most prominent sector within the globally resurrected system of liberalism, so that

"In the event of a conflict between Main Street and Wall Street, the latter [will] be favoured" (Harvey 2011: 33).

McChesney said concerning this situation, "Neoliberalism is the defining political economic paradigm of our time – it refers to the policies and processes whereby a relative handful of private interests are permitted to control as much as possible of social life in order to maximize their personal profit" (McChesney 1998; quoted in Chomsky 1999: 7). As a system of wealth creation, neoliberalism has been able to generate vast sums of capital for the owners of large corporations, and particularly American corporations. It is for this reason that "the advocates of the neoliberal way now occupy positions of considerable influence in education (the universities and many 'think tanks'), in the media, in corporate boardrooms and financial institutions, in key state institutions (treasury departments, the central banks), and also in those international institutions such as the International Monetary Fund (IMF), the World Bank, and the World Trade Organization (WTO) that regulate global finance and trade" (Harvey 2011: 3).

Neoliberalism as a theoretical position justifies itself by claiming that all prior to systems, and any future system, would be inferior to its own functionings; for which cause it seeks to consume and destroy anything that runs contrary to its own mechanisms of dynamic wealth production whether they be social, political, religious, cultural, or economic. The resurrection (*ba'th*) of liberalism as neoliberalism is basically the rule not of a culture, religion, party, or people but of wealthy individuals connected to corporate power. Thereby it is not the American government that rules, it is Corporate America that rules, and as McChesney said, such a rule infringes unscrupulously on democratic institutions, "corporations themselves are effectively totalitarian organizations, operating along nondemocratic lines. That our economy is centered around such institutions severely compromises our ability to have a democratic society" (McChesney 1998; quoted in Chomsky 1999: 13). What this ultimately shows is the demise of democracy at the hands of neoliberalism and its being subsumed into capitalism and submerged with it to become a plutocracy.

This subsuming of democracy into capitalism was not an equilateral subsuming: democracy lost most of its key components while capitalism's pre-existing totalising and universalising dimensions became deregulated and unrestricted. Indeed, "proper attention to the *ab origine* universal or universalizing dimensions of capitalist development should not blind us to the rupture or shift in contemporary capitalist production and global relations of power. We believe that this shift makes perfectly clear and possible today the capitalist project to bring together economic power and political power, to realize, in other words, a properly capitalist order" (Hardt & Negri 2000: 9). This capitalist order is a plutocratic order, or what I call "capitalism with teeth."

Friedman explained this more apparent form of the metamorphosis by stating, "The hidden hand of the market will never work without a hidden fist" (Friedman 2000; quoted in Callinicos 2003: 50). It is the threat of state violence that allows the market and the marketeers to maintain the system of universal market control. There is no doubt the personifications of Capital, the capitalists, have become, in our time, something more than businesspersons. They, in our time, literally rule. Though their rule is not in the form of open politics, regardless of the successes of the Musks or the Trumps, but of the biopolitics of subjective (*muttasil*) reproduction.

According to Hardt and Negri, "The great industrial and financial powers … produce not only commodities but also subjectivities" (Hardt & Negri 2000: 32), these industrial and financial power players became superordinate to all governmental bodies and agencies, including inter-governmental bodies and agencies, thus further compromising culture (*thaqafah*) and biopolitics. Biopolitics actually occurs when politics is used to control and discipline people's bodies: when life becomes political and when the political, economic, and cultural "overlap" into everyday life (Hardt & Negri 2000). The expansion of capitalism into the biopolitical realm transpired when media, culture, religion, and politics all became commodified and commercialised.

Callinicos (2003: 27) explicated in particular how "this direct subordination of cultural production to the priorities of profitable accumulation can be witnessed daily on television, where lust, greed, celebrity, and lifestyle fuse in a mutually reinforcing circuit of nightmarish banality." Though multimedia mechanisms truly work in favour of capital, capital supersedes the media – even media empires – by becoming inexorably biopolitical and intertwined with governing institutions. As capital and its personifications now rule with a hidden fist it becomes evident that the people not only have no power over them, but are themselves the subjects of their plutocratic governance.

I

Neoliberalism, as a revived and resurrected (*bu'itha*) form of liberalism, basically instigated the turning of the countries of the world into sections of a global plutocracy; which itself started out as nothing more than an alternative perspective on economic policies that sought to revive neoclassical liberalism in the post-war era. "During the Long Boom of the 1950s and 1960s, most of these policies [were] dismissed as the fantasies of economic heretics dreaming of a return to the nineteenth century" (Callinicos 2003: 2). At that time, the

Keynesian orthodoxy ruled the day; for neoliberalism to replace Keynesianism as orthodoxy it took a major international crisis to open the hearts and minds of the world leaders. Effectively, "The IMF and the World Bank … [were] centres for the propagation and enforcement of 'free market fundamentalism' and neoliberal orthodoxy. In return for debt rescheduling, indebted countries were required to implement institutional reforms, such as cuts in welfare expenditures, more flexible labour market laws, and privatization" (Harvey 2011: 29).

But the revived liberalism of our time has thus become plutocratic, which equates to neoliberalism; just like when Islamism has become anarchic it equates to neo-Islamism. When one adds the discourse of White superiority to the biopolitics of a White plutocracy the end product will be White privilege. Consider it well, as long as the industrial and financial powers and the economic and military super-ordinates are predominantly White, and perpetuate the discourse of White superiority; then both discourse and practice will be White privileging, regardless of the ideological ruse that is used to hide both hand and fist from the masses. The fact that neoliberalism is also a global order of capital accumulation and capital domination simply means that the method of maintaining a reality of privilege, even if only in an inherent form, is to allow some non-Whites to share a measure of privilege and propagate that as globalisation; and seeing as how they also propagate and instigate the subjectivities of the people through biopolitics, the people get deluded into believing that submitting to a non-White exploiter or oppressor (who conveniently happens to be subordinate to some White power player or other) is freedom.

Shari'ati even furthered the point, stating, "As men were possessed by spirits in the old days, today a man is reduced to the position of a cog in a strict, monotonous and ruthless bureaucracy due to perpetual contact with a certain mechanical tool. He no longer feels and comprehends his individuality; he has 'lost' himself" (Shari'ati 2006: 15). In order to explain what he meant by all this he continued, "When I feel my own religion, literature, emotion, needs and pains through my culture, I feel my own self, the very social and historical self (not the individual self), the source from which this culture has originated. Therefore, culture is the expression and super-structure of the real being of my society, actually the whole history of my society" (Shari'ati 2006: 17). In all, we can see here two subjectivities: one based on the biopolitic of the bureaucracy and the other based on the *thaqafah* of *al-mujtama*. The first is a false culture (*al-thaqafah al-za'if*) created by the Western power players, the second is a real culture (*al-thaqafah al-haqq*) created by the history of the people.

Shari'ati (2006) was clear that the self (*al-nafs*) created by *al-thaqafah al-za'if* is birthed by different conditions, conditions that involve another history, another background, another economy, and another social setting. This *al-thaqafah al-za'if* is extremely problematic as "when I wish to feel my own real self, I find myself conceiving another society's culture instead of my own and bemoaning troubles not mine at all" (Shari'ati 2006: 17). To further clarify what he meant Shari'ati continued, "The dark skinned man of Africa, the Berber of North Africa, the Persian and Indian in Asia, each has a particular past and unique present. However, they feel inside particular pain and concern which they regard as their own, but which are actually offshoots of problems of periods following the Middle Ages" (Shari'ati 2006: 18). Europe's world dominance began after the Middle Ages with the time of the Renaissance. Following that time Europe became the global power that dominated all global non-powers. The repercussions of this were that all global non-powers, including those in Africa, Asia, and Latin America, would seek to imitate Europe as best they could. However, what they ended up imitating was actually only the false culture (*al-thaqafah al-za'if*) of neoliberalism.

So it was internationally, even so nationally; in the countries of the West neoliberal ideas emerged due to the propagation of ideals like "human dignity" and "individual freedom." "In so doing [neoliberalism] chose wisely, for these are indeed compelling and seductive ideals. These values, they held, were threatened not only by fascism, dictatorships, and communism, but by all forms of state intervention that substituted collective judgements for those of individuals free to choose" (Harvey 2011: 5). Basically, for liberal theory to resurrect (*bi'thah*) as a system it had to make itself a biopolitical option legitimate for the people. It is for this cause, "The central role previously occupied by the labor power of mass factory workers in the production of surplus value is today increasingly filled by intellectual, immaterial, and communicative labor power." However, "the problem of [these] new figures of subjectivity, [is] in both their exploitation and their revolutionary potential" (Hardt & Negri 2000: 29). Without a doubt the gatekeepers of late modernity, as with most other historical epochs, are the intellectuals, the thinkers, the mental workers; they can be used to either perpetuate or undermine the existing social order, which in our case is a global order.

The power of the intellectual circus became apparent to capital during the 1970s, after the protests for Civil Rights and against the Vietnam War that took place on the campuses of America and the protests of the '68 movement that took place on the campuses of Paris – both cases in which students, scholars, and the academic strata began to display their power in more radical expressions (Harvey

2011) – had dissipated. In these movements authority – personified by the representatives of Capital, the State, the Church, and the University – was considered the primary target. What occurred during the time of transition between the 1960s rebellion and the 1980s sell-out was an important historiographic moment called the 1970s; when Capital and certain elements within the University made an alliance to help establish and perpetuate each other, and concentrate all the frustrations of the students onto knowledge systems.

Accordingly, academics of the calibre of Foucault devoted their attention to "fighting the power" while becoming themselves autocratic power players. Foucault's hypnotic syntax and prolific writing concealed the discursive nature of his own anti-discursive polemics: the Foucauldian web is highly discursive while duping the people into believing it liberates them from discourse. Still, the magic trick of Foucault is nothing compared to the Hat Trick of Jean-François Lyotard, who (i) convinced everyone that the shift from the differentiation between democracy and capitalism to their converging to become a plutocracy, was, at the same time, a leap from modernity into a postmodernity; (ii) convinced everyone that this postmodernity marked an end to all metanarratives like religion, ideology, and philosophy (systems that conveniently happen to be the only ones capable of critiquing and challenging the plutocracy); and (iii) convinced everyone that his postmodern theory was neither itself a neoliberal metanarrative nor simply a ruse for what was really just liquid modernism.

The fact is, the central institutions of modernism were not done away with or surpassed, but were in fact either accelerated, liquefied, or subsumed into more powerful institutions. The intellectuals (*al-daki*) of the 1960s and 70s – that were introduced to students as left-wing – were categorically neoliberal, and it was their responsibility to provide the intellectual legitimation for the domination of Capital. On the other hand, Capital would provide a market for their ideas and universalise their names and credibility. Of particular interest in this case is Foucault, Christofferson (2016: 12) intimated how, "Foucault had a history of taking philosophico-political stances that seem to be based more on a desire to situate himself within the intellectual avant-garde than on sincere conviction." It is evident that Foucault and many others within the Foucauldian establishment sacrificed credibility for celebrity.

It must at this point seem rather strange to read one who uses terms like biopolitics, governmentality, and discourse critiquing the very man who popularised those terms, however, my critique is not of the terminology he used but of the ideas and theoretical positions he promoted and highlighted; and the reasons behind that promotion. While it may seem to some that Foucault sold-out to neoliberalism the seeds of his change were always present within his theoretical enterprise (Behrent 2016). It also appears that the very celebrity Foucault received for these theories would be the tipping point, "Foucault had, in the 1960s, converted his academic credentials into cultural celebrity by increasing his visibility in intellectual reviews and the cultural press, eventually achieving intellectual superstardom with the publication of *The Order of Things: An Archaeology of the Human Sciences*, which was extensively discussed in the mass media and became a bestseller in the summer of 1966. ... Although [men like] Glucksmann may have distorted Foucault's ideas, he was a useful ally in Foucault's bid for recognition ... Glucksmann praised Foucault to the sky in books that sold in large numbers and were well promoted in the media" (Christofferson 2016: 11).

Though it might seem harsh to say, it appears that Foucault's moral compass always pointed south, an embellishment first revealed in his debates with Noam Chomsky, where he said, quite unapologetically, "One makes war to win, not because it is just" (Chomsky & Foucault 2006: 51). Thus, further emphasising what Shari'ati said in the 1970s, "as long as beliefs are not accompanied by awareness not only are they of no use, but they are harmful because they will waste our energies" (Shari'ati 1981: 578). When science and philosophy are used to promote valueless beliefs, which is what has happened to philosophy since Foucault, then they have nothing left to do but side with the bourgeoisie even if appearing to be fighting against them (Shari'ati 1981).

Foucault, for all his Marxism and individualism, had come to the place of rejecting the concept of justice as a bourgeois decorative only useful in a bourgeois system, as he also said quite plainly, "Rather than thinking of the social struggle in terms of 'justice,' one has to emphasize justice in terms of the social struggle" (Chomsky & Foucault 2006: 50); that is to say, justice, to Foucault, only exists in accordance to the social situation accentuated by the social struggle: if the bourgeois are ruling then it will be a bourgeois justice, if the proletariat are ruling then it will be a proletarian justice. Hereby, Foucault's conception of justice, and of morality in general, was based on the Western model. Using this Western standard Foucault had all the leeway he needed to make a transformation from Maoist contender to neoliberal defender without undermining the core of his system. And though his initial works presented an alternate history of knowledge and institutions in society, the way in which that history was presented remained no more than "an intuitive and empathetic retelling" (Rehmann 2016) than an eidetic critique – though admittedly such was implied.

Foucault's earlier works actually represent an anti-structuralist structuralism. He consistently displayed tableau

– minor tableau no doubt but tableau nonetheless – finding and using features linking them to systematically organise them. The tabular and epistemic structures Foucault presented are thus just that, structures. However, far from critiquing the architecture of the tabular structures he developed Foucault spent more time considering how these systems have been effective in creating our world.

An example of this is perceptible to one who reads *Madness and Civilization* expecting to find a railing critique against the system of psychiatry or against the systems used to determine normality and abnormality. In the end they will have only wasted their time scrolling through endless reams of historical, aesthetic, and literary accounts before they get even a glimpse, a very vague one at that, of a critiquing of the reasoning behind the institutionalisation of the mentally affected. All this giving truth to Behrent's (2016: 181) rather provocative statement: "Foucault's methodology and its philosophical underpinnings account (at least in part) for his attraction to neoliberalism" and also for his denial of legitimate concepts like justice.

But Foucault's turning to neoliberalism was not a betrayal as much as an awkward acceptance of the intellectual's lot, articulating that lot as such: The fact that they could be manipulated by power groups like parties and unions; the fact that they may not be able to develop these groups "for lack of a global strategy or outside support" (Foucault 2006: 166); and the fact that they may not be followed at all, or by only a minority. While Foucault appreciated that in late modernity intellectuals (*daki*) had "the same adversary as the proletariat, namely, the multinational corporations, the judicial and police apparatuses, the property speculators, and so on" (Foucault 2006: 162); not to mention other intellectuals who are obliged to serve the interests of the State or Capital (Foucault 2006). Nevertheless, for Foucault the temptation to join Capital "to win," so to speak, was too irresistible and as he had never really approached a genuine critique of society as much as an alternative history of society he was able to switch sides almost seamlessly, bringing with him a tidal wave of intellectuals and academics.

Ultimately, the Foucauldian web, while not necessarily being an apologetic for neoliberalism does invariably have affinities with it. In this, Foucauldian influence can be held responsible for many of the neoliberal turns that transpired in the years following his death as explicated by Daniel Zamora (2016: 75), "Colin Gordon, a leading translator of and commentator on Foucault in the English-speaking world, does not hesitate to declare that 'parts of the formulae of Clinton and Blair for a "third way" may have effectively carried out a form of the operation which Foucault might have been taken as challenging the socialists to contemplate – the selective incorporation, in an updated and corrected social democracy, of certain elements of neoliberal analysis and strategy.'" At the same time, "his thought [also led] to the breakdown of the social realm into a myriad of singularities, which proved unable to coalesce into a force that could achieve emancipation for the many" (Amselle 2016: 167). Indeed, Foucauldian fragmentation leads inexorably to the Thatcherite summation that society (*mujtama*) and the social (*ijtima*) do not exist at all. True, the fragmentation of late modern society cannot be blamed entirely on Foucault, but his thought still played an effective role in encouraging it, thereby he legitimated one of the more intricate aspects of neoliberalism to his followers.

There is no doubt that Foucault was also a vital influence on the postmodernist turn that transpired in the wake of his early writings: "It is difficult to generalize about the numerous discourses that go under the banner of postmodernism, but most of them draw at least indirectly on

Jean-François Lyotard's critique of modernist master narratives, Jean Baudrillard's affirmations of cultural simulacra, or Jacques Derrida's critique of Western metaphysics ... [Nevertheless] postmodernist theories are defined by many of their proponents as sharing one single common denominator, a generalized attack on the Enlightenment" (Hardt & Negri 2000: 139); this derives from the Enlightenment's exigency to create theories based on a binary logic which separates self from other thereby being the breeding ground for such discourses as misogyny, sexism, heterosexism, cis-sexism, racism, and colonialism (Hardt & Negri 2000).

Indeed, "the postmodernist insistence on difference and specificity defies the totalitarianism of universalizing discourses and structures of power; the affirmation of fragmented social identities appears as a means of contesting the sovereignty of ... the modern subject" (Hardt & Negri 2000: 139). Here we can see how Foucault's influence affected postmodernism, fragmenting social identities and thereby making it more difficult to organise a structured and effective opposition to the *thaqafah al-za'if*. Moreover, Shari'ati called all this an exercise in futility, saying, "While the spirit ruling over the 19th century used to be ideology, the soul dominating the 20th century is futility" (Shari'ati 1981: 537). Further, as Shari'ati continued, in the age of ideology, "Each ideologue [was] responsible to change the status quo relative to his ideals and convictions. Therefore, accepting responsibility to an ideologue [was] a predetermined matter" (Shari'ati 1981: 1837). Something that has changed dramatically since Foucault.

Foucault effectively birthed the post-structural, post-colonial, and postmodern traditions – all three equating to what I call "the existentialist school" or the neoliberal intellectual automation, calling them such, as, all function under the same neoliberal spook, and like automatons are all organically unconscious, while having the appearance of consciousness through the operation of that spook. This neoliberal intellectualism is based largely on the alliance between Capital and the University. Shari'ati lamented this predicament, saying, "We are now witnessing that science has become the stooge of those who control the world's money and power. Science is at the service of Capitalism. Science and money have married each other and it is obvious which one runs the show" (Shari'ati 1981: 1996). This sell-out of the University to Capital is the playground on which the neoliberal intellectuals play unburdened by conviction or responsibility.

Moreover, the neoliberal intellectuals prove to be the opposite of what he called enlightened souls, explaining how, "In a nutshell, the enlightened soul is a person who is self-conscious of his 'human condition' in his time and historical and social setting, and whose awareness inevitably and necessarily gives him a sense of social responsibility." Indeed, "Although not a prophet, an enlightened soul should play the role of a prophet for his society" (Shari'ati 2002: 10, 12). In this sense, the enlightened and the intellectuals represent two very different opinions. While the intellectuals of our time are the neoliberal intellectuals, the prophets of our time are the enlightened souls, and the key distinction between them is their perspective of biopolitics. Here the neoliberal intellectuals represent the pseudo-intellectual spokespeople for the *thaqafah al-za'if*.

Moreover, the revival of liberalism as neoliberalism appears to have been unaffected by the turn towards representational politics and fragmented social identities as we can see from a quote by Naomi Klein from Goldman and Papson (1996), "noting that 'we have, after all, no idea what punk or grunge or hip hop as social and cultural movements might look like if they were not mined for their gold...' ... For the most part, however, branding's insatiable cultural thirst just creates more marketing. Marketing that thinks it is culture" (Klein 2010: 66). There is in fact no better example of this mining for cultural (*thaqafi*) gold than Black culture, "Over the past decade, young black men in American inner cities have been the market most aggressively mined by the brandmasters as a source of borrowed 'meaning' and identity. This was the key to the success of Nike and Tommy Hilfiger, both of which were catapulted to brand superstardom in no small part by poor kids who incorporated Nike and Hilfiger into hip-hop style at the very moment when rap was being thrust into the expanding youth-culture limelight by MTV and *Vibe*" (Klein 2010: 73). If anything is blatantly clear it is that fragmented identity alone is incapable of challenging the system.

But neoliberal intellectualism is not simply a celebration of fragmentation and difference, in its opposition to binaries and boundaries it seeks above all to acknowledge and celebrate hybridity, "however, [this] is liberatory only in a context where power poses hierarchy exclusively through essential identities, binary divisions, and stable oppositions. The structures and logic of power in the contemporary world are entirely immune to the 'liberatory' weapons of the postmodernist politics of difference" (Hardt & Negri 2000: 142). In fact, as we have seen with Black culture being used by marketers and neoliberal entrepreneurs to reinforce the power structure, even so hybridity and the attack against modernist boundaries has also proven ineffective.

"If diversity is what we wanted, the brands seemed to be saying, then diversity was exactly what we would get. And with that, the marketers and media makers swooped down, airbrushes in hand, to touch up the colors and images in our culture" (Klein 2010: 111). What must be respected is how subtly this change took place within the Western world. That is not to say, however, that all forms of *thaqafi* rebellion are useless or futile, but that hybridity and fragmentation, due to their lack of substantive political capital – because their only capital was in opposition to modern essentialisms – was destined to degenerate into a neoliberal free-for-all, along with Foucault's other projects, due to the intellectual sell-out of their master.

Yet, as academia could not honestly legitimate the domination of neoliberalism to anti-establishment students they simply called into question all legitimacy and authority, so that, in the words of Foucault himself, "neo-liberal governmentality appear[ed], at least in part, as a sort of major economic-political alternative which, at a certain moment at any rate, [took] the form of, if not a mass movement, at least a widespread movement of political opposition within American society" (Foucault 2010: 193) and thus, with the philosopher's stone he turned rebellion against authority into a neoliberal rebellion. The task at this point was in hiding its hand, fist, and logic from the masses under the rhetoric of individualism. "Neo-liberalism was well suited to this ideological task. But it had to be backed up by a practical strategy that emphasized the liberty of consumer choice, not only with respect to particular products but also with respect to lifestyles, modes of expression, and a wide range of cultural practices" (Harvey 2011: 42). Basically, neoliberalism gave to students a *belief* that they were rebelling against authority by quoting Foucault, Lyotard, or Said when really they were submitting unconsciously to it and to the status quo by actually standing for nothing

II

There are three prerequisites that have to be appreciated before one can go any further in a genuinely comprehensive evaluation of neoliberalism: (i) Neoliberalism is the resurrection (*ba'th*) of a neoclassical liberalism that was superseded in the 1940s by Keynesianism. (ii) The spirit and philosophy of neoliberalism existed long before it became the revived political economic orthodoxy it became in the 1980s. (iii) The neoliberal intellectualist movements *are* neoliberal in orientation regardless of how opposed to neoliberalism they claim to be. Neoliberalism therefore exists as the cultural, social, political, and economic somatisation of post-1970s market apperceptions but its process of development and its rise to power is a narrative worth exploring before we consider any deeper its propositions and its opponents.

After the economic crisis of the Great Depression and the geopolitical crisis of World War II the global powers began to seek a supranational juridical institution, or institutions, to ensure economic and geopolitical stability. What Callinicos (2003: 60) called "a fountain of multi-lateralist acronyms" – the UN, IMF, GATT, NATO, EC, and G7 were all created to establish a new global order based on what Harvey (2011) called a "class compromise between capital and labour" or bourgeoisie and proletarian. "What all of [their] various state forms had in common was an acceptance that the state should focus on full employment, economic growth, and the welfare of its citizens, and that state power should be freely deployed, alongside of or, if necessary, intervening in or even substituting for market processes to achieve these ends. Fiscal and monetary policies usually dubbed 'Keynesian' were widely deployed to dampen business cycles and to ensure reasonably full employment. A 'class compromise' between capital and labour was generally advocated as the key guarantor of domestic peace and tranquillity" (Harvey 2011: 10) and effectively a post-war social, political, and economic consensus was framed.

On the geopolitical level this "class compromise" was an international compromise between the First World of capitalist powers and the Second World of communist powers. The formation of the First World alliance occurred mainly because after World War II the US faced an interesting dilemma: the problem of European debt repayments without German reparations, "This time around, the U.S. Government did not extend unilateral credits to Europe and other nations without forming new institutions to facilitate their repayment, and specifically their repayment in convertible foreign exchange. In July 1944 the IMF and World Bank were established at Bretton Woods, New Hampshire, as permanent financial and debt-management consortia. Foreign governments held shares in these institutions, but not enough to match the dominating veto share held by the U.S. Government" (Hudson 2021: 161).

American economist Michael Hudson was very clear, "It was primarily to solve [the problem of debt repayment] that the United States took the lead in forming the International Monetary Fund and World Bank to supplant German reparations as the mechanism through which to provide the Allies with institutionalized means to sustain their demand for U.S. products and to maintain the discipline of gold in international relations. Formal mechanisms were established to permit continued borrowing from the United States on much sounder bases than after World War I. The foundation of U.S. lending capacity was its enlarged stock of monetary gold, which had soared during the prewar and wartime years" (Hudson 2021: 160). It is this monetary gold that played a major part in America's rise to dominance in the post-war years. Moreover, the US government felt that they could exploit Europe's weakened position after the war to ensure they acquired all the legroom they needed to establish the right terms of agreement for these bodies.

The American negotiators entered Bretton Woods believing that they would be fulfilling America's global destiny, creating a world economy of peaceful co-operation under United States leadership (Hudson 2021). Indeed, "in the diplomatic meeting rooms the American negotiators made it clear that cooperation among the world's central banks would be based on the financial status quo as it existed upon the return to peace. This status quo found the U.S. Treasury holding 60 per cent of the world's monetary gold, giving it unique advantage in a world desperate for hard currency" (Hudson 2021: 302). According to Hudson the fundamental reason behind the IMF was to stabilise international currency: to do this they needed reserves sufficient to do so. "It was [also] critical that the IMF members agreed to stabilize their currencies 'in terms of gold as the common denominator or in terms of the United States dollar of the weight and fineness in effect on July 1, 1944,' that is, at $35 an ounce" (Hudson 2021: 305).

Effectively, these negotiations at Bretton Woods would have fallen apart without Britain. Britain, at that time, was in the strongest non-American position to lead the discussions. Sterling was strong enough and international enough to allow the IMF to work. Even though they were entering into the Bretton Woods negotiations at a slight disadvantage, the war had ravished the country; Britain, still at war and still under Winston Churchill, was considered an international hero as well as still being at that time a global empire. However, Britain bowed to all US concessions.

According to Hudson:

> *These concessions started with the breakup of the Sterling Area. Multilateralism for the United States*

> *had [thereby] come to connote the end of the British Empire and the forging of a concentric Dollar Area revolving around American gold, American economic power, and American full-employment levels. Lend-Lease, the British Loan of 1946 and the Bretton Woods agreements called for the dollar to supplant sterling as the world's reserve currency. The Sterling Area was to be absorbed into the Dollar Area, which would be extend throughout the world.*
>
> *"The British Loan [of 1946] served as the economic setting for introducing the IMF and its program for stabilizing world currency parities ... it essentially ended Imperial Preference for the British market by opening up the Sterling Area's reserves to be spent on U.S. exports. At the Bretton Woods meetings there had been general agreement on two points: competitive devaluations of national currencies must not occur in the postwar world, and all major trading currencies must be tied to gold" (Hudson 2021: 302).*

Then, what occurred in the early 1970s changed the course of global history. First, "President Nixon suspended all further sale of U.S. gold to foreign central banks. Henceforth the $61 billion of liquid debt owed to foreigners would be paid only in the form of other paper evidences of debt. By suspending gold payments, the United States was, in effect, repudiating its foreign debt" (Hudson 2021: 377). This was the genius of the Bretton Woods agreements, the IMF declared currency convertible not only into gold but into gold and US dollars at their gold parity of 1944, which at that time was $35 per ounce. The agreement did not say that the US had to continue buying and selling gold at that price.

This "Shock Therapy" caused many global currencies to plummet. Currency since then has been based the US dollar and only the US dollar, and so long as foreign central banks continue to "rely on the dollar for their international reserves, the effect is to finance the U.S. balance-of-payments deficit and, incidentally, the domestic U.S. budget deficit" (Hudson 2021: ix). All money is currently nothing more than a US IOU, money is no longer based on value – which is why its own value keeps on decreasing – but is based on the US Treasury bill.

Next, after the Arab-Israeli War, also in the early 1970s, the oil rich Muslim countries in the Organization of Petroleum Exporting Countries (OPEC) agreed to boycott the United States, Holland, and Denmark, "The resulting oil shortage enabled OPEC to respond to the rise in world grain prices by quadrupling its oil export prices. The oil embargo and the sharp increase in oil prices changed the pattern of international payments, driving a wedge between America and Europe" (Hudson 2021: 418). Basically, with OPEC oil price rises and US grain price rises the Dollar Area was hit hard and suffered a huge financial breakdown.

Finally, as the Keynesian paradigm was never fully accepted by all sections of Western society its detractors became restless. To the left of Keynes were the Euro-Communists (the Stalinists), the Western Marxists (the Lukacsians), the neo-Marxists (the Gramscians), and the Maoists. All four felt that Keynesian theory had not gone far enough, it nationalised the "commanding heights" but it needed to nationalise all industry, trade, business, and finance. They also felt it needed to abolish the market and institute a centralised planning system in its place. During the 1960s these groups teamed up with the students and trade unions to form mass movements throughout Europe and America, the result was the new left: also including elements from the women's movement, the Gay movement, the Civil Rights movement, and the Green movement. The new left was very broad-based and led the demand for social justice and personal freedom, mainly centring on the Vietnam War (Harvey 2011). Thus, the Labour movement began to march and to fight, but without having a plan to implement the changes they believed in, by the time all First World economies fell into crisis in the early 1970s they were completely unprepared and incapable.

On the other side of the debate another group was completely prepared and completely capable. They felt that Keynes' institutions were too interventionist and too paternalist, and that the class compromise was also a compromise on entrepreneurship and economic stability. They sought the abolition of Keynesianism and the resurrection of neoclassical liberalism. The most notable of these right-wing rivals to Keynesian theory was Friedrich von Hayek. Von Hayek felt that Keynes' system was too close to communism and thus to totalitarianism, he believed the only way for society to clear itself of its past phantasms would be to expunge Keynesianism and anything else remotely related to communism. They had a clearer vision and more practical means of fulfilling that vision.

One of the central means of ensuring personal and individual freedom, to von Hayek, was through maintaining and strengthening the market. Von Hayek put his ideas into practice by founding the Mont Pelerin Society, a group that "depicted themselves as 'liberals' (in the traditional European sense) because of their fundamental commitment to ideals of personal freedom. The neoliberal label signalled their adherence to those free market principles of neoclassical economics that had emerged in the second half of the nineteenth century (thanks to the work of Alfred Marshall, William Stanley Jevons, and Leon Walras) to displace the classical theories of Adam Smith, David Ricardo, and, of course, Karl Marx" (Harvey 2011: 20).

Though Karl Marx's social, political, and religious theories will be challenged in a future chapter the failure of Marx's economic theories would strengthen the hands of these neoclassical adherents giving them all the leeway they needed to launch a counter-revolution. In his theories of capitalism Marx followed the Ricardian model of David Ricardo, a nineteenth century economist who laid the foundations of economic theory in England until the early twentieth century. But according to Skousen, "David Ricardo had a dark side. His analytical modeling is a two-edged sword. It gave us the quantity theory of money and the law of comparative advantage, but it also gave us the labor theory of value, [and] the iron law of subsistence wages" so that, ultimately, "First Ricardo and then Marx claimed that labor is the sole producer of value" (Skousen 2017: 54, 84), and that consequently all the profits of a company came from reducing wages to subsistence level.

Indeed, based on his theory of surplus value Marx perceived that all the monies of the capitalist were stolen or exploited from the workers, and due to the prominence of Ricardo's labour theory of value no economist of his time had any answer they could give him. Thus, the theoretical framework of economics went from being based on the labour theory of value to being based on the theory of surplus value, which value was presumed to have been stolen from the workers. But the labour theory of value itself came from a dilemma within capitalist theory: "the famous diamond-water paradox. Why is it that an essential commodity like water is so little valued in the marketplace while impractical diamonds are so highly prized?" (Skousen 2017: 50). According to Ricardo the value of diamonds comes from the labour expended to acquire and refine them, the same with units of water, and with all other commodities. "It was only a short logical step to conclude, therefore, that capitalists and landlords were exploiters of labor. If indeed all value was the product of labor, then all profits obtained by the capitalists and interest obtained by landlords must be 'surplus value,' unjustly extracted from the true earnings of the working class" (Skousen 2017: 84). Thus, leading to Marx's theory of increasing exploitation. Yet Marx's theoretical positions never really saw the light of day in classical or neoclassical economics, instead suffering the stillbirth of being beloved only by radicals.

The stillbirth of Marx's economic theories was due in part to the work of Eugen Böhm-Bawerk. At the time when Marx's *Das Kapital* was starting to make headways Böhm-Bawerk challenged the notion "that workers deserve the full value of the products they produce" (Skousen 2017: 110). First, he introduced the "waiting" argument: here, the entrepreneur uses their savings and gains to improve and grow the company. They therefore do not get a chance to spend income on personal consumption but put all but subsistence earnings towards the company. The interest accrued from this recycling of funds, gains, and profits back into the company thus means that the entrepreneur is justly rewarded when the company grows.

As an example, manufacturers have to wait till their goods are made, distributed, and sold, and their company is making stable profits before they are paid. The same with investors, they have to wait before they earn back their investment. But while this may be true of the bourgeoisies it is not true of the workers, who are paid every month or every two weeks "regardless of whether the products they produce are sold or not. They do not have to worry about accounts receivable or accounts payable, about investment debt or changing markets. They get paid like clock-work, assuming their employers are honest and solvent" (Skousen 2017:111).

Second, Böhm-Bawerk also proved that bourgeoisies take on a lot more risk than workers. There is no guarantee their products or services will sell on the market, that the market will remain stable, or that the company will survive a downturn in either the market, the market niche, or their personal sales. Yet "Workers get paid regularly and, if the business goes under, the most they will lose is a paycheck; they only need to search for another job. But the business entrepreneur may face financial ruin, heavy debts, and bankruptcy" (Skousen 2017: 111). Böhm-Bawerk thereby showed that while workers did not deserve to be defrauded a good wage, they, at the same time, did not necessarily deserve the full revenue of the company, or even the lion's share of the revenue of the company. Still, it would not be until John Bates Clark solved the joint-input problem that it became clear how those wages were to be determined.

Capital, Labour, and their personifications were both considered to be responsible for production, yet who deserved more pay was a debacle that frustrated economists sorely. The socialists, Marxists, and radicals sided with Labour and its personifications; the neoclassicalists, particularly after the popularity of Böhm-Bawerk's defence, sided with Capital and its personifications. Clark solved the riddle by showing how "each factor of production – land, labor, and capital – is paid according to the 'value added' to the total revenue of the product" (Skousen 2017: 118). Thus, to Clark, value neither lay totally in the hands of either capital or labour, value was determined by the market and what each contributed to that value on the market.

Clark's theory was based on the marginal theory of value, "In short, customers have to be willing to pay a certain amount before producers will employ productive resources to produce a product, enough to make a reasonable profit" (Skousen 2017: 108). The marginal theory of value made mincemeat out of the labour theory of value and the theory of increasing exploitation by resolving once and for all the diamond-water paradox. They effectively showed that "the difference in value between water and diamonds is due to the relative abundance of water and the relative scarcity of diamonds (given the demand for each). Since the supply of water is abundant, the demand for each additional unit (marginal utility) is low. Since the supply of diamonds is extremely limited, the demand for each additional diamond is high" (Skousen 2017: 108). By thereby resolving the issue of value Marx's theory of surplus value tumbled like the proverbial house of cards.

What the marginalists did was show that in a capitalist economy value actually comes from market forces and not from productive forces. Hence why communist economies always fell apart in the end, they were based on the faulty labour theory of value and not the marginal theory of value. Yet that is not to say that the market is the best of all possible guarantors of financial security. What we are actually saying is that in a capitalist economy market forces trump productive forces as the fundamental mechanism. Indeed, you abolish the market you abolish capitalism. Due to the failure of Marxism to answer the marginalists' critique after the early 1970s the class compromise between Capital and Labour abruptly ended and everything came to a head; it is here that the seeds of America's current imperialism were beginning to germinate.

Now when I speak here of an American Empire, it is obviously not as Hardt and Negri spoke, assuming that the Empire has no fixed location; as, to assume such would be to disqualify the whole concept of Empire altogether: was not the Holy Roman Empire located in Germany, though possessing in its title a location that was relatively fixed, its location may have changed with time but the general truth is that an empire always has territoriality. In its present form the title matches the location: the Great United States Empire (GUSE), nevertheless, quoting Hardt and Negri, "Along with the global market and global circuits of production has emerged a global order, a new logic and structure of rule ... Empire is the political subject that effectively regulates these global exchanges, the sovereign power that governs the world" (Hardt & Negri 2000: xi). Indeed, aside from deterritorialising the current imperial system what Hardt and Negri explained regarding Empire is considerably useful: that the world we live in today has undergone dramatic transformative pressures which have caused a new system of global sovereignty, organised by national and supranational bodies, to set a new paradigmatic standard.

III

In order to further understand how America evolved from a republic into an Empire (or from an eagle into a GUSE) it will be necessary to now consult the writings of John Perkins, who from 1971-1981 was an economic hit man for Chas. T. Main Inc. (MAIN). Perkins explained concerning the requirements of his position thusly, "Economic hit men (EHMs) are highly paid professionals who cheat countries around the globe out of trillions of dollars. They funnel money from the World Bank, the U.S. Agency for International Development (USAID), and other 'aid' organizations into the coffers of huge corporations and the pockets of a few wealthy families who control the planet's natural resources. Their tools include fraudulent financial reports, rigged elections, payoffs, extortion, sex, and murder. They play a game as old as empire, but one that has taken on new and terrifying dimensions during this time of globalization" and, "I should know; I was an EHM" (Perkins 2006: ix). Because Perkins had the inside track on what was going on during the process of empire building I shall be drawing from his story in order to explain its growth.

As mentioned, neoliberal practices existed long before the name and method was actually able to resurrect (*bi'thah*) the economic system of liberalism to economic orthodoxy. The neoliberal foreign policy on development began in the 1970s – Perkins himself was a chief architect – and it is one of the most sophisticated forms of empire building history has produced; as Perkins noted: "The subtlety of this modern empire building puts the Roman centurions, the Spanish conquistadors, and the eighteenth- and nineteenth-century European colonial powers to shame" (Perkins 2006: xx). It is an empire of cunning, chicanery, and hypnotism; Perkins front role was "to forecast the effects of investing billions of dollars in a country", however, "the unspoken aspect of … [the projects thus forecasted] was that they were intended to create large profits for the contractors, and to make a handful of wealthy and influential families in the receiving countries very happy, while assuring the long-term financial dependence and therefore the political loyalty of governments around the world" (Perkins 2006: 15). The system has been remarkably effective allowing the US to gain international superiority from the 1970s to this very day.

Perkins (2006) spoke on how the US has secured this massive Empire mainly through providing loans to the so-called Third World of the post-colonial powers for the purpose of developing infrastructure "electric generating plants, highways, ports, airports, or industrial parks" (Perkins 2006: xvii), however, the string attached to these developments is that a US company must be the builders and engineers involved. "In essence, most of the money never leaves the United States; it is simply transferred from banking offices in Washington to engineering offices in New York, Houston, or San Francisco" (Perkins 2006: xvii). But that does not mean the debtor countries are free from having to pay off their debts, thus debts get piled up, preferably with interest, for projects the debtor country probably had no need for and will never really have need for in the future. According to Perkins, a good EHM's goal is to make the loans so large and the debts so high "that the debtor is forced to default on its payment" (Perkins 2006: xvii) at which time the US swoops in and demands something they find more useful: "control over United Nations votes, the installation of military bases, or access to precious resources such as oil or the Panama Canal" (Perkins 2006: xvii).

The chain of deceit runs long and it has captured many powerful individuals: as Hardt and Negri explained concerning what took place when US power began its expansion globewise, "Juridical transformations effectively point toward changes in the material constitution of world power and order ... [the] transition we are witnessing today from traditional international law, which was defined by contracts and treaties, to the definition and constitution of a new sovereign, supranational world power (and thus to an Imperial notion of right), however incomplete, gives us a framework in which to read the totalizing social processes of Empire" (Hardt & Negri 2000: 9). The GUSE is effectively the empire that debt built. Yet "what we were perpetrating through this new, highly subtle form of imperialism was the financial equivalent of what we had attempted to accomplish militarily in Vietnam" (Perkins 2006: 128). Both Vietnam and 1951 Iran taught America a valuable lesson, in order to build an empire they had to do it without appearing to be building an empire.

Perkins explained how he was instructed by his superior that his job involved encouraging "world leaders to become part of a vast network that promotes U.S. commercial interests. In the end, those leaders [will] become ensnared in a web of debt that ensures their loyalty. We can draw on them whenever we desire – to satisfy our political, economic, or military needs. In turn, they bolster their political positions by bringing industrial parks, power plants, and airports to their people. [While] owners of U.S. engineering/construction companies become fabulously wealthy" (Perkins 2006: xi). There is a lot of talk about how corrupt the so-called Third World leaders are, but there is not a single thought about who the people are corrupting them. If the so-called Third World is corrupt it is the West, and particularly the US, that has corrupted them; and as Perkins (2006: 105) also stated: "A system based on corrupting public figures does not take kindly to public figures who refuse to be corrupted."

Yet Shari'ati also noted concerning this situation that, "Islamic ethics have always struggled and resisted [these kinds of] aristocratic dispositions to the point where it has extremely weakened the aristocratic sumptuousness with regard to richness, opulence, comfort, showing off and belittling others" (Shari'ati 2011: 179). The reason he gave for this was that "it is the feeling of poverty which starts a movement. The necessary factor that would persuade a social class to arise is the feeling and awareness of being exploited rather than the mere fact of being exploited" (Shari'ati 2011: 133). Herein lies the rub. Islam teaches against the idea of corruption and showing off because these highlight the contradiction in society between rich and poor. It does not abolish these contradictions but hides them. Thereby most so-called Third World leaders, even in the Islamic world, have been corrupted by EHMs. Indeed,

Perkins himself mentioned certain Saudi leaders who he himself had corrupted.

Perkins (2006) also pointed out how subtle EHMs became after the 1970s. By that time they were no longer being trained by the NSA (National Security Agency) like he was, but were business employees, yet still performing similar roles. The similarities resulted from what he and other EHMs had done to train the next generation and how they encouraged them, not to be EHMs like he was, "We had gotten better or more pernicious. The people who worked for me were a different breed from me. ... No one had spelled it out for them, what they were expected to do to carry on the mission of global empire. They had never heard the term economic hit man or even EHM, nor had they been told they were in for life. They simply had learned from my example and from my system of rewards and punishments. They knew that they were expected to produce the types of studies and results I wanted." "Every one of the people on my staff also had a title – financial analyst, sociologist, economist, lead economist, econometrician, shadow pricing expert, and so forth – and yet none of those titles indicated that every one of them was, in his or her own way, an EHM" (Perkins 2006: 138, 139). Trained or not those that worked for the expansion of US interests globally through promoting "aid", "development" and "economic progress" in the so-called Third World were EHMs.

If we consider now the articulation of political economic networks being propagated around the world during the 1970s four significant events prove that the West, and particularly the United States, actually had another agenda which allowed for the revival of neoclassical liberalism as resurrection (*ba'th*) to transpire, thus giving the new right a substantial victory in the brief but decisive class war. (i) Nixon's taking America, and thereby the entire Dollar Area, off the gold standard and onto the standard of the US Treasury bill. (ii) The aftereffects of the oil price rise on the Dollar Area and the global crisis it caused. (iii) The ineptitude of the new left in their willingness to strike and march at this time but not to seize power. The new left's inability to capitalise on the economic breakdowns of the 1970s meant that their constant striking and mass movements were nothing more than annoyances for the people who were now beginning to tire of powerful trade unions and unpacified students and Blacks, longing instead for times of peace. (iv) US economic expansion into the so-called Third World through EHMs and the consolidating of their neo-colonial Empire gave new right policies all the credibility they needed.

At this point, the middle class began looking to new right opinions, any new right opinions, to quell the raging battles going on in the streets. Shari'ati pointed out that, "For the same reasons … capitalism, [was] able to [take] control over such factors as self awareness or scientific awareness and become familiar with the laws of the historical revolution and cause its path to deviate in such a way as to safeguard its own capitalistic direction" (Shari'ati 2011: 78). And so, by the 1980s the socio-elastic revival of neoclassical liberalism was taken to the next level with just the right man (and woman) for the job. The Reagan-Thatcher alliance – unlike the Carter and Callaghan governments that preceded them – were strong enough and willing enough to implement the social and economic changes desired by the ideologues of neoliberal reform, and give to the middle class the illusion of peace and security they so fervently desired.

IV

By the 1990s the social order had transformed so dramatically that the resurrection (*ba'th*) of liberalism as a form of undisputed revivalism allowed businesses to no longer simply be on the defensive but now to be actively on the offensive. The alliance between Capital and State also continued as both Bill Clinton and Tony Blair sold out to the neoliberal agenda: "The Third Way originated as a slogan intended to differentiate Bill Clinton's New Democrats from both Reaganite Republicanism and the statist approach to economic and social problems represented by earlier Democratic presidents such as Franklin Roosevelt and Lyndon Johnson. In fact, the Clinton administration's commitment to the neo-liberal agenda was soon confirmed by its strenuous and successful efforts, in close alliance with big business and the Republican right, to persuade ... Congress to approve the North American Free Trade Agreement (NAFTA) in 1993" (Callinicos 2003: 3).

NAFTA was never the golden bullet it is considered to be today by certain historians, as Chomsky informed us, "The NAFTA agreement was rammed through Congress over strenuous popular opposition but with overwhelming support from the business world and the media" (Chomsky 1999: 102). If NAFTA is the expression of American neoliberal policy in action then it helps to remind ourselves of what it meant on the ground. Firstly, Chomsky (1999: 142) noted, "under NAFTA rules, which permit corporations to sue governments, according them in effect the rights of national states (not mere persons, as before)", the central goal was to "cement Mexico's economic reforms" (Levinson 1996; quoted in Chomsky 1999: 105); and to disallow any deviation from the neoliberal programme then in operation throughout the country. The opposition was not weakened by its ratification, however, "The New Year's Day uprising of Indian peasants in Chiapas can readily be understood in this general context. The uprising coincided with the enactment of NAFTA, which the Zapatista army called a 'death sentence' for Indians" (Chomsky 1999: 122).

The cry of the Zapatistas turned from oppositional to prophetic as the post-NAFTA Mexican crisis of 1994 would later prove. Only the economic titans of Mexico and the US really escaped the breakdown – due largely to government bailouts. NAFTA effectively cost the Mexican proletarians many of their "hard-won labor rights" (Darling 1994; quoted in Chomsky 1999: 124), further demonstrating the necessity of the uprising; though among the Mexican bourgeoisie there was a "mixed" response as some lauded it and others feared its potential to take profits and business away from Mexican people and transfer them to foreign (read, American) investors. It was also perceived by some to be an attempt to lock Mexico into the American imperial system then on the rise. In fact, according to certain Mexican polls there was huge support for the reasons the Zapatistas gave for their uprising; and even in the West many felt the Zapatistas were justified for their rebellion, facing virtually the same situation themselves under the not too dissimilar order of the World Trade Organization.

Chomsky, in evaluating an article by then *New York Times* political analyst, David Sanger, wrote, "Going beyond the traditional reliance on the UN, the Clinton administration is turning to the new World Trade Organization (WTO) to carry out the task of 'exporting American values.' Down the road, Sanger [explained] (quoting the US trade representative), it is the WTO that may be the most effective instrument for bringing 'America's passion for deregulation' and for the free market generally, and 'the American values of free competition, fair rules, and effective enforcement,' to a world still fumbling in darkness" (Chomsky 1999: 65). Sanger used as his case in point the WTO agreement on telecommunications. Accordingly, "The agreement 'empowers the WTO to go inside the borders of the … countries that have signed it,' and it is no secret that international institutions can [only] function insofar as they keep to the demands of the powerful, in particular, the United States. In the real world, then, the 'new tool' allows the United States to intervene profoundly in the internal affairs of others, compelling them to change their laws and practices" (Chomsky 1999: 69).

The implementation of these kinds of neoliberal readjustments did not only affect foreign policy and global power relations but were also detrimental to US domestic policy, as during the 1990s and even into the 21st century, workers either accepted low wage incomes or accepted income reductions to meet the needs of greedy shareholders. "Inequality [even] reached levels unknown for seventy years [prior], far beyond other industrial countries" (Chomsky 1999: 28); all while those same shareholders received huge bailouts from their governments. Apparently, "at least twenty companies in the 1993 Fortune 100 would not have survived at all as independent companies, if they had not been saved by their respective governments" (Ruigrock & van Tulder 1996; quoted in Chomsky 1999: 38). Tellingly, big business knows that trusting in market regulation is economic suicide and that without government help capitalism on its own is nothing more than an anaemic hope, yet they continue trumpeting the glories of neoliberalism, or revived liberalism, to emerging markets and economies in the hopes of stealing their wealth away "legally."

This system of what Chomsky called "socialism for the rich" is in fact "misery for the poor" who, even in the United States, found their standards of living steadily declining. "The corporate media, the Clinton administration, and the cheerleaders for the American Way proudly offer themselves as a model for the rest of the world; buried in the chorus of self-acclaim are ... the 'basic indicators' just published by UNICEF, revealing that the United States has the worst record among the industrial countries ... by such standards as mortality for children under five. It also holds records for hunger, child poverty, and other basic social indicators" (Chomsky 1999: 112). All this recapitulates the point that America in the 1990s was a First World country with so-called Third World conditions. Veritably, while it has been the spatial delimitation of global territories and identities and the vitality of biopolitical global forces determining how rights and responsibilities are defined within the GUSE (Hardt & Negri 2000); as we can see, it is the rights of the wealthy and their corporations that currently outshine those of the citizens and their social bodies.

In sum, globalisation has played a major role in reorienting the structures of distinct national laws with the United States having the power to effect changes to the constitution of (inter)national law and commerce. The sovereignty and authority of national-states within the global Empire of the United States is therefore extremely questionable. Here Hardt and Negri offer a reasonable description of the situation: "Our basic hypothesis is that sovereignty has taken a new form, composed of a series of national and supranational organisms united under a single logic of rule. This new global form of sovereignty is what we call Empire" (Hardt & Negri 2000: xii). Here the late modern passage to Empire has caused a re-summation of the concept of sovereignty, inadvertently causing penality and national security to overcompensate. Invariably, if we track "the roots and modalities of America's stupendous drive to hyperincarceration [it] opens a unique path into the *sanctum* of the neoliberal Leviathan ... *the penal apparatus is a core organ of the state*, expressive of its sovereignty and instrumental in imposing categories, upholding material and symbolic divisions, and molding relations and behaviors through the selective penetration of social and physical space" (Wacquant 2016: 126).

Clearly, Foucault is thus proven somewhat of a false prophet in declaring in the mid-1970s that the penal system was vanishing, it was, indeed, to expand – in America's case by 500 percent (Daulatzai 2012). But Foucault's blunder was due to his taking penal reformers and theorists of confinement at their word and not considering the real, living reality of imprisonment and its aftereffects (Wacquant 2016). Even with the diminishing credibility of the national-state due to certain neoliberal policies there is inextricably also an incorporation of the intensifying of national security as counterbalance. It is especially the case in the United States with the hyperincarceration of Black, Brown, and so-called Red-skinned Americans. It is also the case in Western Europe where "precarious workers and the unemployed, postcolonial migrants, and lower-class addicts and derelicts" are targeted by police for harassment and arrest (Wacquant 2016: 127).

There is no denying the surveilling and punitive systems of the West that Foucault thought he had pinned down were far more elusive. Where Foucault presumed the main objective of disciplinary institutions such as: courts, prisons, asylums, factories, classrooms, et cetera. was to produce docile and productive bodies, he was not able to consider the greater exigency for these institutions was actually warehousing. Surveilling itself becomes neither rehabilitative nor operative it is simply voyeuristic, a means of keeping subversive bodies from subverting too much.

In fact, according to Greenberg (2014), FBI counter-intelligence tactics were, from the 1920s onward, used as a necessary means of surveilling revolutionary bodies within the United States, removing and confining revolutionary elements within a sub-spatial locus. They were also used to prevent any left-leaning groups from inspiring a communist revolution either in, or within the vicinity of, the United States. Here, again, Foucault, in his desire to be a step ahead of everyone else, may have actually run off course; far from seeking to produce docile bodies the FBI and the US state-apparatuses seek neutralised consumers, with body and brain intact, but nonetheless still able to wet their voyeuristic appetites.

During the late-1970s Carter's more lenient approach to surveillance may have been refreshing but it was short lived. "In fact, when former California Governor Ronald Reagan defeated Carter in the 1980 election, FBI policies and procedures began to change. Reagan revived aggressive FBI spying within the new terrorism framework for investigations. Rather than limit investigations to political acts of violence, the FBI also considered violent speech by groups or individuals sufficient to advocate surveillance" (Greenberg 2014: 16). The ferocity of the Reagan reforms to surveillance affected not only those within the United States but even foreign policy too.

As Greenberg (2014) explained things did not change much following the Reagan administration, and that Bush, Clinton, Bush, and Obama all seem to have expanded the spying techniques re-instituted in the 1980s, whether by the FBI or the CIA, using the precarious legitimation of combating terrorism. He also stressed that it is of no consequence whether the impetus was derived from White House mandate or from the agencies themselves, the fact of the matter is that from the time of the ending of the Cold War the US engaged in spying activities on its own people for the purpose of containing a specific religious movement, Islam. That which the government called and fed to the public as security, was nothing more than a means of social control and the negative labelling of a religious movement. Therefore the fact that "state surveillance continued to advance even though the Cold War had ended" (Greenberg 2014: 270) is not surprising, especially when we consider the track record of the United States.

In 1994, surveillance was taken to another level when President Clinton signed into law the Communications Assistance for Law Enforcement Act (CALEA); a move which according to Greenberg was pivotal in furthering the "surveillance society." CALEA completely transformed telecommunications as we know it, or as we beforehand knew it: effectively granting the government the right to intercept tele-technic communications for the purpose of law enforcement and "other purposes". Greenberg took note of these "other purposes" considering them to be a euphemism for intelligence gathering. Telecommunications carriers and manufacturers of their equipment were instructed to cautiously implant within their devices means that allowed for surveillance to be continued via telecommunications technology. The CALEA was also used to justify surveillance not only through telephones, pagers, and other earlier forms of text messaging but soon even Internet services, and later social media also fell under the remit of the CALEA as the federal judiciary ruled that it did not violate the Fourth Amendment.

Basically, we can see that from the Clinton *error* onward the privacy of the American public has been severely compromised. According to Greenberg (2014) law enforcement and intelligence agencies used CALEA as a justification for searching through websites as though they were newspapers – considering that they are public spaces that require no search warrant to investigate. In effect, they had the power to join computer chat rooms, et cetera. with fictitious identities, looking for any form of radical or anti-establishment expression from individuals or groups. Greenberg (2014) also noted that this "unwanted gaze" has become a fundamental aspect of law enforcement post-9/11. There is a relevance in this, what was the real necessity for improving surveillance capabilities in the first place? Though I accept the post-9/11 hysteria generated the desire for greater national security among the masses in the United States, in the 1990s it was hardly justifiable. That is unless one takes into consideration the state's need to perpetuate itself. It is the neoliberal world order that has made this necessity ineluctable as social forces generate a multiplicity of theories in society, each one a potential threat to its maintenance, continuance, and effectivity.

Many have praised Clinton as a President who cared for the poor and vulnerable, yet what becomes clear from any non-capricious observation is that the 1990s saw changes to the system that ultimately affected poor and particularly ethnic groups in the United States in such a negative way that it would be impossible to overlook. First, with the Violent Crime Control and Law Enforcement Act (1993) came the largest expansion in policing and punitive organisation. It also encouraged the building of more prisons, the setting up of boot camps for delinquents, denied prison inmates access to higher education, labelled being in a gang a felony (going against the constitutional right to freedom of assembly), and made a provision for a mandatory minimum sentence of twenty-five years to life for any third felony. All signed into law by Clinton in 1994.

Clinton also saw to the passing of the Personal Responsibility and Work Opportunity Act (1996) (the dreaded Welfare Act) which was rushed through Congress in the summer of 1996. The law itself made it compulsory for any welfare recipient to find employment after two years of receiving their benefits and also limited the lifetime reception of social welfare to five years. Consequently, "The cyclical alternation of contraction and expansion of public aid [prior to the Clinton administration, was] replaced by the continual contraction of welfare and the runaway expansion of prisonfare" after it (Wacquant 2016: 118).

V

We the children of the godbody are able to see through the fog of lies that perpetuate national-states and national security. Nationalities and national identities are themselves hugely precarious, there is nothing stable or solid about them or their legitimation, this is true especially in these times of late modernity (or liquid modernity) as national devotion is being displaced by transnational migrations. One of the major problems that is going on in the world today is the question of multiculturalism: is multiculturalism a viable and, indeed, ethical system of identification? If we judge by American standards then multiculturalism appears to be the highest form of ethical standard; however, we are not trying to judge by American standards are we? By investigating and criticising more deeply to find the relevant truth behind the fog it becomes far more feasible for one to judge by appropriate standards. Thus, the question becomes: why does America currently propagate the standard of multiculturalism to the extent that it does?

The solution to this question can be extricated by considering Jacques Derrida's interjection in the early 1990s after the fall of the Second World, "never have violence, inequality, exclusion, famine, and thus economic oppression affected as many human beings in the history of the earth and humanity. Instead of singing the advent of the ideal of liberal democracy and of the capitalist market in the euphoria of the end of history … let us never neglect this obvious macroscopic fact, made up of innumerable singular sites of suffering: no degree of progress allows one to ignore that never before, in absolute figures, never have so many men, women, and children been subjugated, starved, or exterminated on the earth" (Derrida 2006: 106). Regardless of the reasons behind the modern state's abandoning of its rhetoric of civil liberties under the current rhetorical promise of protection, it has done nothing but create a paternalistic discourse that can be used to justify a mass of prohibitions, institutions, and act-species effectively exposing its somatic spookism. While it could also be said that the purpose of the origin of the state in the first place was to do just that: protect the people from the personal liberties of others to harm, cheat, or abuse them, if we consider more in-depth the actual reasons for its origins we will be more able to surmise its teleological conclusion.

Basically, what we see is that the current predicament is caused not by the modern state as such (whether it be a bourgeois state or a proletarian state), the problem is with the state itself, and the "state of permanent exception" implied in its existence through the law. According to Hardt and Negri (2000) international (or supranational) law "over-determines" domestic law. The more an issue is agreed on within the international body of laws and rights the more legitimated it becomes within the domestic sphere. New institutions which have gained global or semi-global credibility are open to acceptance in the domestic sphere. This, however, is too simple an explanation. Although I agree that "the right of the police is legitimated by universal values" (Hardt & Negri 2000: 18), and accept that global forces usually impact in an imperious way the social forces within a nation or society, those global forces themselves must be generated from the social forces of a particular social body (*mujtama*). As social bodies are moved by social forces to create social change, and on a grander scale global forces inspire global changes, even so global forces are nothing more than the impressed forces that have come from a particular global body: and in this case the global body is America.

The transformation is not of the international law into the national, but of the social forces of one social body into the global forces of the global powers. Obviously, not all countries and all nations have submitted to the global forces of the US-cum-GUSE but all accept its ethic and precedent. Thus, the global forces, generated by the global force of one global body (read, America) influence in an imperious way the social forces of all social bodies. In other words, US precedent has become very influential on other Western and non-Western countries causing them to submit, in spirit, to their forms and structures. That is not to say there is no resistance, it is just to show how the global expansion of the GUSE can be seen in an abstracted way.

The transformative nature of forces: whether from environmental to global, global to social, social to astral and astral back to social, social to global and global to environmental, produces an endless and ubiquitous stream of interactions. Nevertheless, "Perhaps the most significant symptom of [this social] transformation is the development of the so-called *right of intervention*" (Hardt & Negri 2000: 18). On a domestic level this is played out by the police, on a supranational level the actors are "peace keepers" mandated by "any type of emergency and superior ethical principles" (Hardt & Negri 2000: 18).

If we consider again the exigencies of the GUSE, after the fear inspired by 9/11 US policy, both domestic and foreign, changed substantially: "Domestically, the threat of 'terror' from the *immigrant* Muslim ... justified a highly racialized crackdown on immigrants in the United States, resulting in the normalization of deportations, detentions, and disappearance" (Daulatzai 2012: 173). Internationally, "the transnational logic of incarceration and the institutional links between the prison regimes around Black Muslims in the United States and the emergence of military prisons in Iraq, Afghanistan, and Guantánamo ... may have come full circle" (Daulatzai 2012: 176). As Daulatzai (2012) acknowledged, while the US has always played fast and loose with the term national security, with the rights of its citizens being only an ephemeral ruse, their treatment of Muslims, from the time of the Bush Sr. administration, has been such that they appear to not have the right to any rights. Indeed, Greenberg (2014) pointed out that the expansion of CALEA during the post-9/11 era was not only against high-profile targets but against anyone in the Muslim community with radical leanings.

In these and many other ways Muslims have been isolated during the post-9/11 outrage; perhaps the most notable exclusionary instance being the notorious October Plan where Arabs and Muslims were specifically selected to partake in interviews with the FBI which resulted in more than 2,000 people's lives being disrupted, "From a civil liberties perspective, religious profiling took place when only one set of religious institutions (mosques) were under widespread surveillance" (Greenberg 2014: 289). Such instances speak to the global population revealing the hypocrisy of US multiculturalism. There is no denying the sham multiculturalism the US is currently trumpeting around the world is merely superficial, especially considering the increase of surveillance that has taken place since 9/11. Daulatzai (2012: 172) explained that "In the post-9/11 era, the rhetoric of 'terrorism' has become a proxy for race, generating tremendous political and ideological capital for U.S. nationalism and the implementation of our whole infrastructure and apparatus of control through the 'War on Terror.'"

Berman made an interesting point too in articulating what was at stake, "Permitting investigations without factual predicate and with limited supervisory involvement is overwhelmingly likely to lead to profiling on the basis of race, religion, ethnicity, national origin, or political belief" (Berman 2010; quoted in Greenberg 2014: 296). She noted that the danger is that in these situations suspicion can be decided based on an FBI agent's personal biases. Or taken to its more logical completion "the more 'devout' a Muslim, the greater the likelihood he is 'violent.'" (Greenberg 2014: 297.)

It is ideas like this that allowed, "The emergence of imperial imprisonment in Iraq, Guantánamo, Afghanistan, and elsewhere, combined with the domestic architecture of mass incarceration and the assault on Black Islam in the United States, [to form] an archipelago of power and geography of violence in response to the possibilities of the Muslim International, as the prison seeks to contain and prevent its power and possibility" (Daulatzai 2012: 175). Yet, "While the Bush Administration proved a disaster for civil liberties, Obama [had] not reined in the FBI, making only symbolic changes. He no longer used the term 'war on terror' and shed the overblown and exaggerated discourse associated with it. … However, not much [had] changed in terms of structure and motive for investigating political activity. Obama [had] not put an end to the practice of political policing. Indeed, in some ways he permitted the expansion of FBI spying capabilities" (Greenberg 2014: 37).

So while the official statements of the United States are towards multiculturalism and integration, their act-species are blatantly anaemic. US targeting of foreign Muslims has thus played a big part in undermining their multicultural (*mushrik al-thaqafi*) rhetoric; immigrant Muslims have not been fooled in the least into believing the hype that the US is a place of tolerance and acceptance, but come to America mainly, though not exclusively, for economic reasons. The Black Muslim, on the other hand, sees the United States for what it is – a falsehood that portrays itself as a land of opportunity while being a land filled with poverty – they are under no illusions, their immigrant Muslim brothers and sisters are escaping the so-called Third World only to re-enter another Third World within the First World.

Daulatzai also elucidated the ways in which American propaganda is being used to suppress the expansion of the Muslim International (*al-umma*) within the United States: "The racial and ideological calculus behind [certain] comparisons helps you generate the necessary fear and political will needed for increased domestic repression, and … the [insidious way] in which the logic of the 'War on Terror' is being mapped domestically and combined with existing narratives of Black criminality through the 'War on Crime' discourse [creating] an alchemy of repression that links Muslims, Blackness, prisons, and gang culture" (Daulatzai 2012: 182). Indeed, US policy on criminality is heavily racialised to the point that the *imaginative culture (al-thaqafah al-khayali)* of a Black person is criminal and the *imaginative culture (al-thaqafah al-khayali)* of a Muslim is terroristic; hence the penalisation of socio-cultural groups inevitably expands into the penalisation of racial groups.

There is ineluctably a somatic concatenation between the penality of culture (*thaqafah*) and the growth of neoliberalism's acceptance and institutionalisation. Invariably, "neo-liberalism correlates closely with the international diffusion of punitive policies in both the welfare and the criminal domains". "But to discern these multilevel connections between the upsurge of the punitive

Leviathan and the spread of neoliberalism, it is necessary to develop a precise and broad conception of the latter" (Wacquant 2016: 127, 128). Neoliberalism is more than simply a resurrected (*bu'itha*) system of political economy, it is also an ideological structure which includes statist, penalist, and imperialist tendencies. Though it cannot be denied the United States has deceptively hidden its harassment and penalisation of the racial and cultural other so as to maintain imperial hegemony and frustrate the growth of Black and Islamic sympathy within and outside its national borders, there is still very present an underlying and inherent promotion of national identity and positionality that is quite veritable.

National identity as a form of rhetoric has constantly shifted from one extreme to the next. From left-wing to right-wing. But such has been the case, and will always be the case, in a plutocracy that disguises itself as a democracy. That is not to say its democratic imperatives supply no actual freedoms; however, the sacrifices to be made to gain those freedoms falsify the meaning or reality of those freedoms. This is the problem with Western nationalism, although it has the appearance of being a standard by which to hold other existing political entities, eidetically it is a hypocritical standard that is good for all other people but has no bearing on the Western countries that seek to enforce it. The national-state is effectively a pseudo-state, which physically looks solid due to the corruption of the media but is eidetically falling apart at the hinges. That does not mean that national identity has disappeared entirely either, but that its logic of privilege, particularly with regard to the dominant racial group, has become more insidious.

As Balibar (1991) explicated, the racism inherent in certain forms of national identification, and in particular in nationalist variations, has its basis in the need and desire to maintain social privileges: Indeed, "Privileges can only be guaranteed by the defence of an exclusiveness that is as restrictive as possible. It seems to me that we can in this way better understand why the crisis conjuncture combines within the popular classes an uncertainty ... as to the 'security' of existence and an uncertainty about collective 'identity'" (Balibar 1991: 226). In this instance it is not national security that is threatened by groups such as Blacks or Muslims; it is invariably White privilege.

What was the need for the beefing up of surveillance and spying techniques during the 1990s after the Cold War had already ended if not to maintain privilege? Therefore because the privileges of the very high few could not be maintained without creating a national enemy, one which could evoke fears concerning national security and create unity concerning national identity, surveillance and repression of Muslims with the excuse of defending national security took on both a domestic and transnational flavour with both Black Muslims and the Muslim International being targeted by US agencies, policing units, and military forces, as Daulatzai (2012) has also noticed.

VI

The United States seeks to promote the dominance and supremacy of a particular culture – the pluralist culture (*al-thaqafah al-mushriki*) – a *thaqafah al-za'if* that fragments society allowing the most privileged class, the very rich, to maintain their system of privilege relatively unhindered. The GUSE has disseminated their *thaqafah al-za'if* mainly due to the global unsettling that has occurred and been occurring since the revival of liberalism as a resurrected orthodoxy and the fall of the Second World that succeeded it. The world is not the same way it used to be, we at one time had a two bully system where two opposed bullies stood against each other and the rest just chose a side, now the two bullies have teamed up (pretty much, I know there are complications in their relationship) and are terrorising the rest.

The countries of the world (*al-'alam*) now look to the GUSE as the last remaining empire, but that in no ways stops America from still seeking to strengthen its own country, its own national exceptionalism. However, as Derrida said, "how can one deny that this conceptual phantom is, so to speak, made more outdated than ever, in the very *ontopology* it supposes, by tele-technic dis-location? (By *ontopology* we mean an axiomatics linking indissociably the ontological value of present-being {on} to its *situation*, to the stable and presentable determination of a locality, the *topos* of territory, native soil, city, body in general)" (Derrida 2006: 102) – a statement in which Derrida's fondness for making up words knows no bounds – the truth of the statement, however, is quite discernible considering the all-encompassing nature of the GUSE.

Bakunin, in his own time, sounded the knell on these ideas of nationalism, national exceptionalism, and the *ontopology* of the nation by stating one of his most obvious perceptions, "it is clear why the *doctrinaire revolutionaries*, whose objective is to overthrow existing governments and regimes so as to create their own dictatorship on their ruins, have never been and never will be enemies of the state. … They are enemies only of existing governments, because they want to take their place" (Bakunin 2005: 137). Interestingly enough, this is exactly what happened with the overthrow of the monarchs, what happened with the overthrow of the imperialists, and what happened every time a Marxist regime took power.

Bakunin (2005) himself believed the only difference between a liberal democracy and a revolutionary dictatorship was that the fraud of elections – in which a privileged handful come to power having been chosen by the "pseudo-popular will" of people who know nothing about the representative they are now choosing to be their dominator (*zalim*) – takes place in one; while in the other the masses are dominated by an all-encompassing power, and all "in the name of the presumed stupidity" (Bakunin 2005: 137) of the people. In either case the people are dominated by a force that is opposed to them, that is contrary to them, and is thus alienation incarnate.

The Marxist regimes that fell in the early 1990s left a void in the United States, on the one hand, and a danger, on the other. It is then that Islam almost seamlessly replaced Marxism as the global threat that marked the danger to Western values and freedoms; however, that did not stop the ending of the Cold War from allowing US expansionist ambitions to soar. At the same time, as the Vietnam War, on the one hand, and the empires of old Europe, on the other, were proving to the US: colonised people were far more resilient than was initially presumed. Their attempts at a new form of colonisation in Latin America were far more effective than they had initially estimated they would be, thus the US realised that for expansion to work there would need to be a level of subterfuge.

Daulatzai (2012) pointed out that the US expansionist ideals and triumphalist emotions came at a time when they were without rival, when they had no competitor. The Muslim threat was hardly a match for US wealth and power, though they propagated it as such. He also noted that as racial inequality was the Achilles heel of US Cold War propaganda, so cultural intolerance is now proving to be the Achilles heel of US War on Terror propaganda. For the US to get over their history of racial and cultural opposition they had to, and still have to, promote the idea of multicultural expansionism (which really just amounts to multicultural imperialism). Daulatzai also explained how the "new Imperial multiculturalism ultimately [maintains] the traditional relations of power, with whiteness still being the invisible norm … as the celebration of a multicultural United States [gives] moral sanction and ethical legitimacy to the country as a global superpower" (Daulatzai 2012: 157). There is no denying that the United States has used multiculturalism as a means of legitimising their own form of neo-colonialism, a neo-colonialism that is rooted in racial undertones and discourses of White cultural and intellectual superiority.

Obviously, it is the sport of most US neo-colonialists to claim Islam is a new form of fascism, but Islam was able to coexist among many religiously and racially different communities for centuries in Africa and Asia, which were genuinely multicultural environments, so why does Islam find it so hard to coexist now? The answer is twofold: the mechanisms the GUSE put in place in its rise to imperial status created an imbalance that heavily favoured people of the same race as those who had colonised the world; and the immorality and immodesty of the Western social order offends the stricter sections of the Muslim community. Nonetheless, as we have seen, the current Western overindulgence in surveillance predated Bush Jr.'s War on Terror and goes all the way back to Reagan's resurrection (*ba'th*) of liberalism in the 1980s: it could even be said to have begun all the way back in the 1920s when the Bureau of Investigations was first organised as a counter-communist agency. Yet it is not until Clinton that the right and ability to spy on private, that is, non-organisational, citizens began. Which brings us again to the original question, if by the 1990s – when Clinton enhanced the FBI's spying capabilities exponentially – the United States was really as tolerant as it claimed to be, why the need for such measures?

First of all, if we consider the objectives of the FBI's counterintelligence program in 1968 we find their true intentionality for increasing surveillance prior to 9/11, I shall quote just a section:

1. Prevent the COALITION of militant black nationalist groups. In unity there is strength; a truism that is no less valid for all its triteness. An effective coalition of black nationalist groups might be the first step toward a real 'Mau Mau' {Black revolutionary army} in America, the beginning of a true black revolution.

2. Prevent the RISE OF A 'MESSIAH' who could unify, and electrify, the militant black nationalist movement. Malcolm X might have been such a 'messiah;' he is the martyr of the movement today. Martin Luther King, Stokely Carmichael and Elijah Muhammed all aspire to this position. Elijah Muhammed is less of a threat because of his age. King could be a very real contender for this position should he abandon his supposed 'obedience' to 'white, liberal doctrines' (nonviolence) and embrace black nationalism. Carmichael has the necessary charisma to be a real threat in this way. (Hoover 2016).

Secondly, "As the 'Black criminal' and the 'Muslim terrorist' have served to give coherence and purpose to U.S. national identity, the recurring presence of Black Islam in U.S. political culture continues to reveal the unresolved contradictions around race and empire that sit at the heart of U.S. state formation" (Daulatzai 2012: 109). Hence, the reason for all this surveillance is that, though White people seek to maintain their privilege, Black people, particularly the strategically placed Black Islam, are capable of and have the capacity to dismantle their entire system of privilege and global dominance.

The politics of surveillance for national security purposes in the United States betrays an underlying insecurity within the system, an insecurity of the powerful, whose power must be maintained by exacerbating any nationalistic contradictions – particularly between different racial groups that if unified could effectively overthrow their system. In point of fact, those in power rarely surrender their power easily or willingly. As an example, the British Empire was unwilling to let go of India though they had an independence movement being promulgated since 1857; and even after the success of the independence movement Britain was still able to maintain a level of control over India through rebranding the British Empire as a British Commonwealth of Nations.

The same will be the case with regard to the GUSE, and they have more subtle tricks to prevent a successful revolutionary movement. Worse still, if a revolutionary movement was to succeed they will immediately begin the process of setting up a counter-revolution: whether through a military coup like they did in Egypt (2013), or through a "people's" uprising like they did in Libya (2011) or their failed attempt at the Bay of Pigs (1961), or through outside invasion like their failed attempt in Iran (1980-1988). Those who think the revolution itself will be the hard part are living in a dream world.

Post-Colonialism in Africa

If one considers late modern African scholarship, arguably the most popular position and methodology is the post-colonial. This position was given popularity by Edward Said, a Palestinian liberal whose family emigrated to the United States when he was young due to the occupying presence in Palestine. Said already breaks boundaries by being a Palestinian liberal, he further breaks boundaries in that he was raised in both Cairo and America. It would be this breaking of boundaries that would characterise the content of his vast oeuvre. Said first offers us a definition of post-colonialism in his essay "Third World Intellectuals and Metropolitan Culture", of which Ahmad gave a full description: "The latter half of this essay consists of the entirely salutary recommendation that non-Western writers be taken seriously by Western readers. The main burden of the argument, however, rests on a rather strange distinction between what are called 'colonial' and 'post-colonial' intellectuals" (Ahmad 2008: 203). Here Said's intentionality was to produce a redefinition of alterity: he sought to show that within this eidetic category called alterego are contained two sub-categories (again, what is meant here by alterego is any ego other to primordial ego).

Ahmad (2008: 205) continued by articulating some of the discrepancies lurking beneath, "These categories have no analytic value, or theoretical status, when they are mobilized to homogenize very complex structures of intellectual productions or the trajectories and subjectivities of individual writers and critics or broad intellectual strata, of the kind Said suggests in his essay." Ahmad mainly appears to have taken issue with Said's labelling with the category of post-colonial mainly those intellectuals who were privileged enough to have reached maturity during and after the process of decolonisation (Ahmad 2008). While also agreeing that such is a blatant form of idealistic tautology the reasoning behind it is not that difficult to put together. The so-called Third World intellectuals who wrote mainly during the period of colonialism would have critiqued colonialism from the position of a Marxist; Said, if not anti-Marxist was at least non-Marxist and desired to make a radical critique of colonialism from a non-Marxist standpoint, thus was born post-colonial theory and the post-colonial perspective.

Post-colonialism took off in what for the non-West were the radical times of the 1970s-1980s and still carries weight in academic disciplines as diverse as English literature, anthropology, cultural studies, and Islamic studies. This is due to Said's refusal to respect boundaries and stay within a specific genre, and seeing its own particular elevation through to the end. Said, in a technical sense, is the father of post-colonial theory, however, if Said is the father then Foucault is definitely the forefather. As Said said in the introduction to his hugely influential Opus *Orientalism*, "I have found it useful here to employ Michel Foucault's notion of discourse, as described by him in *The Archaeology of Knowledge* and in *Discipline and Punish*, to identify Orientalism. My contention is that without examining Orientalism as a discourse one cannot possibly understand the enormously systematic discipline by which European culture was able to manage – and even produce – the Orient politically, sociologically, militarily, ideologically, scientifically, and imaginatively during the post-Enlightenment period" (Said 2003: 3). Not that I have no agreement here with Foucault and Said, indeed, I myself used the discursive conception to show how Black people have been inferiorised, sexualised, and criminalised politically, sociologically, ideologically, scientifically, and imaginatively since the days of our enslavement; my problem is with the solutions offered by Foucault and Said.

It, therefore, becomes necessary for us to return briefly to Foucault to see how he conceptualised discourse and the individuals who develop them. Foucault said concerning the intellectuals who developed discursive systems of truth-finding that they have "a threefold specificity: that of [their] class position (whether as petit bourgeois in the service of capitalism or 'organic' intellectual of the proletariat); that of [their] conditions of life and work, linked to [their] condition as an intellectual (his field of research, his place in a laboratory, the political and economic demands to which he submits or against which he rebels, in university, the hospital, and so on); finally, the specificity of the politics of truth in our society ... it being understood once again that by truth I mean not 'the ensemble of truths to be discovered and accepted' but, rather, 'the ensemble of rules according to which the true and the false are separated and specific effects of power attached to the true,'" (Foucault 2006: 169).

Foucault here, correctly, pointed out that not all things identified as true (*haqq*) are in fact true and that it is the precedent given to what is called true (*haqq*) that ultimately determines what will be its perceived correlates. Foucault's solution, however, gives credence to a statement by Ali Shari'ati, "An intellectual may be an accomplice in the service of a power structure, or he may be a slave of his stomach and his family" (Shari'ati 1981: 2038); either way they are not in the service of the people.

Said's, nonetheless, is more about representational politics – which is another sweetheart of neoliberalism – as Klein intimated, "for many of the activists who had, at one point not so long ago, believed that better media representation would make for a more just world, one thing had become abundantly clear: identity politics weren't fighting the system, or even subverting it. When it came to the vast new industry of corporate branding, they were feeding it" (Klein 2010: 113). It is also for this reason that Shari'ati felt enlightenment was a far more suitable principle upon which to establish a system, as he intimated back in the 1970s, "Given our culture and specific definition of 'enlightened' as a person with a prophetic mission, the objectives and responsibilities of such a person are to transform the existing social conflicts from the context of the society into the feelings and self-consciousness of its members" (Shari'ati 2002: 44). Moreover, "As the Holy Prophet says, 'The scholars of my *ummah* are higher than the prophets of the Bani Israel.'" (Shari'ati 2003: 65).

I

If we were to ask: what then is the diatribe the godbody perspective has against post-colonialism we would find it is not simply in its ineffectiveness at fighting for enlightenment and liberation, but in its potential to reinforce and maintain the neoliberal status quo. In order to verify this presupposition I shall begin my critique with a look at some of the ideas and concepts espoused by Said in his groundbreaking work *Orientalism*. It becomes necessary then to start the debate by first getting an understanding of what Said meant by Orientalism. This is difficult as Said used three consecutive and contradictory definitions. However, neglecting these Said's most consistent, and consistently used, definition is found in the succeeding:

> *Therefore, Orientalism is not a mere political subject matter or field that is reflected passively by culture, scholarship, or institutions; nor is it a large and diffuse collection of texts about the orient ... It is rather a* distribution *of geopolitical awareness into aesthetic, scholarly, economic, sociological, historical, and philological texts; it is an* elaboration *not only of a basic geographical distinction ... but also of a whole series of 'interest' which, by such means as scholarly discovery, philological reconstruction, psychological analysis, landscape and sociological description, it not only creates but also maintains; it* is, *rather than expresses, a certain will or* intention *to understand, in some cases to control, manipulate, even to incorporate, what is a manifestly different ... world; it is, above all, a discourse that is by no means in direct, corresponding relationship with political power in the raw, but rather is produced and exists in an uneven exchange with various kinds of power, shaped to a degree by the exchange with power political (as with a colonial or imperial establishment), power intellectual (as with reigning sciences like comparative linguistics or anatomy, or any of the modern policy sciences), power cultural (as with orthodoxies and canons of taste, texts, values), power moral (as with ideas about what 'we' do and what 'they' cannot do or understand as 'we' do). (Said 2003: 12).*

As a foundation to this critique I shall add a few points on which godbody sociology agrees with Said: Firstly, "To say simply that Orientalism was a rationalization of colonial rule is to ignore the extent to which colonial rule was justified in advance by Orientalism" (Said 2003: 39). It is inexorable, especially considering the avalanche of proofs presented throughout his life's work, that Orientalism preceded colonialism, and provided legitimation for the colonisers to rule over the colonised. Said was smart enough to put together that it was first necessary to inferiorise a social body (*al-mujtama*) before you could subjugate it. Clearly, the discourse of Orientalism played a strong and pernicious role in justifying colonialism and not vice versa. Hence, the theoretical must precede the practical and pragmatic, even as thought when crystallised becomes action, which itself, when crystallised, becomes custom, which also, when further crystallised, becomes tradition. It was the theory of Orientalism that gave way to the governmental Acts of legalised domination, which then created the culture of colonialism, and the tradition of Islamophobia. But these things all start as a seed and, as Chomsky said, it is "in terms of justice; it's because the end that [is sought] is claimed as a just one" (Chomsky & Foucault 2006: 54).

Secondly, "Many terms were used to express the relation: … The Oriental is irrational, depraved (fallen), childlike, 'different'; thus the European is rational, virtuous, mature, 'normal.'" (Said 2003: 40). It is true the West has created a binary in which the Oriental (and, indeed, all non-Whites) come out the loser; thereby "Orientalism [expresses] the strength of the West and the Orient's weaknesses – as seen by the West" (Said 2003: 45). Indeed, since the arrival of late modernity and the postmodern discourse, the dualism and dialecticism that ran throughout mid-modernity with its Manichaean veneer has been slowly getting surpassed. The binaries of self and other, nature and culture, private and public, inside and outside, female and male, foreign and national, oriental and occidental, primitive and advanced,

Black and White, have been facing heavy opposition from the academic and non-academic world of late modernity. The result has been that the barriers separating these bounded and clearly defined groups have been coming down. That is not to say all barriers have been coming down, or that those just mentioned have already come down (that is, completely), but that late modern society has been defined by a desire to eradicate all boundaries and universalise human identity. At the same time, late modernity has been characterised by a desire to particularise and fragment the various groups and categories (*qisman*) of human identification so as to "give a voice to the voiceless."

Thirdly, "there is no doubt that imaginative geography and history help the mind to intensify its own sense of itself by dramatizing the distance and difference between what is close to it and what is far away" (Said 2003: 55). Basically, the working of the imagination (*khayal*) of the Orientalist allows for a distance, both binary and bounded, to be set between the European and the Oriental – even as the Africanist does with the European and the African. Africa, Latin America, and the Orient are fantasised as lands of the backward (both economically and culturally). The people are not as evolved politically or socially as the Westerner therefore they must be carried by Europe and the US toward development and progress. (The consequences of this concatenation shall be analysed briefly).

But this imaginative geography (*al-jugrafiya al-khayali*) is not limited to large geographic bodies like Europe and the Orient. The geographical distinction between the urban ghetto and the suburban heartlands is just as imagined. Here, even ethnographies of the ghetto by university educated social scientists (*al-'ulamaa al-ijtima'iyya*), whether Marxist, feminist, or functionalist, usually end up perpetuating the same imaginative (*khayali*) stories of economically backward, blatantly misogynist, and culturally apathetic illegitimates who are lost in the system. It does not matter whether the writer is for or against the underclass they all seem to borrow from each other the same general structure of composition – abnormalising and distancing the middle class readership from these estranged illegitimates with the same excuses for the separation: poverty, capitalism, machismo, misogyny, deviance, and anomie.

Finally, that in Orientalist writings, "Asia speaks through and by virtue of the European imagination, which is depicted as victorious over Asia, that hostile 'other' world beyond the seas" (Said 2003: 56). Effectively, the Orientalist is differentiated from the Oriental by the fact that the Orientalist is an observing, communicating, commanding subject while the Oriental is an observed, represented, and dominated object captured first in the imagination (*al-khayal*) then in concrete materialisation (*al-hass*). Yet, as the writings of the Orientalist speak for the Oriental so the writings, words, and images (texts) of the Africanists speak for the African (whether pan-Africanist or academic Africanist).

Though it could be said that in pan-Africanism the African speaks for himself or herself, in many ways pan-Africanism turns out to only invert or subvert the narrative of Africanism (which though not a fault in itself, does show that the two narratives are intrinsically linked). Allowing those opposed to us to speak for us, even when we speak for ourselves, shows that we, in many ways, have not come to find ourselves or to take a stand. That is not to say the narrative we do choose to follow will or should be taken from outer space or based on nothing solid and substantial within the dominant narrative, but that simply turning Black devils into White devils or Black weaknesses into Black strengths is not enough to see the overthrow of White racism or Orientalism.

II

In all, the areas of disagreement between godbody sociology and post-colonialism themselves have a profound distinction. Firstly, Said's overemphasis on representation: the conception itself is one of serious importance to Said due to the tendency of some writers and journalists to misrepresent those they are supposed to be representing. Nevertheless, for him "the real issue [with representation] is whether indeed there can be a true representation of anything, or whether any and all representations, because they are representations, are embedded first in the language and then in the culture, institutions, and political ambience of the representer" (Said 2003: 272). It is this question of misrepresentation and the positionality of the representer that has had profound repercussions on the social sciences (*al-'ulum al-ijtima'iyya*).

This problematic is not helped by the internal complications inherent in a group Abu-Lughod (1991) called "halfies" (those bicultural individuals belonging to both an "othered" culture and the Western – particularly academic – culture). She said on the subject, "The problem with studying one's own society is alleged to be the problem of gaining enough distance. Since for halfies, the Other is in certain ways the self, there is said to be the danger shared with indigenous anthropologists of identification and the easy slide into subjectivity" (Abu-Lughod 1991: 468). Thus, by the West questioning the "halfies'" right to represent their own culture and Said questioning the Westerner's right to represent any other culture, it becomes apparent that representation is at once a precarious yet also a very complex issue. If bicultural social scientists (*al-'ulamaa al-ijtima'iyya*) cannot represent their own people then is anyone worthy at all?

The back and forth seesaw over who is worthier to represent a culture (*thaqafah*) or social group (*mujtama*), Westerners or "halfies," is on the whole an incongruent discrepancy. Anyone, whether Westerner or "halfie," has the right to voice a fictive opinion (as opposed to a fictitious one), especially if informed by evidence, of what they believe to be a cultural or societal variation particular to a *thaqafah* or *mujtama*. The idea that science or objectivity can come from the study of either is an illusion. The most that can be hoped for is an intersubjective interpretation of the *thaqafah* or *mujtama* that the social scientist (*al-ʿalim al-ijtimaʾiyya*) empathically constructs and analyses with his or her data. Anything less is potentially stereotyping and prejudiced or hypocritical fantasising. Ultimately, when the primordial ego of the social scientist can see non-ego as both alterego and intersubjective ego – connected to self via various similar mechanisms (when they can see There as Here) – then their fictive descriptions will be as good as they could be. The *ʿulum al-ijtimaʾiyya* are incapable of being genuinely objective (*munfasil*), the most they can hope to be is intersubjective.

It is hereby that in the process of developing and evaluating this and other social static situations that it will be necessary to have the right formula; in this instance two axiomatics of social statics become relevant:

1. The process of stasis for a social movement begins when it has reached its natural limitation and remains constant and predictable, and when there are no external social forces driving it to instigate change or $g(Lm) \leftrightarrow \alpha \searrow o$.

2. When a social movement has decelerated to become a social body all narratives to describe its process of development and

continuance will be fictive and therefore will require some intersubjectivity. Or said another way, $\exists \alpha \searrow o \to x^u \geq g$.

If one is not intersubjective in their research they may end up asking a bunch of interview or survey questions based on Western stereotypes and unrelated to how a people see themselves. Something most White people fail to appreciate is that if we used biased surveys and questions that confirm suspicions concerning stereotypically White behaviour and asked those questions to an assortment of White people, and to a control group of non-White people, it would only perpetuate non-White prejudices concerning White people. The trouble here is, to certain sections of the White population White stereotypes are those that show them as innocent, suburban, professional, and corny, they are unable to assume that large sections of the non-White population see them as self-righteous, privileged, domineering, and arrogant. However, an empathic scholar (*'alim*) studying White people would take into account how White people see themselves and would ask questions based on that perspective.

Notwithstanding, there is a greater necessity for White people to research and analyse non-Whites more empathically than there is for non-Whites to empathise with Whites; as there is no serious difficulty with the powerless empathising with the powerful as empathy is implied in their status. The powerful, in this case the White, have a responsibility, particularly in academia, to empathise with the powerless non-White and to represent them as they see themselves, that is, to re-present them intersubjectively. That is, to present their real subjective (*muttasil*) selves and not an illusory othered self, one created by Western scholarship and moralising principles. At the same time, they are not in the position to demand of the non-White the same favour as the moment the powerful set the terms of how the powerless can study and comment on them is the moment the oppressive nature of the power dynamic becomes totalising.

Furthermore, the central diatribe existing between godbody theory and post-colonial theory is over these issues of objectivity and intersubjectivity; issues that have driven Ahmad (2008: 193) to ask "is it possible to make true statements? [Consequently, there] are powerful traditions, including the Nietzschean, which have denied such a possibility. There are other powerful traditions, including the Marxist, which have said that yes, true statements are possible. Said's equivocation on this key question is delivered in what appears to be a precise formulation – namely, that the line between a representation and a misrepresentation is always very thin" (Ahmad 2008: 194).

Further, Said here "enters the Nietzschean world of questioning not merely positivist constructions but the very facticity of fact, so that it will eventually force a wide range of historians around the globe – some of the Indian Subalternists, for example – to start putting the word 'fact' in quotation marks" (Ahmad 2008: 194). Though to Said, "Perhaps such a view as Nietzsche's will strike us as too nihilistic, … at least it will draw attention to the fact that so far as it existed in the West's awareness, the Orient was a word which later accrued to it a wide field of meanings, associations, and connotations, and that these did not necessarily refer to the real Orient but to the field surrounding the word" (Said 2003: 203).

Secondly, the notion, namely, "that the matter of Identity-through-Difference … points to the primacy of representation over all other human activities" (Ahmad 2008: 182). As an example, Said mentioned how, "In the films and television the Arabic is associated either with lechery or bloodthirsty dishonesty. He appears as an oversexed degenerate, capable, it is true, of cleverly devious intrigues, but essentially sadistic, treacherous, low. Slave trader, camel driver, money changer, colorful scoundrel: these are some traditional Arab roles in the cinema" (Said 2003: 286). It is these kinds of misrepresentations that have led Said to present his anti-Western summations and consolidate his post-colonial theoretics.

In fact, "Said's denunciations of the *whole* of Western civilisation is as extreme and uncompromising as Foucault's denunciations of the Western episteme or Derrida's denunciations of the transhistorical Logos; nothing, nothing at all, exists outside the epistemic Power, logocentric Thought, Orientalist Discourse" (Ahmad 2008: 195). Still, as Klein (2010: 110) already explicated, "many of our demands for better representation [have been] quickly accommodated by marketers, media makers and pop-culture producers alike – though perhaps not for the reasons we had hoped." Far from having primacy over human activities representation has become a tool of Western plutocratic domination.

However, Said and Foucault were more influential in their suppositions, especially during the anti-colonial phase of the tricontinental liberation movements. Mudimbe (1988: 165) said, "All of the social and human sciences underwent [a] radical experience between 1950 and 1980. Fundamentally, the questioning [was] based on 'the right to truth,' implying a new analysis of three paradigms: philosophical ideal versus conceptual determination, scientific authority versus sociopolitical power, and scientific objectivity versus cultural subjectivity." Mudimbe himself being a product of this shift found himself in methodological agreement with Said and so adopted a post-colonial standpoint from which to evaluate the historical redefinition that was occurring in Africa as a result of the futility of the nationalist struggles and the hypnotic allure of Foucauldian suggestions.

According to Mudimabe, "The preindependence generation of African intellectuals was mostly concerned with political power and strategies for ideological succession. Since 1960, and more visibly since the 1970s, a new generation prefers to put forward the notion of *epistemological vigilance*. This generation seems much more concerned with strategies for mastering intellectual paradigms about 'the path to truth,' with analyzing the political dimensions of knowledge, and with procedures for establishing new rules in African studies" (Mudimbe 1988: 36). Yet this generation of post-colonial thinkers in Africa are no more than Foucauldian post-structuralists that happen to be from the so-called Third World. Their substance, indeed, their allure, is no more than the fact that they are critiquing the West in Foucauldian, and therefore academic, language.

For Mudimbe (1988) what was important was the epistemic paradigm shift from political decolonisation to academic decolonisation. At the same time, it may be true that "To teach ... that there are, in Africa, organized social structures, sophisticated systems of relations of production, and highly complex universes of belief, is to express propositions which can be tested. [And to] add commentaries or exegeses on black cultures which are essentially mystical, religious, and sensuous, is to decipher a possibly controversial myth and, at any rate, to elaborate on what is not the immanent significance of the object studied" (Mudimbe 1988: 89); but the solution of the post-colonialists and Foucault to dismiss the whole falsifies the substance of the whole post-colonial argument: that the colonised are silenced by the colonisers and made to speak through the coloniser with the coloniser's voice. This is the third almighty danger of post-colonialism, by condemning all forms of Western articulation for not comprehending the subtleties of African systems and structures they thereby lose or forfeit the opportunity to learn the positive points of Western systems and structures, and to be sure, the West does have positive points in their systems and structures.

Western adoption is what Shari'ati called Western imitation, but, at the same time, he recognised that some forms of imitation are not necessarily bad. The student imitates the professor until they learn and master the subject. The protégé imitates the mentor until they are able to go out on their own. Effectively, "There are two kinds of imitations. One type is when I train a person to blindly follow me, in a master-servant type relationship. In this kind of imitation the terms of servitude are chosen by the master and the more the servant imitates, the more he proves his servitude. However, there is another kind that I have discovered." This "type of imitation […] is the opposite of the first one, since it saves me from servitude, weakness, and falling under foreign influence" (Shari'ati 1981: 1468). Thus, we see that the imitation of some Western forms of articulation does not necessarily mean selling-out or psychological inferiority. We can still maintain a level of independence while adopting certain Western ideas and understandings.

This issue is fundamentally important to me being of Jamaican parentage, on the one hand, and having traced back part of my roots to the Hausa of Nigeria, on the other. Does my having learned from and studied under Western scholarship make me any less African? My heart bleeds for Africa as a child panting after her mother. Indeed, I love Africa more than I love my own soul. Even deeper than that, am I any less of an African because I was not born in Africa? These questions are posed not only to the people on the continent but also to that section of the diaspora that call themselves pan-Africanist. Having countered the colonial power structure after the deception of biological anthropology ran its course – notwithstanding the West's never really letting go of Africa post-independence and only re-imposing colonialism under the guise of "aid" and "development"; the dependency of Africa on the West monetary-wise (though the West is just as dependent on Africa for cheap labour and resources) shows that they lost their independence economically – pan-Africanism has been both inspirational and exclusionary at the same time.

Not that I am against celebrating being African or the transgenerational, transhistorical, transmigrational African soul, but the vast majority of the leaders of these movements have a tendency to be lost in a kind of megalomania, and so violently opposed to anything even smelling White that they shut down and shut you down even if the point you are trying to make is valid. As much as I despise what White people have historically done to us, and as much as I despise the instruments they used to conquer us; and as much as I acknowledge that we are still under a system of White supremacy today, inherent though it may be, as a godbody I cannot accept the absolute rejection of their race as though they have nothing good to offer us just because they are White and "have oppressed our people for centuries." Those who make such an argument know little about White history and just believe the propaganda and narrative White people have told about themselves "for centuries." For White people to reach the pinnacle of civilisation they have reached – not that they are more civilised than the Original nations but that they have built the current ruling and dominant civilisation – they had to have learned from somewhere and they did: from the Muslims.

As racist and Islamophobic as Medieval Europe was they were still willing to learn from the Muslims, especially as the Muslims were willing to teach them. Were it not for Islam Europe would have never adopted the Hindu-Arabic numeral system, in contrast to the Roman numeral system that was being practiced in Europe and still would be practiced today. The West also learned *al-jabr* (algebra), *al-kemi* (chemistry) and gained more accurate maps of the earth and of the motions of the planets and stars from the Muslims. In fact, it was ibn Rushd's interpretation of Aristotle that introduced the scientific method to Europe during the Middle Ages (a method created more so by him than by Aristotle himself). But again, even ibn Rushd was willing to study and learn from this White man when he found the lessons he was providing worthy; and Islamophobic Europe was willing to learn from the Muslims in order to share in their level of knowledge. The pan-Africanists' despising of all things European prevents them from seeing that, like it or not, Europe currently holds the keys to all doors, so, like it or not, we will have to learn from them in order to surpass their current order.

Abu-Lughod made a conclusive point in this wise: "Some anticolonial movements and present-day struggles have worked by what could be labelled reverse Orientalism, where attempts to reverse the power relationship proceed by seeking to valorize for the self what in the former system had been devalued as other" (Abu-Lughod 1991: 470). Even so, pan-Africanism could be called a reverse Africanism. As Shari'ati also noted, "In short, if we chance towards the West, we will be trapped and swallowed. But if we hate her, we will be reactionaries and will fall prey to a surprise attack from behind" (Shari'ati 1981: 1519). This is why the Foucauldian system of denying all truth (*haqiqa*) and making everything academically level will never work: we are not all level. White people are proportionately more powerful in every category and can use that power against us to hold us back. Moreover, Mudimbe's Foucauldian reasoning that, "With the problem of truth, we are confronted with one of the most paradoxical forms of amplification and with the promotion of African alternatives" (Mudimbe 1988: 41), shows that he and many African academics view the power issue as one of knowledge alone and not one of total systemic disempowerment.

Moreover, the totalitarian subjugation of the non-White to the White, and the Africans' and Orientals' struggle to liberate themselves from this subjugation does not mean that we simply succumb to absolute rejection. In valorising our own power structures it is imperative that we do not forsake evidential truth for self-pleasing myths. Therefore, it is also imperative that we imitate the dominant power in this respect and not simply self-gratify by rejecting all things European. The vulgar Foucauldian premise that there is no truth (*la haqiqa*) and that all European systems of knowledge are questionable, while boosting the egos of former colonies also keeps them from proportional growth. As an example, Mudimbe (1988) used Tempels' and Kagame's promotion of Bantu Philosophy to show an affirmation of original alterity and complex cosmological systems. While such may seem innocent enough if taken to its most expanded conclusion Africa will remain impotent and incapable of rivalling any power that builds on the scientific principles discovered by Islam and furthered by the West. We have to be sure that in elevating our ancient cultures we do not spend so much time looking backward that we forget to look forward.

But perhaps the greatest danger of post-colonialism is how it has influenced academic study: for example, the ideas espoused by Abu-Lughod (1991) would prove far more detrimental than remedial if applied. For a start the whole premise of writing against culture – that is, the concept of culture, which she viewed as a contributor to difference and division – is categorically inefficacious. As a theoretical interpretation it obviously had its origins in Said but it takes a rather militant stand against a non-threatening enemy. Culture (*thaqafah*), or the dividing of social groups into cultures, on its own can do no harm to those groups thus divided. It is when we begin to prioritise and hierarchise that the difficulties begin. Writing against culture, in essence, is like writing against employment, or writing against hobbies, or against football teams. It is writing against an effectively neutral force believing that it will produce conclusive results in ending division.

Abu-Lughod's (1991) suggestions for writing against culture are as fallacious as the original premise, firstly, she suggested using the terms practice and discourse in place of culture explaining: "practice and discourse – do signal a shift away from culture. Although there is always the danger that these terms will come to be used simply as synonyms for culture, they were intended to enable us to analyze social life without presuming the degree of coherence that the culture concept has come to carry" (Abu-Lughod 1991: 472). The idea is similar to conclusions like: if you choose not to use a dirty word the word will cease to exist, or that covering over your history can make it less horrific, et cetera.

The real problem, however, is that culture is not a dirty word, or an offensive word, or even a demeaning word, and it has never been. It is only post-colonialists who have any problem with using it as a result of their over-problematising the word, and all to non-effect as culture is still an existent paradigm that shapes how people think, behave, interact, and communicate. In all, the only things to be gained by replacing the word culture with the words discourse and practice would be to limit the range of understanding the readers and listeners will gain from an ethnography you have worked so hard on, and to limit your own level of conversation making you have to use many difficult words to produce explanations for questions that could have been answered with one simple word.

Further, although I have no serious disapproval of Abu-Lughod's (1991) suggestion that connections be made between the anthropologist and the culture he or she studies I do not think she went far enough. An anthropologist, sociologist, and ethnographer should be completely empathic in their choices of wording and questioning during the process of data collection. That means more than establishing connections between worlds, that means seeing the world as they see it and not simply trying to show the West the similarities or differences between the two worlds. This applies to culture, location, and history. Instead of prejudging ancient or transgeographical cultures and then proving or disproving your own hypotheses with documented or collected "evidence" the ethnographer should begin their research as though they were in the world they are examining, begin as though There was Here, so to speak.

To produce honest writing on culture the ethnographer must write as though the world and worldview of their informants is not only real but is also upright – I use the word upright here in the moral, spiritual, philosophical, practical, and judicial senses of the word. It is imperative that the ethnographer, whether anthropologist or sociologist, does not carry personal biases in their research: although such is perhaps necessary when they draw up their conclusions. Here godbody sociology is conclusively superior to post-colonial anthropology in that it starts at the subjects' point of view, then it goes in-depth and, finally, it makes estimations and recommendations based on the conclusions it has drawn from the research.

The final area of disagreement between post-colonial anthropology and godbody sociology is with the issue of generalisation as articulated in Abu-Lughod's (1991: 473, 474) following statements, "Generalization, the characteristic mode of operation and style of writing of the social sciences, can no longer be regarded as neutral description"; "On the one hand, it is the language of those who seem to stand apart from and outside of what they are describing. Again, Smith's critique of sociological discourse is relevant. She has argued … that this seemingly detached mode of reflecting on social life is actually located: it represents the perspective of those involved in professional, managerial, and administrative structures and is thus part of 'the ruling apparatus of this society.'" Although it could be said that broad generalisations and meta-discourses of social act-species are disputable due to the positionality of those making the generalisation that may be a case of throwing out the baby with the bathwater. Any good system employed by dubious individuals to further dubious ends will end up looking dubious. However, generalisation if employed in a credible fashion can be most effective.

An ineffable example which effectively challenges the assumptions made by Smith and Abu-Lughod is when Philips (1991: 102) speaking on female disempowerment said; "Many had thought of problems they had with husbands or lovers in terms of individual psychology – maybe we're not compatible? maybe I want what's impossible? maybe he just doesn't care? – but in the process of exploring individual experiences, they came to identify general patterns of power." As these personal behaviours were not isolated to one or a few men or women, so disempowerments and behaviours for other social groups could also be shown to be more general. This actually reveals one of the big problems I have with Foucauldian philosophy, because it is all about individual truths and fragmenting society into isolated pockets of truth, it leaves intact the reigning power dynamics without giving those individuals or groups the wherewithal to challenge it.

Yet another argument that could be made in favour of the science behind generalisation came from Carl Furtmüller's poignant insight: "The fact that reverses do occur is no counter-argument to [generalisations]. In training a dog we also will observe reverses; yet this will not prevent us from ascribing to the dog a disposition of domesticability which distinguishes him from the wolf" (Furtmüller 1912; quoted in Adler 1964). In any study of typologies (*aqsam*) certain aberrations will be common but that in no ways negates the validity of the typical specimen: even the most untrainable of Great Danes is unlikely to ever devolve into an African wild dog let alone metamorphose into a hyena, therefore determining the archetypal Great Dane behaviour can generally be conceived.

III

The main idea currently running through variations of post-colonial anthropology is that generalisations must be viewed with suspicion due to the hierarchical assertions implied in certain Western interpretations of them. The problem, again, is not the generalisations (*'umumat*) or categorisations (*qisman*), either implicated or explicated, in anthropological writings, but the hierarchical positioning of the reader or writer of the anthropological work. In either case the interpretation will be a fallacy and misinterpretation. To lump all generalisations (*'umumat*) with the falsely interpreted ones is not scientific but cowardly, and it is this dismissive rejection of science (*'ilm*) that is the legacy of Foucault.

It seems that in order to dismantle the scientific edifice on which power relations are built Michel Foucault, and his lackey Edward Said (who, as much as I respect as a man and as a spokesman for the cause of Palestinian liberation, I must critique on his academic premises and all their Foucauldian splendour), attacked the practice of generalising in academia. All the schools of neoliberal intellectualism derive their basis from Foucauldian hypnosis, only, as the sorcerer's apprentice he seems to have lost control of his creation, which has become like an automaton, living without living, alive without being alive, the simulacrum of life. Foucault effectively produced not disciples but replicants, simulations that appear so alive but are actually more machine than human. Such is the neoliberal intellectual and their convoluted answers to anthropological and, indeed, social scientific generalisations (*'umumat*). They reject science fervently while claiming a form of legitimation equal to or greater than science and discourse; but being unable to represent perfectly anyone end up representing no one at all.

As an example of what I mean Abu-Lughod in explaining her ethnographies of the particular wrote, "Anthropologists commonly generalize about communities by saying that they are characterized by certain institutions, rules, or ways of doing things. For example, we can and often do say things like 'The Bongo-Bongo are polygynous.' Yet one could refuse to generalize in this way, instead asking how a particular set of individuals – for instance, a man and his three wives in a Bedouin community in Egypt whom I have known for a decade – live the 'institution' that we call polygyny. Stressing the particularity of this marriage and building a picture of it through the participants' discussions, recollections, disagreements, and actions would make several theoretical points" (Abu-Lughod 1991: 475). She effectively thereby closes her eyes to the general nature of certain customs and, indeed, cultural realities (*al-haqiqat al-thaqafi*), in order to insulate that culture from the racist or Orientalist views of certain readers.

This approach may seem admirable but it actually does more to harm that culture than to protect it. Firstly, the intellectual strata of that culture could do far more to defend or critique it with profuse academic writings acknowledging its existence as a broad and general trend. Secondly, the practitioners of those practices have no insecurity or concern for how the West views their culture (*al-thaqafah*), they will keep doing what they have been doing regardless. Thirdly, it is far better to expose the racism or Orientalism of the reader who judges the culture than to hide the cultural reality (*al-haqiqa al-thaqafi*) of an ethnography, which ultimately hurts the paper itself and not the reader. Finally, what each culture and community actually needs is not to be particularised or culturally declassified. What they need is for their culture to instead be normalised, as in, made less particular, and less "strange." Particularising and writing against cultural practices only maintains their abnormal positioning among the majority of social scientists (*al-'ulamaa al-ijtima'iyya*) that encounter them for themselves.

Effectively, there are more or less three possibilities that can arise from generalisation, of these two of which are unwanted and one which is appropriate to the task: (i) The universalisation of dominant mores intellectually, culturally, politically, and legally. This is inappropriate as it is coercive, however one looks at it. Coercively forcing typical ideas and behaviours on atypical individuals negates their freedom and agency. We are all different regardless of what *thaqafah* we belong to, and should be allowed to enjoy our personal lifestyle choices without being bullied into doing what we personally do not agree with or into not doing what we personally desire to do. Though such is the argument of all neoliberalists, including our neoliberal intellectuals, if it did not have some semblance of truth it would not have the measure of influence it has today. Notwithstanding, the problematic is found in universalising not in generalising.

(ii) The creation of stereotypes. Stereotypes are when typical behaviour is exaggerated or the typicality of a behaviour is misrepresented. Here, however, the problem is not the generalisation of the behaviour as much as the misrepresentation of it. Therefore, rather than struggling to particularise events and behaviours there is no problem with identifying typicality in a *mujtama* or a *thaqafah* so long as it is done empathically and intersubjectively (and not objectively, as there can be no real objectivity in any social science due to politics and opinion running too deep within all forms of narration). The least that we can hope for is intersubjectivity, which is an empathic approach to articulating typical behaviour.

(iii) The benefit of generalisation, on the other hand, is in discovering archetypal ideas, sensibilities, behaviours, and practices. Through discovering and appreciating archetypes one can avoid eternalising social behaviours and norms. Indeed, social archetypes are similar to social superegos, particularly considering that they help us to identify the existing paradigms of a *mujtama*. Moreover, as paradigm shifts usually happen – contrary to the dominant supposition – internal to a *thaqafah*, rather than simply being a product of the West, or of capitalism or modernity, social archetypes help us to understand these shifts more profoundly and less biasedly.

The fact is, in areas of science such as the medical, to not generalise is not only impractical, it is malpractice. The same is true of a godbody sociologist. For a godbody sociologist to not use generalisations (*'umumat*) and typologies (*aqsam*) in order to diagnose would be malpractice. Therefore godbody sociology must encourage the godbody to use social archetypes and social prototypes – which themselves represent paradigmatic shifts – in order to diagnose those who seek their services. Nevertheless, a problematic could become apparent at this point: if generalisations (*'umumat*) and typologies (*aqsam*) can be made in godbody sociology who is it that will be making them? Who defines what is the typical behaviour of a *mujtama* and what is the anomalous behaviour?

Clearly, with regard to defining the typical behaviour of a powerless *mujtama* it is unhelpful to have someone who is not empathic: firstly, to their disempowered position, and, secondly, to the historical circumstances that contributed to their disempowerment. Godbody sociology therefore also encourages empathic and introspective analysis of social stases and aetiology to find typical patterns and prototypical shifts. Through vigilant introspection and intersubjectivity godbody sociologists will be able to keep their data on archetypes from transmutation into a collection of stereotypes. Thereby the sexuality, gender, race, class, age, or ability of the sociologist is not as important as the legitimation of their affectivity.

Still, godbody sociology has ultimately delineated within its own grand philosophy certain similarities with depth psychology's phenomenological philosophy – only instead of accepting without merit the postulations of social constructivism, which removes some of Freud's more naturalising conceptions – godbody sociology reshapes Freud and Adler to expose and demystify the power dynamics, and, indeed, psychodynamics, present in the various forms of social relations. [...] But there will obviously be a lot of knowledgeable Black people out there who will consider some of Freud's misadventures and possible racism, and will at this point question my reasonings for following and quoting from the man Sigmund Freud, such, however, would be a very cynical and inappropriate reaction. Indeed, Dr. Francis Cress-Welsing, one of the most substantial figures of the late modern Black struggle, was a behavioralist psychologist: a perspective of psychology founded by John B. Watson; though Huey Newton said concerning him that, "John B. Watson once stated that his favorite pastime was hunting and hanging niggers, yet he made great forward strides in the analysis and investigation of conditioned responses" (Newton 2002: 184). This is what I call throwing out the baby with the bathwater.

To be sure, the ideas of godbody sociology are also based on similar premises to Auguste Comte's (1986), however, rather than seeing social statics and social dynamics as based on institutions we see them as based on social forces. Let us therefore be clear, godbody sociology is neither social constructionism nor deconstructionism, which try to relativise any comprehensive studies of social phenomena. If I were to place it in any particular Western school of thought I would say that it is a socio-Newtonian, quasi-Freudian sociology. I have basically assimilated a respectable amount of Newtonian physics and Freudian analysis into this metanarrative – and to be sure, it is a metanarrative – and predominantly relied on my knowledge of their theories together with Shari'ati's Islamic conclusions to develop the fundamental principles underlying godbody sociology.

IV

Having, thus, delineated the beginnings of a critique of theoretical post-colonialism it becomes clear that in order to further understand Africa's post-colonial history we must take into account what transpired in African history at the outset of modernity. The colonial powers of the West created the need for foreign investment and foreign capital where none existed. Yet now with the revival of colonialism as the incorporated spook of neo-colonialism investment has increased as many African countries sought for partial import substitution (Engberg-Pedersen et alia. 1996). Big business was where all the money was and while very few in the African bourgeois class could cross the threshold from mid-level to large-scale enterprises; foreign, state sector, and joint-venture enterprises were able to create monopolies in many African countries. Accordingly, these enterprises were predominantly owned by foreigners (e.g. Whites and Asians), the state, or a handful of local African partners. It would be these bourgeois classes that would rise to the position of chief modernisers after the fall of colonialism.

Though there is undeniably real poverty conditions on the continent, within the urban setting several African countries succumbed to what Engberg-Pedersen et alia. (1996) call conjunctural poverty. Here the formal sector, paid employment, and real wage decreases have been the major obstacle. However, in the rural setting Africa has a huge differentiation with poverty becoming far more abject. Here poverty is measured in indicators such as: "food insecurity and malnutrition, lack of proper shelter, physical isolation in inaccessible rural areas, and vulnerability to external shocks, diseases etc. ... The rural/urban gap is also significant in regard to access to safe water, education and health services" (Engberg-Pedersen et alia. 1996: 57). The detriment of the rural/urban gap is in a sense a class war between the peasantry and the bourgeoisie, but while the peasantry are clearly the majority on the African continent it should be the African bourgeoisie that provide those services the West claim they are trying to provide.

In the early post-colonial period many African countries sought for foreign private investment hoping they would bring a form of "development." However, most foreign investment instead came in the form of the joint ventures of private companies with loans and other forms of "aid" from donor countries guaranteed by the African states that were receiving the "aid" (Engberg-Pedersen et alia. 1996). And as we should also be able to conceive from Perkins' stories about EHMs: "the objective of foreign aid is imperialism" (Perkins 2006: 48). To legitimate this statement Perkins used his own involvement with Panama, "I had been sent to Panama to close the deal on what would become MAIN's first truly comprehensive master development plan. This plan would create a justification for World Bank, Inter-American Development Bank, and USAID investment of billions of dollars in the energy, transportation, and agricultural sectors of this tiny and very crucial country. It was, of course, a subterfuge, a means of making Panama forever indebted and thereby returning it to its puppet status" (Perkins 2006: 62).

Perkins' relationship with Omar Torrijos speaks of a relationship between the leader of a so-called Third World country and a colonialism reviving as a corporeal spook. Yet at one point Perkins even wondered whether Torrijos "knew that the foreign aid game was a sham … It existed to make him rich and to shackle his country with debt. … It was there to keep Latin America on the path of Manifest Destiny and forever subservient to Washington and Wall Street. I was certain that he knew that the system was based on the assumption that all men in power are corruptible" (Perkins 2006: 75). Still, though Torrijos was far from corruptible by American standards most African elites have, by the same standards, been considered not only corruptible but blatantly corrupt. "For some neo-liberals the size and character of the [African] state sector are exogenous variables, determined by the rent-seeking behaviour of the local elite; that is, the elite choose a system involving heavy [state] control because this allows them to extract rent by working its control to personal advantage" (Engberg-Pedersen et alia. 1996: 5).

It is this section of African society that has worked hand-in-hand with the neo-colonial powers in their effort to assert effective control over the African continent, its resources and human capital, and have allowed the ubiquitous presence of "aid" and "development" organisations to use progress as a carrot to dangle in front of them so as to have them willingly surrender their sovereignty to the West in the name of good governance. As we also saw earlier "aid" and "development" agencies go to places like Africa in search of LDCs (less developed countries) and LICs (low-income countries) not with the intention of bringing "development" or "progress" but intent on creating economic dependants through debt repayments for "development" and gratitude for "aid." In the case of America this is to enlarge their Empire, in the case of other First World countries it is to further their influence in the region or to develop a history.

However, the interaction between the two global bodies in a bilateral "development" project is not one of a passive, immobile object being acted upon by an imperial or domineering power; when the imperial or Western state goes to an African country they face a state just as proud and domineering as the donor state, and perhaps even more so as they are in their territory. While the one state may be seeking to diminish the powers of the other so as to further its own expansion, the other state seeks to use their powers in order to strengthen its own position in the country. Contrary to Ferguson's (2014) summation that neither "development" agencies, donor states, nor receiving states are complicit in the outcome of the project, such does not denote innocence.

As Perkins stated earlier, he had many people on his team when he went around the world bringing "development," all of them (unconsciously) were EHMs. The fact that they are not making a conscious decision to expand the GUSE, or some other First World country, does not clear them of responsibility. Besides, any keen observer of "development" plans and "development" outcomes should be able to detect the pattern. On the one hand, the donor state gains huge influence in a country that is now indebted to them. On the other hand, the receiving state machine becomes more pernicious and more domineering in the biopolitics and necropolitics of the country. Though neither the donor nor receiver are consciously perpetuating a social kinetics instituted for the purpose of expanding US power interests, if that turns out to be the outcome of all their "development" projects and programmes, together with increased state control over the ordinary citizens of the recipient country, then the "development" staff are to blame, whether sent by a donor state or an international agency.

Along these lines some of the terminology of "aid" discourse must be explained before proceeding any further. "If aid is given directly, it is bilateral aid; if it is given through international agencies, it is multilateral aid" (Degnbol-Martinussen & Engberg-Pedersen 2005: 41). Either way the humanitarian side of "aid" is mostly ostentatious as "a country's government can give foreign aid … mostly motivated by considerations of national security or special commercial interests, but at the same time tell their taxpaying citizens that their motives are altruistic" (Degnbol-Martinussen & Engberg-Pedersen 2005: 7).

This is all the more true of the American government, which promotes itself to the American taxpayer as generous and altruistic when in reality its "aid" is not aid at all but usually a loan with expected returns of exorbitant interest. Indeed, "Most Americans are under the impression that their nation's foreign aid programs supply poorer countries with needed resources, as outright gifts or on easy credit terms at very low prices. But in a travesty of economic terminology, any loan extended by the U.S. Government to any foreign country is classified as 'aid,' *ipso facto*, even when the balance-of-payments effect is from aid recipients to donors, and even when the 'aid' disrupts the recipients' economies" (Hudson 2021: 247).

Moreover, "After 1948 virtually all U.S. aid was bilateral, save for that extended through the World Bank and IMF whose functioning stimulated demand for U.S. exports and opened up the international economy in accordance with U.S. designs" (Hudson 2021: 260). Basically, the economic mechanisms going on in the US have substantially affected and impacted countries like those in Africa in ways that have been detrimental to the African systems in existence. Moreover, "Since the 1960s a major aim of [U.S.] foreign aid has been to help the U.S. balance of payments [of their own foreign debt and to finance and offload the merchandise of] U.S. producers." Furthermore, the impact of US foreign policy with regard to "aid" is not only evident in construction and engineering industries, "The self-interest that characterizes U.S. aid is most blatant in the case of food 'aid' – dumping U.S. crop surpluses on countries. The effect is to reduce recipient countries' food prices, making the farming of grain and other U.S. export crops unremunerative for local farmers" (Hudson 2021: 247).

To further explain this concept of "aid" trickery, Degnbol-Martinussen and Engberg-Pedersen continued, "One of the ways in which business interests in donor countries are taken care of is through tied foreign aid […] In principle, there are several ways in which foreign aid can be tied: to specific projects, for example, or to implementation of certain policies or institutional reforms. But in the debate, tied aid normally refers to a donor's demand that grants or loans must be used to buy goods and services from the donor's own country" (Degnbol-Martinussen & Engberg-Pedersen 2005: 13). An obvious example of tied foreign aid is food aid, another is the private engineering firm Perkins worked for, which, as many consultancy firms do and have done, advised recipient countries to use equipment, engineers, and construction workers specifically from the donor country, or to design infrastructures that would require future maintenance using equipment, engineers, and construction workers specifically from the donor country (Degnbol-Martinussen & Engberg-Pedersen 2005).

In this way colonialism has been able to revive as the incorporated (corporeal) spook of neo-colonialism and thus to obfuscate the foreign "aid" conundrum. Another way colonialism has been revived as the corporeal spook of neo-colonialism has been through structural adjustment programmes. "The term structural adjustment is normally used in one of two closely linked senses. One implies a shift in economic *policies* from an interventionist stance, which permits and sometimes encourages state intervention in the economy, towards a neo-liberal position which aims to minimize it, letting the market allocate resources wherever possible. In this sense, it is a Third World version of policies which have dominated international economic discussion ... But it also stands for the *mechanisms* which have been used since about 1980 to persuade Third World countries, often very reluctantly, to follow such policy prescriptions" (Engberg-Pedersen et alia. 1996: 3). It appears that since the 1980s the idea of using foreign "aid" to reorient political situations in the so-called Third World has lost its distastefulness even though it compromises that country's sovereignty (Degnbol-Martinussen & Engberg-Pedersen 2005).

Furthermore, there appears to be an explicit determination to produce structural changes within these "aid" receiving countries – not excluding African ones. There are even cases of donor countries only providing "aid" to countries that implement 'correct' policies "which [correspond] to a great extent to the Western model" (Degnbol-Martinussen & Engberg-Pedersen 2005: 50); this was particularly the case with President Clinton's 1998 tour of Africa where he agreed to certain investment, trade, and "aid" benefits for specific "role model" countries on the continent. On the one hand, debate in receiving countries concerning bilateral "aid" seems to centre on this idea of tied and politically motivated "aid," on the other hand, on the issue of sovereignty.

The latter is especially the case when one considers that those receiving "aid" usually become dependent on those giving the "aid" and that in many instances ex-colonial powers concentrate their "aid" in their former colonies, usually to their own greater benefit in gaining privileged positions in the procurement of precious resources, markets, and human capital in the ex-colony (Degnbol-Martinussen & Engberg-Pedersen 2005); but more so due to the tied nature of the "aid" and its ability to keep corrupt and puppet governments in power. Debate is even more complex concerning multilateral "aid," as, with this category the "aid" agencies are predominantly US-based and – in the case of the IMF and World Bank – are a part of the Washington Consensus, wherein both bodies are significantly influenced, with regard to policymaking, by the US government.

While it is true Africa has received a large amount of "aid" through loans from their former colonial powers, according to Engberg-Pedersen et alia. (1996: 15) it is also apparent that in situations where "there are multiple donors for particular countries, and [even] where their total aid flows are significantly greater than those of the main institutions sponsoring structural adjustment (the World Bank and the

IMF), ... other donors link their release of funds to decisions made by the World Bank and the IMF", which is usually what happens with African "aid" too. And yet with regard to World Bank policy, "The US president has appointed the World Bank president and has either appointed or been able to block the appointment of the heads of the major UN agencies and regional development banks" (Degnbol-Martinussen and Engberg-Pedersen 2005: 132). The US control of the World Bank, the chief "aid" and "development" agency, has led to a more certain presence of GUSE economic ideologies within the African continent. Thus, the policies of privatisation, trade liberalisation, and currency devaluation can all be traced back to structural changes enforced on African countries by certain US agencies.

We are therefore able to see how colonialism was able to be incorporated – in the sense of being unconsciously active – spook within the countries of African. The clear answer is through the US domineering position in Africa and through the conditions set by their institutions of multilateral "aid." Engberg-Pedersen et alia. (1996: 18) even went so far as to remind us "the introduction of conditionality turns aid from a gift into a contract-based bargain. However, the contract is oppressive, since it is entered into by parties with totally different positions of strength. In the process the national sovereignty of the recipient is abrogated and a 'second imperialism' introduced." And as it is American agencies that hold the position of power in the "aid" debate the revival of colonialism as an incorporated neo-colonial is exceptionally strong in Africa.

V

Moving on now to the issue of why Africa is unable to rise above its current position of poverty, it is obvious to most people that cultural structures have played a big part in this situation. However, according to Shari'ati, "Debates on the definition of culture versus barbarism, or on the question of who is civilized and who is modern, are best discussed in light of Islamic doctrine" (Shari'ati 2006: 7). Herein we find that a non-terroristic Islamism can provide a substantial critique of modernity far greater than what we have thus far considered. Islamism coincides with modernity and actively struggles against it. As on an ideological level modernity is defined by secularism, capitalism, legalism, democratism, and imperialism, Islamism is defined as a form of anti-modernism that is contrary to all these aspects of modernity.

Yet a movement away from modernity would not necessarily mean a retrogression back to medieval times, which in itself is impossible, but an advance towards a true post-modernity. Not one void of metanarratives but one void of White supremacy. Consequently, in the current debate between the modernists, postmodernists, and the anti-modernists the modernists and postmodernists accept late modernity, with all its contradictions (though the postmodernists critique those contradictions). It is only the anti-modernists that actively fight against late modernity. Again, as Islamism is fundamentally anti-modern they actively fight against late modernity and its manifestation in the neoliberal and neoconservative schools of thought.

Moreover, not all forms of Islamism are terroristic. Judging from a non-terroristic Islamist perspective we can see, as Shari'ati noted, that the non-West was divided and ruled by the pan-Europeans, who taught them to unite with those who did not have their best interest in mind and only wanted to use, trick, or manipulate them. One of the main ways that the pan-European tricked these non-Europeans, particularly the Africans, into allying with them against their own Black brothers and sisters was through the concept of a shared humanism.

By claiming we all have a common human ancestry and a common human brotherhood, while yet presupposing a White superiority to Blacks they turned one group of Africans against another and built animosity between two tribal groupings who would otherwise have been unified against the Whites had they known the Whites did not see or respect them as equals. Indeed, "Humanism is a thesis utilized by the powers that be in the world, which control the destinies of other nations to establish superficial and false relationships between the colonizer and the colonized … I am not talking about the scientific and philosophical aspects of humanism, for certainly, the oneness of the human race is a sacred truth. The questions I am raising here are those of by whom, for what purpose, and at what time this sacred truth is being utilized" (Shari'ati 2002: 29).

Shari'ati also pointed out that, "Another example is nationalism. It played a very positive role in European countries toward the end of the Middle Ages, but now it plays the opposite role in Africa. There nationalism is like a dagger that, in the face of colonialism, chops up Black Africa, a continent that faces a common destiny and thus should be united" (Shari'ati 2002: 28). Two central reasons come into play for the national disparity in Africa: The first being the fact that the colonial situation was heavily nationalised, to the point of using coercive and violent means of co-opting and dividing up Africa. The second being the fact that the African bourgeoisie heavily idolised and idealised the European system in its entirety, and therefore sought not to replace it but to replace the people ruling it.

That is not to say the Europeans did not play a huge part in sabotaging the post-colonial efforts of the Africans during the process of decolonisation. They even crippled Africa with the two economic systems of modernity, capitalism and socialism, which only brought about the ruin of African cultures and civilisations, and crushed out all forms of economic opposition. Shari'ati, in articulating the conditions of pre-modern Africa, noted that, "In an Africa society we ... notice [in] their desires, interests and joys [that] their production is equal to their consumption, which is consistent with their traditions, tastes and necessities" (Shari'ati 2006: 25). This system, under which the majority of Africa lived, was ransacked by modernity during the time of colonisation.

The intentionality of Africa's historical progression towards the modern economic systems of capitalism and socialism came at a cost and was forced upon them by colonisation. Shari'ati said of these circumstances, "Unfortunately, modernity has been imposed on us, the non-European nations, in the guise of civilization." "Under the guise of civilizing nations, acquainting them with culture, they presented us with this modernity ... which they persisted in calling 'ideal civilization.' Our intellectuals should have understood years ago and made people realize the difference between civilization and modernity" (Shari'ati 2006: 7). Basically, industrial development was brought to sub-Saharan Africa through modernism, along with new forms of engineering and construction, railways and new agricultural techniques (Engberg-Pedersen et alia. 1996).

It is true that Africa under colonialism went through a rapid modernisation that enforced the entire Western culture onto African, and all non-Western cultures, yet as Shari'ati delineated, "western societies have been able to impose their philosophy, their way of thinking, their desires, their ideas, their tastes and their manners upon non-European countries to the same extent that they have been able to force their symbols of civilization (technological innovations) into these countries which consume new products and gadgets" (Shari'ati 2006: 21), believing them to be superior to their own cultural (*thaqafi*) symbols.

A fourth example of how the pan-European has deceived the African is with regard to production. Production may not be as fundamental to capitalism as the market is but it is still an important aspect of capitalism, and that cannot be denied. According to Shari'ati, "The frantic production rate, rising constantly, exceeds the desire of people to consume. They can't keep up! Thus, since the machine has compulsively produced excess goods, it must step over its national boundary and push goods into foreign markets. When the capitalists gained control of machinery, technology and science in the 18th century, humanity's destiny was [thus] determined". Basically, "Ever since the 18th and 19th centuries when European machines began to overproduce, the surplus had to be sold to Africa, Asia, Latin America, and Australia, but the merchandise such as beauty aids, were made for the European tastes. How could an African woman use it? As an African woman makes her own beauty aids from her farm, the same is true about her clothing" (Shari'ati 2006: 24; 1981: 975). All effectively producing the cultural imperialism under which many non-Western countries happen to currently be.

Shari'ati was basically claiming that what occurred historically as a result of overproduction was that the West pushed their overproduced commodities, and thereby their culture, onto foreign nations in Asia, Africa, and Latin America in the 18th century thereby creating cultural colonialism. Cultural colonialism soon gave way to political colonialism as we moved into the 19th century and mid-modernity. "Strictly speaking, 'modernized' means that one becomes modernized in consumption. One who becomes modernized is one whose tastes now desire 'modern' items to satisfy [their] wants" (Shari'ati 2006: 28). What we see is that production and consumption played a big role in producing the political colonialism that plagued Africa, Asia, the Caribbean, and Latin America till it got replace in the mid-twentieth century with incorporated neo-colonialism.

Moreover, Shari'ati pointed out that these colonised territories fell to colonialism due to the greed of what became the bourgeoisie, "Religiously speaking, the [bourgeois] is a devout and fanatic follower of the faith of 'consumerism', who not only fails to see nature as a world brimming with truth, beauty, and the Lord's hidden secrets, but also does not recognize man as a small world having supernatural and Divine talents, beauty, values, goodness, and mysteries." Yet as Shari'ati continued this bourgeois class needed help in spreading their ideological outlook to the proletarian mass of the people: "They had to change the nation, and they had to transform a man in order to change his clothing, his consumption pattern, his adornment, his abode and his city. What part of him to change first? His morale and his thinking. Who could change the spirit of a society, the morale of a society and the way of thinking of a nation? In this respect, there was little the European capitalist, engineer or producer could do. ... So the big producers and big European capitalists ... let the intellectuals handle this project" (Shari'ati 1981: 726; 2006: 26).

Furthermore, Shari'ati could see the dead-end this was all leading the colonies and incorporated neo-colonies to. The pan-European bourgeois works the overseas manufacturer to the point of overproduction. The overflow from the production gets sold to the colonised world, or in our time neo-colonial Third World. The intellectuals – and in our time the neoliberal intellectuals – convince the masses to purchase these excess goods. To afford these excess goods the overseas manufacturer works extra hard producing more than is necessary, and so on, and so on. The "sociologist calls him a 'circular man' who produces for the sake of consumption and consumes for the sake of production" (Shari'ati 2006: 13). The pan-European powers have not taken this lightly either. To a degree they have felt obligated to palm off their overproduced goods on to the so-called Third World to keep from making any extended losses.

The question then becomes: how do the people of the so-called Third World afford to purchase the goods and services the West provides? This is where the genius of the current system of debt repayment becomes clear. As Shari'ati continued, "Credit purchasing can do miracles … Without increasing the standard of living or purchasing power … it gives him [a] pseudo, false sense of purchasing power, and aides consumption. Loans, bank credits and credits given by the Westerners to the Easterners have a dual purpose. First, these backward people should not become so poor that the list of our goods for consumption be drastically reduced. … On the other hand, they should not become so rich as to become able to produce. They should be in between. That is why we would give them a false sense of purchasing power" (Shari'ati 2011: 245). Due to this weapon of credit and debt being used so often by the Western powers it appears that Africa has fallen deep into poverty with very little means of rising out.

Shari'ati also claimed that religion has been a powerful hindrance to non-Western – and particularly African – progression. In this situation Shari'ati used the analogy of Cain and Abel to explicate the predicament of how religion can be used to corrupt a people. "Abel followed Adam's religion, so did Cain. However, the same religion was divided in two opposite religions in two individuals. One became grounds for justifying Cain's profits and personal gains, and the other became a factor in verifying Abel's truths and virtues. These two religions have been at war with each other throughout man's history" (Shari'ati 1981: 621). These two religions started out as one, the Adamic religion, where Adam, the first prophet, turned his children and his wife towards Allah. However, his children, or at least one of them, corrupted his religion and became an oppressor (*zalim*). In this analogy places like Africa, which had their own religious systems, developed corrupted *zalim* religions.

Shari'ati described the story of Cain and Abel as a scientific analogy to explain humanity at its origins, saying,

> "[T]he story of Cain and Abel in the Qur'an brims with scientific facts. It is the beginning of humanity in symbolic form, resembling Oran city in Camus' [Plague]. Cain and Abel are Adam's children. Adam betrothed two of his daughters to two of his sons. But Cain found his brother's wife more attractive. He coveted her and consequently committed a sin. Abel said, 'I am pleased with what was chosen for me.' But Cain objected, 'No! I must take away what you have.' Due to Cain's encroachments, the war between the two became heated. They complained to their father and he said, 'Each one of you choose a sacrifice and whosoever is acceptable to the Lord, the other will submit.' The proposal appealed to both.
>
> Abel chose a red-camel, the best and the most expensive animal he had, while Cain chose a sheaf of wheat, rotten and moldy. They took their offerings to the altar. Naturally, Abel's was accepted. And since Cain was disappointed, he continued his aggression against his brother, until he deceived him in the desert and

> *murdered him. This is the first human blood spilt in the history of man" (Shari'ati 1981: 588).*

Shari'ati clearly did not take this story of Adam, Cain, and Abel to have been an historical event, but saw it as analogically symbolising what occurred at one time in the distant past. "As Adam (who symbolized mankind's intrinsic unity) was transformed into two poles, Cainian and Abelian, oppressor and oppressed; the world too was divided into two foci of goodness and evil." (Shari'ati 1981: 664). Just as Cain's religion was believed by Shari'ati to be the religion of the oppressor (*zalim*), even so White supremacy could be called the current religion of the *zalim*. Indeed, as the Cain religion of *zulm* led to the corruption of the ancient population, so the modern Cains who oppress (*zalama*) their fellow brothers and sisters have a corrupted religion (*din*).

Shari'ati also explained how this weapon of religion has been used to create a sense of inferiority in Africans as to their place in this world, noting, "religious world-vision provides that the world has an omnipotent God. What is man then? Naught but a toy and a spineless creature in the hand of God (or gods) which is bashed around at His (or their) will" (Shari'ati 1981: 558). Religion (whether Christian or Muslim) only shows the "sin-nature" of the people and unifies them under the common brand of Crusader or Jihadi against some immoral or unhelpful practice that is really just a molehill compared to the real problems of the nation. "We notice also that in the religious world-vision there is a fanaticism which leads to [the] futility and unoriginality of man. In short, the religious world-vision, since its inception, culminates in the negation of man's true essence" (Shari'ati 1981: 558).

Effectively, whether the religion is the religion of the *zalim* or the spook religion of the fanatics, religion has been a powerful tool used by the pan-European to divide and rule

Africa. All these ideologies: humanism, nationalism, modernism, consumerism, and religion have played a big part in causing Africa to remain in the position of subjugation and isolation it currently inhabits. As we can see the neo-colonial Empire of the United States has used debt to incorporate its neo-colonial expansion into Africa and the so-called Third World, and ideology is how they keep them within their neo-colonial stranglehold. Colonialism's corporeal revival as neo-colonialism has thus been through keeping the neo-colonies blind to the truth through the paradigm of ideology, even religious ideology.

VI

If we now consider the European nations, along with Western Russia, they had not begun to develop their own narrative of pan-European distinction until around the time of the Renaissance. It is at this time that they began to differentiate themselves, not so much as a race (a term that did not really exist until the mid-1600s), but as a people. Though religion played the key role in defining what people they were, nationality was beginning to play a much stronger role. It is also clear that during this time three traumas occurred that brought on what Adler would call an inferiority complex, as he said in 1933: "Behind every one who behaves as if he were superior to others, we can suspect a feeling of inferiority which calls for very special efforts of concealment" (Adler 1964: 260). The discourse of White superiority is therefore a product of White feelings of inferiority which can be shown to have originated during a time when White culture was on the ascendency: the Renaissance.

Again, if we consider the social dynamics of what instigated a White inferiority feeling at this time the only way to explain it is through interpolating the occurrence of a traumatic experience, one that is *now* repressed in the global unconscious of White people. However, if it is three traumatic experiences that brought on their inferiority feeling then the psychological effect would be even deeper and the repressions would have to be even stronger to conceal them.

The three traumas that occurred during the Renaissance were: experiencing the fall of Byzantium and the subsequent expulsion of the Europeans from what was then Ottoman territory; witnessing the sexual behaviours and anatomies of the African and Muslim of the fifteenth and sixteenth centuries; and fear of the scientism of the African and Muslim of the fifteenth and sixteenth centuries. (It must be remembered that pre-Enlightenment Europe was anti-science while the Abbasid *Khalifat*, the Fatimid *Khalifat*, the Ottoman Empire, the Malian Empire, and the Moorish settlements were the scientific centres of the time). These three realities: feelings of military inferiority, sexual inferiority, and intellectual inferiority were repressed deep into the global unconscious of White people and overcompensated for in later years after the European Enlightenment. The narrative of pan-European distinction in itself was a mythology to destigmatise Europe, an ostensibly dirty and uncivilised continent at the time, and elevate European opinions of themselves.

As with all mythologies the narrative of pan-European distinction has many permutations, yet all remain relatively faithful to a general thematic: Europe had the Grecian civilisation which brought us the great philosophies, politics, mathematics, and democracies. Greece was superseded by Rome who conquered the known world and brought us republicanism, imperialism, and advanced militarism. After adopting Christianity Rome became Catholic and so did Europe, while Byzantium maintained loyalty to Orthodox

Christianity. The Roman Empire eventually fell and only Catholicism remained of the empire. Europe then went through her Dark Ages of religious dogmatism, during which time were also the Crusades. Europe experienced a Renaissance which culminated in two events: the discovery of America and the Protestant Reformation. Scientific and philosophic knowledge was reborn in Europe sparking the Enlightenment which culminated in the American and French Revolutions. After that the Industrial Revolution occurred justifying and accommodating capitalism. Two world wars and a Cold War then discredited all ideologies thus leading to postmodernism, which is where we presently are now.

While it could be argued that this narrative was written by myself and therefore contains a level of cynicism it is not far from how most people see the history of the pan-European, it is basically what most people consider the important bits, the archetype. Indubitably, the vast majority of the people reading this book would be familiar with most of the events spoken of even if only slightly. That is because these represent the narrative of Europe's global unconscious, its archetypal self-ideation, the story that Europe has told itself to keep itself from the feeling of inferiority it once felt. Obviously, on top of this skeleton each pan-European nation will add whatever flesh they feel most fitting to these stories so as to make them a little more interesting or realistic, however, the general narrative will always feature all of these stories with not one missing.

If we consider now the feeling of superiority felt by large sections of the pan-European population it can thereby be seen as a result of this overcompensation and the spreading of this false narrative. They do not tell the story of the fall of Byzantium, or that it was the pretext to the enslavement of all Muslims and non-Christians. While they may still possess and express feelings of sexual inferiority in comparison to Blacks they are unable to see it as the significant reason for the desexualisation of Europe (during the Renaissance nudity, at least in art, was common; then suddenly it was condemned when they saw it being practiced by the Native Americans and Africans). Finally, the backlash against science in pre-Enlightenment Europe and the convenient amnesia over where the unenlightened European learned science from to enter into the Enlightenment all tell of another trauma repressed into the global unconscious of White people. To take the last argument a little further, there is also a "need" for Europeans to constantly "remind" Black people that they brought us science and taught us cleanliness when actually the reverse is true.

Yet the predominant global traumata experienced by the early European voyagers who encountered the Africans of the fifteenth and sixteenth centuries, which supersedes that of their scientific and hygienic inferiority, one that the tradesmen and slave-owners who encountered them throughout the slave trade also experienced, producing a Saidian *imagined geography*, not only of the Orient but also of Africa, and creating an imagined embodiment of the Oriental and the African person, is sexual inferiority. In order to escape the feelings of sexual inferiority produced by the imagined sexual embodiment of the Africans who were taken as slaves they desexualised their own societies. From the sixteenth to the twentieth centuries White people in Europe, Russia, and America substantially delimited the sexual behaviours of their societies, not simply because the Enlightenment of the eighteenth century was an intellectual movement, but because feelings of sexual inferiority to Black people had to be concealed. Any sign of weakness could have undermined the whole edifice of the discourse of White superiority to Blacks necessary to justify slavery. Thus, notwithstanding the fact that sex and sexuality were hugely popular in Medieval and Renaissance Europe, by the nineteenth century sex had become completely side-lined. There was also a knock-on effect on women, who were also substantially side-lined during the eighteenth and nineteenth centuries so as to maintain the illusion of White male superiority.

Another effective means of maintaining the myth of White male superiority was through another mythology: the narrative of pan-African inferiority, which worked along the lines of what was taught to us by White scholars and historians. In many ways the narrative is a complete fabrication, however, in the hopes of exposing it I shall delineate its entirety: Black people come from the villainous Ham, who was cursed by Noah to suffer servitude forever. Ham and his descendants migrated to Africa where they lived in naked, promiscuous, and primitive tribes worshiping idols and spooks until some of them converted to Islam. Those that converted no longer went about naked, began to practice marital unions, albeit polygynous, and worshiped one god (a false god); though large numbers maintained the primitive pagan traditions. Then the White man came and took them as slaves to the Americas. After several rebellions, a White led Abolition movement, and an American Civil War the slaves were finally emancipated (some add, though rarely, the Haitian Revolution). Immediately after the slaves were set free the Blacks of Africa were colonised and the Blacks of the Americas were segregated. From the 1950s to the 1970s the African liberation movements in Africa and the Civil Rights movement in America overcame colonisation and segregation, except in the southern parts of Africa. By the 1990s southern Africa had finally gained liberation from colonisation, segregation, and apartheid. But Africa since decolonisation has decayed into abject poverty due to corrupt leaders, and the Blacks of the Americas have decayed into extreme criminality and Black-on-Black villainy.

The lie of this oversimplified fiction may seem somewhat obvious when written down yet it is an unconsciously believed narrative that the largest majority of people, White and non-White, have accepted as truth and have accepted for decades. On the one hand, this narrative, though a fictitious lie, has given large amounts of pan-Africans an inferiority complex. On the other hand, it could be said that Africa is a vast continent with many distinct countries, cultures, and institutions, therefore what is to be gained by speaking about the pan-African as though we are one homogenous whole? At least such was the argument of Frantz Fanon (1965).

To such a challenge I will now use the analogy of the human body: as the human body is a whole with many parts so Africa is a whole with many countries. The differences of their countries are like the differences of body parts in the human body; as each part of the body possesses a teleological function that is of service or disservice to the whole; even so, the uniqueness of an African people does not separate it from the wider community but serves a function that either strengthens or weakens the body, just like when a person breaks their arm, the whole body is affected not just the arm. Moreover, if the body as a whole works predominantly in agriculture or in mining, then the body belongs to a farmer or a miner and all other activities are negligible. Africa, at least at the beginning of the 21st century, had three-fifths of its population in agricultural labour (Encyclopædia Britannica 2015: Standard Edition) showing that Africa, as a continent, was not as technological as Europe or America.

VII

It is impossible to speak about Africa in the 1990s without mentioning that event that shook the world from the early- to mid-1990s: the ending of apartheid. The beginnings of apartheid's end may have been due to certain home-grown noema and noesis such as the 1984 constitution, which received opposition from both right and left for going either too far or not far enough, respectively. Of particular interest to us is the left who formed a then somewhat legitimised coalition called the United Democratic Front (UDF) that unified many left-leaning South African groups and organisations as well as working in alliance with the Congress of South African Trade Unions (COSATU). But most importantly they worked in alliance with many exiled and non-exiled (but secretive) ANC members. UDF protests and uprisings began to occur led mainly by the youth, predominantly male, who were disaffected with apartheid and inspired by Mandela's struggle.

By the late 1980s, the Botha government had suppressed the UDF substantially, and Botha himself having had a mild stroke was forced to cede leadership of the National Party to an up-and-coming named Frederik Willem de Klerk. When de Klerk was elected to the Presidency it was presumed by most that he would maintain the hardline on the ANC and PAC (both rival and warring factions of the liberation movement); however, to the surprise of everybody "when Parliament reconvened on 2 February 1990, De Klerk announced that the bans on the ANC, the South African Communist Party, the PAC and all other proscribed organisations were to be lifted forthwith. Nine days later, Nelson Mandela walked out of Victor Verster prison and was driven to Cape Town" (Ross 2014: 196). Negotiations ensued from that time but proved relatively futile. The first

Convention for a Democratic South Africa (CODESA) meeting in December 1991 and the second in May 1992 both collapsed with no significant progress. On top of that, clashes between the ANC and other Black organisations, like Buthelezi's Inkatha Natal-Zulus, put added pressure on their progression.

Ross (2014: 204, 205) articulated how, "Through the complicated negotiations, three matters were at the centre. The first was the nature and powers of the body which would take over from the tricameral Parliament, which was still the *de jure* legislative assembly of the country." "Secondly, there was the position of the employees of the old governments, of both South Africa and the Bantustans, in the civil service, the police and the defence forces. These people made up an enormous constituency, for the National Party above all. Forty per cent of employed Afrikaners worked for the government." "Thirdly, how was South Africa to be divided, and what were to be the powers of the provincial government?" Once these issues were settled a date was agreed upon to hold national elections, elections in which the ANC gained a substantial majority – about 62 percent of the vote.

Thus apartheid came to an end in South Africa, but the realities of White domination and White supremacy were far from over. Majavu (2008) elaborated that "due to the cumulative effects of longstanding racial discrimination and oppression, which result in direct barriers to black capital formation; the white households [today] are far more likely to inherit or otherwise benefit from family wealth than black households. Looked at from this angle, one is able to explain the socioeconomic developments in post-apartheid South Africa more adequately than the empty claim that South Africa is moving away from race to class apartheid." Indeed, "83 percent of those trained for operational occupation in

South Africa are black Africans compared to 4.9 percent of whites. Further, 71 percent of those trained for managerial and professional positions are white, compared to 16 percent of blacks" (Majavu 2008: 117, 125).

What Majavu (2008) proposed as a solution, at least in the South African context but also applicable to the continent and perhaps even to the entire global community, was a participatory economy (parecon) in which productive property is socially owned, companies and businesses are self-managed, councils are set up to co-ordinate the production and distribution of goods, services, and information, remuneration is provided based on sacrifice and effort, and there are changing and fluctuating job responsibilities. While adopting the whole is rather idealistic and would be incredibly fallacious, there are two aspects of parecon that are thoroughly helpful: the syndicalist structure of setting up councils and the self-management method it encourages.

Though it is clear that Majavu received the parecon philosophy from its visionary and architect Michael Albert it is also clear that his explanation of it is based on his attempts to apply it in South Africa, stating: "In the South African context, councils would not only help eliminate the corporate hierarchy but would destroy the racial and gender hierarchy that characterizes the South African society" (Majavu 2008: 123). To be sure, councils are the central and most essential aspect of the parecon programme. What therefore Majavu (2008) was proposing here was a kind of Black syndicalism thereby making Majavu's programme a far more legitimate form of liberating corporeally neo-colonised Africa from plutocratic America.

Africa has thus far dealt with the corporeal revival of the colonial spook by submitting to it and further by migrating to the neo-colonial heartlands, particularly to America, to become business men and women in the informal sector (Stoller 2002). They have also assumed that by critiquing in a profoundly pretentious and magniloquent way the pretensions of the West that they will be able to further the liberation, or at least the empowerment, of the neo-colonised people. Nevertheless, as the corporeal revival of colonialism as neo-colonialism has compounded and prolonged African dependence, a programme for socio-economic change is in order: one that does not benefit either the elite circle of the middle class or perpetuate the neoliberal benefits of the capitalists.

As Majavu (2008: 122) explained, "In a pareconish society … for workers to do their jobs responsibly and in an empowering way, workers ought to consider what they would like to contribute to the social product, both by their own efforts and in association with those they work with. In addition, workers ought to address how to combine their efforts and the resources and tools they have access to, to generate worthy outputs that other people will benefit from." "The same logic [also] applies to consumers. Consumers ought to consider what they would like to have from the social product, either as individuals or in collective association with neighbors for example. They ought to address what to ask for to advance their lives as best they can in line with the impact their choices will have on the people producing their outputs." While workers' parliaments can definitely function toward co-ordinating the work aspect of the social product, consumers' parliaments can serve the function of co-ordinating the consumption aspect.

This is the vision Majavu had toward post-colonial South Africa, for a Black syndicalism to be organised in order to co-ordinate work and consumption. The premise being to agglomerate South African racial and social equality and to depreciate and ultimately abolish the hierarchical structure that has existed in South Africa since it was colonised, and continues to haunt South Africa to this day: "As has been pointed out in this essay, research conducted by HSRC has shown that the fact of the matter is that whites still dominate ownership and management positions in business, social, and cultural institutions. The councils [or parliaments] could serve as a force to oppose this white domination and institutionalized racism" (Majavu 2008: 123). Not only so, but workers' and consumers' parliaments will be effective in generating a form of self-management and self-organisation – the lowest levels of each being workplace for workers' parliaments and neighbourhood or floor level for consumers' parliaments – and allow for a decentralised planning system to function in Africa.

Within the godbody I am also proposing a kind of Black syndicalism in which we put workers' parliaments in every godbody business and consumers' parliaments in every godbody neighbourhood (and we should also have students' parliaments for godbodies at universities). All these parliaments should meet once a month having three members chosen for key responsibilities: a chair, who would oversee and co-ordinate; a secretary, who would take the minutes of the meeting and transcribe the conclusions, and a delegate who should present their conclusions to the district godbody parliament – that delegate could be a member, the secretary, or the chair if the parliament so decides but the chair cannot be the secretary under any circumstances – these positions should be applicable to all parliaments (students', workers', and consumers').

The district parliaments – e.g. the Manhattan fishmongers' parliament – should also meet once a month at a confirmed location to discuss what the Gods and Goddesses of that town, borough, or city will be likely to contribute to the social product of their town, borough, or city and what they will need in order to contribute to it. They should also send one delegate once a month to a regional godbody parliament to discuss regional needs, concerns, and the likely contributions of its Gods and Goddesses (there will be four regions for these parliaments: Northeast, Northwest, Southeast, and Southwest). Each regional parliament should send out five of its members as delegates to a national parliament four times a year to discuss what will likely be needed and what the Gods and Goddesses are prepared to do. Again, anyone running a successful business knows that goals and plans are essential to its survival and growth. What this decentralised planning system of parliaments does is it provides planning not from the top-down but from the so-called bottom-up.

This form of the parecon structure will be necessary within our movement, but it will ultimately prove to be neither Majavu's nor Albert's utopian versions but what I believe to be a far more realistic and pragmatic version. Having spent a little time in the co-operative movement I can see the striking similarities between both. However, there is a main and central area in which the co-operative and the parecon movements fail: decision-making. While agreeing that ownership should be common and remuneration based on investment (as with the co-operative movement) and that there should be a form of self-management and a syndicalist structure with regard to labour and allocation (as with the parecon movement); as concerns business and industry, that is, the decision-making within the overall companies or organisations, such things need a board headed by a single chief executive who has the final say. Such may seem far from anarchistic, but then, this is not full anarchism, this is thearchism.

The Spectre of Marxism

In his book *Specters of Marx* Derrida spoke about certain other spooks haunting the pan-European world, the spooks of Marx, spooks that exist because of the death of communism and the mentality it sparked. "Many young people today (of the type 'readers-consumers of Fukuyama' or of the type 'Fukuyama' himself) probably no longer sufficiently realize it: the eschatological themes of 'end of history,' of the 'end of Marxism,' of the 'end of philosophy,' of the 'ends of man,' of the 'last man' and so forth were, in the '50s ... our daily bread. We had this bread of apocalypse in our mouths naturally, already, just as naturally as that which I nicknamed after the fact, in 1980, the 'apocalyptic tone in philosophy.'" (Derrida 2006: 16). Such an eschatological exists even in our time some 40-odd years later though not in the least as ferocious. The coming to an end of an entity is always signalled by a crisis in that entity, almost like the death-pangs of one who is aged and demented, the system also goes through its own form of dementia in which it becomes a simulacrum before it mutates or decomposes. Nonetheless, due to socio-elasticity, even after it's dementia, even after it has become a simulacrum, even after it has formally entered the crypt of social extinction and has begun to decompose, a social system can still revive (though in a mutated form) and reassume its former position and glory.

The fall of communism in the early 1990s and the post-Cold War triumphalism of the Western powers signalled what to many was an end of Marxism, whether as movement, philosophy, or as ideology; such a yearning to bury Marxism as a narrative – indeed, a metanarrative – this anachronistic funerary of Marxism, based on the praecox dementia of the Marxist system was indelibly destined to produce spooks: spectres with the determinate will to revive the similitude of Marxism even if but by academia: "Marx ... was despite everything a philosopher" (Derrida 2006: 38); a statement Derrida made derisively to those who sought to make Marx an aberration, academic only, activists not at all; but a statement nonetheless true. For this cause, the end of Marxism was considered the end of philosophy, or, at any rate, philosophy as we then knew it. But the phantom of Marxism signals a rupture within the premature celebrations (or commiserations) going on in the West; a rupture that has the potential to rewrite the philosophy of these late modern times.

Derrida, in speaking of these prophecies of the end of philosophy said: "a funerary note already echoed there – crepuscular, spectral, and therefore resurrectional. Re-insurrectional. It is indeed a question of the philosophical 'spirit': its very process consists of visibly heading the march at the moment of its 'disappearance' and its 'putting in the ground,' it consists of leading its own funeral procession and of *raising* itself in the course of this march, of hoping at least to right itself again so as to stand up" (Derrida 2006: 43). Such may be true for philosophy but it is more so true of social systems. Their burial, their being "put in the ground," is merely prelude to their resurrection, their phantomisation, or their apocalyptic reappearance (I use the word apocalyptic here and throughout based on its original Greek translation as manifested or revealed). The philosophical rupture that Marxism's revival as phantom constitutes will no doubt affect the triumphalism that neoliberalism and neo-colonialism have generated in the post-Cold War era as there is, still, a voice crying out in the wilderness, and it is crying out for justice. Indeed, the phantom of Marxism (anti-capitalism) currently stands as the primary opposition to the resurrection of liberalism (neoliberalism) and the incorporation of colonialism (neo-colonialism), even if systematically it still has its faults.

Having already shown the reader the power of revivalism to return dead institutions such as liberalism and colonialism from the crypt I shall now attempt to demonstrate that revivalism not only resurrects and incorporates *jinn* but it can even phantomise *jinn* – that is, revive them without instituting their movement back to orthodoxy. Firstly, it is important to know the possibility of discovering the structures inherent within a social movement by learning the narrative the social movement has about itself. Once the self-narrative of a social movement has been found the next step is learning the thematic conclusions that can be drawn from that narrative, both positive and negative.

Any author of a social group's narrative – or in this case, the narrative of Marxism – must do so empathically not with the desire to prove, disprove, or challenge a theoretical position. The sociologist should go blind into their research with no biases or ideal stereotypes. Any archetypes discovered during the process of research must be intersubjectively appropriated, even if the sociologist wishes to delineate critique or invective towards the social movement. The ultimate aim should be to identify the psychic processes of the social group (*al-mujtama*), their conscious and unconscious, so as to substantiate and enumerate their empathic disposition.

Secondly, if we are to speak presently about the phantomised revival of Marxism we must also speak about its exorcism, not due to his call for justice, obviously, but due to its misguided methodology: anti-theism. Marx, according to Shari'ati, took the Promethean narrative and ran with it, creating a calamity and a travesty of ideological outlooks, as Marx said in one of his earlier writings, "Philosophy makes no secret of it. Prometheus' admission: 'In sooth all gods I hate,' is its own admission, its own motto against all gods, ... Prometheus is the noblest saint and martyr in the calendar of philosophy" (Marx 2015; quoted in Encyclopædia Britannica 2015). Marx did not see in this an idiosyncratic acceptable only to European minds (as he himself was a European mind) but made this a sweeping statement universalised for all humanity.

It is hence that Shari'ati could say without even a hint of sarcasm, "Marxism shares the bourgeois world-view, anthropology, and morals ... inasmuch as it appeared in a Western bourgeois cultural setting" (Shari'ati 1980: 72). There is actually very little distinction between the two because ideologically Marx was taught in the school of Western bourgeois philosophy, he was a product of Western bourgeois philosophy. The animosity of the West towards that which is divine echoes through in Marx's works, his bitter fight against the conceptions of morality, his determination to elevate the material world to the position of prominence, all stem from his philosophical education.

The revival of Marxism as phantom coincides with the revival of philosophy as outlook, the question could even be asked whether philosophy ever passed away in the first place. "Marx ... was despite everything a philosopher", is not such a statement one of the most indubitable and yet inevitable statements one could speak? Marx, for all his revolutionism, for all his politicism, for all his historicism, for all his scientism, for all his economism, was, first and foremost, a philosopher. It is in fact the philosopher Marx that gives birth to all the other Marxes, thereby rendering them all secondary. The metanarrative of Marxism is a philosophical conglomeration of monolithic proportions, the epitome of Western humanism: which is itself a philosophical tradition started during the Renaissance that, as Shari'ati said, united several schools of thought trying "so hard to replace the ancient religions [yet falling] short of answering the basic human needs, and … in the end, they either [led] people to a sense of futility, or [drew] them into bondage" (Shari'ati 1980: 16). Here Shari'ati took the clear distinction in his polemic, "We see that Marxism makes use of all the anti-religious arguments brought forward to its day from earlier times and adds nothing original to them" (Shari'ati 1980: 62).

Marx's own anti-theism was deeply rooted in the Western philosophical tradition, and there is no doubt that the anti-religious/anti-theist position or opposition of the Marxists is itself based on that of their master. The truth is, atheism is just Christianity for those unwilling to admit *they are*, in fact, Christian. Their only superiority to Christianity is their claim to objectivity, a claim that is falsified by their argument that to be objective (*munfasil*) you must be disinterested in the results, yet many of the results they gain are tampered with from the beginning simply by the quality of questions being answered. For example, if you ask: are all Muslims terrorists? that is a very loaded question. Marx, as an atheist, or even an anti-theist, betrayed his Christian leanings by subscribing to most of the Christian doctrines only in a more "objective" way. His philosophy was thereby Christian millenarianism without the Christ.

Yet for Marx the philosophical standard was set by Prometheus, whose story is best articulated again by Shari'ati, "Prometheus, who gave the 'divine fire' to mankind, first robs the gods of the fire as they sleep and brings it secretly to earth, then is sentenced for this sin to suffer tortures at the hands of the gods" (Shari'ati 1980: 18). An aspect of Greek mythology that bears great similarity to the 22nd degree of the 1-40 in the 120 lessons: "How old was the founder? When Yaqub was six years old, while playing with two pieces of steel, he discovered one piece had magnetic in it and the other piece did not. Then he learned that the piece with magnetic attracted the piece that did not have magnetic in it. Then he told his people that when he was old enough, he would make a nation that would be unalike, and he would teach them *tricknology*, and they would rule for six thousand years." Even as Prometheus rebelled against the gods by giving to humanity the divine fire, so Yaqub rebelled against the Gods (Original people) by creating and teaching an unalike people *tricknology*, thus showing that even as Western philosophy is opposed to all gods, so all Gods should also be opposed to Western philosophy, particularly that of Marxism.

But Marxism is a spook, a daemon, a phantom that rises from the crypt, not only to speak, but also to haunt, to horrify, to become horror to those who relished in its downfall. The downfall of Marxism, which signalled the beginning of a new era, a new world order if you will, did not end the story of Western philosophy (nor of Marxism for that matter) but birthed a phantomatic Marxism, a spook Marxism, a haunting Marxism. "This logic of haunting would not be merely larger and more powerful than an ontology or thinking of Being … It would harbour within itself, but like circumscribed places or particular effects, eschatology and teleology themselves" (Derrida 2006: 10).

The question thus arises: what was the destiny of Marxism? And, were the signs of its last days perceptible in its earlier days? This destiny of Marxism, this teleology of Marxism, though technically non-linear in orientation, can be distinguished in its curvilinearity, therefore the signs of its last days *were* identifiable even from its inception.

I

In order to understand Marx's scientific development we must first venture into his conception of reality. Shari'ati explained how, "Marx in one of his phases is a materialist, and thus in no position to regard the being man as anything but an element within the confines of the material world." "In another phase, he is an extreme partisan of sociologism. Thus, he grants society its independence vis-á-vis naturalistic and humanistic tendencies and then, by arbitrarily and categorically grouping its elements under the headings of either infrastructure or superstructure ... he in effect presents man as equivalent to this superstructure" (Shari'ati 1980: 35). Marx, as any true Marxist should know, saw the mode of production, the economy, as the infrastructure of society and the ideological, indeed, the sociological, as its superstructure; the fact that he placed humanity, according to Shari'ati, in the category of superstructure shows that Marx to Shari'ati was, before anything, still a materialist. We Gods, however, do not make such a blunder; we see the foundation of all things, particularly of all societal things, as knowledge – whether it be knowledge of self or knowledge of the universal order of things. Marx's theory of the infrastructure and the superstructure is the basis for the economic determinism inherent within Marxism.

Taken from Marx's Preface to *A Contribution to the Critique of Political Economy*, for us to get the most out of it I shall quote it at length:

> *In the social production of their life, men enter into definite relations that are indispensable and independent of their will, relations of production which correspond to a definite stage of development of their material productive forces. The sum total of these relations of production constitute the economic structure of society, the real foundation, on which rises a legal and political superstructure and to which correspond definite forms of social consciousness. The mode of production of material life conditions the social, political and intellectual life process in general. It is not the consciousness of men that determines their being, but, on the contrary, their social being that determines their consciousness. At a certain stage of their development, the material productive forces of society come in conflict with the existing relations of production, or – what is but a legal expression for the same thing – with the property relations within which they have been at work hitherto. From forms of development of the productive forces these relations turn into their fetters. Then begins an epoch of social revolution. With the change of the economic foundation the entire immense superstructure is more or less rapidly transformed. In considering such transformations a distinction should always be made between the material transformation of the economic conditions of production, which can be determined with the precision of natural science, and the legal, political, religious, aesthetic or philosophic – in short, ideological forms in which men become conscious of this conflict and fight it out. (Marx 1978: 4).*

It is contained within this theory of the infrastructure and the superstructure one of the major flaws of the Marxist system; and though Marx the philosopher may have valued knowledge as important, as a materialist he designed a system in which it was secondary to money, which he hailed as the primary substance of society. Although Marx gave us clues in this quotation as to his belief that productive forces have played the leading role in social development throughout history, it is also clear from the *Communist Manifesto* that he held the current deification of money down to the fact that we are living in a bourgeois society: "The bourgeoisie, wherever it has got the upper hand, has put an end to all feudal, patriarchal, idyllic relations. It has pitilessly torn asunder the motley feudal ties that bound man to his 'natural superiors', and has left remaining no other nexus between man and man than naked self-interest, than callous 'cash payment'" (Marx & Engels 2012: 37).

For Marx the changing of society from medieval to modern was due to a shift in the productive forces in which feudalism could no longer bear the effects of industrialism bringing about a change to the relations of production – the overthrowing of feudalism. In like manner Marx also felt that in his own time capitalism, being based on privately owned means of production and socially organised relations of production was an aberration and therefore destined to fall, creating a system in which the means of production matched the relations of production. If this is the case we cannot fault Marx for his logic, I would even dare to say we cannot fault Marx for his ethics (but only in a figure), however, that does not negate the fact that Marx's materialism was as misguided as his anti-theism.

If there is an infrastructure it would more likely be a psychological infrastructure and the economy would be simply another part or aspect of the sociological superstructure – the socio-economic. Therefore Marx's giving ultimacy to the economy as the justifying principle was hugely fallacious. Shari'ati commented on the dangers such an outlook produces when he stated concerning Marx, "he transfers all the values that humanity has created, or at any rate possesses, to the means of production, which makes the primacy of man, in the Marxists' version, a primacy of economic tools. Within the narrow bounds of the impoverished materialist world-view, no element is more honored than that of production" (Shari'ati 1998: 70). It was Marx's denial of humanity – his turning humanity into a cog in the wheel of the productive infrastructure – that would allow future Marxists to turn humanity into a cog in the wheel of the State. In this capacity we are able to see how Marx invariably led to Lenin, and regrettably also to Stalin.

But Marx's phantom, the revival of Marxism even if only as spectre, is something some intellectuals – among them some of the calibre of Derrida and Sartre – saw as noble. Yet Derrida, in speaking of a revival of Marxism and of the spook of Marxism, did not lose sight of how such a thing would be perceived, least of all by Marxists: "It is easy to imagine why we will not please the Marxists, and still less all the others, by insisting in this way on the *spirit of Marxism*, especially if we let it be understood that we intend to understand *spirits* in the plural and in the sense of specters, of untimely specters that one must not chase away but sort out, critique, keep close by, and allow to come back" (Derrida 2006: 109). These spectres, these Marxist spooks, are here defined, however, as spook – that is, as one, as singular, as non-plural. Though it may be said that Marxism has many forms and many interpretations, due to the fact that it is a perspective not only of all of the social sciences and of various philosophical and aesthetic schools; but that it has also been, and still is, a social movement and figuration with its own institutions and public bodies. Nevertheless, there is something, or are some things, that remain identifiable within all strands of Marxism due to the fact that Marxism has one central aim, which aim is communism.

It is by appreciating this determinable quality that we can perceive and unify the many different shades of Marx's thought. Marx the philosopher, Marx the historian, Marx the sociologist, Marx the economist, and Marx the revolutionist all converge on the central subject of communism. Communism was Marx's life-long dream. A dream that though he never saw completely fulfilled, he laid the foundation for throughout his works: communism was never too far from what Marx wrote and spoke about. Marx sought for and fought for a communist society, however, he had no idea what one would look like so he trusted that by learning and understanding the functionings of capitalism he could help lead society towards that certain goal and towards that end. But the Marxist phantom is found in more than simply its aim, the spectre of Marxism is also seen in its outlook and culture. As Shari'ati noted: "the difference between Marxism and the western bourgeoisie lies in the fact that one promotes a bourgeois *class*, and the other a bourgeois *society*". Indeed, "Isn't Marxism really just the other side of the coin of Western capitalism?" (Shari'ati 1980: 72, 43). What is Marxism if not the obverse of the Western bourgeoisie?

But if we accept the meiosis of the bourgeois outlook and culture – indeed, the Marxist desire to universalise this outlook and culture to all sections of society – it becomes clear that Marx's praise of the bourgeoisie in the *Communist Manifesto* was far from mere theatrics. Marx was the bourgeoisie *par excellence*, a bourgeois totaliser, bourgeois in spirit and in destination. Therefore Marxism should no longer be held as the antithesis of capitalism as such, but as the totalising of it. This creates a markable distinction, for while Marxism has had these variations since its beginnings, Marxism has been open to huge levels of critique and polemic from the bourgeois community. Interestingly enough, Derrida could state very succinctly that what he believed should not be open to critique in Marxism "is, perhaps, a certain experience of the emancipatory promise; it is perhaps even the formality of a structural messianism, a messianism without religion, even a messianic without messianism, an idea of justice – which we distinguish from law or right and even from human rights" (Derrida 2006: 74).

It is true that what Derrida spoke of here was justice from a class basis but it is easy to see how such a basis can consume the entirety of one's life. It may be somewhat unnecessary at this point but I shall now quote a section from Shari'ati (1980: 116) to further emphasise this dilemma: "Whenever I see some acquaintance, friend, or student so anxious and upset about the question of class exploitation that he comes to see all the questions of the world only through this peep-hole and thinks of nothing else day and night, I feel sorry for him, for he is so very eager to sacrifice himself, and he shows such a strong aptitude and spiritual leaning. He has sacrificed his whole life to one idea. Why should he be deprived of all the experiences that are available in culture, history, religion, or just in life, and that are conducive to the growth of man's other dimensions? Why should he think of nothing but this one question?" This danger inherent in Marxism of focusing one's livelihood and strength towards nothing else but the seeking of class justice, the hermitising of radicals and students for this one goal, though honourable, is also pitiable and, contrary to Derrida, avoidable.

But Marxism must be seen in context as a bourgeois philosophy rebelling against the bourgeois mode of production, it was Marx's means of pushing the then global economy, and particularly the German economy, to its furthest limits. As a totalising bourgeois philosophy

Marxism was invariably fated towards a bourgeois outcome, hence why the communists went down the road of adopting capitalist measures. Shari'ati even said: "Bourgeois liberal society and organized communist society ultimately converge in a single view of humanity, human life, and human society. The bourgeois tendencies of the advance communist societies – which can no longer be simply dismissed – are no accident, no aberration, no revisionist deviation, because … it is only natural that those philosophies that have a similar conception of man, no matter what their starting point, should finally enter upon the same road and have the same final destination" (Shari'ati 1980: 21). It is thereby obvious to any keen observer that the secret of Marxism is that as a messianic without messianism Marxism perceives justice (*adl*) as the bourgeoifying of all humanity, not the abolition of the bourgeoisie but the totalising of them.

Is it not obvious that such a messianic system would be ultimately incapable of saving anyone as it delivers them right back into the captivity from which it had rescued them? Shari'ati went on to show the depth of this "messianic" salvation by exclaiming, "Those very men who, fleeing mechanism, were caught up in Marxism (which issued the strongest attacks on mechanism), became, after the triumph of that ideology and the rise to power of communist regimes, still more trapped in mechanism. For 'material abundance' was proclaimed the essential prerequisite for realizing the real communal society, and the prerequisite for this abundance, in turn, was the transformation of society into a massively industrialized system" (Shari'ati 1980: 43). Was it not true and inevitable that the Marxist project eventually fail seeing as how the enemy it promised to deliver them from was the very enemy it would eventually deliver them right back to, only with one invariable all-consuming exception: the overriding presence of the dictatorial state?

II

While Marx and Engels were spreading their systematic conclusions among the proletariat their strongest critic, the Russian anarchist Mikhail Bakunin, was struggling to win the masses over to social revolution. Bakunin could see the Marxist project as a dead end, or a cul-de-sac if you will, in that it shared so much in common with the bourgeoisie, particularly with regard to the state. Bakunin gave no airs to culpability, "the last word of the Marxists, as well as of the democratic school – is a lie behind which the despotism of a ruling minority is concealed, a lie all the more dangerous in that it represents itself as the expression of a sham popular will." "Therefore we will refrain from urging our Slavic brothers to join the ranks of the Social-Democratic Party of the German workers, which is led first and foremost by Marx and Engels in a kind of duumvirate vested with dictatorial power, with Bebel, Liebknecht, and a few Jewish *literati* behind them or under them" (Bakunin 2005: 178, 50). Bakunin's polemic against Marx stands out as an historical and necessary beacon for the time in that he was the only creditable critic of Marx's who was not of the liberal strata.

Being himself a Russian born Slav, Bakunin started his adult life as a nationalist, but realised later on that nationalism only added up to statism, which would prove to be nothing more than another fetter for the proletarians. Therefore Bakunin turned from nationalism to anarchism and sought to lead the rest of his Slavic brothers and sisters toward an anarchist future, against the desires of the bourgeois liberals and the proletarian Marxists, who Bakunin lumped together under the category of statists. Indeed, the main class Bakunin sought to appease was the peasants of

Russia – at a time when Marx saw the peasantry as counter-revolutionary – as Bakunin noted: "For the German communists or social democrats the peasantry, any peasantry, stands for reaction, while the state, any state … stands for revolution. … Moreover, Marxists cannot believe otherwise. As statists come what may, they are obliged to curse any popular revolution, especially a peasant revolution, which is by nature anarchistic and leads directly to the abolition of the state" (Bakunin 2005: 147). We cannot presume that due to the absence of a peasantry today anarchist theory has become obsolete; it has in fact become more impenitent, more impermeable, more imperturbable. With the rise of plutocratic Empire the modern state has reached its absolute limits, thereby reviving the necessity of anarchism.

In the case of Marxism the state still exists but is believed to be in a process of "withering away" so that the communist society can be produced. Derrida corroborated this equivocation of Marx's when he said, "The universal Communist Party, the Communist International will be, said the *Manifesto* in 1848, the final incarnation, the real presence of the specter, thus the end of the spectral. This future is not described, it is not foreseen in the constative mode; it is announced, promised, called for in a performative mode" (Derrida 2006: 128). Marx, like the skilled necromancer, sought to conjure spirits and animate bodies, however, Marxism has itself become a spirit, a spectre, a disembodied phantom. Nevertheless, for Marx the spectralising of communism, and also of Marxism, in no ways spelled the end: the spectre can be incarnated, the abstract can be concretised; this is the cornerstone of Marxism. The end of Marxism to a Marxist is only in a communist society, they will settle for nothing less. But what performative act brings about a communist society? How does one revive the phantomatic? How does one incarnate the spectre of communism? Marx does not seek to answer these questions he merely announces their answer as promise.

Inasmuch then as the spectre of communism has been announced as materialising, the advent of this incarnation was a promise Marx gave for the promotion not of justice (*adl*) but of scientific principles, as Shari'ati (1980: 77) pointed out by asking: In Marxism "is humanity anything other than the aggregate of those ideological, cultural, and moral values which in turn are the superstructure and the product of the mode of work?" If morals like freedom, justice, and equality, were to Marx nothing more than products of the superstructure, and the basis of his whole theory was the mode of production, then the salvation announced, the promised advent, was never going to bring about a genuine deliverance to humanity psychologically or even socially. Yet Derrida still protested "if there is a spirit of Marxism which I will never be ready to renounce, it is not only the critical idea or the questioning stance … It is even more a certain emancipatory and *messianic* affirmation, a certain experience of the promise that one can try to liberate from any dogmatics and even from any metaphysico-religious determination, from any *messianism*" (Derrida 2006: 111). In point of truth, Marxism is an anti-theistic messianism based not on a call for justice (*adl*) but on a liberation from theism (*ilahani*).

In this case, Derrida got Marx completely confused as he assumed the messianic hope, the promise delivered by Marx, was genuinely one of justice and not simply one of anti-theistic economism. On a closer examination of Marxism we find its dementia, its praecox dementia, all the more obvious, thereby eliminating any fears of its haunting us in future or of its revival as phantom. Derrida's examination of Marxism lightly analysed various Marxist documents providing a prognosis for the social variations occurring in the post-Cold War situation. Derrida was speaking to an exuberant West that had lost sight of what Marx meant to so much people: "Ascesis strips the messianic hope of all biblical forms, and even all determinable figures of the wait or expectation; it thus denudes itself in view of responding to that which must be absolute hospitality ... waiting for the event as justice, this hospitality is absolute only if it keeps watch over its own universality. The messianic, including its revolutionary forms (and the messianic is always revolutionary, it has to be), would be urgency, imminence but, irreducible paradox, awaiting without horizon of expectation" (Derrida 2006: 211).

Marx's promise was the incarnation of the spectre (*al-jinni*) of communism, the arrival (*takawwun*) of a system in which the mode of production would be as social as the relations of production, that is not to say that Marx ever believed the concept of justice (*adl*) was necessary or real (*haqq*). To Marx the incarnation of this spook (*jinni*) was nothing more than the fulfilling of scientific principles, the science of sociology. According to Derrida, Marx sought to bring about this incarnation through the act of exorcism: "effective exorcism pretends to declare ... death only in order to put to death. As a coroner might do, it certifies the death but here it is in order to inflict it. ... The certification is effective. It wants to be and it must be in *effect*. It is *effectively* a performative" (Derrida 2006: 59). Here again we see the performative, what could essentially be called the bodily discursive, we see that exorcism comes about through exercise, through work, through the working of the body. Something must be done. Marx, like the capable sorcerer, sought to incarnate the spectre of communism through a kind of necromancy. The exorcism he sought to perform was instead an incarnatory, and the work Marx announced to be performed in this necromancy was the act of revolution. But like with any deceitful sorcerer, the eventual act of the performative, the coming of the revolution, actually brought about not salvation: freedom, justice, and equality; but subjugation to a new oppressor (*zalim*), one that had the mask of the proletarians.

Bakunin was able to foresee the teleology of Marxism even from its inception; he foreknew that the incarnation of the spectre of Marxian communism would amount to nothing but oppression (*zulm*) to a new form of domination simply by the titles with which he labelled their movement. "The words 'learned socialist' and 'scientific socialism,' which recur constantly in the writings and speeches of the Lassalleans and Marxists, are proof in themselves that the pseudo-popular state will be nothing but the highly despotic government of the masses by a new and very small aristocracy of real or pretended scholars" (Bakunin 2005: 178). To further articulate Bakunin's fears over this inevitable leadership question Chomsky explicated how: "Bakunin predicted that these people would fall into two categories. On the one hand, … the 'left' intellectuals … would try to rise to power on the backs of mass popular movements, and if they could gain power, they would then beat the people into submission and try to control them. On the other hand, if … they couldn't get power that way themselves, they would become the servants of what we would nowadays call 'state-capitalism,' though Bakunin didn't use the term. And either of these two categories of intellectuals, he said, would be 'beating the people with the people's stick'" (Chomsky 2003: 226).

Herein lies the fundamental flaw of the incarnation of the communist spook: Marx may have provided a kind of promise for justice (*adl*), indeed, for salvation (*najat*), but ultimately his system led to an oppression (*zulm*) even harsher than that experienced under democracy – and is not disguised subjugation better than any blatantly harsh subjugation? Consequently, the contradictions inherent within Marxism are highlighted through the tragic drama of one of Marx's most influential pupils, Ferdinand Lassalle. To tell his story I quote further from Bakunin. In Germany, where Karl Marx was originally from, the social democratic movement had two wings: one led by Lassalle (and thus by Marx), the other led by Franz Hermann Schulze-Delitzsch. Schulze-Delitzsch's opinions were challenged heavily by Lassalle, who fought hard to win over the proletarians to his point of view.

"Lassalle showed them [the proletarians], in the first place, that under existing economic conditions not merely their liberation but even the slightest improvement in their lot is impossible and its deterioration unavoidable; and, in the second place, that as long as the bourgeois state exists, bourgeois economic privileges will remain unassailable. But then he came to the following conclusion: in order to obtain real liberty, liberty based on economic equality, the proletariat must seize the state and turn the state's power against the bourgeoisie for the benefit of the workers, in just the same way that it is now turned against the proletariat for the exclusive benefit of the exploiting class" (Bakunin 2005: 175). Lassalle, although little known in socialist history other than as the theorist Marx challenged heavily in his *Critique of the Gotha Programme* – though by that time Lassalle was long dead – was perhaps the most successful Marxist in the West to effectively put into practice the Marxist ideals. As Bakunin continued, "he founded a sizable and primarily political party of German workers, organized it hierarchically, and subjected it to strict discipline and to his own dictatorship – in short, he did what Marx in the last three years wanted to do in the [Workers'] International. Marx's endeavour proved a failure, but Lassalle's was a complete success" (Bakunin 2005: 175).

Lassalle, however, only differed with Marx on the means of achieving Marx's vision. Whereas Marx saw the incarnation of communism as only possible through violent revolution, Lassalle saw it as possible through legal reform: by getting social democrats elected into government the proletarians could institute laws that would eventually "swallow up" the bourgeois state (Bakunin 2005). "That was Lassalle's program, and it is also the program of the Social-Democratic Party. Strictly speaking, it belongs not to Lassalle but to Marx, who expressed it fully in the famous *Manifesto of the Communist Party*, which he and Engels published in 1848" (Bakunin 2005: 176). He speaks here of where Marx and Engels said, "The proletariat will use its political supremacy to wrest, by degrees, all capital from the bourgeoisie, *to centralize all instruments of production in the hands of the state*, i.e., of the proletariat organized as the ruling class" (Marx & Engels 2012: 60; emphasis mine). Basically, what Marx was saying here, Lassalle, and later Lenin, tried to put into practice. The fault was not with Lassalle, nor with Lenin, the fault was within Marxism from its very inception.

Not that communism must always be oppressive and harsh, but the dictatorship of a ruling intellectual (*daki*) strata will inevitably oppress and dominate the people, even Marx's hope of a dictatorship of the proletariat proves to be a misnomer and an absurdity, as Bakunin rightly pointed out, "If the proletariat is to be the ruling class, it may be asked, then whom will it rule? There must be yet another proletariat which will be subject to this new rule, this new state." "Will the entire proletariat have the government? The Germans number about 40 million. Will all 40 million be members of the government? The entire nation will rule, but no one will be ruled. Then there will be no government, there will be no state;" "If there is a state, then necessarily there is domination and consequently slavery" (Bakunin 2005: 177, 178). Yet is it not the hope – the promise – of a kind of dictatorship, a messianic dictatorship; that has inspired many of the religious movements around the world? And has Derrida not described Marxism as a kind of atheistic messianism?

Bakunin, however, masterfully polemicised Marx's ideas of a proletarian state with his conclusory remarks on the subject, "According to Marx's theory … the people not only must not destroy [the state], they must fortify it and strengthen it, and in this form place it at the complete disposal of their benefactors, guardians, and teachers – the leaders of the communist party, in a word, Marx and his friends, who will begin to liberate them in their own way" (Bakunin 2005: 181). And as Marx suggested that "all capital" be wrested from the bourgeoisie and centralised into the hands of the state as a means of accomplishing the proletarian revolution – and considering that Marx himself never explained what a proletarian system should look like, only what the capitalist system of his time already looked like, any Marxist system would inevitably be, and could not be anything but, a proletarian *state*. Bakunin (2005) also articulated that, by aligning themselves and their movement with the state, Marx and Marxism were in turn aligning with reaction, they were in turn becoming reaction. Hence, Bakunin saw in Marxism not a flawed proletarian movement but an already phantomatic bourgeois movement; thereby allowing men like Chomsky to say, "There's nothing about socialism in Marx, he wasn't a socialist philosopher – there are about five sentences in Marx's whole work that refer to socialism. He was a theorist of capitalism" (Chomsky 2003: 228).

So what is the teleology of Marxism? It is a faulty "proletarian state" structure: and considering that Marx defined communism as the proletarians consolidating their "political supremacy" by fortifying the state with the instruments of production (all productive forces), and considering that this consolidation was to be enacted – not for some higher good like freedom, justice, or equality, but following the cold scientific logic of the pseudoscientific theory of materialism – based on the "laws" of the dialectic, "in practice it … turned out to mean [nothing more than] state primacy and worship of the state, which in turn have become primacy of the head of state, the leader. Now, even if this leader is a witless functionary like Stalin, the people must acquire all their philosophical notions concerning socialism, which is a scientific discipline, from their esteemed leader!" (Shari'ati 1980: 111). All the intellectuals and all the functionaries who ran the Marxist states "beating the people with the people's stick" may have spoken the language of liberation (*najat*) but when it came to the crunch they did nothing more than replace a former *zulm* (oppression) with a new form of *zulm*, a far more harsh form of *zulm*.

III

The thearchist system, as opposed to the Marxist, is fundamentally founded on the establishment of love, peace, and happiness. The rule of the Gods and Goddesses (Earths) is thus effectively the rule of love (which brings about peace and happiness). But for love to be perfect it must be libidinal (*hubbiyya*), which is where the unique thearchy of the godbody becomes most powerful: it could even be said of us godbodies that our central law is libidinal love (*hubbiyya*). As we see love as the highest form of understanding, we appreciate that to understand something is to be intimately acquainted with it, even empathically connected to it. Hence, *al-muhibb* to us is a combination of empathic, agapic, and erotic love. Here our thearchy of *al-muhibb* is larger than a society (*mujtama*), expanding even into the whole universe (*'alam*), hence we acknowledge a *tawhidic* inter-connection (that is an empathic/agapic/erotic inter-connection) of all things in existence (of everything in life) with the Black man. We, as humanity – one Original people of the Original nations – have been able to build civilisations superior to the current European paradigm based on thearchy, and if we hope to ever truly be free from the iniquities of the current system (all its sorcerers, spectres, and daemons) we will have to return to a thearchist system; and accordingly the most efficacious thearchy for our time is the godbody thearchy.

Nevertheless, having grown up in *Madinatullah* (Brooklyn, New York) and being surrounded by godbodies one thing always stood out to me in my youth: the Gods would not accept any ideas, words, or statements that were not backed up by proof. Everything was *now cipher*, they said that a lot. The main reason everything had to be proven and backed up was the pervasiveness of trick knowledge. But the central element of trick knowledge is that it is based on falsehood, which has an ultimate aim of dehumanising, or effectively undeifying, the non-White, particularly the Black. The dehumanised Blacks, then, from this basis or beginning, develop an ideological structure of acculturation. These acculturated Blacks being psychologically and ideologically degenerated then proceed toward societal exclusion and marginalisation.

The godbody reject anything that creates power relations where one race is superordinate and another subordinate; true indeed, to the Gods the true and living God is the Black man, but he also manifests himself in all Original people (that is, all non-White races). What we stress about White people being a result of genetic modification and an artificial racial selection process does not negate our understanding that White people can become and behave righteously through accepting the civilised teachings of Black people, particularly the Black people of the Five Percent. Though there could obviously be a back and forth as to the validity of either science by its converse, the fact remains that most of the theories of the godbody have multitudinous evidences from modern scientific discoveries to back them up, whereas most of the racial theories of Enlightenment and colonial sciences were more often than not disproven. The Gods would stand by their philosophy regardless, they are far from acculturated, but our cultural (*thaqafi*) dynamics takes its strength not from dehumanising and denigrating White people but from empowering Black people to the point of deification, therefore it is not a genuine converse.

The science of the Gods and Goddesses identifies the acculturating elements within *tricknology* and counters them with a Black current that magnifies all that is non-White showing that they not only have value but that they have high levels of sacredness. After centuries of the non-White being denigrated and expropriated, for we godbody to offer them a high position within our own cultural standard shows much progress, the problem, however, is that while psychologically the Gods and Goddesses have power, that power has not affected the power structure of the *mujtama* around us. In New York, let alone in America, or in any other nation in the world, the godbody hold no structural powers. The fact is, in relation to the rest of society we are a small minority. Our individual *thaqafi* mechanisms may affect those within our system but they do not affect the rest of New York or America – and as the godbody have only tiny pockets of support in the rest of the Americas and are virtually non-existent outside the Americas, it shows that whatever psychological empowerment we provide to our members is of non-effect outside of our communion.

This is the reality of subcultures: though they may provide a level of comradery and empowerment to their members, they are not the dominant culture (*'adab*). The orientation of a culture from the level of subculture to high culture (*'adab*) is not based on proof, popularity, or all the things valued in this late modern system. *Thaqafah* becomes *'adab* through the mechanisms of the power relations. Power relations allowed culture to be justified first as an aesthetic of the distinguished class and as a measure of just that, class, or better still, high class. Whether the working class have become the ruling class or the capitalist class are still the ruling class is debatable, but the masses have definitely defined their own all-encompassing culture. Popular culture and bourgeois high culture are currently rivals for ultimate supremacy; notwithstanding pop culture itself is an amalgam of many different subcultures from around the world, mainly from the working class.

With that in mind the hope of an individual subculture seizing societal power and becoming the ruling class – the delineation of which is the *thaqafah* that personifies high class in their *mujtama* – is not an easy one to fulfil, for which cause the premise of we godbodies representing a new standard of high class in our day may seem somewhat farfetched, but I encourage the reader to not judge us all too quickly just yet. That said, as I personally see it the current standard of culture (*thaqafah*) is still bourgeois culture (*thaqafah*) so the bourgeoisie remain the personification of high class; however, their power has been weakening substantially.

The working class, with or without a revolution, can take their place as ruling class any generation now. The more dominant popular culture becomes – which coincides with the theory that aesthetic progress precludes historical progress – the more impotent the bourgeoisie become. The irreverence of history for things deemed sacred cannot be overemphasised, and the bourgeois power structure, like the aristocratic power structure before them, could change with just one new law. All it took to diminish the power of the aristocracy was the abolition of slavery. The situation, produced as a result of the propaganda wars as well as the financial deflation after the passing of the actual Act of abolition, heavily affected the aristocracy. And who were the chief White abolitionists? The bourgeoisie.

Just as the bourgeoisie were the gravediggers of the aristocracy with and without revolution – by making Acts of parliament and Congress that severely diminished their power – so the working class need only create an Act that abolishes all monies to severely diminish bourgeois power. Interestingly enough, bourgeois power was much on the rise long before the abolition of slavery removed the aristocracy from any substantial positions in society (*mujtama*) they held, and made them effectively an impotent class. The setting up of the three republics in America, France, and Haiti played a big role in creating the conditions the bourgeoisie needed to rule, but the aristocracy still existed in France and feudal style plantation owners still existed in America. It was not until slavery was abolished completely that aristocracy was overcome proper by the first seeds of democracy. Even so, the working class are not too far from overthrowing the capitalists as a class without a revolution, at which time culture (*thaqafah*) will, indeed, be based on the most popular, which would still be a result of power relations. That most popular subculture, however, would most likely be White. For the godbody to become a contestant within the *Black* community it will need to, at least, be popular outside of the United States.

Godbody *parliaments* are exemplars of *thaqafah*. We also have a verbal aesthetic and a visual aesthetic. The verbal aesthetic is based on the honour we give to the spoken word. The word once it is spoken is now born, it is also our bond – or better, we are bound by our word. The visual aesthetic is in our clothes, our possessions, and our graffiti. The godbody verbal aesthetic is generally based on the manifestation of wisdom (*hikma*) and the spreading of lessons. As it is the God's duty to civilise the savages and uncivilised within all races we have an obligation to teach correct knowledge (the knowledge of 120) as we fight against trick knowledge. We are not acculturated in this but represent a higher level of culture based largely on the bourgeois standard, who though claiming science (*'ilm*) as their criteria, have in practice proven to be upholding only a pseudoscience (*al-'ilm al-za'if*).

While we godbody could also be said to be upholding *al-'ilm al-za'if* that idea has proven to be wrong at each turn. We have been proven in fact to have been teaching either actual facts (*haqiqat*) or the most plausible scientific truths all along. We highly value the sciences (*al-'ulum*) and even tend to speak the jargon of science (*al-kalam al-'ilm*) – though obviously with street slang and within street contexts – never losing sight of concrete, empirical realities and structuring our theories and our words on such. In this instance, though the working class are set to overthrow the bourgeoisie it seems that the godbody has a more immediate connection with the doctrinal prerogatives considered in current high culture (*'adab*) than has thus far been appreciated. True indeed, like with Marxism our verbal aesthetic is more agreeable with the bourgeoisie than most of us would like to admit; but such only makes the case that we are closer to overthrowing them within the Black community than any other cultural groups that stand today.

My memory of the godbody visual aesthetic was also in keeping with bourgeois aspirations: in the case of clothes especially. We bought street fashion and sportswear, but in particular we also bought high fashion, if we could afford it, to show we could afford it. It was almost like making the statement: I have arrived and I am no lesser than the White man. Sportswear like *Nike* and *Adidas* were complemented by moderately high fashion *Tommy Hilfiger*, *Ralph Lauren*, and *Donna Karen*. The higher one rose monetary-wise the more Italian their fashion became, this is very upper class. Though, yet with the Earths (or Goddesses) fashion usually stayed at the moderate level or drifted toward the Afro-chic (which will be considered more thoroughly in Chapter 6).

But bourgeois clothes was just a start, bourgeois or moneyed possessions like cars, accessories, and technologies were also quite regular among the Gods. Although such was not supposed to be the case, and, indeed, was condemned as activities of the 10 percent – who like ghetto vampyres were considered the Black bloodsuckers of the poor – Gods in practice would buy as much moneyed products as they could to show that, even if acquired illegally, they had wealth. Perhaps the only aesthetic articulation we Gods had to our credit that was not in actuality upper class in origin was our graffiti art work. Obviously, if we look simply at *bombing* (name tagging) we find the efflorescence of godbody symbols, but the artistic representation of God as a Black man, or a Black man with codified as God, is more specifically a godbody manifestation.

All these aesthetic methods are to accomplish two ends: to show that the godbody counterculture is in fact very cultured (by subverting the culture of the class that defines high class we godbody are able to demonstrate that we, in spite of being *poor righteous teachers*, are actually cultured and civilised) it is almost the adopting of the symbols commonly in our time recognised as civilised to show ourselves also civilised, and to subvert the meaning behind these symbols to our peers of the same class. Moreover, it challenges the standard views of class: is class a social division or a standard of elegance? Does cultural capital give one class acceptance or is class only economically defined?

One could obviously consider this a very complex question. Firstly, those of the working class who become rich and so have access to social mobility have a tendency to not consider themselves middle or upper class – even if they own several companies or large stocks – if they have not adopted the cultural capital of the class; while those who adopt the cultural capital and signs of the middle and upper classes without having money tend to feel inauthentic and "douchy" in certain communities for such. Secondly, is class as a category still effectively delineating structures in our time or is class distinction a term that should remain relegated to mid-modernity?

We Gods and Goddesses have clearly accepted early twentieth century symbols of class as signifiers of culture (*thaqafah*) and civilisation (*hadara*), but could this mean that we too have fallen the victims of trick knowledge? Could we have been, to a certain degree, acculturated? To be sure, moneyed possessions, moderately high fashion clothing, and a discourse that is an obverse of the colonial age are all signs of White bourgeois influence; for we underclass street lifers to include them in our repertoire is a demonstration of some form of subversion. But maybe that is it. Maybe the godbody movement has the intention of upsetting the general ideas of representation the best way it can: by adopting the racial and class symbols of the White middle class we can thereby ruin any opportunities that may be used against us to attack our most central thesis, that of the Black man being God. This is where the distinction between Marxist capitulation to bourgeois culture and godbody capitulation to bourgeois culture becomes recognisable. Marx capitulated to bourgeois culture because he saw in bourgeois culture the epitome of culture (*'adab*); the godbody capitulate to bourgeois culture mainly to show we are neither inferior to White people nor to your average Black man.

IV

If Marx's spook still haunts us to this day it is not because his phantom is in a genuine sense working class, Marxism speaks from beyond the crypt because it is believed by many, Derrida and Sartre included, that Marx left an injunction, that Marx called for justice (*adl*), that Marx, like the living Messiah (*al-Masih*), must rise from the crypt to overcome the corruptions of injustice. Yet those of the Marxian canon who sought to put into practice Marx's ideas were far from messianic. To be sure, Engels, Lassalle, Bebel, Lenin, Trotsky, Stalin, and Tse-Tung were all hard-core materialists, not prone to giving air to such concepts as justice, except to denounce the bourgeois version of it. In sum, they all fit into a critique Shari'ati (1980: 88) levelled in his own time: "Marxism, remaining fiercely loyal to materialist realism, relinquishes its right to speak of values or to make judgements on the basis of them." While some people may try with all their might to dissociate Marx from the systematics of all these revolutionary Marxists, the fact still remains that all of them followed the blueprint of Marx to the letter; any failings in the systems they organised were thus rooted in the master, not the disciple.

Such an argument could also be made of other institutions too; indeed, am I not a cultural Muslim? and is not the injunction on all Muslims to "fight in the way of Allah those who fight against us" only an *eschaton* of endless wars? True, Islam's current terrorist string has distorted the

Prophet's initial liberating message; but herein ends the similarities: the Prophet spoke excessively about righteousness: freedom, justice, and equality; love, peace, and happiness; while Marxism, as Shari'ati said, quoting Berth, "is the philosophy of the producers". Moreover Shari'ati, in comparing the two, noted that, "Islam and Marxism completely contradict each other in their ontologies and cosmologies. Briefly, Marxism is based on materialism and derives its sociology, anthropology, ethics, and philosophy of life from materialism." "Islam, in holding to the worldview of *tauhid*, is able to justify man as a divine essence, grant him transcendental attributes, extend his evolution to the infinite, and thus situate humanity in a living, meaningful, and infinite universe whose dimensions extend far beyond what even the sciences can represent" (Shari'ati 1980: 65, 87). The truth is, Marx's extreme materialism created within the Marxist tradition not only an anti-theism but also an anti-humanism.

Shari'ati (1980) pointed out how Marxist humanism dehumanises humanity delimiting us to the claustrophobic prison of materiality: there is no transcendence, no evolution (*takawwun*), no infinite potentiality, there is only productive relations and their determining qualities. Marx in his desire to exorcise the spookish *jinn* of religion and morality ended up subjecting humanity to the oppression (*zulm*) of the *jinni* of materiality – an oppression he himself was victim to. Yet because Marx's was also a philosophy of performance, and as Derrida (2006: 38) said: "people would be ready to accept the return of Marx or the return to Marx, on the condition that silence is maintained about Marx's injunction not just to decipher but to act and to make the deciphering ... into a transformation that 'changes the world.'" Herein lies the trouble: if Marx's anti-theism is ultimately dehumanising then the performative of Marxism, the materialising of the phantom, will only end up producing systematic and operatic automatism and self-alienation. Not only so, but Marx's anti-theism, his polemics against religion, apply only to Western religions, namely of the Judaeo-Christian type.

Has not Shari'ati commented on the distinction between Islam and these religions? "[The] popular religious approach always seeks God outside natural, rational laws, in unintelligible courses of events; it sees proofs of His existence in extraordinary occurrences and in unscientific and unnatural sources. By contrast, the scriptures, and particularly the Qur'an, have made a rational case for *tauhid* on the basis of nature, custom, the constant laws of life, and the ordered and intelligible quality of events in the universe"; and again, "why should Marx, like the priests, seek to impugn Islam by making much of the disgraces of the Caliphate? Weren't the first and most outstanding of those martyred by the Caliphate likewise the first and most outstanding of those brought up within the Islamic religion?" (Shari'ati 1980: 55, 61). Not only so, but by denying Islam its heritage of outstanding and noble personalities Marxism invariably forfeits its ability to recognise that nobility that is of the highest order: the nobility that draws one to sacrifice.

The contrast becomes all the more pronounced as Shari'ati explained how, "We see that … Islamic humanism ascends to a kind of awareness, while Marxist humanism proceeds to a kind of production." Is it not also true "that man in the Islamic world-view is a governing will in relation to nature, and might be termed the god of nature; in relation to God, he fulfils the role of His vice-regent"? (Shari'ati 1980: 73, 69.) In this sense, Islam supersedes Marxism with regards to uplifting human dignity, humanity's divine potential is evident within the Islamic tradition. Thus, while Islam upholds conceptions like freedom, justice, and equality (*taharrur, adl, wa musawa*); Islam does not negate the self, it seeks to actualise the self, to create a self-awareness – a knowledge of self – that allows one to see self as connected to the divine. "Islam situates humanity in a world of *tauhid*, where God, man, and nature display a meaningful and purposeful harmony. It presents Adam as the principal essence of the species humanity, as dust into which God has breathed His spirit, as intermediate between spirit and matter" (Shari'ati 1980: 86).

All these arguments that Shari'ati pointed out are clear evidence that, though Islam and Marxism both have all-encompassing systems that have been corrupted by certain elements, their similarities end there. The truth is, Marxism is the messianism of a deceptive justice, of a pseudo-justice; Islam, on the other hand, is the messianism of a psychological liberation, of the liberation of the self. Put another way: when the concept of *tawhid* is fully appreciated it leads to a system of Islamic messianism. And Islamic messianism is not hard to be fulfilled: it is not the waiting for a saviour to come from heaven to save us, but the becoming of your own saviour. It is allowing the saviour to rise within you; in other words, the Second Coming is to us internal: thus every eye shall see him because they will see him in you.

Did not *al-Masih* himself say: "Behold, I stand at the door, and knock: if any man hear my voice, and open the door, I will come in to him, and will sup with him, and he with me" (Revelation 3: 20). We can be sure of one thing, he was not talking here of a physical door. If *al-Masih*'s return is in the heart and not the physical plane (*al-'alam al-hissi*) then the dictatorship of the thearchist movement is also not in the physical plane (*al-'alam al-hissi*) but in the astral. In which case, we now have to ask ourselves: who is the *Masih al-ma'nawi* (the astral Messiah) if *al-Masih* is to enter into our heart to "sup with us"?

The answer becomes clear when we take note of *al-Masih*'s own words to the woman who lived an immoral lifestyle, "Thy faith hath saved thee; go in peace" (Luke 7: 50). Again, *al-Masih* did not say to her *my* faith has saved you: "And he said to the woman, Thy faith hath saved thee;" does this not include all those with faith, a word which has been corrupted over the years to denote belief but in its Arabic and Hebraic original actually comes from the word *iman* and means faithfulness, loyalty, and most importantly hope. Then again, to most godbodies faith is just an illusion given to the 85 percent to blind them from the truth (*al-haqiqa*) or to make up for shortcomings in actual knowledge (*al-'ilm*). The reason I say hope is the most important translation of faith, however, is that I see faith as based on what is written in the Scriptures: faith is the substance of a hope.

True, one with faith shows that they lack actual knowledge but that is neither a crime nor a shortcoming. When a God buys a book on electrodynamics he does not *know for sure* whether he will read it, he does not *know for sure* whether he will understand it if he reads it, and he does not *know for sure* whether the book that he has chosen will help him to master the subject matter; he buys the book in faith hoping that these things will happen. Accordingly, we become our own saviours through faith (*iman*) that we have become one with *al-Masih*; when he rises in our hearts it is then that we *know for sure* that we have become little messiahs. So, the dictatorship *al-Masih* sets up is not a physical or earthly dictatorship but an astral dictatorship internally within us; not as an oppressor (*zalim*) but to remove from us those astral forces that are oppressing us and putting themselves in the place of Allah to us.

Through "opening the door" to *al-Masih* you become one with him and he with you, and you open the door to him by having faith that he is in you and that you *have become* him.

This is knowledge of self as messiah, or, on an even deeper level, knowledge of self as Allah. How do I prove this? It says in the Scriptures: "Glorify the name of thy Lord, the Most High! Who creates, then makes complete," and again, when "(Pharaoh) said: Who is your Lord, O Moses? He said: Our Lord is He Who gives to everything its creation, then guides (it)" (Quran 87: 1, 2; 20: 49, 50). The pertinent question at this point would be: if the Lord makes everything complete (that is, perfect) and guides it (to its destiny), where is perfection (*kamal*) found? Where is our final destination?

Indeed, our destiny itself could be called perfection (*kamal*) even as Allah himself is the perfect one (*kamil*). Yet if Allah is perfect then that means the universe must be perfect as the universe is encompassed with Allah. This is true but it is not so simple. The universe (*al-'alam*) is in a perpetual state of becoming or evolving, therefore the universe's perfection is actually impossible. *Al-'alam* will always be in a state of imperfection (*naqs*) as it will always be in a state of becoming (*takawwun*). If *al-'alam* was to ever reach a state of perfection (*kamal*) it would cease being *al-'alam* and enter *al-Dhatullah* (the Supreme Essence). There would from that time be no more development left for the universe to go through, any further evolution would, in fact, be devolution. Yet though *kamal* is impossible for *al-'alam* (the universe) it is possible for those who are reaching for the state of *Dhatullah*. But this is not easily done, let alone maintained. It can be said that perhaps the Prophet reached this level, and the Messiah, and the Buddha, and Abinavagupta, and maybe Steven Rogers; yet it is not a usual thing for one to overcome the urge to change with the times. The good evolve, the perfect let the world evolve around them.

Again, it can be asked, if Allah is perfect and the universe is encompassed with Allah then why is their evil in the universe? First of all, the universe must be understood from the perspective of Allah's Being (*wujud*) and Allah's command (*amr*). Ibn al-Arabi spoke of two types of commands given by Allah. The first command he gives is the command "Be!" This command brings into existence that which Allah intends and wishes. He calls this the engendering command (*al-amr al-takwini*). The second command he gives is the command which comes by way of an intermediary and is given purely to human beings. He calls this the prescriptive command (*al-amr al-taklifi*). "Since man follows the engendering command in any case, it is the prescriptive command which brings into existence the possibility of opposing God" (Chittich 1989: 293). Indeed, ibn al-Arabi would prefer to reserve the word command for only the engendering commands as they cannot be disobeyed. Even so, a command has been written into each of our natures which cannot be changed or removed. This commanded destiny we must evolve into. Hence, we will become what we are destined to become.

Secondly, nothing that is born from *kamal* (perfection) can contain *naqs* (imperfection) in the absolute sense. Whatever *naqs* (imperfection) it contains is therefore actually *kamil* (perfect). Effectively, the *kamal* of *naqs* is visible to those who are able to understand that Allah is in everything and therefore all things are good. It is written, "Our Lord is He Who gives to everything its creation" (Quran 20: 50); thus, absolute perfection (*al-kamal al-mutlaq*) exists even in imperfection (*naqs*). The thearchy comes when this truth reaches a community, a city, a country, the globe; and encompasses those that have a quality of life significantly different – perhaps even millenarian in nature – from the apologetics of Marxism. Again, the Quran says, "And that to thy Lord is the goal: And that He it is Who makes (men) laugh and makes (them) weep: And that He it is Who causes death and gives life: And that He creates pairs, the male and the female: From the small life-germ when it is adapted: And that He has ordained the second bringing forth" (Quran 53: 42-47). So, the Lord is our destiny; and our second "bringing forth" – our *ba'th* – is unto oneness with him. Therefore the internal Messiah brings us not only to resurrection but also to re-incarnation.

Yet the dispensationalists believe the Messiah (*al-Masih*) is going to come down from the skies to carry them up in a "rapture" to heaven; the word itself coming from the Latin word *raptus* – which means to seize – and being based on the Vulgate translation of two key Scriptures: "Two women shall be grinding together; the one shall be *taken*, and the other left. Two men shall be in the field; the one shall be *taken*, and the other left." "For the Lord himself shall descend from heaven with a shout, with the voice of the archangel, and with the trump of God: and the dead in Christ shall rise first: Then we which are alive and remain shall be *caught up* together with them in the clouds, to meet the Lord in the air and so shall we ever be with the Lord" (Luke 17: 35, 36; 1Thessalonians 4: 16, 17; emphases mine).

However, the intentionality thematised in these Scriptures was never for this taking, seizing, and capturing to be physical; the actual presupposition presented in them was of the non-physical. It is said of *al-Masih*, "And when he was demanded of the Pharisees, when the kingdom of God should come, he answered them and said, The kingdom of God cometh not with observation: Neither shall they say, Lo here: or, lo there: for behold, the kingdom of God is within you" (Luke 17: 20, 21). Though God is seen and heard everywhere his thearchic dominion does not come by looking up or waiting for someone to come down and save you. The thearchy starts within and manifests itself outwardly.

Still, it is currently the view of the dispensationalists that the rapture must be a physical seizing of the righteous and taking them to the skies to be with *al-Masih*; but it is more likely that the rapture is a non-physical carrying into ecstasy: when the self leaves the physical body and "sups" with *al-Masih*. Thus, the second advent of *al-Masih* (the Messiah) is not a physical (*hissi*) one in that somebody flies down from the sky and takes us into the heavens. The second advent of *al-Masih* is to be within the physical person of everyone who gains knowledge of self as messiah. On a more advanced level this apocalypse must and will reach to all the Original nations regardless of their corruption over the years or the judgment they have received after death: "On the day when it comes, no soul will speak except by His permission; so (some) of them will be unhappy and (others) happy. Then as for those who are unhappy, they will be in the Fire; for them therein will be sighing and groaning – Abiding therein so long as the heavens and the earth endure, *except as thy Lord please*. Surely thy Lord is Doer of what He intends" (Quran 11: 105-107; emphasis mine). Two key ideas are instantly apparent here: basically, the Day of Judgment is spoken of here as taking place during the heaven's and the earth's endurance, thus before a new heaven or new earth and before any resurrection (*ba'th*).

Another interesting point is that the Fire (or hell or Sheol) is explained in the Quran as enduring for an individual until "the Lord please." In the Quran hell is not an eternal punishment for wrong, it is a place of purging and purifying. Indeed, it is written in the Quran, "Allah promises the hypocrites, men and women, and the disbelievers the Fire of hell to abide therein. It is enough for them. And Allah curses them, and for them is a lasting chastisement" (Quran 9: 68). The purpose of chastising is to purge something until it reaches perfection (*kamal*). It is not God's intention to condemn forever but to perfect (*kamil*) us, to make us one with him. It even goes on to say in the Quran, "On that day no intercession avails except of him whom the Beneficent allows, and whose word He is pleased with" (Quran 20: 109). One can even intercede for you at your judgment; and as the Bible continues: "the Lord *will not cast off for ever*. But though he cause grief, yet will he have compassion according to the multitude of his mercies. For he doth not afflict willingly nor grieve the children of men" (Lamentations 3: 31-33; emphasis mine). This is the general message of the godbody movement: that the God of the Scriptures is not a cruel judge on a throne in the sky, he is in our hearts desiring for us to wake up to the knowledge of truth (*al-'ilm al-haqiqa*) so that we can be one with him, that is, become Allah himself. Any chastisement we receive is to help us reach that point of oneness.

V

One of the central imperatives of godbody sociology is the assumption that all humanity has a precognitive, ahistorical, and amoral essence that is *mithali* (perfectible). This essence though relatively impermanent, is still noetic and is more impermeable than the astral body: which we godbodies call the self, the psychologists call the *psyche*, the Christians call the soul, the ancient Hebrews called the *khadj*, and the ancient Egyptians called the *ka*. Putting aside these semantics they all add up to the same thing, which has structures and systems that are similar to, yet distinct from, those of what scientists call an essence.

Here Islam presents us with an interesting form of essentialism incomparable with the Western tradition. To Islam the essence (*al-dhat*) is also *mithali*, and is adaptable to relational and correlational communications within the universe too, i.e. it can evolve (*takwin*). Moreover, there is also a Supreme Essence (*al-Dhatullah*), which is noetic, precognitive, and ahistorical. While Allah himself may be defined by all the names and attributes of him used in the Quran, the *Dhatullah* itself is based on one name: al-Muhibb (the Libidinal) so that just like with the light side and the dark side of the Force, the *Dhatullah* always sides with the light, and the *Dhatullah* never changes. It is written in the Quran, "And there endures forever the person of thy Lord, the Lord of glory and honour" (Quran 55: 27).

The fact that all existentialists believe that human existence precedes any human essence shows that to them origin and destiny are not determined before physical manifestation but are historical attributes that are developed after birth, or said another way, "It is not the consciousness of men that determines their being, but, on the contrary, their social being that determines their consciousness" (Marx 1978: 4). This mantra of materialism was accepted by Sartre and all existentialists post-Sartre bringing to light an even more comprehensive statement: "No one knows or can know the future." Regardless of foretelling and predictive capabilities, who we are, though somewhat malleable and impermanent, does have an unchangeable quality about it. Now I am not saying that history has no effect on our consciousness, nor that systems and structures are not socially constructed through human interactions with astral forces, social forces, global forces, and even environmental forces. What I am saying is, firstly, that those forces, and, secondly, our human psyches are ontologically viable agents before birth, during life, and after death.

We also have to remember that every theoretical position is positioned, is motivated, is loaded, and Sartre's reinvention of existentialism was also positioned. Sartre was a middle-class, White, male, intellectual whose motivation was intellectual grandeur: to both make Husserl digestible to

French academics and to remove the "thingness" from human existence. His teachings were also loaded with individualism, subjectivism, and ontological humanism. Still, that might be presenting too simplistic a definition of Sartre.

He did write a number of essays on anti-Black racism in the United States, and supported both the Algerians and the Vietnamese in their respective struggles; he even wrote introductions to both Léopold Senghor's *Black Orpheus* and Frantz Fanon's *The Wretched of the Earth*. He was also an Ashkenazi in a world where being Ashkenazi was still unpopular. Surely Sartre was more than a bigshot seeking intellectual grandeur? While to a degree that may be so that is still no excuse for holding to his faulty system. Existentialism, post-Sartre, tends to believe that human existence (*insan al-wujud*) precedes any human essence (*insan al-dhat*), and that humanity (*al-nas*) therefore has an absolute freedom to determine its own essence. We are effectively not born a certain way, or at the very least if we are we have the freedom to be different to how we were born, and the circumstances or realities (*haqiqat*) we were born into.

It seems to me that since Sartre, de Beauvoir, and Fanon it has become quite popular to be existentialist. The common reason is that the idea of ascribing to a group an essential (*dhati*) quality like White superiority, Black power, or feminine mystique dehistoricises their development and takes no consideration of the individual and their freedom to choose. This hyper-individualism of existentialism blinds its practitioners to the reality of the group matrices that develop and drive even individuals. The idea of abandoning the whole system of essentialising may appear commendable due to the historically accepted hierarchical positions that were created by essentialising and the rebellion against it. But the solution of the existentialists has been to deny the sovereignty and primality of essences and to deny and oppose any form of essentialism that should arise, particularly in the human (*al-insan*) sphere. However, this philosophical addition when confronted by the other sciences (*'ulum*) faces a problematic: surely the Periodic Table of Elements, the Table of Common Acids and their Methyl Esters, and the Table of Less Common Acids and their Methyl Esters are essentialised categories (*qisman*)? What about the polynucleotide chain that was used to identify the DNA structure, surely there is an essentialised quality in there? Or the Classificatory Table of the Four-Kingdoms, taxonomy would fall apart without those essentialisings.

Yet the central argument of existentialism is that there is no pre-existing or primordial *human* essence (*insan al-dhat*) that chooses a physical host or manifestation. Again, all things are material first and then they are defined and given a *dhati* quality, whether that definition is self-given or imposed from above it is socially constructed and not eternal. There is no essential (*dhati*) human quality that is being demoralised by capitalism, or racism, sexism, heterosexism (homophobia), cis-sexism (transphobia), or any other established system. Basically, dehumanisation is an absurdity as humanity (*al-nas*) would have to be defined existentially, in which case what is occurring is actually a critique, a deconstructing if you will, of socially oppressed (*mazlum*) or undermined groups. The potency and problematic are removed. The generalised nature of the critique is ignored. Instead it is a simple criticism, or worse, a comment, by an alterego. On a deeper level, if Blackness is not legitimated on an essentialist basis then those behaviours that are general to most Blacks, behaviours that are criticised with such fierce invective, will still be viewed as pertaining to the vast majority of Blacks and the contrary will simply be seen as an aberration.

The three main fears that have caused most social scientists (*al-'ulamaa al-ijtima'iyya*) to view essentialism with suspicion are: (i) essentialising was used to justify slavery, segregation, colonialism, racism, sexism, heterosexism, and cis-sexism; (ii) thanks to the materialist nature of their argumentation essentialism appears to them to actually be non-scientific; and (iii) the idea of a natural disposition whether through biology or psychology scares most social scientists as it undervalues the influence of socialisation. The implications of these three arguments produces the anti-essentialist sentiments that exist within the social sciences making most social scientists wary of trusting anything that has even a hint of naturalism.

The suspicion the existentialists have produced has even found its way into human sciences (*al-'ulum al-insan*) like psychology, where psychologists, and even psychoanalysts, view the natural sciences and human sciences as two separate schools with two separate outlooks: one based on drives, properties, and mechanisms; the other based on systems, structures, and interpretations. Though neither science (*'ilm*) can be so simply defined, and I am indulging in the basest of generalisations (*'umumat*), the dichotomous distinction the anti-essentialists intimate between the natural sciences and the human sciences ultimately derive from the arguments articulated originally by the social scientists (*al-'ulamaa al-ijtima'iyya*).

In order to challenge them I shall confront each of these issues one at a time. As concerns the first argument by the existentialists: that essentialising was used to justify so many deplorable systematic violations like slavery; such is a reasonable concern but a faulty one. The problem is not the system used to justify the wrong but the wrong itself. The justification is innocent. It could be said that Christianity has also been used to justify those same wrongs, along with others, yet we can also agree that Christianity itself was innocent of the wrong in itself; corrupt men took an innocent system and corrupted it. It is far from wise to say that a perfect (*kamil*) system would be incorruptible (*mutqini*) as all systems are at the mercy of the people who employ them.

Again, there are systems that could be called corrupt from the beginning for which cause I agree that there are corrupt systems, but one must apply intersubjective perceptions to know whether the system they are examining is a corrupt or innocent system. Case in point: slavery and the Holocaust were corrupt from the beginning, however, Christianity and biology are not inherently corrupt. Their corruption (*naqs*) into enslavement and Nazism was a product of corrupt people. So, again, how does one discover whether essentialism is inherently corrupt? Can essentialism ever be used for good or by good people to promote a good outcome? The question itself ultimately implies the answer. Essentialism could be respected as inherently innocent and corrupt people have just been using it to justify and further their implacable ends.

The second argument by existentialists is that essentialism is unscientific, by their standards, as it is from an abstracted basis and not a materialist basis. Yet as I demonstrated earlier using the examples of scientific tables and maps to essentialise and generalise can, in some senses, be more scientific than not to. But the following argument is then used to challenge this notion: "Even if scientific tables and maps are used to essentialise categories, that does not negate the fact that *humanity* existed before we were given an essential quality by science. In fact, all entities must exist before we can apply an essential or ontological or teleological quality to them." Such an assessment of the situation may seem undeniable, nevertheless it can be problematised.

Firstly, if we consider the concept of human nature (or the human archetype): a true existentialist would say no such thing exists because for such a thing to exist it could only do so in the abstract as a product of a pre-existing mind, whether human or otherwise. But again, all this is based on the perspective of the finite. From the perspective of the eternal we are able to see that the distinguishing qualities that make up *al-nas* came about due to the right genetic and cultural combinations. For example, 2+1 will always equal 3, whether the human mind conceptualises those numbers or not. Again, one electron wave circling one proton wave will always be a hydrogen atom, and if it loses one of those waves it will always be a hydrogen ion; regardless of whether such entities ever actually do exist or not.

Secondly, essentialism gives substance to ontology and teleology. For example, those characteristics that make humanity distinct from other mammals, whether they be biological, psychological, or sociological, contribute towards producing a human essence (*insan al-dhat*). Further, there are things biological and psychological that distinguish male from female (they are not all simply sociological as even de Beauvoir (2009) accepted). Because of our unique biological and sociological combinations we humans have a teleological purpose and destiny that need not be as religiously suggestive as it at first sight appears.

As to the third argument: that a natural predisposition undermines the value of socialisation; yes it does, to an existentialist. In psychology the debate takes a completely contrary turn. Here the question is asked in the form of whether nature or nurture is the key factor in a person's psychological development. To make the debate a little clearer neurologists claim the nervous system, geneticists claim genes, behaviourists claim social conditioning, and psychoanalysts claim the tripartite intrapsychic mechanisms. The debate, however, goes even further back than modern psychology: and it has taken new theorists like Steven Pinker (2002) to show that in fact the two, nature and nurture, can work together. Socialisation should not be undermined, but nor should it take priority. Existentialists give priority to socialisation; essentialists, on the other hand, give priority to both biological *and* sociological factors. Whereas existentialists to a greater degree deny the place of biology, essentialists do not necessarily deny sociology's presence in human relations.

VI

The preceding explication of various Marxian theories has been to, firstly, show the teleology of Marxism: that Marxism had a destiny from its very foundations towards the end that it reached – though such may not have been the aim or hope of its adherents, least of all Marx himself. Secondly, to apocalypticise the spectre (*jinni*) of Marxism: while it remains hidden it can haunt, horrify, and possess; when exposed it loses the sorceries of the undead and becomes powerless. Thirdly, to exorcise the spectre of Marxism, that is, to undo the revival of the Marxist phantom, not through the performative of a Marxian revolution but through allowing the dissipation of interest in the Marxian project to exorcise its effectiveness. Finally, to show that any social movement can contain the seeds of its own self-destruction from its very inception. True indeed, all movements inevitably have an expiration date. The goal is to have your movement last as long as it can without self-destruction. Thus, we can see that what brought on the self-destruction of Orthodox Marxism was in fact the failures within Marxism as such.

It must be remembered that in the 1980s the concepts of neoliberalism and late capitalism were being carried by the West to the world. On top of that, the idea of a unified Europe – the European Community (EC) – was gaining huge popularity at the time too. These two: economic improvement and political integration played a big part in the turn of events of the early 1990s. Again, as Fukuyama noted, "By the late 1980s, a remarkable intellectual revolution had occurred within the Soviet economic establishment" (Fukuyama 2012: 29); a revolution or counter-revolution that he stated was orchestrated by the fact that many of the leading Soviet economists were starting to get educated in the basic principles of marginalist theory in the West. The new ideas acquired from their schooling caused them to initiate economic programmes that would draw into the Soviet economy certain market mechanisms. However, the multiplicity of opinions coming from these liberal theories when combined with the Soviet system as it then stood caused a breakdown which led to economic disaster.

The *eschaton* of Orthodox Marxism in the early 1990s, however, is perceptible by three facts: (i) Marx surmised that with the foundation of all social systems being an economic infrastructure, if the power relations just centralised ownership of capital into the hands of the state, thereby effectively transforming the economic system, the state would eventually "whither away" as the primary aetiologic of inequality would have been transcended. (ii) Marx provided a detailed, albeit wrongheaded, account of capitalist production believing that by mastering the intricacies of the capitalist system his followers could design an economic system superior to capitalism; however, as he did not explain at any length what this new system would or should look like but left it up to history to design it, the architects of the first socialist system only ended up creating nothing more than a proletarian state of centralised state-planning instead of markets for their transactions. (iii) Marx emphasised the scientific, almost inevitable, nature of his system using scientific terminology and comparative research methodologies, so that when the state failed to "whither away" but instead became more oppressive, and when the economic system began to go through its own economic dysfunctions due to the War in Afghanistan, new forms of social organisation were sought for by the people.

That is not to discredit the individuals within the top echelon of the Soviet Bloc who also played the major role in bringing about the fall of Orthodox Marxism. Fukuyama (2012: 27) articulated how it was never assumed that Orthodox Marxism would fall so easily – and in hindsight it can be seen based on the exegesis of Marx's own words that as a system it was closer to an authentic orthodoxy than has been appreciated by most of his later disciples – yet for the Soviet Union the writing first appeared on the wall with "the election of Boris Yeltsin as president of the Russian Republic in the spring of 1990, who with many of his supporters in the Russian Parliament subsequently left the Communist party. This same group then began advocating the restoration of private property and markets."

Thus though it could be said that European Communism began to fall in November of 1989 with the fall of the Berlin Wall, Orthodox Marxism did not really meet its actual death until Yeltsin was elected to the top seat. Then, "By early 1991, all formerly communist states in Eastern Europe, including Albania and the major republics of Yugoslavia, had held reasonably free, multiparty elections. Communists were initially turned out of office everywhere except in Romania, Bulgaria, Serbia, and Albania, while in Bulgaria, the elected Communist government was soon forced to step down. The political basis for the Warsaw Pact disappeared, and Soviet forces began to withdraw from Eastern Europe" (Fukuyama 2012: 27). Effectively, the system that was able to take Russia from the most backward Eurocentric country prewar, and the most devastated by World War II with the most casualties, to within ten years able to compete with the US as a global superpower in its own right, was abandoned and torn down in both Russia and Eastern Europe by the early 1990s.

It is thereby from Marxism, and from the rise and fall of certain other historical movements, that we are able to find three axioms of social dynamics:

1. All social movements are finite and cannot continue indefinitely, as all social movements must have a purpose and therefore have an end (no social movement, regardless of how courageous, can endure beyond its natural limitations: the aim is to find those limitations) or written mathematically: $Lm > g$.

2. Social movements are caused by and succeed through the social forces they have acting on the social bodies involved – thus whether they will succeed or fail can be determined by how long they maintain the consistency of their social force (and not their size, nor wealth, nor smoothness, nor scalability, nor durability, nor medium, nor cunning, nor any other spatial factor). Hence: $\exists(\alpha > Lm) \rightarrow g \nearrow$.

3. Social movements (whether they be resistance or reaction) become completely

> inert as new systemic boundaries and societal limitations replace old ones causing the social forces to decelerate, or $\exists Lm \to \alpha \searrow +g \searrow$.

From these it can be seen that social movement, the basis of social dynamics as defined here and throughout, functions as a vessel housing various social forces whether these forces are resurrected, incorporated, or *phantamatic*. Further assumptions could also be intimated as to why countries such as the United States, while having many uprisings, have so few revolutions; while several countries in Africa and Latin America go through endless waves of revolution after revolution. (That is not to say the West has not had a hand in the revolutions, revolts, and civil wars that have happened in Africa, Asia, and Latin America; but to say there is no smoke without fire. Countries like America, in all things, are extremely patriotic. Identification as a unified nation is relatively new to the African states, and Latin America's identity shifts from class to nation constantly. The Arab Spring also shows that while it was social forces that won the day, as they gained power those forces began to dissipate. The US controlled military regained power easily).

I write all this not in agreement with the Marxian assumptions, as noted I am a Black thearchist; just to show how a social movement once inert can die. Then again, Marxists do have a tendency of calling any movement that is not Marxist counter-revolutionary as they hold to the delusional belief that Marxism is the only way to social progression. The truth is, however, whether resurrected, incorporated, or phantomatic, Marxism will always be an advancement toward captivity and not toward liberation. Though it spoke the language of liberation the final outcome was depersonalisation into the all-encompassing monolith of the state, which embodied and took on a universal mechanisation. Though Marxism appears to be undead, that is, is a haunting phantom, it has very much so died and needs only the funerary performative of revolution, or counter-revolution in the few locations that have it as orthodoxy, to be markedly recognised as dead. Even though its hangers-on can protest that Orthodox Marxism was not the true intentions of the real and living Marx, the actual outcome of his philosophy could lead nowhere else.

On the other hand, America avoids inertia by constantly renewing its patriotic devotion to both its political and its economic systems. This also explains the reason for so much fragmentation in Western societies; it is necessary so as to maintain the illusion that the state is the primary force over society: the illusion of liquidity in all subcultural in-groups keeps the social system of neoliberal plutocracy from adopting any new high cultures to replace the unthreatening popular culture of pluralism. Nevertheless, there is also a tendency within Marxism that they share with most feminists, critical race theorists, and post-colonialists: the tendency to assume that their theory has a monopoly when it comes to the liberation of their social group (*mujtama*), the rather arrogant and snooty idea that somehow their way is the only way for their *mujtama* to understand *al-'alam* and how to overcome the social oppression their group has historically experienced.

In contradistinction Islam – by valuing the soul of the individual first, then considering the existing power structures of their social situation – could never fall into this trap; and the thearchy, being, primarily, an internal revolution and, secondarily, a structural revolution, has the means to avoid this kind of fallacious and potentially oppressive situation. And while it could be said that there is still an element of necromancy within the thearchy due to the incarnatory of a form of anarchism, anarchism itself being equivocally a phantom. Indeed, thearchism itself could also be called phantomatic – though not in the godbody manifestation of it – as thearchies have existed deep into antiquity. Yet the thearchy's archaic presence is more an assurance of their potential and successes than their failure. Both Dynastic and tribal thearchies were, and in some cases still are, able to last for thousands of years. The only reason Europe's initial thearchy failed was because the European gods were mainly malevolent.

A New Philosophy of Man

As stated earlier my personal philosophy as a godbody is based on *tawhid* (theocentric monism), but is also based on *al-muhibb* (the libidinal); on the other hand, my personal ideology of Black thearchism (the godbody ideology) – which employs the programme of Black syndicalism (participatory economics) and the discursive of Black eroticism (sexualised embodiment) – also informs my definition of godbodyism. Here the Black thearchy is the ideological opponent to the White oligarchy – which itself employs the programme of White neoliberalism (late capitalism) and the discursive of White superiority (biological distinction).

Now when I use the qualifier Black for the ideology of the Black thearchy I am not trying to say that it is exclusively for Black people. It does, however, make up the system of a Black *umma*, just like the godbody system that spawned it. This system, while being Black developed, seeks to be multiracial and transnational in orientation. The qualifier Black is only used as I am a Black man speaking mainly to Black people; in the non-Black communities this qualifier can be replaced by the word ethnic; thereby the ethnothearchy should also be based on Allah, *al-Islam*, *al-tawhid*, and *al-habba*, which are all represented in an *umma* that is ideologically thearchist, programmatically syndicalist, and discursively eroticist. All patently showing that our system is also in blatant opposition to what passes for Islamic in the so-called Third World. Whereas the fulfilment of fundamentalist Islam is in an Islamic State, the fulfilment of cultural Islam is in an Islamic Anarchism.

To understand this Islamic anarchism in relation to godbody sociology we must first take into consideration the Islamic perspective it is derived from. During the 1990s, around the time the communist regimes were beginning to fall at an incredible rate the US was left with a difficulty, "with the threat vacuum created by the fall of the Soviet Union, questions arose as to who or what would begin to define [the] new U.S. military posture … While debate raged, a consensus began to develop that later emerged from the buildup to Gulf War I, as the one-time U.S. ally Saddam Hussein was being compared to Hitler" (Daulatzai 2012: 154). Islam's becoming the new global threat to American expansionism was long in the making: In the mid-1950s after the Suez incident, in the 1960s with the rise of the Ba'th Party, and in the 1970s with both the Arab-Israeli War and the Iranian Revolution. However, the existence of the Soviet Union was far more immediate; once the Soviet machinery was beginning to crumble the old Islamic threat could be re-propagated.

I

The religion of Islam came under serious scrutiny in the West, and in particular the United States, during the early 1990s as a result of two events: Iraq's invasion of Kuwait and Samuel Huntington's analysis of the post-Cold War world as a result of it. Prior to those events, though Islam and the Orient were signified with relatively backward codes, Arabs and Orientals were still largely distinguished from Blacks as a much higher class. What those two events accomplished was the relegating of Arabs and Orientals to a position far closer to Blacks than their initial state.

In all the West's Orientalism and racism, Islam still held the imaginary (*al-muttasil al-khayali*) and illusory (*al-munfasil al-khayali*) of a civilising force, superior to witchcraft and promiscuity, which were heavily Africanised signifiers. Even in Huntington's delineation of Islamic civilisation there are still remnants of respectfulness accorded to the *thaqafah* and unifying quality of Islam, but there is also identifiable a shift. Muslim countries were no longer seen as allies against communism or partners in economic negotiations, they were now a threat and an opponent that must be brought in line with Western civilisation. Though, obviously, Saddam's invasion of Kuwait was neither his first invasion of another country, nor an Islamic country's first atrocity against the United States: the Iranian Revolution of 1979 in which a fundamentally Islamic government came to power, having as its first order of business revenge against America by taking hostage various American workers at the embassy, was obviously far more atrocious to Americans than a Muslim country invading another Muslim country.

It was Kuwait's status in OPEC (the Organization of Petroleum Exporting Countries), not with regard to oil – Iraq could possibly have more oil even than Saudi Arabia, something the US has known for decades – but with regard to influence over other OPEC countries, that played a key role in causing America to consider the invasion a priority. America effectively had a choice: they could either support one OPEC ally or the other. The fact that they chose Kuwait had repercussions across the Islamic world that we are still feeling the effects of today. Not least of all in Huntington's analysis of the situation.

Surely had America allowed Iraq to get away with the invasion there would have been no Gulf War – something

Bush Sr. capitalised on to change his image from a weak leader into a strong leader – and therefore the weight of Huntington's argument, that the post-Cold War conflicts will no longer be ideological but civilisational, would have lost some serious strength. Indeed, his central hypothesis: that there is a "clash of civilisations," may not have even been born were it not for the three main factors of Iraq's need for money as a result of attacking the also Muslim, but Shi'a, Iran; Bush Sr.'s need to look strong amid speculations that he would be another Jimmy Carter; and the EHMs' failed attempts to bring Saddam under the heel of America as they had done with Saudi Arabia.

If Saddam had just "played ball" with America and submitted to the Empire for a mutually beneficial deal then the general thesis that civilisations are in conflict would have seemed preposterous. Yet he does present two points as a disclaimer: the so-called Confucian-Islamic alliance and a comment that his hypothesis is not that the civilisations will necessarily war, or even clash for that matter, but that they exist and will hold the central fault lines for the future. Yet, while it is true that Islam has played a major role in global politics since Gulf War I and 9/11, North Korea, China, and Russia have also been problematic to the United States in its drive for world domination.

Though I agree with Huntington's general thesis that cultures have their value, far more value than in the West they are given, I do not see the current or future fault lines as being between his fictitious civilisations (some of which were quite ridiculous) but between Islam and *Ishrik*. In this, where Huntington speaks of the Iron Curtain being replaced by a Velvet Curtain, I prefer the term Silk Curtain for three reasons: Firstly, it employs the old Orientalist signifiers of what one imagines (*takhayyalat*) of the Orient – close to the imaginative (*khayali*) and fictitious geographical and geopolitical ideas the West has of Islam. Secondly, there is a pre-modern, candidly ancient referential with regard to silk – even as the division between West and East travels as far back as Philip and Alexander, and even further back to ancient Sparta and Persia. Thirdly, silk, as opposed to velvet, is light, sometimes even transparent, thus it can go unnoticed with an almost invisible, unconscious air to it – even as the boundaries demarcating and segregating the Muslims from the *Mushriks* are light, invisible, and somewhat flimsy.

It is therefore not a clash of civilisations as such: according to the Prophet Islam has always been in the world, and even the forces of nature and the universe are in perfect Islam. If Islam is the distinguishing characteristic of the universe (*al-'alam*), there is therefore a need to articulate various propositions and suppositions with the Islamic derivation that actually enumerate the eidetic intentionality of Islam and its correlation to Western religious and scientific apperceptions.

Shari'ati spoke of a powerful consideration that is very important to Islam, the consideration of knowledge: "A person's character may be judged in accordance with his degree of knowledge concerning his beliefs, for the mere holding of a belief is no virtue in itself. If we believe in something that we do not fully know, it has little value. It is the precise knowledge of that in which we believe that may be counted a virtue. Since we believe in Islam, we must acquire correct knowledge of it and choose the correct method of gaining that knowledge" (Shari'ati 1979: 60). Indeed, most godbodies would say that belief should be excised from our vocabulary and mentality entirely. A person should be guided only by what they *know for sure*. Therefore, knowledge of Islam, more so than belief in Islam, should be what we endeavour to achieve.

Shari'ati articulated a central means to acquiring knowledge of Islam, making clear that his scientific method of developing a knowledge of Islam can be used to develop a knowledge of any religion (*din*) or culture (*thaqafah*) in society: "[T]here are various ways of knowledge of Islam. One is the knowledge of Allah, and comparing Him with the objects of worship in other religions. Another is the knowledge of our book, the Qur'an, and comparing it with other heavenly books (or books that are said to be heavenly). Yet another is the knowledge of the personality of the Prophet of Islam and comparing him with the great reforming personalities that have existed throughout history. Finally, one more is the knowledge of the outstanding personalities of Islam and comparing them with the prominent figures of other religions and schools of thought" (Shari'ati 1979: 42).

Now there is an essential eidetic apperception that must be acknowledged about Islam before we proceed any further: there is a distinction between practicing Muslims and pious Muslims. Muslims in general have four basic indicators while pious Muslims have five. The four indicators that someone is a practicing Muslim are belief in a beneficent and merciful God (*Allah*), belief in the oneness of God (*Tawhid*), belief in all the prophets of God from Adam to Muhammad (*Nubuwwa*), and complete submission to the person of God (*Islam*). The five indicators of a pious Muslim are testifying to the oneness of God and the prophethood of Muhammad (*shahadah*); praying five times a day (*salah*); giving a portion of what you earn to those in need (*zakah*); fasting during the month of Ramadan (*sawm*); and going on the pilgrimage to Mecca, when you have the means to do so (*hajj*). This essential apperception shows that the category of Muslim is far richer than simply the pious brand that most people acknowledge as our representatives.

Nevertheless, we godbodies have our own *shahadah*, we have a *hajj* to our own Mecca, many of us practice *sawm* during Ramadan, we give a kind of *zakah* to those godbodies in need, and as far as *salah* goes, though we do not pray, let alone five times a day, it is written in the Quran, "Recite that which has been revealed to thee of the Book and keep up prayer. Surely prayer keeps (one) away from indecency and evil; and certainly the remembrance [*dhikr*] of Allah is the greatest ... And Allah knows what you do" (Quran 29: 45). Now this *dhikr* is in fact the Arabic word for meditation or mindfulness, and *al-dhikr* Allah is Arabic for the mindfulness of the sacred. As the Quran says this mindfulness of the sacred is of greater value than prayer (regardless of the amount of times a day it is done) those godbodies that practice that mindfulness of the sacred regularly, and many of us do, are actually in a greater position Islamically. In that sense, we godbodies can also be classified as pious Muslims, though we godbodies actually reject religious labels and would rather be called cultural Muslims.

But we godbodies can gain a greater intimacy with the depths of Islam, which we do claim as our culture, through following Shari'ati's list; in so doing an overtly presented conclusion can be deduced immediately that Daulatzai captured when he said "God – via Christianity – came to be associated not only with whiteness but also with the powerful imperialist aggressor of the Western world, including the United States. Allah – via Islam – however, was 'out of power' and understood as Black" (Daulatzai 2012: 18). Shari'ati (1979) also concluded that what demarcated all the Abrahamic prophets (*anbiya*) from the non-Abrahamic prophets was that their missions and their systems were usually anti-establishment and "out of power," sometimes even to the point of invoking war and martyrdom. As Islam is the seal of the Abrahamic faiths it is only right that the God of Islam be an anti-establishment and anti-imperialist God. In all, the first thing we know for sure about Islam is that the God of Islam, Allah, is a God for the non-established.

"As for the book of Islam, the Qur'an, it is a book that like the Torah contains social, political and military provisions, even instructions for the conduct of warfare, the taking and setting free of prisoners; that is interested in life, in building, and prosperity, in struggling against enemies and negative elements; but it is also a book that concerns itself with the refinement of the soul, the piety of the spirit, and the ethical improvement of the individual" (Shari'ati 1979: 80). Ultimately, we can see conclusively therefore that the perspective of Islam is defined based on the book of Islam and the God of Islam.

In turn it can be perceived that the book of Islam is a book that comprises information about how to live in the world here and how to improve yourself for the world hereafter, and that the God of Islam is a God of the non-established and particularly of Black people. Yet Islamic history begins with the knowledge of this God and what sort of people he works with. According to Shari'ati he works with *al-anbiya* (the prophets) to send a message to *al-nas* (the people). Again, Islamic history is long, dating as far back as the creation, but the personages of Islamic history have a standard definition: they were all prophetic. Moreover, "Prophets were individuals who transformed history and societies and they revolted as well as fomented a revolution. Who was Abraham? He was neither a philosopher nor a scientist. His father made idols and he would sell them. Later, he became a shepherd and finally he led the greatest movement in history. Or, look at Moses, he was an abandoned child who was brought up in Pharaoh's

Palace. He took off and went to Shoeyb and began to herd his sheep. Finally, he started his struggles with Pharaoh with his gnarled staff and he won! The same is true about Jesus, Muhammad, and all the Prophets" (Shari'ati 1981: 2058).

The personages of Islamic history: the prophets, caliphs, and Imams, all trace their lineage back to Abraham, and, as can be seen, served a non-pretentious and non-established deity. Indeed, it is when their movements became the establishment that Islam would historically begin to fall. We see this throughout Islamic history, however, we learn just as much by studying the book of Islam: the Quran. Therefore, what we have learned about the God of Islam is that he is anti-establishment, anti-imperialism, and anti-intellectualism. We learn the same also by studying the history of Islam and the personalities of Islam: from Abraham, to Moses, to Jesus and Muhammad, to the caliphs and Imams.

But we do not learn completely the place and identity of man in the plan of Islam. From here Shari'ati went on to ask a quite pertinent question, "Can we deduce the status and nature of man from the manner in which the creation of man is described in the Qur'an, the Word of God, or in the words of the Prophet of Islam? From examining the story of Adam – the symbol of man – in the Qur'an, we can understand what kind of a creature man is in the view of God and therefore in the view of our religion" (Shari'ati 1979: 71). It will thereby be through the Quran that we will learn the true Islamic philosophy of man.

II

The first and most important detail the Quran teaches us about man (and I use the masculine not to undermine women but to make the distinction) is that he was created by, and therefore must be subservient to, Allah: "Allah is the Creator of all things and He has charge over everything" (Quran 39: 62). The *'alam* and everything we know was created (*khalaq*) by Allah and for a purpose; though there is categorically some teleological significance in that idea it is not to say that Allah does not allow the world (*al-'alam*) a measure of agency. If *al-'alam* did not have any agentic capacities then all beings would be merely automatons doing the will of Allah not by choice but by necessity. That said, Allah has nonetheless also appointed for everything in the universe (*al-'alam*) its measure, as it is written: "And there is not a thing but with Us are the treasures of it, and We send it not down but in a known measure." And again, "He said: Our Lord is He Who gives to everything its creation, then guides (it). ... He said: The knowledge thereof is with my Lord in a book; my Lord neither errs nor forgets –" (Quran 15: 21; 20: 50-52). The Quran thus teaches us that God set and knows the limits of all things in *al-'alam*.

Nevertheless, there is an ultimate question that arises from the understanding, according to the book of Islam, that man was created by Allah and was appointed by structures that he set in place natural limitations he could not transgress: In what way was man created (*khalaq*) when Allah *khalaq* Adam? It is written, "And surely We created man of sounding clay, of black mud fashioned into shape" (Quran 15: 26); a proposition made no less evident by the discovery of the earliest fossils of humanity in East Africa. Again, the original Eden was most likely a savannah in East Africa and not some astral garden in the netherworld (Muller 2013). Here the evidence of the Quran and modern science agree that humanity's origin is as Black and that Adam or the Original man was fashioned from minerals in the African soil.

Indeed, virtually all the elements of our planet are found in the human body, though the elemental distributions may vary. Again, the most plenteous minerals of the earth are in brown or black colours and rarely, if at all, in pink or white. If Adam was made from black mud fashioned like clay into a human body – the story is an analogy – he would have had to have been Black. Yet it also says of him that he was created from dust, "When thy Lord said to the angels: Surely I am going to create a mortal from dust. So, when I have made him complete and breathed into him of My spirit, fall down submitting to him" (Quran 38: 71, 72). Two implications can be drawn from these statements: (i) the spirit of Allah has always dwelt within man, (ii) "All the angels of God, great and small, are commanded to fall down in prostration before this creature" (Shari'ati 1979: 75).

Thereby, what we can see is that in Islamic sociology: (i) Allah created all things, including Adam; (ii) Allah created Adam from dust and black mud; (iii) Allah breathed into Adam "not His blood or His body – so to speak – but His spirit, the most exalted entity for which human languages possess a name" (Shari'ati 1979: 74). The duality by which humanity is composed is based on being in a sense a dual nature: divine and profane. Man, however, is not distinguished by this duality: every creature (*khalq*) has the breath of life; and while Shari'ati reasoned that humanity's "splendor and importance derive precisely from [this]" (Shari'ati 1979: 74), such is not the case.

In Genesis it says "And they went in onto Noah into the ark, two and two of all flesh, wherein is the breath of life" (Genesis 7: 15); and though I recognise the analogous nature of the Noah narrative – that the species of animals are too numerous and diverse to have fit into a literal ark, and that the existence of Noah himself may be questionable – that is beside the point. The point is that all creatures and species contain the breath of life not just humanity. Indeed, the breath of life or spirit of Allah flows throughout nature.

Finally, the angels were all commanded to bow before Adam: "This prostration of the angels before Adam serves to clarify the Islamic concept of man. Man knows certain things that the angels do not know, and this knowledge endows man with superiority to the angels despite the superiority of the angels to man with respect to race and origin. In other words, the nobility and dignity of man derives from knowledge and not from lineage" (Shari'ati 1979: 75). In fact, as I shall try to prove later on what distinguishes humanity as a species is knowledge.

The Quran also teaches that the woman was also made by Allah in similitude to man, "And Allah has made wives for you from among yourselves, and has given you sons and daughters from your wives, and has provided you with good things. Will they then believe in falsehood and deny the favour of Allah?" (Quran 16: 72). Incidentally, to refine our understanding of this exegetic text Shari'ati (1979: 75) articulated, "Another point to be considered is the creation of woman from the rib of man, at least according to the translations usually made from the Arabic. But the translation 'rib' is incorrect, and the word so translated has the real meaning, in both Arabic and Hebrew, of 'nature, disposition or constitution.' Eve – that is, woman – was created, then, out of the same nature or disposition as man." What is remarkable is that it was translated as rib in the first place, the idea of man's dual nature of divinity and profanity being embodied in a female of the same physical and sensual constitution, but with certain composite biological distinctions: chromosomes, hormones, breasts, vaginas, wombs, and ova; shows a greater depth than mythological ideation. It is the basis of our relation to the world (*al-'alam*) and to Allah who created the world.

At the same time, I must say at this point that contrary to popular opinion I am sympathetic towards the ideology of feminism, particularly abolitionist pro-sex feminism, and by no means hope to eradicate it. However, there is an issue within their theoretical propositions that might be preventing their progression as a movement in the future: there is a tendency among some feminists to use the concept of man for an idealised evil. To say all the problems of women, if not of the world, are a result of men. Men become the absolute oppressor, manipulator, tempter, or womaniser. In this case, like with the anomalous theory of the devil, the essentialised become the essentialisers.

Even when done from an historical perspective, so as to point out male-centred/male-created structures, it is done so with the absolutised evil men deceiving an idealisation of an absolute innocence – a just as historically constructed – version of the feminine, for example, in de Beauvoir's statement, among many, that "Lord-man will materially protect liege-woman and will be in charge of justifying her existence: [so that] along with the economic risk, she eludes the metaphysical risk of a freedom that must invent its goals without help" (de Beauvoir 2009: 10). There is a danger here of essentialising all men under the position of absolute corrupter/deceiver without respecting the power dynamics of the time and who were the ones subjecting and who they were subjecting.

Also there is a feeling that many of these feminists have a "cut off your nose to spite your face" mentality. They hate men so much that they have no desire to see or produce any benefit for them at all. What do I mean by this? I have heard women say that they do not want sexual liberation because men benefit from it. The way I see it, that would be like a slave saying they do not want emancipation because the slavemaster benefits more than the slave. You may say, in what ways? They no longer need to preserve and protect the slave. They no longer need to feed, house, and clothe them. They no longer need to pay for ownership of them. They no longer need to pay exorbitant fire insurance prices. They are no longer condemned by the North as slaveholders, et cetera. These benefit may have accrued to the former slaveholder but man would they rather have maintained slavery. Same with female sexual confidence, polyamory, sensual freedom, light exhibitionism, seductionism, and hypereroticism. Though obviously men gain certain small benefits from these and women gain only one, but like with slave emancipation that one is so big that it trumps the gains men get. Herein I see the anti-sex feminists as those who are trying to cut off their nose to spite their faces.

So, as godbodies we must now ask: Why have certain ideas become so widespread within certain social bodies, and what will be the circumstances of their decay or development? If all that is considered is the failings of a particular section of *al-mujtama* or the constructing of a group as absolute failure/evil as a reverse of having been constructed or marginalised by them as inferior, then the most that can occur is a reversal of circumstances where the oppressed (*mazlum*) become the oppressors of their former oppressors (like Marx's expropriation of the expropriators). Such may seem fitting but it will not be as fulfilling as hoped, it will inevitably only create an insatiable lust for more power until the pendulum swings back in favour of the former oppressors.

Furthermore, as the Quran continued, humanity's rebellion against Islam began with both Adam and Eve, saying: "But the devil made them [Adam and Eve] slip from it, and caused them to depart from the state in which they were. And We said: Go forth, some of you are the enemies of others. And there is for you in the earth an abode and a provision for a time. Then Adam received (revealed) words from his Lord, and He turned to him (mercifully). Surely He is Oft-returning (to mercy), the Merciful" (Quran 2: 36, 37). The symbolic and figurative nature of the Adam and Eve story does not diminish the value of it; Adam fell from Islam because of the devil, Adam rose back to Islam because of Allah's mercy.

This is a central distinction between the Islamic philosophy of man and the Christian. In Christianity humanity is born wicked because of Adam's sin and needs the coming of Jesus to be saved, in Islam Adam's sin affects only Adam and only for a brief moment until Allah forgives him, therefore humanity is neither born wicked nor in need of a saviour. *Al-Masih* came to redeem humanity from open rebellion to Allah, but such was a result of the devils' corrupting each of us individually through *shirk*. What the godbody perspective does is it exorcises the mysticism from Islam: a Muslim becomes simply anyone who believes in and teaches *tawhid* and a *Mushrik* becomes anyone who believes in and teaches *shirk*.

Nevertheless, as the purpose of the Adamic analogy was to explain to new generations that the Original people were Black people created (*khalaq*) by Allah in his own image, that also puts a twist to the Noah analogy too, where it says, "And it came to pass, when men began to multiply on the face of the earth, and daughters were born unto them, That the sons of God saw the daughters of man that they were fair [in Hebrew *towb*, literally meaning good, that is, good to look at, beautiful]; and they took them wives of all which they chose" (Genesis 6: 1, 2). If Adam was an Asiatic Black man then the daughters of Adam would have been beautiful Asiatic Black women, women that looked so good that even the angels were unable to resist them. In fact, in my opinion Allah only created the Black woman to show off.

Yet, as the Quran teaches, they were created for us. "And of His signs is this, that He created you from dust, then lo! you are mortals (who) scatter. And of His signs is this, that He created mates for you from yourselves that you might find quiet of mind in them, and He put between you love and compassion. Surely there are signs in this for a people who reflect" (Quran 30: 20, 21). Moreover, this love and compassion were never meant to simply be taken as sterile concepts but active realities within human affairs even as they were with the first couple. It is said in both the Bible and the Quran that Adam and Eve dwelt in Paradise before the fall, and that all their godly children will one day return to Paradise having completed their worldly travels. This Paradise, coming from the Hebrew Eden and Arabic Edin is, however, a lot more beautiful than most Christian interpretations have appreciated. Accordingly, the word Eden in Hebrew means voluptuous, luxuriant, and given to pleasures. Furthermore, its Hebrew root Adan means: ecstatic and pleasant. Even its feminine *Ednah* in its original Hebrew means ecstasy, voluptuousness, and pleasure; yet here it is in the *erotic* sense of the words.

Basically, what can be seen by a true definition of the word Paradise, in its Hebrew and Arabic original meanings is that it is more a place of delights, both sensual and spiritual, and all these are promised to the righteous children of Adam. But though it could now be said that we Black people hold a special place being the authentic children of Adam, in order to enter this Paradise we, and all humanity, will one day have to give an account of what we have done with the good Allah has given us, as it is said, "And surely We have honoured the children of Adam, and We carry them in the land and the sea, and We provide them with good things, and We have made them to excel highly most of those whom We have created. On the day when We shall call every people with their leader: then whoever is given his book in his right hand, these will read their book; and they will not be dealt with a whit unjustly." "So wait patiently for the judgment of thy Lord, and obey not a sinner or an ungrateful one among them. And glorify [*dhikr*] the name of thy Lord morning and evening" (Quran 17: 70, 71; 76: 24, 25).

III

On a deeper level, what all the above Scriptures are saying is what certain schools of psychology also teach: that remembrance (*dhikr*) of the Lover (al-Muhibb) can lead one into Paradise. While this conclusion is itself charged with affectivity, identifying its scientific externalities requires us to look deeper into psychology — and ultimately into the ontology of nature — before we can continue on articulating the variations within godbody sociology.

Interestingly, while it has been recognised in classical sociology that there must be a use of the terminology of other sciences for the purpose of communication, it has still been very difficult for most classical sociologists to accept the principles of other sciences, particularly the natural sciences. Nonetheless, I have taken three of depth psychology's concepts and applied them to sociology — which is a sociological anathema. This kind of scientific snobbery existing in sociology has no place in scientific exploration and does not exist in any of the natural sciences. For example, quantum physics sometimes uses ideas and theories from molecular physics, molecular physics sometimes uses ideas and theories from biophysics, and quantum physics sometimes uses ideas and theories from astrophysics and vice versa. Yet though sociology sometimes uses the terminology of anthropology, history, political science, jurisprudence, and economics it refuses to apply the pre-existing principles of biology, psychodynamics, or social psychology, or any elements from drive and striving theory.

In psychological study, as in sociological study, it is imperative to first choose a perspective from which to make our analysis. For godbody sociology it shall be the perspectives of depth psychology: in particular Freud and Adler; therefore if we hope to go any further in the godbody perspective it will be necessary to receive a brief grounding in Freudian and Adlerian theory and how they interconnect. To begin with, Freud saw all affectivity as discharges of sexual energy, that being the basis of how a person related to the world exterior to them. "For Freud, a person's interest in the world is a manifestation of his investing it with sexual energy, which he called *libido*. The world's ceasing to exist for a person and his withdrawal of libido from the world are, for Freud, two aspects of the same process" (Lear 1998: 133). Or basically, "The world exists because we invest it with sexual energy" (Lear 1984; quoted in Lear 1998: 140).

Lear could make such a statement based on his understanding of Freudian analysis, particularly of "primary narcissism" the state by which libido (*habba*) is invested in the self to create a self-identity, that is, primordial ego. However, the libido has an even greater personification within Black thearchism. Thereby the libidinal (*hubbiyya*) becomes the divine (*ilahani*), which is based on the very essence of Allah, the *Dhatullah*. Moreover, within Black thearchism the *Dhatullah* is based on the combining of three Greek concepts that are personified in the libido (*habba*): the erotic, the agapic, and the empathic. However, in Freudian theory, it is also through libido (*habba*) that an infant begins to differentiate itself from the world; but it is also understood that the same libido is then invested back into the world by the infant as a manifestation of divinity *(ilahaniyya). Again, this thesis was not to propose some complicated infantile masturbatory theory or to promote some paedophilic stimulation, it was developed to explain human psychic development.*

To Freud the libido (*al-habba*) was the sexual energy formulated by the sexual drive. Though the root of sexual energy may be located in the erotogenous zones – like the root of the nervous system is located in the brain and the root of the circulatory system is located in the heart – the hormonal distributions aroused by the pleasant sensations are relational to the endocrine system: the sexual drive itself, from whence the sexual energy derives, nevertheless, comes from the hypothalamic part of the brain. Obviously, to a prepubescent sexuality is an innocuous ideation; but that, however, does not negate the possibility of a prepubescent sexual drive. Again, "It seems probable that the sexual drive is in the first instance independent of its object; nor is its origin likely to be due to the object's attractions" (Freud 1981; quoted in Lear 1998).

The sexual drive is therefore independent of the sexual object it desires and so exists like other drives in the human body without any form of malicious or devious propositions. As an example, even before we learned how to use the toilet we had a drive to urinate; even before we learned the usefulness of food to our bodies and our lives we had a drive to eat; and even before we learned how to use language we had a drive to be social (Adler 1964). All these drives are improved by a family that invests love into the infant; the infant's response thus becomes clear, to invest libido (*habba*) back into the world it has come to differentiate from itself.

Sexual objectification is not necessarily a negative as such, at least in Freudian theory, investing sexual energy into something is to give it value, to internalise within the self that the object is meaningful. Interestingly, the discharge of sexual energy does not necessarily mean having sex with a sexual object, but simply agreeing that it is a pleasurable object, that it excites and stimulates your libido (*habba*). "For a person to be able libidinally to invest in an object, the object must be something *for* the person. The object must have psychic reality. This must be true even when the 'object' is the [ego] or the self" (Lear 1998: 134). During the developmental process a parent's or family member's display of love nurtures the infant and creates their first sexual object. Because an infant has no idea what sex is they manifest their sexual desire through archaic dreams – at least in Freudian theory. This sexual energy soon gets internalised as the infant learns to differentiate its primordial ego from the world outside of itself.

Sexual energy can be discharged without the act of sex or masturbation ever taking place. Conversely, when the infant's sexual object becomes the self, such does not lead to infantile masturbatory self-stimulation but to primary narcissistic development. Freud also "insisted that a developing infant must experience frustration if he is ever to perceive an independently existing world. ... And it is through all the frustrating descendants of [their] primal frustration that the world comes to have psychological reality for him" (Lear 1998: 157). For an infant to come to a point that they are able to differentiate themselves from an independently existing reality they have to go through a level of disappointment. They have to experience disappointment in order to develop the mental capacities, and the desire to develop the mental capacities, to overcome their disappointment.

This is a fundamental aspect of human development: the will, or as Freud called it, the death drive, and as Adler called it, the striving for power. It is the second product of the developmental process, even before the self-identity has been constructed and identified the striving for power is developed by the libido. This occurs usually when the object of the infant's affective desire is not immediately consumed by the infant, the frustration at trying to acquire or consume the object causes them to realise that they do not have the power to do whatsoever they want to do; their immediate response is a kind of inferiority feeling, which for the infant gets instantly translated into a striving for that power. All these affects – the frustration, the inferiority feeling, the perception of reality, the striving for power – occur at the speed of femtoseconds, making it impossible to decipher when one ends and the other begins.

Accordingly, Lear (1998: 165) presented a complete summarisation of the developmental process of an infant: "At the beginning of life there are no firm boundaries between self and world, nor are there firm boundaries between wishing and reality. The newborn's wishes suffice his 'world.' Each recognition of the mother's separateness is by its nature also of frustration and disappointment. In response the mother is taken in, but so are the child's wishes! For where they once held sway over the world, they are now evermore confined to the interior of the child's developing soul." It is at this point that the infant's sexual energy goes from being invested purely externally to being invested internally and the infant's sexual object goes from being the mother to being the self, i.e. narcissism.

Significantly, during all succeeding instances of the now narcissistic sexual energy being invested into an external sexual object the boundaries of differentiation again get severely blurred. According to Freud, in most romantic relationships, "we see that the object is being treated in the same way as our own [ego], so that when we are in love a considerable amount of narcissistic libido overflows on to the object. It is even obvious in many forms of love-choice that the object serves as a substitute for some unattained [superego] of our own" (Freud 1981; quoted in Lear 1998: 197). Thereby, sexual energy gets invested in the world outside of ourselves, outside of primary narcissistic libido, due to us seeing ourselves, whether our current selves or our ideal selves, in someone else.

The preceding ideas were all preliminary and necessary to fully understand and appreciate the Freudian system of developmental psychology, now we come to the crux of the matter. Libido or sexual energy is the central source of our affective disposition to the world, our sexual objects, being independent of our sexual drives, are malleable but when coupled with disappointment (or rejection) can cause mental interpretive development of the similitude to our archaic mental development. While in infancy the disappointment was advantageous in many ways, it is less so in adolescence and adulthood and may even be traumatic. In either case, it will produce change.

When our sexual drive desires a sexual object that it cannot attain the consequences could be very substantial, "we libidinally invest the world and it comes to have reality for us. Were we to withdraw libidinal investment in the world, it would come to an end (for us)" (Lear 1998: 139). The eschatological implications inherent in this statement impose a radical supposition: the End of the World – as well as any eschatological paradigm shifts – is an individually and socially experienced transition that occurs as a result of libidinal inhibition. *Habba* (libido) is thus a necessity if we are to avoid meaninglessness.

Consequently, Freud thus developed his libidinal theory into something all-encompassing:

> *'Libido is an expression taken from the theory of the emotions. We call by that name the energy, regarded as*

a quantitative magnitude (though not at present actually measurable), of those instincts which have to do with all that may be comprised under the word 'love.' The nucleus of what we mean by love naturally consists (and this is what is commonly called love, and what the poets sing of) in sexual love with sexual union as its aim. But we do not separate from this – what in any case has a share in the name 'love' – on the one hand, self-love, and on the other, love for parents and children, friendship and love for humanity in general, and also devotion to concrete objects and to abstract ideas. Our justification lies in the fact that psycho-analytic research has taught us that all these tendencies are an expression of the same instinctual impulses; in relations between the sexes these impulses force their way towards sexual union, but in other circumstances they are diverted from this aim or are prevented from reaching it, though always preserving enough of their original nature to keep their identity recognizable ..." (Freud 1981; quoted in Lear 1998: 140.)

Though sexual energy is the basis of libido the concept itself is far broader. Indeed, libido (*habba*) could in fact be considered a divine (*ilahani*) principle. Moreover, Allah's essence is considered to be *Habba* within this Black thearchic theory. Further, the vast majority of social relations between individuals and the world could actually be articulated as libidinal (*hubbiyya*); it is only when we come to social bodies that we reach a point of competitive – possibly even conflictual – articulation. While a person may individually invest the world with sexual energy a *mujtama* initially invests the world with personal aggrandizement, every social body (*mujtama*) gives itself a personal mission – we godbodies being no different – to define *al-'alam*. The social kinetics of in-group relations shows that though libidinal energy (*hubbiyya*) flows to the group and its members it is denied to out-group social bodies and individuals.

Such is the case because the stability of *al-mujtama* (the social body) is compromised by inter-group relations. Though not completely, sometimes there are alliances, unions, or mergers that transpire as a result of inter-group communication, such, however, is not the initial case and in the vast majority of inter-group relations the initial confrontation is usually hostile or non-hostile competition, each seeing itself as the superior social body. Once lines of communication are opened and offending systems and practices are removed or adjusted libidinal energy (*hubbiyya*) is then able to be transmitted to the second social body as to one's own. Such a transmission coincides with erotic agency as narcissistic libido can be coerced from a social body (*al-mujtama*) by erotic expropriation. Indeed, "in its origin, function, and relation to sexual love, the 'Eros' of the philosopher Plato coincides exactly with the love-force, the libido of psycho-analysis …" (Freud 1981; quoted in Lear 1998: 141).

If there is a Paradise in the universe then it is reached only through eroticism and its fulfilment is in orgasmic ecstasy. Erotic seduction is resoundingly affective and attracts the sexual drive, thereby blurring the boundaries of differentiation. As libido is coerced from the social body it effectively surrenders its offending qualities and attempts union with the second body. In both cases there is sacrifice and in both cases there is the expending of sexual energy, but the ultimate objective is inter-group unity and solidarity. Again, Lévi-Strauss (1972) theorised that the initial bond unifying the different tribes of antiquity was also sexual in nature, whether this is true or not sexuality is capable of playing an effective, and, indeed, affective, role in removing the differentiation between out-groups and the in-group. Furthermore, as Lear (1998: 153) stated, "if our tie to the world is genuinely erotic, we can no longer conceive the world as a mere receiver or inhibitor of our discharges. Love is not just a feeling or a discharge of energy, but an emotional orientation to the world." Thereby demonstrating that our opinions, ideologies, and perspectives of the world are determined, and can be changed, by our libidinal disposition.

While Freud's libido theory may have received heavy criticism: any truth (*haqiqa*) that offends is a truth (*haqiqa*) nonetheless. We can also see in it the substantiation of the Islamic belief that love, particularly the love between a man and a woman, that is, sexual love – not excluding homosexual love – is a sign from Allah. But humanity is not alone in possessing this kind of love, most mammals are both erotic and empathic. Indeed, according to Lear (1998: 147) Freud's theory of love "did not confine itself to the human soul; it was occurring throughout animate nature, even within a single living cell", thus reasoning that it transcends humanity and encompasses all organic life. There is no disagreement here with the Quran either, as it is written: "And there is no animal in the earth, nor a bird that flies on its two wings, but (they are) communities like yourselves. We have not neglected anything in the Book. Then to their Lord will they be gathered" (Quran 6: 38).

Basically, the breath of life of Genesis is not necessarily breath in the lungs, or even in the nostrils – though such has been used in conjunction with the breath of life (the word for nostril in Hebrew is *aph*, which can also mean face or forehead. This is interesting as the word translated as breath of life when it is used in conjunction with the word nostrils is *neshamah*, which actually means intellect or divine inspiration – as opposed to the word *ruakh*, which translates from the Hebrew as wind, breath, or spirit) – thus could in fact be very libido (*habba*) or libidinal energy (*hubbiyya*).

IV

As we now see, the godbody interpretation of the philosophy of man agrees in many ways with certain schools of scientific thought: (i) man has an organic relation to all living things which in essence contain a similar if not the same origin; (ii) the Original man was made of the same elements found in the earth; (iii) our earliest human ancestors were Black people; (iv) humanity, like all organic nature, has the spirit of life, which is libido; (v) the forces of nature (angels) are able to be mastered by humanity; and (vi) when the libido is inhibited the world becomes meaningless. Returning to the Quran we also find out that man was given authority in Quranic exegesis: "And when thy Lord said to the angels, I am going to place a ruler in the earth, they said: Wilt Thou place in it such as make mischief in it and shed blood? And we celebrate Thy praise and extol Thy holiness. He said: Surely I know what you know not." "And when We said to the angels, Be submissive to Adam, they submitted, but Iblis (did not). He refused and was proud, and he was one of the disbelievers" (Quran 2: 30, 34).

It is clear from these verses the eminence accorded to man by Allah in the Quran; as a result Islam sees man as the highest of Allah's creatures on the earth "a ruler in the earth" and as high also in the heavens "We said to the angels, Be submissive to Adam," even European humanism does not accord humanity so high a position (Shari'ati 1979). Again, the word translated in the verse above as ruler is the Arabic word *Khalifah*, which means successor, trustee, or viceregent. Therefore, "The same mission that God has in the cosmos, man must perform on the earth as God's viceregent. The first excellence that man possesses is, then, being God's representative on earth" (Shari'ati 1979: 73). The narrative of Adam, being an analogical symbol of humanity (Adam in both Hebraic and Arabic translates to Original humanity) imposes upon *al-nas* (the common humanity) the responsibility of trusteeship over the earth. In a sense, even from the origin Allah appointed Adam, and thereby the Original people, to be *darwishi* (poor, righteous, teachers), from whence we also get the term dervish.

Moreover, Shari'ati believed that man was distinguished from all other creatures under the sun by three qualifiers: (i) the breath of life, (ii) the *Khalifah*, and (iii) the Trust (*Amanah*) that Allah gave to Adam (which he believed to be the ability to go against our instinctual nature). It is written in the Quran, "Surely We offered the trust to the heavens and the earth and the mountains, but they refused to be unfaithful to it and feared from it, and man has turned unfaithful to it. Surely he is ever unjust, ignorant" (Quran 33: 72). This trust (*amanah*) that was given to man separates him from all things in heaven and on earth. However, as far as the ability to go against our instinctual nature, humanity is very instinctual, particularly in our affectivity, therefore I believe that the trust is actually the *Khalifah*. So, what actually distinguishes humanity from the animals in my opinion are three somewhat different qualifiers: (i) the *Khalifah* (which is our trusteeship), (ii) libidinal sublimation, and (iii) knowledge.

Perhaps the key attribute of man that separates him from all other species is knowledge. It is written, again, in the Quran: "And He taught Adam all the names, then presented them to the angels; He said: Tell Me the names of those if you are right. They said: Glory be to Thee! we have no knowledge but that which Thou hast taught us. Surely Thou art the Knowing, the Wise. He said: O Adam, inform them of their names. So, when he informed them of their names,

He said: Did I not say to you that I know what is unseen in the heavens and the earth? And I know what you manifest and what you hide" (Quran 2: 31-33). Like with Durkheim and Mauss (2009), the Quran therefore agreed that what distinguishes humanity as a species is our ability to classify and our ability to categorise.

We godbodies have, therefore, expanded this conception of classifying capacity into an internal striving for knowledge and a receptivity (*qabul*) to retain deep knowledge. Basically, to us godbodies humanity has an interaction with knowledge unavailable to any other creature. Knowledge is the key to our evolution (*takawwun*), once humanity began learning and mastering their surroundings, they became truly human. In fact, Homo sapiens is Latin for the thinking man, even as Homo habilis is for the handy man, Homo ergaster is for the working man and Homo erectus is for the upright man. The distinction of humanity from these earlier hominidae is thus our ability to acquire, develop, and apply knowledge.

Furthermore, the angels and *jinn* themselves are not as knowledgeable or intelligent as humanity. Indeed, they are relatively simplistic in comparison. They exist by the formula of love, peace, and happiness, which is why some of them fear humanity. We murder, oppress, torture, rape, abuse, and deceive. Such practices are unknown to the angels and are only used strategically among the *jinn*. Allah and the angels may be wise, but deep intelligence is a human phenomenon. Allah's omniscience is primarily a result of his omnipresence, which is really, again, just panopathic understanding. In this sense, Allah knows what digitised, materialised, and idealised beings could never know. Herein, Allah's knowledge may be considered primitive, and even simplistic, to our complex human minds, but it is still total and completely unfathomable.

Here is an interesting thought: Allah creates an artificial intelligence in a lower dimensional plane whose intelligence vastly exceeds anything that those on the higher dimensional planes could possibly comprehend. A section of those higher dimensional beings then rebel against Allah and his AI beings and begin a war with Allah and his AI beings because they feel superior to them. Hundreds of millennia later those same AI beings now create, on an even lower dimensional plane, their own artificial intelligences that vastly exceed even their own vast intelligence. If you can see the signs, it's like poetry it rhymes.

Now the word *scientia* is the Latin word for knowledge and intelligence, yet scientific elevation does not negate human artistic capabilities. The artistic and the cultural are just as unique to humanity as knowledge, though while other animals are able to learn (e.g. horses, dogs, beavers, and mites) their ability to enact cultural performances is purely instinctual, even when they perform a transformative of nature it is based entirely on instinct. Humanity, on the other hand, performs cultural and technical works based only to some degree on instinct. What really occurs, according to Freud, is that the instincts, effectively the sexual drives, get sublimated into something more socially acceptable.

In this, all the activities, all the achievements, all the progresses that have been made by humanity are a result of a moral dilemma: the desire to have continual sexual relations in a world that condemns, or at least deplores, those that do. When a bee or a beaver builds their constructions they are following their illimited instinctual drive to do so; when a person builds an architectural feature or a work of art it is because they are sublimating their delimited instinctual drive. Consequently, "Our greatest cultural achievements, Freud speculated, may be due to

[this] sublimation" (Lear 1998: 179); therefore, whereas it could be said that humanity possesses more knowledge (*'ilm*) and cultural genius (*al-daka al-thaqafi*) than the other animals, humanity is not as autonomous or as uninhibited.

But if such is true of our cultural and technical narratives and performatives could it not also be true of all cultures in general? Are all human *thaqafah* in fact just a sublimation of our instincts? If it is true then what is commonly considered the conscious mind is in fact a result of many generations of inhibitors – particularly European inhibitors – which have gained global credibility. Furthermore, the striving for power's elevation to the forefront of our conscious thinking is hereby shown to be the result of nothing more than the sublimation of our sexual energy.

The striving for power (which Freud called the Thanatos), according to Adler is the prerequisite of human psychological functioning, which is only beneficial so long as it is based upon the social interest. Adler, in his summation of psychological impetus, pointed out two potentially disconnected potentially interconnected drives in humanity, presenting his "evidence to show that the line of movement of human striving originates in the blending of social interest with the striving for personal superiority (Adler 1964: 145). These drives or motivations when they are interconnected (*tarabut*) influence a person toward socially progressive developments and are what I shall call the striving for empowerment.

Then again, "In all problem people, excluding the feeble-minded, we find that their goal of personal striving for power has miscarried but that all their movements are 'intelligent.' ... Accordingly they will lack the developed social interest and the courage which are necessary for the useful solution of the problems of life" (Adler 1964: 153). When the striving for power takes place without the social interest to chase it it is no longer the striving for empowerment but the striving for personal superiority. Again, if the social interest is really just another name for the *habba* (libido) then there is actually shown here a gradation of the *habba* within us.

The gradation system of the *habba* is a means of measuring an astral or social body's level of psychological stability, not based on normality, or what is commonly considered normal by societal standards, but what the conscious and unconscious mind strive for. (i) At the highest the *habba* is enacted as sexual exhibitionism, thus the superego becomes libidinal (*muhibb*) thereby allowing for the already libidinal (*hubbiyya*) instincts to have freedom of expression: at this level there could possibly even be a conscious or unconscious development of clairvoyance, clairsentience, clairaudience, or all three. (ii) When the *habba* has been sublimated by the striving for power then the astral forces of the individual or the social forces of the social group push them to strive for empowerment. (iii) When the striving for power begins to inhibit the *habba* then there is what Adler called the striving for personal superiority, which can manifest any one of these neurotic symptoms: megalomania/superiority complex, depression/hypersensitivity, phobia/anxiety, or all three. (iv) At the final stage the inhibition is significant and the striving for power becomes prohibitive to the *habba*, at this time any one of these three symptoms of psychoses may then become evident: delusions of grandeur, hallucinations, paranoia, or all three. (As a disclaimer I must mention that I am neither a doctor nor is this the opinion of any doctoral theorists; however, it is a first step towards a godbody psychology).

What transpires in the psychic figurations when different cultures are created (*khalaq*) is their libido usually gets sublimated and their striving for empowerment gets ameliorated, as this striving for empowerment usually means the empowerment of the social group (*al-mujtama*), the cultural parameters of the social group become more defined along with the empowering of the culture (*al-thaqafah*). It is written in the Scriptures concerning each culture: "… For everyone of you We appointed a law and a way. And if Allah had pleased He would have made you a single people, but that He might try you in what He gave you. So, vie one with another in virtuous deeds. To Allah you will all return, so He will inform you of that wherein you differed" (Quran 5: 48). Allah has thus appointed for each *thaqafah* its own structures and systems. Nevertheless, they are each based entirely on the level of striving for power. Low levels of this striving means they can focus on sexual emancipation, higher levels means the sexual drive of those in that *thaqafah* will be repressed by it.

V

As future generations join a new culture they will learn to exhibit, inhibit, or sublimate their sexual drives within the social body so as to attain social acceptance. Whereby we can see that the first inhibition of human sexual energy must have been the establishment of the patriarchy. Not to buy into the whole social evolution theory, especially as it always seems to favour White culture over all non-White cultures – I speak using the colonial definitions – but as one studies what we know of the pre-dynastic Egyptian and pre-dynastic Kushite cultures they were matriarchal long before they became patriarchal. If in fact the more ancient the culture the more matriarchal it was likely to be, then what took place to change that?

At this point an even more pertinent question would be: what is it that allowed the patriarchy, such a precarious and desultory form of governance, to maintain not only an existence but even a dominance in the world for so many thousands of years? Sexual inhibition to a certain degree answers that question. Although I cannot say I know the initial act that caused women to fall into subjection (and such has been an issue of debate since Europeans first discovered matrilineal tribes in the Americas) it is clear how the domination of women was maintained: by essentialising women as *nothing more than* sexual objects and then making sex and sexuality publicly taboo, thus men were able to prolong their domination over women. There are some obvious discrepancies though, a wife still has some influence over her husband – nevertheless, the dominance of man in general still proves the greater.

The inhibitive nature of the struggle of the sexes created the current repression of human libido. While the libido (*habba*) in itself is still the strongest force in all organic nature, including human nature; as the libido (*habba*) gets inhibited by Eurocentric trick knowledge, the striving for power innate within all human beings becomes the more dominant pursuit of conscious activity, diverting all the energies of our consciousness towards that end: in which case both inhibition and sublimation could be considered the cause of all European industriousness and cultural achievement. Albeit thanks to Eurocentric trick knowledge the libido (*habba*) is now substantially inhibited, thus they cannot genuinely be called alive, or at least not living with meaning, as without *habba* life has no meaning.

Not only so, but with the *habba* now given indirect outlets, precarious narratives like that of pan-European distinction, and objectionable performatives like those of slavery, colonisation, segregation, and criminalisation do and will manifest themselves more readily. That is not to say that all narratives are precarious or that all performatives are objectionable, just that while sexual sublimation may, on the one hand, be the cause of some of our greatest feats and triumphs; sexual inhibition and sexual repression could be the cause of some of our most unfortunate and unnecessary failures. All human systems may in fact be indirect exhibitions of human sexuality, therefore by deploring direct sexual exhibitionism, the *mujtama* – that is the patriarchal *mujtama* – has created so many unnecessary systems and institutions. Very few systems have really been of any serious benefit to humanity thereby making most of them in a genuine sense meaningless.

Another interesting question arises from the matrix: what allows a social system to move beyond the transient and so perpetuate itself? The reason for this question should be evident to anyone who has been paying attention to what has been written so far: if the patriarchy, an obvious form of male-domination, has been able to endure for thousands of years virtually unchallenged with only minor pockets of matriarchal revival in some African, Native American, and pagan cultures, while on the whole, the world, including those very cultures, have only been getting more patriarchal, how do we keep White supremacy, an obvious form of White-domination, from also lasting thousands of years, while, at the same time, fighting against the patriarchy?

These issues are of great importance within Islam as it was commanded of Allah: "And fight in the way of Allah against those who fight against you but be not aggressive. Surely Allah loves not the aggressors. And kill them wherever you find them, and drive them out from where they drove you out, and persecution is worse than slaughter. And fight not with them at the Sacred Mosque until they fight with you in it; so if they fight you (in it), slay them. Such is the recompense of the disbelievers. But if they desist, then surely Allah is Forgiving, Merciful. And fight them until there is no persecution, and religion is only for

Allah. But if they desist, then there should be no hostility except against the oppressors" (Quran 2: 190-193).

Although such a message may sound too violent for our oversensitive, "turn the other cheek" ears, we are still willing to let the police and the military use violence in the way of preserving White society and for the cause of White society. What the Prophet was basically saying was that we instead should be willing to use violence to fight for our own society and against all aggressive and oppressive systems that may arise in our society. Indeed, it has been incumbent upon all Muslims to fight against oppression since the time of the Prophet. Thus, giving Islam an actual history of fighting against oppression and persecution.

In this case, we may now need to ask: how were the male chieftains, kings, Pharaohs, and Amirs able to hold back the female population, who at that time held all the secrets to knowledge, science, mysteries, and mysticism? Are White people able to do the same thing they did? And, if they are how can we stop them? These are all issues to be studied in social dynamics, which analyses the beginnings and endings of various social bodies. The study of social dynamics, just like the other methods of social mechanics, is based on formulaic computation and application. As mathematics works on the principle of formulae – once the correct formula has been discovered and applied any problem can be solved, but if an incorrect, inappropriate, or unfruitful formula is applied it will only lead to confusion, or worse, deception – so the branches of social mechanics are formulae for solving social problems.

Looking at social mechanics allows us to develop from an infinitude of non-linear events and ideas a curvilinear progression from idea to event to new idea to new event. Thereby, in considering what we have been discussing so far, whereas with the patriarchy we may not know the exact cause of the male rise to power we are able to define a veritable concatenation with regard to White supremacy to devise theoretically the circumstances under which White people rose to power. If we consider the history of European and pan-European domination certain historical events become evident: Europe before the Renaissance was going through its Dark Ages, what the Renaissance did for Europe was to give to Europeans a unified identity and a common enemy in the Muslims. That is not to say there was no internal conflict, the Northern Renaissance is commonly known as the Reformation, in which many northern European countries separated from the Catholic Church, instigating in some cases all-out war.

Nevertheless both Catholics and Protestants were united against the Muslims – whether the Muslim was Turk, Arab, Indian, or Moor – thus the climax of the Renaissance was *the enslavement of West Africans in 1441* and its justification in 1442 by Pope Eugene IV as anti-Muslim heroics. Popes Nicholas V, Sixtus IV, and Innocent VIII continued the anti-Muslim rhetoric instigating in Spain and Portugal a Reconquest, the culmination of which occurred in the early 1490s when the last of the African Moors were expelled from Spain, an event that was epilogued by Columbus' voyage to find the east of India. Indeed, the desire to find a back way to India was in itself nothing more than the result of his own anti-Muslim and anti-pagan proclivities: Columbus was a would-be Crusader, as were all the Conquistadors and the Reconquistadors; he set out to find a back way to the East coast of India as a spy for appropriate attack positions. Any form of slavery that was inflicted was justified by the Popes so long as it was against a non-Christian, and Luther had no argument with this kind of slavery either.

From these humble positions Europe began its rise to domination, these are the events that began White supremacy. Prior to the Renaissance, the Reconquest, and the Trans-Atlantic Slave Trade; Africa and Asia were not going through Dark Ages like Europe was but were going through a period of immense enlightenment. Europe's enlightenment, which came over 200 years later, was based on lessons stolen and sometimes even plagiarised from Muslim intellectuals who wrote during Europe's Dark Ages. Europe was never able to compete with the Muslim world until they adopted Muslim systems such as Hindu-Arabic numerals, the Islamic algebraic systems, Muslim chemistry, Muslim economics, Muslim geography, and Muslim astronomy.

Both Copernicus and Newton owed their knowledge of the motion of the planets to studies done originally by Islamic scholars like ibn Sina. But if Islam was the then dominant culture why was it surpassed by Europe during the 1700s and the European Enlightenment? And what has caused White people to maintain a form of supremacy ever since? Again, according to the Quran, "Allah never changes a favour which He has conferred upon a people until they change their own condition – and because Allah is Hearing, Knowing" (Quran 8: 53).

The European gained and maintained supremacy because the non-Europeans changed their condition; but that is only because White people demoralised and devalued them in a similar fashion to what was done to women. First, the so-called Negro, as Fanon said, for "the majority of white men ... represent[ed] the sexual instinct (in its raw state). The Negro is the incarnation of a genital potency beyond all moralities and prohibitions" (Fanon 2008: 136). This stereotype was created by various White explorers and intellectuals due to the freedom and exhibitionism of the African *thaqafah fariyya* they encountered. According to

Fanon there exists to the White man, "Two realms: the intellectual and the sexual" (Fanon 2008: 127).

It was mainly by relegating the so-called Negro to the sexual realm, while, at the same time, devaluing sexuality, that White people were able to create the fiction of our racial inferiority; and though, "One can hear the glib remark: The Negro makes himself inferior … the truth is that he is made inferior" (Fanon 2008: 115). Yet, though such was true for the so-called Negro it was soon expanded to all Muslims as Said also noted, to the post-Enlightenment European, "An Oriental lives in the Orient, he lives a life of Oriental ease, in a state of Oriental despotism and sensuality, imbued with a feeling of Oriental fatalism" (Said 2003: 102). Effectively, the discourse of White superiority was always based on making the non-White an inferior player.

As we read earlier, Said presented a good argument with respect to Orientalism and its effect inside and outside the West: "My contention is that without examining Orientalism as a discourse one cannot possibly understand the enormously systematic discipline by which European culture was able to manage – and even produce – the Orient politically, sociologically, militarily, ideologically, scientifically, and imaginatively during the post-Enlightenment" (Said 2003: 3). Said also explicated how the transmutation of typology into stereotype took place in Europe with regard to the Oriental. Yet if this is the case for the Oriental it was even more so the case for the Black, "In Europe the Negro has one function: that of symbolizing the lower emotions, the baser inclinations, the dark side of the soul", "the Negro is only biological. The Negroes are animals. They go about naked" (Fanon 2008: 147, 127). Thus, White supremacy is maintained first through devaluing sex, then by sexualising the other, whether it be women or Blacks. What is therefore needed is not the desexualisation of the other as such, but the revaluing of sexuality.

Notwithstanding, the Quran opens up new levels of racial interpretation worthy of our investigation, as the Prophet said, "And of His signs is the creation of the heavens and the earth and the diversity of your tongues and colours. Surely there are signs in this for the learned" (Quran 30: 22). Almost with a sense of irony this argument is presented to the learned, who in modern times, that is late modernity, seem to be in a controversy over the "race relations problematic." What the Prophet hereby showed was that the problem is not, and never was, racial categorisation, the racialisation of different human peoples; the problematic stems from racial stratification, the hierarchical arrangement of races into ascending layers.

Although most late modern social thinkers argue that the problematic lies in racial categorisation and the distinguishing of the biological, that is, physiological, differences between us, this Quranic statement showing that the different racial categories are a sign from Allah forces godbody sociology to look deeper. Though such evidence as Quranic exegesis will not be enough for a scientific mind I will begin here to illuminate the historical distinction between modern and Islamic thinking. Shari'ati said on the subject, "Why is Islam, despite the lack of any capital investment or propaganda, so popular among African blacks? Because Islam is an ideology. What kind of an ideology? Whatever the black man's needs are. What are his needs? Freedom from discrimination and his longing for human equality" (Shari'ati 1981: 1932). Islam was able in its earlier years to encourage the brotherhood of all people and to embrace many races without disempowering or subjugating any for the sake of their racial differences, in spite of having a quasi-racial categorisation system, because they saw what we would call racial distinction as a sign from Allah. In fact, the racism many Arabs now possess comes primarily from Western education, whether directly or indirectly.

One of the central arguments presented by academics and social thinkers against racial categorisation is that the classical and the scientific race theorists who initially attempted to categorise the races could never agree on the number of races. While such is a cute reason it is far from scientific and seems more lazy than thorough. Class is a categorisation system just as "socially constructed" as race, just as hierarchical as race, and just as controversial as race (most social scientists have not agreed on the number of classes or, indeed, the description of what constitutes a class, or what constitutes the existing classes of late modernity), yet the vast majority of social scientists (*al-'ulamaa al-ijtima'iyya*) and academics (*al-daki*) recognise the need for identifying class distinction and using such to explain social reality (*al-haqiqa al-ijtima'iyya*).

VI

What we can ultimately understand is that knowledge brought forth Adam's greatest exaltation and knowledge brought forth his greatest failure, Allah trusted Adam with knowledge of self and thereby made him his *Khalifah* but Adam, through trick knowledge, fell, together with his wifey, from all that grace and abundance, having been corrupted by the prideful Iblis. And so "he caused them to fall by deceit. So, when they had tasted of the tree, their shame became manifest to them, and they both began to cover themselves with the leaves of the garden [Jennah]. And their Lord called to them: Did I not forbid you that tree, and say to you that the devil is surely your open enemy? They said: Our Lord, we have wronged ourselves; and if

Thou forgive us not, and have (not) mercy on us, we shall certainly be of the losers" (Quran 7: 22, 23).

Notice that in the Quran they did not blame Allah, saying, "You made us like this," "You made our circumstances like this," or "You made the world like this." Nor did they say, "It is not our fault for, 'His is whosoever is in the heavens and the earth. All are obedient to Him' (Quran 30: 26) therefore we are not to blame." Neither did Adam blame the woman, saying, "It was 'The woman whom thou gavest to be with me' (Genesis 3: 12) that caused me to fall." Instead they were wise enough to seek mercy after their fall; and as they sought mercy, even so they received mercy, "Then Adam received (revealed) words from his Lord, and He turned to him (mercifully). Surely He is Oft-returning (to mercy), the Merciful. We said: Go forth from this (state) all. Surely there will come to you a guidance from Me, then whoever follows My guidance, no fear shall come upon them, nor shall they grieve" (Quran 2: 37, 38). Blame and irresponsibility pepper the biblical story of Adam and Eve but not the Quranic. Furthermore, guidance is promised to those who accept Allah's teachings.

When knowledge comes from Allah it completes us just as it completed Adam, but when we forget the teachings taught us by Allah we become vulnerable to trick knowledge; again just like Adam, "Supremely exalted then is Allah, the King, the Truth. And make not haste with the Qur'an before its revelation is made complete to thee, and say: My Lord, increase me in knowledge. And certainly We gave a commandment to Adam before, but he forgot; and We found in him no resolve" (Quran 20: 114, 115). Thus, Adam's fall was more an issue of forgetting the knowledge he gained from Allah's teaching, and his trusting in the *tricknology* he gained from his enemy, than of his eating a fruit in the eternal Jennah.

Indeed, Iblis has always been an enemy of Adam, as it was written, "He said: O Iblis, what is the reason that thou art not with those who make obeisance? He said: I am not going to make obeisance to a mortal, whom Thou hast created of sounding clay, of black mud fashioned into shape." Again, when asked the reason he would not make obeisance to Adam Iblis did not say, "And whoever is in the heavens and the earth makes obeisance to Allah only" (Quran 15: 32). It says in the Quran, "He said: What hindered thee that thou didst not submit when I commanded thee? He said: *I am better than he*; Thou hast created me of fire, while him Thou didst create of dust" (Quran 33; 13: 15; 7: 12; emphasis mine). Herein, the reason for the fall of Iblis, and of humanity, was racism. Iblis felt superior to Adam and so became a sworn enemy of Adam.

Moreover, the Prophet also recognised a preordained aspect to this racial heterogeneity, saying, "O mankind, surely We have created you a male and a female, and made you tribes and families that you may know each other…" (Quran 49: 13). Nevertheless, to present a tabular image of the hierarchical structure of the current racial categories of our time, they are, in ascending order: (i) Blacks: the people of African and Aboriginal descent; (ii) Browns: the Muslim and Hindu people of Near Eastern and South Asian descent; (iii) Red Indians: the people of Native American, Meso-American, and Latin American descent (though most people call Latin Americans Brown such a misnomer is unfeasible as most Latin Americans are descended from Native or Meso-Americans who were either raped by their oppressors or forced to adopt their oppressors language); (iv) so-called Yellow people: the people of Mongol, Indochinese, Polynesian and Far East Asian descent; and at the apex (v) Whites: the people of European and Caucasian descent.

Within each racial group but the Blacks there is a belief that Black is the lowest level. There is not a place on this planet, not even in Africa, where Black people are not classed as lesser than the non-Black inhabitants. At the same time, in each racial grouping but the Blacks there is also a belief that White is superior, to the point that each racial group but the Blacks classifies themselves as White in their own country. Invariably, we Black people have an inauspicious position in *al-'alam*, in *al-mujtama*, and in *al-fikr*, a position that we are constantly fighting to oppose with insurmountable odds measured against us. Again, with these situations the problematic is not in the category Black, or in the other categories (*qisman*) used to define other racial groups, but in the hierarchy, which is itself rooted in what I theorise to be a *global White neurosis* that goes all the way back to Iblis himself.

It must be stated to qualify this statement, first of all, that not every White person suffers from this global neurosis but every White person is affected by it and has a high potential of acquiring it. Second, White people did not always have a global neurosis but at one time suffered from global psychoses which was even worse. The distinction between the two is that pre-Enlightenment White people were more adventurous and a lot less scientific, as they became less adventurous, by an Adlerian definition, they became more neurotic. And as the Prophet said, "… Surely Allah changes not the condition of a people, until they change their own condition. And when Allah intends evil to a people, there is no averting it, and besides Him they have no protector" (Quran 13: 11).

The European psychosis pre-Enlightenment should be obvious to anyone who studies European history: delusions of grandeur with a sense of Christian destiny; paranoia in launching a million and one crusades against Islam which predominantly failed; and hallucinations (an idea that is proven in that the apparitions, voices, and miracles that would canonise saints, during those times, were usually racist and Islamophobic, and thus were pseudo-spiritual). Yet by a Freudian definition psychosis does not come from heredity or subjectivity but from traumata. As we have already articulated, the origin of the three pan-European traumas began before they scattered to several different continents, that is, their traumas began at the time of the Renaissance.

The current global White neurosis is not the result of a new trauma but the result of gaining too small a level of *habba* during the Enlightenment. The level of *habba* was somewhat insignificant or at least incapable of overcoming their collective striving for power, called by Freud the death instinct, therefore their hallucinations subsided only slightly becoming depression or hypersensitivity, their paranoia diminished only slightly becoming phobia or anxiety, and their delusions of grandeur morphed into their megalomania and superiority complex. Again, this is not global *individual* neuroses but a *global collective neurosis*; individual Whites may manifest non-neurotic symptoms but as a collectivity their history and present manifests neuroses. Basically, as a global body White people have a collective neurosis and manifest symptoms of neurotic behaviour, which can be dangerous for both themselves and for those global bodies othered by them.

As Adler commented, "In a neurotic we are always confronted with a highly placed goal of personal superiority. … That such a highly placed goal of personal superiority betokens a lack of the proper measure of social interest and precludes the development of a healthy interest in others is understandable. The striving for personal superiority and the nondevelopment of social interest are both mistakes.

However, they are not two mistakes which the individual has made; they are one and the same mistake" (Adler 1964: 240). Consequently, what Adler called the social interest I have chosen to call the libido (*habba*), and as the pan-European has a discourse of White superiority, they, as a race, have a global neurosis.

That is not to say that a form of neurosis, or at least sexual sublimation, does not exist between all social bodies when they first encounter another social body, however, this inhibition or sublimation is diminished as libidinal (*hubbiyya*) repressions are removed. *Habba* unbounds all demarcations and illimits solidarity between the two social bodies. On the other hand, though they may not recognise it, White people in general have a superiority complex, denoting neurosis. Yet, a White person could always say that I (Shahidi Islam) am in no position to diagnose what I believe to be neurotic symptoms as I am no doctor and have neither studied nor seen an actual manifestation of genuine neuroses. They could say all my knowledge is book knowledge, and that as I am no student of psychology I have no place commenting on White actions and behaviours as though I were an expert. To them I would say I have been researching psychoanalysis independently since 2003, that is long enough to be neither a novice nor an amateur, also I will say that all the information I express concerning White people is highly documented.

While White *habba* may individually be either exhibited, sublimated, or inhibited in their interactions with non-White individuals, the *habba* of the *global body* of White people is undeniably inhibited with regard to the other races and has been for centuries. On top of that, a section of White people have a tendency to this day to carry around the effects of one of the three traumas mentioned earlier: the fear of Black and Muslim sexual behaviours and anatomies. While personally an *individual* may never have seen either, the fear of both still remains strong within the global unconscious, particularly toward the Black. Moreover, as Fanon articulated, in spite of the fact that the Ashkenazi "is feared because of his potential for acquisitiveness. ... As for the Negroes, they have tremendous sexual powers"; "here the Negro is master. He is the specialist of this matter: Whoever says *rape* says Negro" (Fanon 2008: 121, 127).

Not that Black people are naturally any better in bed than any other race, but the fear, and therefore the hope, is there: "That is because the Negrophobic woman is in fact nothing but a putative sexual partner – just as the Negrophobic man is a repressed homosexual" (Fanon 2008: 121). Negrophobia and Islamophobia are directly related to the fear of violence but indirectly related to sexual desire. While Fanon's homosexual theory may be taking it a little too far, the centuries of raping the Black woman belie the White man's inhibited desire for the Black woman. In this case, though sex is had it is not done libidinally but aggressively; it is a result of striving for personal superiority-cum-dominance.

The sexual desire for the Black man and the Black woman creates their actually existing Negrophobia (that is not to say all White people are Negrophobic, or even the majority of White people are, but most Black men can relate, when walking down the street during the day in front of a White woman who suddenly grips tight to her handbag, or the look of disgust on the White man's face as a pair of Black women hold a conversation on a bus) which contributes to the lowly position of Black people in the racial stratification system. On the one hand, sex is inhibited in White society; on the other hand, sex with a Black person is out of the question for those individuals.

These factors also affect their psychological disposition, "when a white man hates black men, is he not yielding to a feeling of impotence or of sexual inferiority?" (Fanon 2008: 122). Negrophobia, as a symptom of their global neurosis, is in fact a result of an inferiority feeling that triggers an overcompensating in the area of study, the fabled mind/body dichotomy in which White people are the mind and Black people are the body; as Fanon delineated, "There is one expression that through time has become singularly eroticized: the black athlete. There is something in the mere idea, one young woman confided to me, that makes the heart skip a beat. A prostitute told me that in her early days the mere thought of going to bed with a Negro brought on an orgasm" (Fanon 2008: 122).

Another aspect of global White neurosis is White hypersensitivity, which manifests itself as a response to White guilt. This is where White people take offence at us Black people using broad generalisations (*'umumai*) to describe our subjugation and believe that not all White people are to be blamed for the current Black predicament and that we Black people must take responsibility for our own actions. To challenge this perception I shall use, again, the analogy of the human body: a single cell may not know the plans of the brain but being a part of the body its complicity is implied. An individual cell may feel like it cannot destroy the whole body by its actions, but by the simple act of "doing its job" it serves as a means of perpetuating the body and thereby the actions of the body. Indeed, does not a cancer begin with just a single cell?

At the same time, a single cell may think it is doing great harm to the body when in reality it is only providing a mild form of irritation, while, still perpetuating and benefiting from the same body it believes itself to be damaging. The same can be true even with a global body like the White race: if the whole global body reproduces and benefits from the system of White supremacy then even if one White person or a few individual White people disagree with it, by them doing nothing more than holding up a picket sign to fight against that White supremacy they are actually just perpetuating it with something so simple as "doing their job." Herein, if a body as a whole is privileged then the body as a whole is implicated in reproducing and benefiting from the system that privileges it, even if its individual cells are disconnected from the centres of power. So, like it or not every White person, who is born into privilege regardless of how rich or poor their individual circumstances, must therefore eventually find their own way of responding to the actuality of their White privilege, which will determine their judgment when their book of life is opened.

Those Whites who are incapable of seeing White privilege – having unconsciously adopted White hyper-sensitivity – instead view the body of White people, at least in our time, as innocent of any wrongs done historically by their ancestors, and as benefiting from personal grit (something that must therefore be inherent to most White people in order to explain so much White success stories). Those Whites who can appreciate that while the rhetoric is less racially charged and the institutions are less racially homogenous, the superiority complex has become internalised and the biases have become more inherent, and put their reputation and *their lives* on the line to change these circumstances – as knowledge without action is useless – are genuinely anti-racists and are worthy of a just narrative in their own book of life.

As the reader may have surmised, I do not take issue with the creation of racial *qisman* for the different races, I take issue with the hierarchical system of stratification implicit in the *qisman* (categories). I do not personally feel the Boasian denial of races is helpful in confronting the issue, in fact, it may turn out to be more fallacious to the overcoming of racism in the long run as it ultimately blinds White people to White privilege. The Prophet said again on the subject, "And for every nation there is a messenger. So, when their messenger comes, the matter is decided between them with justice, and they are not wronged" (Quran 10: 47). This philosophy allowed the Muslims of the Middle Ages to live relatively peacefully in the communities they inhabited, without domineering over the people of different faiths, that they called the *dhimmi*.

As noted, the racial hierarchy came about in an historical context as a result of the global White psychosis of the Renaissance, in order to insist a position of superiority to the other races, thus they had to prove, at least to themselves, that the closer a racial group was to the White paradigm the more likely it was to be beholden to superior qualities. Though the intermediary *qisman* varied based on the theorist, as Blacks were the furthest racially from Whites, they were naturally considered the most inferior by all classical and "scientific" standards of race theory; for which cause, in Fanon's eyes, "Ontology ... does not permit us to understand the being of the black man. For not only must the black man be black; he must be black in relation to the white man ... [that is] in conflict with a civilization that he did not know and that imposed itself on him" (Fanon 2008: 82).

Yet the conflict was not a clear Black and White conflict for Fanon, who "took the discussion of race to a very different place from that which UNESCO" and the Boasian school desired: "Race still had a place for Fanon insofar as it could contribute to the overcoming of racism" (Bernasconi 2011: 92). What anthropology was attempting to do by "passing the buck" to biology, and biology in denying outright its scientific validity was to cover over the sins of old Europe; this social absolution provided by science, absolving Europe of responsibility for the crimes of Nazism, where science and racism went completely hand in hand, was a pseudo-absolution, an absolution by denial of responsibility. Instead of acknowledging the real sin (the delusions of grandeur on the part of the Nazis) they denied the existence of the real sin and acknowledged the method of its justification as the real sin.

On a deeper level, the symptom, if that was acknowledged, would have shown the real root of the problem to be a superiority complex stretched to its furthest limits: a Nazi collective psychosis. It must also be remembered that the sense of destiny acquired by the Nazis against Ashkenaz was a hugely deluded and demented development based on some assumed persecution by the Ashkenazi. The superiority they ascribed to themselves was crushed by the trauma of having lost in World War I, thus to compensate they, firstly, created the invisible enemy, and, secondly, expanded their internal sense of destiny. Science only became a tool to verify their delusions, in which case science was not the problem, race theory was not the problem, the problem was the delusions of grandeur.

Fanon took as a given the White feelings of racial and cultural supremacy, yet he also foresaw the demise of both in the post-colonial realities then beginning to emerge. Such a politics called for a new evaluation of the theories being employed, not least of all the racial theories. "However, Fanon was not about to declare the advent of a postracial society. As he emphasized in 'Racism and Culture,' his speech to the First Congress of Negro Writers and Artists delivered in 1956, the way forward was not to abandon race, to deracialize (*déracialiser*) oneself ... He knew that the effects of past racism remained and that, for all the exceptions, 'what divides this world is first and foremost what species, what race one belongs to'" (Bernasconi 2011: 91).

VII

The purpose of this chapter has been to reflect on the constitution of godbody sociology and what makes it fundamentally an Islamic sociology. As we can see from all this, Islam is beyond what we can describe with human words, and that it takes a special tongue, one of divine origin, to speak the words of Islam. Yet there have been many to do just that. True Adam was the first human Muslim, *Khalifah*, and *Nabi* (prophet), but in a technical sense every prophet was also a Muslim and a *Khalifah*. This is the area of prophethood (*nubuwwa*), that state that is beyond what we in our time are able to reach. Indeed, the ancient prophets were guides and showed us how to find truth: for this cause we seek Allah, not in new *anbiya* (prophets) or in new *nubuwwat* (prophecies) but in the fulfilment of his truth (*haqiqa*). Indeed, the *haqiqa* of Allah is Allah himself. Allah is *al-haqiqa al-mutlaq* (the Absolute Truth and the Absolute Reality). Beyond Allah there is nothingness, yet, at the same time, Allah reaches into nothingness and pulls out creation.

It is written in the Quran, "And there is not a thing but with Us are the treasure of it" (Quran 15: 21). Again, there are many treasures in heaven and on earth, but we shall focus now on the treasury of imagination (*khizanat al-khayal*). Ibn al-Arabi spoke of three forms of imagination (*khayal*): non-delimited imagination (*al-khayal al-mutlaq*), objective imagination (*al-khayal al-munfasil*) and subjective imagination (*al-khayal al-muttasil*). *Al-khayal al-mutlaq* is also called the astral world (*al-'alam ul-ma'nawi*), while *al-khayal al-munfasil* is the physical world (*al-'alam al-hissi*) and *al-khayal al-muttasil* is the imaginal world (*al-'alam al-khayali*). Each of these worlds are encompassed in the *tawhid* even as Allah is Lord of all worlds (*Rabi 'alamin*). Moreover, each of these universes are parts of the body of Allah while the face of Allah could be called *al-Dhatullah*.

Again, as Allah is the Real or the True (*al-Haqq*), his thoughts are a reality unto themselves. But some of what Allah imagines he then brings to life. It is written, "Our word for a thing, when We intend it, is only that We say to it Be; and it is" (Quran 16: 40). Allah adds being to his intentions by taking of his own Being, even as he is the Supreme Being (*al-Mawjud*). Ibn al-Arabi said, "God made imagination a light through which the assumption of forms by all things – whatever it might be, as we said – may be perceived. Its light penetrates into sheer nonexistence and gives it the form of an existence" (Ibn al-Arabi 1972; quoted from Chittick 1989: 122). Allah, who is Existence/Being (*al-Wujud*) injects being into his intention by saying to it "Be!"

Allah is Existence (*Wujud*) in its raw estate. Allah is also the *Haqq* (the Real or the True), even as it is written, "And We created not the heavens and the earth and what is between them but with truth [*haqq*]" (Quran 15: 85). What we can see from this is that Allah took of himself as *al-Haqq* to create the physical universe. As noted, the universe (*al-'alam*) is effectively the body of Allah. The *'alam* itself is, however, in a state between existence (*wujud*) and nonexistence (*'adam*) called becoming (*takawwun*). Even deeper still, between *wujud* and *takawwun* there is another *barzakh*, what ibn al-Arabi called the Supreme Barzakh. It stands between the Real and the coming to be. It is the realm of non-delimited imagination (*al-khayal al-mutlaq*) that many scientists call the astral plane and that the ancient people used to call the heavens.

Basically, in the beginning was Allah, the *Haqq*. The *Haqq* had a thought, *al-khayal al-mutlaq*. As it was his thought it was close to his reality, though it did not exist in existence as the only existent thing (*al-wahad al-mawjud*) was Allah. Then Allah said to some of his thoughts, "Be!" and they came to be, thus they became his creation (*al-khalq*). However, none of those thoughts came to be immediately. In fact, their coming to be was and is a process. Nothing comes to be, fully developed. Everything evolves till it becomes what it was supposed to be. Thus, the realm of Being is the Real (*al-Haqq*), the realm of non-delimited imagination is the Astral Realm (*al-haqiqat ul-ma'nawi*), the realm of constant evolution is the physical universe (*al-'alam al-hissi*), and the realm of personal thought is the subjective imagination (*al-khayal al-muttasil*). Each *barzakh* containing its own rules, its own laws, and is a part of the body of Allah.

William Chittick said on the subject of the law that, "The Law is an outward dimension (*zahir*) of the Reality, while the Reality (*haqiqa*) is the inward dimension (*batin*) of the Law" (Chittick 1989: 260). Indeed, ibn al-Arabi said, "The Shari'a is identical with the Reality" (Ibn al-Arabi 1972; quoted from Chittick 1989: 260). Yet as we have said in previous chapters there are two kinds of commands that come from Allah: the engendering command (*al-amr al-takwini*) and the prescriptive command (*al-amr al-taklifi*). Based on this understanding there are also two kinds of Shari'a: *al-Shari'at u'llah* (the Laws of God) and *al-shari'at ul-nabu* (the laws of a prophet). Like the *amr al-takwini* the *Shari'at u'llah* cannot be broken. Some call it the laws of physics, some the laws of nature, but either way they are the laws of Allah. However, just like the *amr al-taklifi* the *shari'at ul-nabu* are prescriptive and while they can be disobeyed such is not recommended. The *shari'at ul-nabu* provide the best ways to fulfil the *Shari'at u'llah*, therefore it is beneficial to walk in them.

Nevertheless, there have been many *anbiya* (prophets) all of them with methods for their own time on how to fulfil the divine Shari'a. In our time we have the *'ulamaa* (scholars) who can tell us what the divine Shari'a is in more conclusive terms. The scholars have the words of all the *anbiya* and the lessons of former scholars throughout history. Through these they have been able to narrow down the *Shari'at u'llah* into twelve Universal Laws of Existence (*Shari'at ul-kulliyya al-wujud*):

1. The *law of interaction (whose corollary is the pleasure principle)*,
2. The *law of intersubjectivity (whose corollary is the vibratory law)*,
3. The *law of self-organisation (whose corollary is the identity law)*,
4. The *law of opposition (whose corollary is the feedback law)*,
5. The *law of repetition (whose corollary is the inertia law)*,
6. The *law of self-similarity (whose corollary is the correspondence law)*,
7. The *law of conservation (whose corollary is the reciprocity law)*,
8. The *law of evolution (whose corollary is the power law)*,
9. The *law of devolution (whose corollary is the entropy law)*,
10. The *law of self-destruction (whose corollary is the phase-transition law)*,
11. The *law of interconnectivity (whose corollary is the synchronicity law)*, and
12. The *law of interrelation (whose corollary is the eternalist law)*.

And again, like with the *amr al-takwini* these *Shari'at ul-kulliyya* (Universal Laws) cannot be broken, therefore they are not only the laws of the Supreme Barzakh but are also the laws of the entire *khalq*.

Yet within the reality of these *Shari'at ul-kulliyya* can also come miraculous abilities (*karamat*). Within cultural Islam there are four main types: *panopathy* (*al-rahma al-mutlaq*), which comes by mastering the second Universal Law of Existence; acting through resolve (*al-fi'l bi'l-himma*), which is another way of saying telekinesis and comes by mastering the third Universal Law of Existence; manifesting into engendered existence (*takwin*), which comes by mastering the eleventh Universal Law of Existence; and supersensory perception (*ma'nawi idrak*), which comes by mastering all twelve Universal Laws of Existence. While these are all achievable through falling into states (*hal*) they become permanent attributes only through entering into a station (*maqam*).

According to ibn al-Arabi "'state' is every attribute which you have at one time but not another," "'station' is every attribute which becomes deeply rooted (*rusukh*) and cannot be left behind" (Ibn al-Arabi 1972; quoted from Chittick 1989: 279). Effectively, when one finds oneself performing miraculous signs (*ayat*) it generally means they have entered upon a state (*hal*) and are in that moment expressions of Allah's power, but *ahwal* (states) themselves are only achievable through release of libidinal energy (*hubbiyya*). The more libidinal energy (*hubbiyya*) you feel towards someone (or the One) the more likely you are to enter upon a state (*hal*).

Still, it is also found written in the Quran, "And there is none of us but has an assigned place, And verily we are ranged in ranks" (Quran 37: 164, 165). This assigned place is what ibn al-Arabi called your station (*maqam*) and each of us has one. Even so, as we godbodies also identify as poor, righteous, teachers (dervishes), so there are four *maqamat* (stations) we should acknowledge within our own social development: *Hakim* (Arabic for foresight, insight, and hindsight user, or even for a wise one; though better translated as an omnivisionary sage), which means becoming a master of the science of life. *Karim* (Arabic for clairvoyance, clairaudience, and clairsentience user, or even for a noble one; though better translated as an omnipotent mage), which means becoming a master of the Supreme Mathematics. *Rahim* (Arabic for climateopathic, biopathic, and panopathic user, or even for an empathic one; though better translated as an omnipresent hage), which means becoming a master of the Build Allah Square. *Allah* (Arabic for omnivisionary, omnipotent, and omnipresent deity, or even for a Supreme Being; though better translated as a divine one), which means becoming a grandmaster of the science of life, Supreme Mathematics, and the Build Allah Square.

Though it is true that *anbiya* no longer exist in the world as an established office, we in the godbody do have dervishes possessing one or more of these gifts: *rahma al-mutlaq* (*panopathy*), *himma* (telekinesis), *takwin* (manifesting), and *ma'nawi idrak* (supersensory perception). These gifts exist to those who enter upon a state, and can be reached through them taking the sexual energy they achieve in orgasm or multiple orgasms and focusing it on mastering the practices of the station they are currently in. They should not try to seek to skip stations. Though while it could technically be said that our fate is already written, the relativity of our agency allows for some leeway, and just as for the male, achieving a state (*hal*) or reaching a station (*maqam*) is interdependent on their relation with their sexual partner, so to a woman, achieving a state (*hal*) or reaching a station (*maqam*) is interdependent on their relation with their sexual partner. Ultimately, however, whether one has reached a station or is simply in a state one is still able to do what all the *anbiya* (prophets) were able to do even in our time.

The main distinction in our time is that we have received unveilings (*kashafat*) rather than prophecies (*nubuwwat*). One who has not reached a *maqam* can still fall into a *hal*, while *ahwal* (states) become less likely as one rises up the *maqamat* (stations). Chittick (1989: 278) said on this subject, "the 'state' (*hal*) or present spiritual situation of the individual is by definition transitory, while a 'station' (*maqam*) may have the same attributes as a state except that it is a fixed quality of the soul. States are 'bestowals' while stations are 'earnings.'" Conversely, it is impossible to reach a station outwardly (*zahir*) that you have not also reached inwardly (*batin*).

This *batin al-qabul* (inward receptivity) comes about by angelic insight even as Allah did for Moses. Effectively, "We ordained for him in the tablets admonition of every kind and clear explanation of all things" (Quran 7: 145). Thus, the rising from one *maqam* to the next or even the receiving of a *hal* comes about only with angelic help. However, when we receive a *maqam* it is by knowledge or science and we rise up the *maqamat* through lessons we gain from Allah. Accordingly, as ibn al-Arabi said, "Passing from station to station does not mean that you abandon a station. On the contrary, you acquire that which is higher than it without departing from the station within which you dwell. ... When someone passes from one knowledge to another knowledge, this does not imply that he becomes ignorant of the first knowledge. On the contrary, it never leaves him" (Ibn al-Arabi 1972; quoted from Chittick 1989: 280). Conversely, as the individual, male or female, rises in their *maqam* they decrease in their *hal*, in both the *zahir* and the *batin*. For example, the individual who reaches the *maqam* of *Rahim* (empathic) no longer relies on *iman* (faith) to accomplish *shahad* (clairvoyance), they now use empathy (*rahma*).

Effectively, what we have learned from this chapter is that in Islam there are several theories of humanity that are addressed: (i) humanity has the same origin as all other things in nature, (ii) the Original people were made from the same elements as are found in the earth, (iii) the Original people were Black people, (iv) the forces of nature can be mastered by humanity, (v) what gives life meaning is libido, (vi) what differentiates humanity from the animals is knowledge, libidinal sublimation, and the *Khalifah*, (vii) the different races and languages all exist as a sign to teach us how to live, (viii) Original people are the *Shaitan* of Iblis and Iblis is the *Shaitan* of the Original people, (ix) racialisation was an Islamic practice but racial stratification was not, (x) racial awareness and the vying with different races was seen as virtuous, (xi) all cultures are transient and will all one day come to an end, (xii) all cultures are based on the shari'a of a prophet or group of prophets, (xiii) the universal laws are based on the shari'a of Allah, (xiv) there are signs one can perform through mastering different aspects of the shari'a of Allah, (xv) one who performs signs by faith has entered into a state, and (xvi) one who performs signs by knowledge has entered into a station. Based on all this we can see that Islam has a far more viable sociological framework from which to view different social and racial groupings. Thereby the godbody sociology, as an Islamic sociology, has a philosophy of man far superior to what humanism could ever be.

Resistance Through Sensuality

Peace to the Gods and the Earths,

In *Black Divinity* and *The Black Threat Theodicy* I spoke of a Black theodicy and the part it played in necessitating a Black thearchy. Soteriologically the aim was to prove that a Black thearchy is the answer to the question of Black suffering and what is to be done about it. However, after the publishing of those two I soon came to realise that what I imparted to the issue of Black theodicy was a very shallow examination. Black theodicy is far more complicated than I fully considered. One of the main issues that was not considered in the theodicies of *Black Divinity* and *The Black Threat Theodicy* was micro-Black suffering. Though I have dealt with Black suffering throughout my entire oeuvre that has mainly been from a macro level: like issues of modernity, slavery, capitalism, colonialism, segregation, poverty, illegitimisation, criminalisation, incarceration, and eschatology. These forms of Black suffering are important for all Black people and face the majority of Black people, if not all; nevertheless, within Black culture, there is another kind of Black suffering that affects a sizable portion of us: underclass Black suffering.

I personally consider myself an expert with regard to this situation: I grew up in what we called *Madinah* (Brooklyn, New York); I was raised in relative poverty; I have been expelled from high school; I dropped out of my next high school; I have been to jail, prison (both state and federal), and the psychiatric ward; I have been certified as schizophrenic; I have been an immigrant and a deportee; I have been from homeless shelter to homeless shelter; I have slept on the open streets numerous times; I have been a drug dealer and abuser; I have had a sexually transmitted infection; I have been an Original Gangsta Crip; I have been in countless fights; I have been stabbed in the face three times; I have been betrayed by close friends; I have been betrayed by my church; one of my parents had a stroke in front of me; I have been abused and harassed by police and correction officers; I have been on welfare and in social housing; and on top of all that I have been plagued by the racism that affects all Black people; I basically fall into the category of virtually every underclass Black male stereotype but one: both my parents participated in raising me (though my mother died when I was nineteen) – and while that may distinguish me from the Black American and Black Caribbean underclass it does not affect my connection to the Black African underclass, which in most cases also have both parents to raise them.

Seeing as how I have such an advanced rap sheet of micro-level Black sufferings one would expect that I would be bitter or would have just given up, yet what has gotten me through all these has been three phenomena that I cherish very dearly: my relationship with Allah (who I define as the Black Mind), Black music (in the form of Gospel, Reggae, Soul, Funk, R&B, Dancehall, Hip-Hop, but mainly, and especially since I have grown older, Neo-Soul) and Black women. Of the three Allah is definitely the dearest, but I must repeat, it is not that I believe in a mystery god but that I acknowledge that while knowledge is God and the Black man is God, there are forces outside of knowledge and the

Black man that are also God (not more so or less so but very God). Allah is the universe, and though I am also the universe the universe is also beyond me. The universal force is electromagnetic and the universal essence is also electromagnetic: this force and this essence abide by universal laws, laws which have become so inherent to them that they rarely break them. This is why I love Allah more than all things.

If, however, we consider again the fact that we live in a world of White supremacy and plutocratic Empire, we may lose faith (*iman*) in our potential to ever elevate above it. For example, we have seen that the American monolith of resurrected and incorporated domination has permeated our reality (*haqiqa*). But it is also here where the second assistant in my own struggle for self-development, Black music, has played its major part. Obviously, in most orthodox versions of Islam music is considered *makruh* (disliked), if not then haram (prohibited), which makes this statement rather strange within a Muslim treatise. Such an idea, however, should be considered nonsense due to the form of Islam we come closest to, Sufism.

Within Sufism is understood the concept and practice of *sama'* (hear or listen), which they apply to listening to music. Chittick (2013: 97) even called the Sufis, the Folk of Sama', saying, "The 'Folk of Sama' ' are those Sufis who employ music to transport themselves into ecstatic states." Indeed, even the Quran says of the disbelievers, "Allah has sealed their hearts and their hearing [*sami'*]; and there is a covering on their eyes, and for them is a grievous chastisement" (Quran 2: 7). It could be said that this hearing or listening that the Sufis call *sama'* Allah has hidden from the hearts and minds of those Muslim scholars who have determined to give precedent to the Hadiths, and to misinterpretations and mistranslations of the Quran.

At the same time, the Black community has had a tradition, from the days of slavery to the present, of using song and music to acquire a deeper understanding of the mystery of God's grace and his severity. Yet, by the 1990s Black music had become far more nuanced, and while sacred and spiritual songs were still being performed in the Black Church, far more realistic and sensual songs began to be developed within the Black community. The 1990s was also the era of R&B's development into maturity as a classy yet overtly sensual form of written and performative discourse, and this all came to the fore amid the triumphalism of post-Cold War counter-revolution. This sensuality began for the Black woman in 1992 with En Vogue's extremely popular single "Giving Him Something He Can Feel." The song itself, originally written by Curtis Mayfield in the 1970s, but re-released in the '90s by En Vogue and mainly sung by Dawn Robinson, with the chorus sung by the rest of the group; is about a Black woman's devotion to her Black man and her willingness to "give him something he can feel" so to speak. As a rather safe seller, particularly in the Black community, there appears to be no controversy, yet its music video was filled with sexually charged motions, actions, and visuals that cannot be denied.

The music video for "Giving Him Something He Can Feel" is one of the first instances, at least since the era of Donna Summer and Diana Ross, when Black women looked both sexy and classy at the same time. If we consider from here the perception of Mimi Sheller that, "To analyse this sexual praxis would require going beyond a scribal literary reading of lyrics; it requires a reading of the entire embodied performance, including the glittery sequined clothes and gyrations of the male performers as much as of the female performers" (Sheller 2012: 263); we can discover more intricate and salient points about sexuality in the 1990s music industry. Interestingly, the sexualised embodiment of these women was not a disempowering tool used against them by an oppressive patriarchal system – though male figures probably played a big role in designing their outfits – as we can be certain they had a measure of agency with regard to their own sexual expression. And as sexual agency can, on the one hand, be used as a means to subjugate women and reinforce their domination by men, on the other hand, it can be used by women to assert their own power and transgress social boundaries and prohibitions (Sheller 2012).

Featuring scenes of the quartet in long red dresses with knee-high slits performing a steamy burlesque tease on a stage in front of a room full of Black men all in awe of their performance – the video marked a turning point in R&B and hip-hop. Although the impact of the video did not fully materialise until around 1994, the performance of sexually charged actions in classy costumes played a substantive role in creating the counter-discourse of erotic agency within the Black community. Sheller articulated this discourse as such: "Erotic agency ... is the antithesis of enslavement. It appears not only in the context of sexual relations, but also in the context of other forms of creativity, including all kinds of work" (Sheller 2012: 245). En Vogue's use of erotic agency as a means of Black female empowerment allowed them to soar to the heights of culturally creative distinction. Not only was their employment of sexuality a catalyst for the Black sexual revolution of the 1990s, it also showed Black women that they could be sexy in a world that over-vaunted White female models and actresses as the standard of femininity.

The exhibition of the sexual energy and erotic agency of the Black woman was taken to the next level through the light sensual performance of Jade's music video for "Every Day of the Week." Like with "Giving Him Something He Can Feel" "Every Day of the Week" challenged the master narrative of the modest or shy Black woman – a narrative that was already under pressure from hip-hop's female prodigies Salt-N-Pepper and from other underground artists like Roxanne Shante – and presented the Black woman as an independent, confident, and sexy agent who is free to play pursuer. In the video the trio merged images of the ghetto, sexually vibrant, hood rat with those of the sensuous, classy, girly-girl, and the confident, independent, businesswoman to express their own form of nuanced and yet active sensuality: mainly through the assortment of outfits they wore throughout. The video starts out with the trio wearing tight jeans and casual tops with their slim torsos exposed, walking through the streets. Following that scene the trio are in an open studio with microphone stands wearing extremely short dresses: Tonya Kelly wearing a black dress, Joi Marshall wearing a silver one, and Di Reed wearing a copper toned one. And scattered throughout are also scenes of each of the girls individually standing or sitting wearing black suits with white shirts.

The erotic agency of this video is found in their freedom and also in their outfits, particularly in the shortness of their dresses. The confident exhibition on the public space of television of various sexualised parts of the female body created a new narrative for the Black woman: that of the independent vixen. Indeed, it may be considered by some to come close to endorsing hetero-male voyeurism, but such comments and criticisms miss the point. Jade were not objectifying themselves in the video, their playful and light-hearted sexuality did not negate their inherent personal strength, which is obvious throughout. Not to mention that Jade's light sensuality was nowhere near as distasteful as some of the virtually softcore pornography in most of the hip-hop videos I grew up watching.

The rewritten (or remixed) narrative of the Black woman, being infused with this soft sensuality and classy sexuality, did not fade when we entered 1995 as Xscape's "Feels So Good" music video showed. The video was shot perhaps in a café or at a bar of sorts, a rather classy semipublic space, where the two lead singers: Kandi Burruss and LaTocha Scott sang about how their perfect man made them feel. Though the sexuality of this video is not as playful as that of Jade's, it is as light. Burruss and LaTocha Scott are in collared shirts and exposed bras with loose trousers explaining how having the perfect man has affected their lives. However, the attention of the viewer is mainly, and perhaps even intentionally, focused on Tameka "Tiny" Cottle and Tamika Scott as they do a wet counter-performance in a public shower. The subtlety of the video thus creates a kind of sexuality denuded of vulgarity and based on simplistically sexy representation. Further, their counter-performance also resembled what Sheller (2012) called an "elaborated spatial category" of the similitude to classical blues, Caribbean dancehall, and South African Kwaito. Such dances, while recognising the male gaze, use its objectifying qualities as a means of reasserting power and rebalancing the power relations in the context of sexuality.

Yet it cannot be denied that this male gaze also has the potential to morph into what is called the pornographic gaze. Herein lies the danger of Xscape's video: though presenting a sexually denuded video it also has the potential to be judged and viewed through a pornographic lens. The men who do this, however, are such to view most things women do through a pornographic lens. This brings us to a new concept presented by Pierre Bourdieu (2010): that of the pure gaze. The pure gaze is when male and female view texts and signs not as moral or immoral but as aesthetic. "The pure gaze implies a break with the ordinary attitude towards the world, which, given the conditions in which it is performed, is also a social separation" (Bourdieu 2010: xxvii). Indeed, the pure gaze exists without judgment and without ethos. It is truly separate from the popular aesthetic, it is an aesthetic based largely on beauty and detached from economic necessity. Xscape's "Feels So Good" is thus not a trap for the male gaze nor an entry point to the pornographic gaze, if looked at aesthetically it can produce the pure gaze from those with the class to see it with such.

All these ideas would then be driven home in the music video to SWV's song "Use Your Heart" released in mid-1996. One of the most incredible and aesthetically captivating music videos of the 1990s, "Use Your Heart" features lead singer Cheryl "Coko" Clemons singing about her relationship wearing mainly black dresses, but also wearing a grey dress with white straps and a white upper section. She seductively draws the viewer in with her non-verbal/non-literary discourse of sexual embodiment. Her soft eroticism and light flirtiness gives the subject of the song a sense of irony, as, though saying very explicitly "use your heart and not your eyes," the eyes are drawn in by the radiance of the trio and their aesthetically elegant performance. The song ends with Tamara Johnson-George closing with a hauntingly beautiful ode to her relational partner as she wears a white blouse and tan loose trousers.

The video for "Use Your Heart" took the full ensemble of what went before: En Vogue's classy elegance and erotic agency; Jade's light sensual embodiment; and Xscape's denuded sexual representation and made a masterpiece. It presented the Black woman as a lover in the main relational senses of the word: a sexual lover and a loving companion. It also destroyed all sexual stereotypes of the Black woman as inferior to the White woman, whether in class, beauty, sophistication, or femininity with its embrace of a non-verbal, highly sensual bodily discursive.

But it would be SWV's innocuous articulation of erotic agency that would capture visually as well as verbally an eroticism that expresses one of the more prominent lines of the song, "real love purified." As Sheller also articulated, "The erotic … is clearly more than the sexual, though it may encompass the sexual. It includes the power of love, knowledge, creativity, and life force itself" (Sheller 2012: 244); a statement that exculpates Black erotica as an empowering libidinal force (*hubbiyya*) that can be used within the Black community for the construction of practices both sexual and non-sexual. And while the critique can be made that a Black erotica will only encourage further the male gaze on women within the Black community, if said Black erotica is able to live up to the standard set by videos like "Use Your Heart" such fears can easily be put to rest.

In fact, their articulation of Black erotica captures one of the more general perceptions discussed by Black American feminist Audre Lorde, "The very word erotic comes from the Greek word eros, the personification of love in all its aspects, born of Chaos, and personifying creative power and harmony. When I speak of the erotic, then, I speak of it as an assertion of the life force of women; of that creative energy empowered, the knowledge and use of which we are now reclaiming in our language, our history, our dancing, our loving, our work, our lives" (Lorde 1984; quoted in Sheller 2012: 244). Lorde's view of the erotic shares obvious similarities with Freud's view of the libidinal (*hubbiyya*), a relation that reveals the attractive intentionality of the trio's expression of sexual sophistication. Yet the video also manifested the nature of the erotic to bring order to the chaos, to abolish the chaos and generate raw creativity and life in the human mind. There is even an almost voyeuristic nature contained within the video as the eye is so sensually stimulated and impacted by their choice of actions, gestures, clothing, and performances that even though they do not engage in the levels of overtly sexual iconography that can be seen in some music videos their sexual exhibitions are far more potent.

Coming from this background the R&B girl groups of the 1990s created a controversial storm with their erotic discourse and heightened sensuality. Still, since the 1990s sensuality has lost its edge in R&B. Solo artists now predominate going for the instant kill rather than the subtle stalk. That is not to say that artists like Rihanna and Ciara are not sexy, but the eye captivating, sense stimulating videos of the 90s do seem to have faded, even though the girl group has definitely been resurrected (*bu'itha*) in recent years. In 1996, En Vogue were able to retake the flag of distinction with their sensually charged music video for "Don't Let Go (Love)". The song talks about taking a friendship to the next level, but the video itself is classic Black eroticism – in the all-encompassing sense. All four girls are in a relationship of sorts with Mekhi Phifer. All four represent a level of elegance and class with him (while still being sexy) that also deserves recognition. Indeed, this video features performance (as opposed to counter-performance) in the dramatisation of the love story. And though it does get intimate, there is nothing overtly lewd within the video itself. Even in the opening scenes, as Robinson flirts with Phifer for a sexual home-movie they are making, she is still tasteful.

Now when we look into the cultural variation of all these women from the 1990s R&B world, we find it was most likely a generically non-sexual Christianity that spawned them. The transgression of sexually permitted boundaries made in the 1990s by the Black woman – whether in the light form displayed in the videos discussed or in the more aggressive form of certain rap artists – was not an outward articulation of an essential drive of the race towards raw sexuality. Nor can it yet be blamed purely on marketing companies, music video directors, record labels, or neoliberal capitalism. The fact is, blaming it on one of these undermines these women's personal agency and lightly erotic potential. To be sure, though the music video directors may have made suggestions on what to do, the actual sexual movements of the women, whether in gesture, insinuation, or some other form of act-specie, were all performed by the women themselves as defiant demonstrations of their erotic agency. And by practicing, verbally and bodily, said erotic agency within the context of Christian cultural identification they were advancing and contesting normative Christian interpretations of sexuality, and thereby turning their erotic praxis into a sacred praxis (Sheller 2012).

I

I personally feel that rather than simply condemning women like those mentioned here as 85 percent we godbodies should recognise them as examples to be emulated: they were classy while yet being sexy, and they set the standard for sensual resistance using Black eroticism as a means of challenging the system of White *female* supremacy. Again, sensual resistance, erotic agency, and embodied sexuality are proven means of fighting White supremacy internally. They are also able to create a determination and drive within our godbody brothers and sisters – when they are used as a form of resistance to socio-cultural White supremacy – to continue the struggle, come what may.

Fanon reported a similar drive within the Algerian National Liberation Front (the FLN) when he stated, "The female cells of the F.L.N. received mass memberships [as a result of the anti-colonial struggle]. The impatience of these new recruits was so great that it [would] often [endanger] the traditions of complete secrecy. The leaders had to restrain the exceptional enthusiasm and radicalism that are always characteristic of any youth engaged in building a new world. As soon as they enrolled, these women would ask to be given the most dangerous assignments" (Fanon 1965: 108), an attribute that dies down with experience. Indeed, the war against White supremacy is more complicated and subtle than the Algerian war against colonialism. In that war they overcame the violence of colonialism with the counter-violence of revolutionism. In our struggle we overcome the discourse of White superiority with the counter-discourse of Black eroticism, spoken through discursive embodiment.

But perhaps one of the greatest strengths of Black eroticism is not simply that it is a counter-discourse that challenges the grand discourse of White superiority but that it empowers Black people spiritually, psychologically, mentally, and sexually. It is clear that any Goddess who develops the level of sensuality articulated by any of the R&B divas mentioned in this chapter could become to us a paradigm setter; mainly as we Gods seem to have followed the world's definition of God, the godly, and righteousness rather than accepting the more ancient definition: that based on the sensuality of the ancient Egyptians, who themselves learned righteousness from ancient Kush.

The gods and goddesses of these Nilotic Black cultures were sensual by nature and definition. They displayed their divinity through their sensuality. Obviously, the system of Egypt, and the whole of East Africa (except Ethiopia), all fell to conquest and colonialism and need to be adjusted to the times we are currently in now, but that does not negate the truths of sensuality's significance within the global Black unconscious. We Gods must accommodate for its influence and effectuation. Moreover, though with regards to religious structure we godbodies are not necessarily non-religious nor anti-religious – we are more supra-religious, in that we go beyond all religions seeing God in the Black man from Asia – our sensual development as a movement is such that most religious bodies would reject it.

To be sure, we do not knock the Scriptures of any religion, we just see all Scriptures as pointing towards us. We are the Chosen People of the Bible and the People of the Book of the Quran, or on an even more revolutionary basis, we are the God of the Bible and the Allah of the Quran. Indeed, First Born Prince Allah purportedly said that "Allah [the Father of our movement] allowed participation in any tradition, as long as the Five Percenter knew that he was the locus of whatever transcendent power the tradition presented: the black man, when in a mosque, must know that he is Allāh; in a church, he is Christ; at a stupa, he is Buddha" (Knight 2011: 194).

Due to this self-identification we do not reject any religion but have the freedom to attend any religious gathering we feel most comfortable in. In this sense, we are hidden within the masses of the people in a situation that gives us the ability to talk face-to-face with the people *where they are*. Furthermore, we also fulfil degree 18 of our 1-40: "What is the duty of a civilized person? To teach the uncivilized people – who are savage – civilization, righteousness, the knowledge of himself, and the science of everything in life, which is love, peace, and happiness." For which cause, any God or Goddess that goes to church should know the Bible well enough to quote it, and any God or Goddess that goes to mosque should know the Quran well enough to quote it.

Consequently, our dress code, for the most part, allows us a level of invisibility to outsiders, as Abu Shaheed once said, "for those who know and those who need to know the Quran says: 'Blessed is he who believes in the seen and the unseen.' And I say ... We, the people, are the seen and the unseen. You could pick an F.O.I and the M.G.T out of the crowd because of their appearance. But you couldn't tell the difference in us" (Shaheed; quoted in Allah 2015). This is one of the strengths of the godbody movement, to the majority of the people we are invisible just like they claim Allah is, though he is seen and heard everywhere.

However, there is also a fundamental flaw within our system, as, though this dress code applies to the men, our women are forced to cover three-fourths of their body and to wrap their head with the headscarf. In this sense they are very visible. When we see a Goddess in church (though maybe not at mosque) or when we see a Goddess attend a social gathering or cultural event: whether it be a club, dance, meeting or celebration, or just on the streets; they should be as unseen (that is, unseeable) as the Gods they associate with. Herein, as I have stated in my former books, it is my opinion that sexuality with class is missing from our current identification.

To explain this idea a bit further: when a God is in the world he may see the females of the 85 percent, usually they are dressed very sexy and in very revealing clothing. This will then drive his imagination wild and create all manner of sexual lusts as a temptation for him. But if that sexy woman was to also have wisdom (*hikma*) in conversation she would be able to keep his mind right so that he would not allow those thoughts to consume him. Or to put it another way: the problem is not with how she dresses, the problem is how he responds to how she dresses and what he thinks of her as a result of how she dresses. If the Original woman is really the *beautiful* Asiatic Black woman then why should she not be allowed to display that beauty and get complements from other men for displaying that beauty?

Again, we Gods for the most part dress strong and thugged out: if a Black woman was to judge us based on our outer garments she would see us as thugs; but when we open our mouths and they hear wisdom (*hikma*) they know they have just spoken to God in the flesh. Us dressing strong and acting strong does not detract from our wisdom (*hikma*). Well, just as the God can dress strong and be wise, so a Goddess should be free to dress sexy and be wise, and in manifesting that wisdom she will show that she is a Goddess and that, as with the R&B singers, the godbody movement can be sexy and still have class.

At the same time, the debate on the dress code of our Goddess sisters does not stop with her freedom to wear more or less than three-fourths but goes into the issue of the Goddess' right to be more sexual within the godbody movement. Indeed, sexuality as a subject is most definitely shunned within the Muslim world, at least as a matter of public discourse – and though the Five Percent are generally supra-religious we still consider ourselves to be righteous Muslim – the reality of sexuality is highly emotive and elusive, if not outright rejected as the devil's means of corrupting our people and our civilisation. Nevertheless, Sheller stated, "counter-performances of citizenship can sometimes deploy sexual and erotic agency to undo the gender, racial, and sexual inequalities that uphold normative moral orders, legal systems, and state practices, both national and trans-national." Indeed, "mainstream historiographies of slavery, emancipation, freedom, and national politics must be reconsidered in view of the erotic politics of citizenship" (Sheller 2012: 27, 30).

Sheller, coming from the position of a sociologist and Caribbeanist reinterpreted Black sexual codes and bodily discourses in the Caribbean to show how erotic agency has actually been a weapon for Black people, and Black women in particular, to attain liberation amid the delimiting struggles of slavery, colonisation, segregation, and criminalisation: "Beneath the dominant citizenship regimes of liberalism and republicanism and the noisy politics of the public sphere are hints of an alternative Caribbean ideology of freedom, one grounded in the living sensual body as a more fully rounded, relationally connected, erotic, and spiritual potential" (Sheller 2012: 23).

But the wearing of sexy clothes has a more blatantly revolutionist thematic to it, "because racial and ethnic politics is played out sexually, and sex is played out through a racial and ethnic politics, a politics of the body and of sexual citizenship must be central to any liberation movement and to any theory of freedom" (Sheller 2012: 241). The question of women's clothing and the form, style, or length of her clothing carries huge political, as well as social, connotations. Firstly, as alluded to, it makes her as invisible as Allah. She becomes just another Black woman, and such is not even speaking of her sexuality, she becomes just another sexy Black woman. The intransigent nature of the sexy Black woman, however, is something that carries far more political implications.

Take, for example, the case of the Algerian woman in the anti-colonial struggle, her form of clothing represented several expedients when juxtaposed to different scenarios. Fanon, speaking on these cases stated how, "The way people clothe themselves, together with the traditions of dress and finery that custom implies, constitutes the most distinctive form of a society's uniqueness, that is to say the one that is the most immediately perceptible" (Fanon 1965: 35). Thus, clothing traditions, customs, or prohibitions at once demarcate a cultural group from others of similar orientation. This is complicated though, as we have already established two things: (i) that we godbody men (the Gods) are the unseen and what demarcates us from those in the street life is our wisdom, and (ii) that I am trying to create and establish this standard for our godbody women (the Earths or Goddesses). Yet I am not seeking for us to be completely indistinguishable from the people, what I am looking to do is remove the prohibition of certain female clothing and cause a debate to allow her the freedom to wear clothes as long or short as she desires, while still maintaining the tradition of the headscarf.

The sexuality of the Black woman, particularly of a Goddess, shows to the world and to the Black man, her divinity. As an example, everyone from old New York remembers them or has seen them: the lost Black men on the bus to Rikers Island. I can guess it was the same in other Black communities too. One thing that was intuitively unexpected was the love and appreciation coming from Black and Latin women as they saw the buses drive by. The sexual and erotic (or at least friendly) displays and gestures made by Black and Latin women to show the solidarity these Original women felt towards the men on these police buses in their struggle against the system of White supremacy – which was the underlying cause of their then current situation of criminalisation and incarceration.

Obviously, New York is no longer the same place since gentrification: developers have basically gone into the Black areas of New York, bought out all the prime locations in Brooklyn, Queens, Harlem, and the Bronx and priced Black and Latin people out of the housing market, thereby forcing them to move out of New York. The ruff areas I grew up in have now been redesigned and refurbished into White havens such that the Black and Latin people, who used to be side-by-side, can no longer afford to live there. But back in the 1990s and early 2000s the Black and Latin women were under no illusions, they knew the Black and Latin men were being locked up for a form of resistance to White supremacy – albeit a terrible and unfruitful form of resistance.

It is under these circumstances that our Black eroticism becomes a far more promising form of resistance. But why? The answer to this question is threefold: (i) Black eroticism is one of the most effective forms of *dhikr* Allah (though not called by that name) practiced within the Black community surpassed only by gospel music; the main difference being that the performance of Black eroticism is far more potent in that it takes the Black person, who sees the performative, directly into either the Paradise of Allah or the essence of Allah. (ii) Black eroticism leads to the union of man and woman, not only in a heteronormative way but also integrating the two most necessary forces of cohesion within the Black community: the Original man and the Original woman; which is a force that is strong not simply because it produces the Black child but also because it balances out the gendered propensities of the one on its own. (iii) Black eroticism as a bodily discourse effectively shuts down all White feelings and boasts of superiority, as, with regard to sexuality they have already subconsciously placed Black people in the seat of victory; we thereby ruin their efforts to claim absolute supremacy by dominating in the area of sexuality.

One of the greatest lessons I have learned about White people in my life's journey is that they cannot stand losing, it drives them crazy. Anytime they find an area they are incapable of dominating in they will just devalue it on the scales of importance. This is what they have done with the areas Blacks are most dominant in. As articulated earlier, we have been placed into a mind/body dichotomy in which to be body is considered lower than to be mind. Victorian anthropologists all concluded that the White is the mind, the rational, the intelligent; the Black is the body, the sensual, the physical. Though such a notion is now repudiated within the social sciences I consider it to be very much so still present in society outside of academia (and even in certain pockets of academia to a degree). As we Black people played no part in taking the idea public we will be ineffective at destroying it. The best thing for us to do is use it to our advantage, become more body and highly value our sexuality while, at the same time, refusing to have any sexual relations with a White person so as to deprive them of the privilege of that experience. This will give White people a fight they are incapable of winning and will ultimately drive them mad.

The main reasons behind this encouragement to become more body, become hyper-body, basically, become the stereotype they have relegated us to, rather than fight the stereotype: become hyper-mind, become knowledge incarnate, are, firstly, because the godbody already value knowledge above all else and possess a high degree of intelligence (are hyper-mind) so by joining the godbody we already put ourselves in a position to prove mind in a verbal dialogue. The trouble is most White people will never get the chance to engage in dialogue with a godbody or a Five Percenter, and even if they did would still see the Black *race* as body regardless. Secondly, remember, White people's greatest weakness is that they cannot stand to lose. They will always find a way to devalue anywhere they are weak. What we need is a way to take the fight to the White community that all Black people, high and low, can participate in without losing.

Nevertheless, there is also a tendency, within the White community to weaponise the idea of some hypothetical daughter figure in order to gain some kind of control over the Black woman's body. However, in this case I am not referring to young women or girls but to adults. Yet it seems that to certain White people, male and female, gaining a level of control over how an adult Black woman dresses has become a method of regulating the movements of the Black woman's body. The conception that she corrupts Black children with her sexuality or with her hypersexuality is a weak and hypocritical excuse as very few White people complain about all the real pornography that exists on the internet, or the sexually explicit television shows featuring White people. No, they complain about Black culture and Black women. The truth is, her level of respectability gains no outward credibility by her inhibiting the sexuality of how she dresses.

Moreover, those Black men who also use the hypothetical daughter figure only do so following the example of White people. They are so embarrassed by the Black woman's sexual emancipation and liberation that they tell her to behave appropriately or "respectably", et cetera., in fear that the race be judged as inferior, or looked down on for our sexual permissiveness or behaviour. What is worse is the eyes of the world are viewed as on us, or at least on those in the middle class, so they desire to impress their non-Black counterparts that have no understanding of our ways and actions. These Black men, and their middle class Black female counterparts, however, are the ones that have been corrupted.

Like a ventriloquist dummy they are basically speaking the White man's words out of their Black mouths. Even if in most things their ideals are Black, in this particular area, the area of Black sexuality, their ideals are Victorian. Not simply White, but Victorian White. The same with the Muslim, Indian, and Southeast Asian who uses the revered daughter figure to justify their "respectable" crusade against Black sexuality. All these peoples have in their history and in their past traditions that were very sexual and very erotic. It is only post-Victorian influence during the days of colonialism that caused these peoples to become more sexually modest and promote sexual modesty as though they had done so since the beginning.

This is the anachronism of culture, it creates a distortion field causing all within to believe that their existing practices were always practiced as such, and that their existing beliefs were always their beliefs. The truth, however, is that in all of the Islamic empires of the medieval age there was a high level of sexual liberation and sexual expression. The same with the ancient and medieval Indian cultures (particularly those influenced by Tantra). Even in Southeast Asia women were far more sexually liberated during the ancient and medieval times than the post-Victorian Asians. The women of all these Asiatic cultures would be completely naked underneath fine spun elegant clothing and perform sexual and erotic dances and activities, and in public and semi-public spaces, freely, without fear of non-respectability or stigmatisation. True, they did not, in those times, live in havens of female social or political empowerment despite their sexual empowerment. However, there was no fear or excuse made in those times of corrupting some mythical or hypothetical daughter figure, or of disrespectful or unethical degeneration.

Still, as with Algeria and the White tactic of using the respectability argument (in Algeria's case, defending and empowering the Algerian woman; in our case, protecting and maintaining the innocence of Black children – and what Black woman would fight against that?) When they begin to see that it is no longer working on Black women, and that not only are the ones professing respectability the most disrespectful, corrupt, and hypocritical people on the planet; but that their frame of respectfulness and use of Black children to undermine our sexual freedom is only a tactic of war, never used against White sexual exhibition but only against Black sexual exhibition whenever we prove to be far better at it than them; then they will truly be free, not only to be more sexual but even to be hypersexual. In fact, all inhibitions of their hypersexuality will weaken. Not to say they will be completely removed, but with their weakening the Black woman will feel and desire less of a need for validation from White society, and more of a desire to exhibit her instinctual eroticism.

II

Though the value of Black eroticism to our movement should thereby be self-evident, especially considering the preceding arguments, I shall now use myself to present another example – and I know a lot of you Gods will be able to relate. When I was in Greene Correctional Facility I received no visits from anybody: my mother was dead, my sister was in England, and the rest of my family either had no idea I was locked up, or wanted nothing to do with me. It was during the night hours when it got its loneliest. But what helped me, and a lot of us brothers, get through our time was softcore porno magazines, *Black Tail* in particular, and a spot in the boom-boom room – that to us, or at least to me, was as good as ten visits – and to further qualify this I shall now present the words spoken by *al-Masih* himself, "I was in prison, and ye came unto me" (Matthew 25: 36).

Obviously, when *al-Masih* said that he was speaking mainly of his disciples locked up (but are we Gods not also his disciples?) As much as some of you Gods and Goddesses may condemn those sisters in the magazines as sluts, freaks, emotionally damaged, or some other kind of unworthy, when we Gods were at our lowest those *Black* women who posed for those *Black* porno magazines – knowing that the central readership for *Black pornography* was those locked up in prison – not only held us down but gave to us a *dhikra* Allah (reminder of Allah). If you are incapable of seeing the righteousness, beauty, love, and peace in that then you must be as blind as you claim the 85 percent to be.

As another example – and she may not be too proud of it now – a couple of decades ago Damon Dash's cousin Stacey Dash released some sexy photographs and we Black brothers were happy to give her praise up to the heavens for this act, especially those of us who were locked up. But once she switched to the Republican side we condemned her as a sell-out. Now I personally may not be Conservative, Liberal, Republican, or Democrat, et cetera., being an anti-state thearchist, but, though Dash may have been talking a lot of foolishness that was a bit unbearable to listen to, she is still one of us and will go through, and has gone through, the same struggles as a Black person – as a Black woman – in a White man's world.

We Black males should never cast someone aside who has sacrificed for us. That would be ungrateful. It is written in the Scriptures: "He that receiveth a prophet in the name of a prophet shall receive a prophet's reward; and he that receiveth a righteous man in the name of a righteous man shall receive a righteous man's reward. And whosoever shall give to drink unto one of these little ones a cup of cold water only in the name of a disciple, verily I say unto you, he shall in no wise lose his reward" (Matthew 10: 42). What Dash did back then was for what she considered righteous men, no matter what her story is now. She is from New York and undoubtedly knew about the godbody, and knew back then that we would be the main ones seeing those pictures, yet still took them in spite of her Hollywood status.

We godbodies need to prove her right – that we were genuinely righteous brothers – therefore it is only right that we learn to disagree without condemning or casting out someone, unless they have actually caused the life of a revolutionary to be put in danger, either through arrest or death, at the hands of the slavemaster. Splitting into Toms and Turners has only perpetuated the divide-and-rule situation we currently happen to be in. It was ineffective in the 1960s – though disagreeing with his vision and tactics both Malcolm X and the Elijah Muhammad came to respect Dr. King – and it will be ineffective to our cause if we continue it now. I say this as one who has been a Black revolutionary for over a quarter of a century now: though there are many Black militants there are very few Black revolutionaries. A lot of militants talk but have no action or if they have action it is no better than what most White people do – protests, marches, boycotts – as their only intention is to bring about a reform to the existing system.

Being in this position has allowed me to see that both the militant and the reactionary are sleeping – one is sleep talking the other is sleep walking – but because the militants are so loud they think they have a monopoly on what Black is. It is easy for Black militants to say that the Black people, those who are conservative in anyway, are not real Blacks; but those Blacks who choose to be conservative usually only become reactionary because they see no other way to survive in a White man's world. To say they should just rebel like the rest of us is beside the point: as someone who is doing it now, rebelling on your own is not for the fainthearted, and the militants prove no surety as they do a lot of militant talking but very few or only reformist actions.

Conversely, the Black militants talk against the system but change nothing, the Black liberals agree with the system while trying to change it, and there are too few Black revolutionaries to present an actual alternative to the system. It is just an opinion mind you, but, maybe one of the main reasons so many of our Black people are in the church today is not because they are deluded by the slavemaster's religion but because in the church they have acceptance, an alternative to the world system, and, at least concerning God and the Messiah, they do not feel condemned for their choices in life.

Notwithstanding this, many of us Gods who sell drugs *to survive* have the nerve and hypocrisy to condemn those Black women who become strippers *to survive*. We will use 120 to justify selling drugs, saying, "Will you sit at home and wait for that mystery god to bring you food? Emphatically no!" And yet we are unable to see how this applies just as much to the Black women who strip. As much as I love you Gods as my teachers, many of you are in no position to judge a Black woman's lifestyle choices if your lifestyle is no better. Her stripping, modelling, posing, or acting has nothing to do with her enlightenment or her potential for enlightenment. (I say all this not to be overcritical of our movement but to show that the same empathy I have suggested academics should employ when analysing and judging other cultures is also applicable to the Five Percenters when analysing and judging the 85 percent, particularly their women).

The ultimate truth is, those Gods, Goddesses, and Black people who do judge or condemn those Black women that strip, hook, or behave sexual in any way have actually, more or less, been deceived by a version of trick knowledge. In effect, they are articulating White fears over Black behaviours. When we say things like, "I don't want my son to be a thug..." "...gangster", "...hoodlum"; we are expressing White fears of the ghetto and ghetto culture. White people have never been to the ghetto and avoid it at all costs because they fear the ghetto and the aggressions of the men living in the ghetto so they call them thugs and criminals and set fears among each other about us.

Again, when we say, "I don't want my daughter to be a slut…" "…hooker", "…prostitute"; we are underestimating and undervaluing the realities of the ghetto based again on White fears. Most of us men grew up with young girls and women that were sexual, some even hypersexual, and it did not damage or ruin us or them, in fact, it made ghetto life beautiful, interesting, and exciting. The violence and sexuality of the hood was not scary, intimidating, or vile for us as youths, nor were we thugs and hookers, nor did we grow up to be thug and hookers. Thereby, where does this sudden fear of Black boys becoming thugs and Black girls becoming hookers come from?

Moreover, in virtually every age and every generation of Black culture the same thing happens. Black boys become no more dangerous or violent, and Black girls become no more erotic or sexual, but the fact that they express any level of violence or sexuality scares White people, who transmit their fears to the older generation of Black people. Herein lies the truth of Black eroticism: it is the ultimate exhibition of divine love, whether articulated by Black men or Black women. Conversely, if we consider a situation in which *al-Masih* was confronted by a woman with a bad reputation in town, he did not judge or condemn her but said concerning her, "Wherefore I say unto thee, Her sins, which are many, are forgiven; for she loved much: but to whom little is forgiven, the same loveth little" (Luke 7: 47).

Again, when he asked the Pharisees concerning a parable he spoke to them, saying, "Whether of the twain did the will of his father? [And] They say unto him, The first. Jesus [then] saith unto them, Verily I say unto you, That the publicans and the harlots go into the kingdom of God before you" (Matthew 22: 31). Now for a start, the word he used here for harlot is the Greek word *porne* showing that the lifestyle so many of these ghetto females have taken up is justified. Also *al-Masih* was very much aware of the lifestyle of these *porne* and was also aware that *many of them had no other means to survive* and so were *unlikely* to stop living that lifestyle; therefore in his eyes their loving much was in the very lifestyle they were then living and the very exhibition or their erotic behaviour (these were real people not cartoon characters). So, to him the exhibition of their love, even the erotic love they practiced through their lifestyle, was effectively able to bring about not only the remembrance of Allah, but reveal the very face of Allah.

Regrettably, nowadays sites like Instagram and X are filled with the sexy pictures and videos of amateur models, "baddies", and superstar wannabes starving for attention and likes. At the same time, that does not necessarily mean we should be ashamed of the sisters who do this. Instead, we should try to view them as our beautiful counterparts who, by showing-off their beauty reveal the essence of Allah. Again, their sexuality should be seen as beautiful and as a libidinal (*hubbiyya*) expression displayed primarily for Black men to stimulate within us the *dhikr* al-Muhibb. These performances of Black erotica are thus a living presentation of libido (*habba*); a practical exhibition of love and passion rather than the simulacrum of either. They are also the reunification of the Black lover to the Black lover. With both displaying and practicing Black erotica the beauty of Black love will help develop our relationality to each other: love and sex would also be united in Black relationships and not simply the dominance of one or the other.

Nonetheless, the central corrosive in Black relationships is lack of trust, on both sides, and the cure for it will not be found in greater commitment or displays of commitment, nor in marriage (the ultimate display of commitment). If one or both partners are unable to trust in their relationship, for whatever reason, their partner could display all the commitment they wish it will just be ignored or outright rejected. What is needed is a change of perspective. There is nothing wrong with seeing the Black body, male or female, as a sexual object (in the Freudian sense); there is also nothing wrong with having a relationship with one you have sex with. The danger comes from the Victorian definitions of what a relationship is and how it should look. To be sure, the current way of defining a relationship is a social construction designed essentially to favour men, it opened up to women during the 1970s and 1980s, and particularly during the 1990s, as a result of feminism but it still maintained huge remnants from its original male-centred structure.

We godbodies are able to see through the marriage and relational system of the West due to our prohibition of marriage (though not all follow it). The desecration of modern relationality as a means of re-appropriating *our* common practice as counter-discourse shows, as Hardt and Negri articulated, "The will to be against really needs a body that is completely incapable of submitting to command. It needs a body that is incapable of adapting to family life, to factory discipline, to the regulations of a traditional sex life, and so forth" (Hardt & Negri 2000: 216). Through our contrasted perspective we are able to show the Black community the possibilities open to us beyond the standard contemporary ideas prevalent in the Western world. The Black embodiment of sensual and sexual interactivity can thus bring to us an insubordinate form of freedom and justice, the equality comes when both Gods and Goddesses participate in the eroticism.

Thus, Black erotica can be seen as a form of resistance that benefits both genders, while at the same time de-gendering both, allowing for an equality to be established that recognises our overt biological differences while not using these differences against either. Essentially, Black erotica allows for our erotic agency to be used mainly for the cause of empowering each other with the *dhikr* Allah: it thereby becomes a weapon we can capitalise on not only to fight against the injustices and inequalities of the current system of inherent White supremacy, Black racial dehumanisation, and Black psychological inhibition; but also a means to fuel, inspire, and motivate, ourselves and our partner to fight longer. As Sheller noted; "The notion of erotic power appears in the work of several Caribbean and African American feminist theorists and derives from the practices of embodied freedom that emerged out of the African diaspora experience of enslavement" (Sheller 2012: 243).

Ultimately, allowing within the framework of the godbody for the Original woman to dress as sexy as she desires can provide huge benefits for the Gods locked up – and to be fair, most of the Gods are either locked up now or have been locked up in the past. However, though in the short term a more liberal dress code pattern among the Goddesses allows the Goddesses and the Gods certain levels of improvement, in the long run we still lose that distinguishing quality Fanon (1965) spoke about that can demarcate the Five Percent from the 85 percent. To be sure, the *kufi* and the headscarf are traditions practiced within the male and female dress code of the Five Percent, but we will require a defining feature among us that transcends generations and can be used by any as an automatically recognisable trait connected to our movement. For this cause I make two suggestions: first, an injunction to wear a bandana of the universal flag on our left bicep and only our left bicep (not our forearm or hand) everywhere we go – as with a Mandalorian's helmet. Second, an injunction to never wear underwear again, ever – as with a vegetarian and meat.

III

To those new to the conception of not wearing underwear I make this assertion not to be perverted but to, firstly, expose the pseudoscientific justifications for the adoption of underwear such as hygiene and cleanliness. Secondly, to challenge European perceptions of modesty and morality. Thirdly, as a way of internalising Black sensual and sexual stereotypes in a movement that uses our strengths – indeed, one of our greatest strengths – as a means of correcting the social wrongs in society; and considering that not wearing underwear is already a counter-cultural act of immense proportions it makes for a fresh addition to Black erotica and the systems of the godbody movement. The Original people who adopt this approach will ultimately be doing for their fellow Original people what the Black women did for the Black criminals (so-called criminals) on the bus to Rikers Island. Such a concept has the potential to inspire Original people everywhere as it is easily practiced and easily identifiable.

Naturally, the idea of prohibiting underwear appears at first glance as very restrictive, but on closer examination it is actually quite liberating and disinhibiting, hence why I call it "light exhibitionism." It is to a certain degree exhibiting the Black body, and the private areas of the Black body, in a way that is yet and still classy. Within the White community they call this act "going commando," for whatever reason, but it has no social or revolutionary connotations behind it. It is done just for its erotic value. The Black community has pretty much followed the White thus far with regard to this subject; they wore underwear when Whites told them to wear them and they considered it erotic so long as White people considered it erotic. As far as the counter-culture of not wearing it: such is practiced by a minority of Whites, let alone Blacks, though not consistently and mainly among women.

Conversely, while erotic agency will play a central role in bringing down the systems of plutocracy and inferiority; even as "intimate inter-bodily relations are the fundamental basis for human dignity[,] and thus for freedom in its widest sense" (Sheller 2012: 22); even so, light exhibitionism will be a method of unifying and inspiring the Black community towards manifesting that agency. Hence, within the struggle against White supremacy the Black woman will play a dominant and imperative role in both frustrating and complicating the White man's socio-sexual, heteronormative imagination.

In this, the Black woman will thereby become for him a Goddess of sexual ecstasy and counter-discursive erotica, thus reclaiming from him the offensive by using her attractive, indeed, seductive, charms as a means of prostrating the Beast to her divine nature. That said, a Beast of this calibre will unlikely prostrate himself easily, he will try to dominate, try to degrade, try to insult and belittle. But any negative reactions to the emotions she will be stirring in him will just be his instinctive and his normative drives working against each other: his libidinal drive going against his striving for domination and control. But the fact that this striving is not as prominent in the other races is no proof of the White *man's* destiny (teleology) to rule, it is more proof of his collective neuroses.

At this instance, we can see that light exhibitionism is a form of militant self-exposition – a meta-discursive militancy no doubt, but a militancy nonetheless. Again, as we are not infants we have no need to wear diapers. This is said in spite of the doctrine of hygiene that has been spoon-fed to large quantities of us as a people, but I repeat, it is far more hygienic to thoroughly clean your private areas, before and after you bathe or shower. Indeed, the golden rule of light exhibitionism is: whenever you take a shit take a shower. Add to that the added responsibility for Black women to start using tampons over panty-liners and it becomes even more complicated. Obviously, the Black woman may object, saying, tampon makers use unhealthy substances in their products. To this I will say that if you as a Black woman were to write to the tampon manufacturers and brands, not via email but through either Insta or direct mail, and complain about this discrepancy demanding that they make a more natural tampon they would eventually correct it.

Moreover, with the technical undiapering of Original people this sexualised act becomes infused with socio-political indices. Within the Black woman, thus placed in the position of sexualised agent, her agency to do or to refuse to do the act of light exhibitionism sets her in a place of being at once the *zalim*'s enemy and also his fantasy. She becomes the dream woman: the vision of socio-political freedom fighter, while yet the symbol of sexualised and erotic freedom, an unattainable other that drives to sexual frustration and psychological traumata at the Black woman's sexual availability to her Black man and her determination to fight the White man's position of dominance in the existing world system.

This desexualising of such a hypersexual act will create for the Black man at one time a hesitation and at another an ideal. It is a consternation, on the one hand, due to the public prohibition of bare bottoms: "What if my wife were looked at in a lustful way. I would have to be ready to kill every man she walked passed." This fear of the Black man is tempered by his own sexual admiration for those women who do indulge in this pastime, particularly those who do it for counter-cultural reasons. However, this admiration is not enough to convince any man to tolerate such a licentious theory; sexuality used as a form of resistance seems too dangerous, and subjects our women to danger. If we were unable to protect her from the White man's advances and murders before this light exhibitionism then why do we think we can protect her from its own inevitable negative impacts?

Fanon spoke of a similar consternation and hesitation to involve women in Algeria's struggle against colonialism: "The decision to involve women as active elements of the Algerian Revolution was not reached lightly. In a sense, it was the very conception of the combat that had to be modified" (Fanon 1965: 48). The new Algerian that came into being as a result of the anti-colonial struggle affected both male and female. New dimensions of the struggle had to be unfolded, new spatial and cultural norms had to be constructed. Here the Algerian woman was as much a factor as the male combatant. For example, Fanon mentioned how, "in the mountains, women helped the *guerrilla* during halts or when convalescing after a wound or a case of typhoid contracted in the [mountain]" (Fanon 1965: 48).

In this phase of the anti-colonial struggle the woman was a nurse or at best a therapist, albeit unqualified, she took care of the male combatants physically as well as emotionally. As mentioned the Black woman plays a similar role in the Black man's struggle against White supremacy. True indeed, that struggle has not entered the combative phase, but that is not to say it is not alive. The current role of the Black woman in the struggle is a source of support and strength but she is also an organiser, promoter, agitator, inspiration, and militant. Not all Black women can fill all these posts in the struggle but all Black women have a body. The Black body is instinctively sexualised by the White and other non-Blacks. Rather than fear or challenge this perception we should instead use it to our advantage – as any combatant uses the enemy's propaganda to their own advantage – to bring down White supremacy.

The non-verbal/non-literary forms of discursive interaction – that is, the discursive embodiment of the Black woman – operate on a far more libidinal, subconscious, pre-cognitive level. They entrap and captivate minds with profound effect. This discursive embodiment, the use of sexuality to articulate rebellion and resistance, is nothing new though. Sheller (2012: 26) articulated that throughout Black history "gender and sexuality … were not peripheral concerns; they were *central* to the practice of slavery, to antislavery movements, and to the reorganization of post-slavery societies. At each step along the way, gender and sexuality were also racially and ethnically charged, electrifying daily conflicts, sparking collective protests, and adding voltage to armed struggle." It is without doubt that the sexuality of the Black body, particularly that of the Black woman, has caused White imaginations to be driven to near madness throughout our shared history together.

Nevertheless, the Black Gods should discard their underwear together with the Black Goddesses and also take to light exhibitionism. In this, both would have made, not only open rebellion against the West, but affirmed their seat in the imagination (*khayal*) of the non-Black, particularly the White, as both deity and emancipator. We show that our culture is freedom, we reveal the uniqueness of our struggle, that it is not only a socio-economic struggle against the plutocracy nor yet merely a discursive/counter-discursive struggle against White superiority; we are waging an all-out struggle on both fronts: the discursive and the socio-economic. Such a fight, a counter-cultural fight, requires techniques that are controversial, maybe even counter-intuitive, but are nonetheless effective.

Light exhibitionism, however, should ultimately, be seen as nothing more than a mark of distinction, a seal showing that one belongs to the thearchist movement, and not simply as a combative counter-performance used to weaken White people. Moreover, rather than us Gods fearing and paternalistically trying to protect our Goddesses from potential trouble; like with the MGTs we should provide them with the means and training to protect themselves (with regard to armed training and unarmed training, teaching them to strike hard at the private areas of the body to provide maximum damage), thereby raising them from the position of dependence on us to one of liberated Black siren – let the devil touch her at his own risk.

Consequently, while we Blacks, from the time we were stolen from Africa, have been the victims of racially motivated attacks, we now face something far more pernicious, there is a right-wing school of thought based on vulgar Kingism – the using of Dr. King's words and ideals against the very people he fought so hard to defend. That is not to say that Dr. King had no care or concern for non-Blacks, but he would definitely hate that his ideals and principles were being used to condemn and demonise his own people – who are still the victims of murder, attack, hate crimes, and discrimination – by the same type of people who would have condemned him and his movement were they alive during that time.

White supremacy, based on socio-economic and psycho-discursive positionings, can only be challenged when the world no longer sees White people as worthy of their position. It will take people to overthrow a people; it will take Allah to inspire the people to do it. The motion of the Black struggle from adolescent to its more mature phases will need to adopt this cultural reality not simply as a phase of the struggle but as a part of the divine Black repertoire. This means abandoning underwear permanently as a means of establishing theocentric cultural freedom.

IV

In all, the spatial affinities of the Black person to the opposite sex in heteronormative encounters qualified the Black man and woman for instances of non-verbal/non-literary bodily discourses. One of the loudest things that could be spoken in this way is the sexually evocative statement. But yet such a statement can also effectively change institutionalised norms and balance socio-political indices, as Sheller mentioned: "intimate bodily encounters within disciplined workplaces (including domestic ones), organized public and semipublic spaces, and counter-spaces of performance and counter-performance can sometimes reproduce governing ideals of respectability yet can also deploy sexual and erotic agency to undo the gender, racial, and sexual inequalities that uphold normative orders" (Sheller 2012: 26). The sexual space thus inhabited by the light exhibitionist is one of the revolutionary not only in the battlefield but in all fields available.

Notwithstanding, it will be important for the sexualised Black woman to remember that it is not her goal, in light exhibitionism, to simply attract the White man, though such will happen; nor to simply nurse the Black man, to be his emotional and sensual support and resurrection (*ba'th*); but to self-identify, to basically become fully real and fully self. At the same time, the moment that Black women (and Black men) take off their drawers they put themselves in the firing line. First, they will need to begin the practice of shaving, lotioning, and perfuming or cologning their private areas. Second, they will need to prepare themselves for the accusations of manipulation, deceit, blindness, corruption, discrimination, racism, sexism, sexual slavery, and primitivism that will come flying from all places.

Again, it could be asked: *how can you fight primitivism by doing something so blatantly regarded as primitive and uncivilised?* The issue is that *they* set the rules, so no matter what *we* do that is our own it will be criticised as either infantile, abnormal, criminal, barbaric, savage, primitive, or uncivilised. Rather than trying to run from these labels let us meet them head on by showing White people what hypocrites they are in condemning our Black sexuality, while lusting after the Black body. This form of the struggle, the discarding of underwear, is an attack on all things White people, and particularly White men, claim make them civilised. When it comes to the heart of the matter, they are just as instinctual and savage as they claim the Black man is.

Returning to the case of the Algerian woman, Fanon gave a brief history of her position, particularly with regard to the veil, in the anti-colonial struggle. Indeed, the symbol of the veil became as important in their struggle as the symbol of underwear could become in our struggle: "In the beginning, the veil was a mechanism of resistance, but its value for the social group remained very strong. The veil was worn because tradition demanded a rigid separation of the sexes, but also because the occupier *was bent on unveiling Algeria*. In a second phase, the mutation occurred in connection with the Revolution and under special circumstances. The veil was abandoned in the course of revolutionary action. What had been used to block the psychological and political offensives of the occupier became a means, an instrument" (Fanon 1965: 63).

Fanon (1965), in speaking of the experience of the Algerian woman during the course of the Algerian struggle against colonialism articulated issues that will most likely occur for the Black woman during the Black struggle against White supremacy. In the Algerians' determination to struggle for their humanity, for their dignity, they made headways within global identification. Worldwide, Algeria had sympathisers and apologists willing to support their cause. The Algerian woman, determined to struggle for the same humanity as the Algerian men in their dehumanised, acculturated situation, made very clear that gender was a feature of warfare and revolution that is ignored at the peril of the revolution.

At the same time, we godbodies fight not simply for re-humanisation but for deification. This means we face a foe more tenacious than even the White man, we face the astral powers of Iblis and his *jinn* who gave White people their power in the first place. The Algerian woman faced her own challenge, and to a different extent. The climbing of the Algerian woman to the position of the European woman (a position that was at the time higher than that of the Algerian man), was something that would mean her whole posture would have to change, as would her mannerisms. She now had to see self not only as important, but, with a European arrogance, as all-important.

In similar vein, the exhibitionist Black person, particularly the Black woman (though including the Black men), would now be in the position to be sensual, to radiate sensuality, to manifest the sexiness that comes from an internal confidence. Here our inhibitions, along with our underwear, must be discarded. We basically become in the struggle a fantasy; and the now exhibitionist Black women, in similitude to the unveiled Algerian woman, will now have to adjust herself to this level of struggle. Fanon explained this adjustment as such, "The unveiled body seems to escape, to dissolve. She has an impression of being improperly dressed, even of being naked. She experiences a sense of incompleteness with great intensity. She has the anxious feeling that something is unfinished, and along with this a frightful sensation of disintegrating. The absence of the veil distorts the Algerian woman's corporal pattern. She quickly has to invent new dimensions for her body, new means of muscular control" (Fanon 1965: 59).

Now, that is not to say the Black woman will necessarily feel such extremities when she practices light exhibitionism, but it is never fully appreciated by men the courage it takes for a woman to go without wearing underwear. Even while wearing underwear many Black women still feel levels of anxiety when wearing something simple like a short skirt or dress. However, to be genuinely seductive one cannot be timid, and to make a bold bodily statement like not wearing underwear one must be unoffendably and unapologetically audacious. Therefore, if she is confronted on it she must make very clear that she knows what she has done and that she stands by what she has done.

Still, our Black women will also undoubtedly face another difficulty in practicing light exhibitionism from what the Algerian women faced, according to Fanon, in unveiling. As Fanon pointed out concerning what she went through in her transition, "She [had to] overcome all timidity, all awkwardness ... and at the same time be careful not to overdo it" (Fanon 1965: 59). The brave Black women who take to this form of combat will effectively be frustrating the sexual appetites of White men and indulging the sexual proclivities of Black men thereby creating in Black eroticism a militancy that will affect social positionings. The shift from martial resistance to erotic resistance and back again to martial resistance will thereby shift spheres of attack and wreak havoc on the White conception of the Black. While we will still be looked on as daemons in their eyes, we will no longer be ashamed daemons hiding from our natures, but proud daemons unabashedly displaying our sexuality.

Then again, Fanon also articulated another dimension of the struggle of the unveiled Algerian woman that will no doubt affect the Black woman too: "In the course of her comings and goings, it would happen that the unveiled Algerian woman was seen by a relative or a friend of the family. The father was sooner or later informed. He would naturally hesitate to believe such allegations. Then more reports would reach him. Different persons would claim to have seen 'Zohra or Fatima unveiled walking like a ... My Lord, protect us! ...' The father would then decide to demand explanations. He would hardly have begun to speak when he would stop. From the [young woman's] look of firmness the father would have understood that her commitment was of long standing" (Fanon 1965: 60). The resolute determination of the unveiled Algerian woman must be an example to the exhibitionist Black woman.

To be sure, Fanon expressed that the main roles of the unveiled Algerian woman during the pre-terrorist phase of the Algerian Revolution were simplistic: "The regrouped Algerian woman, cut off from her husband who ... remained with the combatants, [took] care of the old and the orphans, [learned] to read and to sew and often, in a group of several companions, [left] the camp and [joined] the Army of National Liberation", "among the tasks entrusted" to her was "the bearing of messages, of complicated verbal orders learned by heart, sometimes despite complete absence of schooling. But she [was] also called upon to stand watch, for an hour and often more, before a house where district leaders [were] conferring" (Fanon 1965: 117, 53). When the battles were fought using terrorism she also distributed bombs and weapons, and though the French settlers soon caught wind of this tactic her resolve still remained.

Though Fanon claimed that the veil was taken up again later, having been "stripped once and for all of its exclusively traditional dimension" (Fanon 1965: 63); it is my hope that underwear will not have to be taken up again after our struggle, by either men or women; so that the beauty of the Black body will not become again an aesthetic mystery, but will endure like a sentinel guarding our minds against the threat of any form of White supremacy. These ideas also coincide with Malcolm X's aesthetic vision for the Black community, when he said, "Black artists need to recapture our heritage and our identity if we are ever to liberate ourselves from the bonds of white supremacy" (Malcolm X 1992; quoted in Daulatzai 2012: 105). The artistic beauty of the Black body is captured by no greater paint brush than the human eye, and its image has no greater beauty than when it is uncovered.

For this cause it cannot be overemphasised how imperative it is that any Black man or Black woman who participate in light exhibitionism – those under the age of 18 should be restricted – should clean thoroughly both private areas of their body so as to keep their aesthetic value. Exhibitionism will also mean they will have to drop activities like sagging their jeans. Leave sagging of jeans to the kids. In fact, practicing light exhibitionism even forces us to be more sanitary than those who wear underwear, so as to avoid public humiliation or personal uncleanness. We will basically reach a point where we despise filth so much that we soap our anus at least a hundred and eighty times rinsing it after soaping it sixty times after every time we defecate thus showing ourselves more hygienic than our opponents.

V

It may be asked at this point: what is the overall purpose of practicing light exhibitionism? The purpose is, firstly, as a weapon to fight against inherent White supremacy, secondly, to encourage Black people to act libidinally toward their brother or sister till we overthrow this inherently White supremacist system, and, thirdly, as a sign of proof one belongs to our movement. As an example of what I mean here: underwear actually causes more hygienic harm than good for both women and men in the long run. A woman's genitalia, as a result of underwear, can actually breed fungi and bacteria. By practicing light exhibitionism women can keep their genitalia from being over-moist, overheated, and underventilated, thus reducing the risk of contracting urinary tract infections and yeast infections.

For men, on the other hand, tight fitting underwear can overheat the testes and affect semen quality. Urologists have even found that going commando allows temperature regulation and testosterone optimisation. Warmer testicular temperatures can even impede testosterone production, which affects healthy masculinity, being itself the primary male hormone (obviously, women do not have testes, so they have no need to worry about their testosterone increasing). Not to mention the fact that for both men and women, maintaining a healthy genital environment contributes to endocrine function, which increases hormonal balance and stability. These are the medical benefits of not wearing any underwear, a product invented during Victorian times by the colonisers to control the bodies of the colonised.

Again, contrary to Dr. King's hopes, this system will not change by turning the other cheek. To assume that White people will not use any kindness we show them against us is to blind oneself to the history and sociology of those we are laying down our lives for. The world has no need for another Jesus, let alone a race of Jesuses. The first Jesus did his job and fulfilled his destiny. Our destiny is not to lay down our lives so White people can succeed and prosper, our destiny is to divinity. In the current social kinetic White people have all the power and use their position to perpetuate their supremacy and to denigrate all non-White people, and particularly us Blacks. The other races have seen and now share their contempt for Black people. To some White people it is even seen as a God-given right and privilege for them to have a level of exclusivity. The only way we can fight this current system of disempowerment is by asserting our own power. The counter is to do nothing at all and just tolerate while they get worse and worse in their superiority complex.

I must now at this point also warn the Black people who join in this erotic form of combat of two potential dangers that we may have to face: First, many in the White community may also choose to practice light exhibitionism and thereby dilute the power of the protest. Which thus brings us to the elephant in the room: the idea that going pantyless is already synonymous with European women. Can Black people really steal this practice from Europe and apply it to their own circumstances. Such a difficulty should not prove too bothersome though. Accordingly, White practitioners will not be able to outdo Original people should we maintain our position, as the calibre of Original people practicing light exhibitionism will make all the difference.

Furthermore, as Klein (2010: 85) said concerning the corporate adoption of revolutionary personas: "More indifference has met Apple computers' appropriation of Gandhi for their 'Think Different' campaign, and Che Guevara's reincarnation as the logo for Revolution Soda (slogan: 'Join the Revolution'…) and as the mascot of the upscale London cigar lounge, Che. […] Why? Because not one of the movements being 'co-opted' expressed itself primarily through style or attitude." Even so, it is not about the quantity, it is about the quality of people doing it. If we Gods and Goddesses begin to add light exhibitionist practices into our discourse then we will produce a higher class of revolutionist; thus it should not take too long for us to become synonymous with it even as Black people are already synonymous with sex right now (Fanon 2008).

Second, many in the White community may become so enamoured with those Blacks who do practice light exhibitionism that they will go out of their way to seduce us. Therefore any Black person incapable of resisting a White person or who gets paid in their line of work for having sex with White people, rather than compromise the movement should just keep out of it. That is not to say that White people can never join our movement, we obviously have lots of White Five Percenters, that is to say Whites need to work twice as hard to distance themselves from their position in *al-mujtama* and *al-'alam*, and need to work even harder to fight against their fellow White brothers' and sisters' position in *al-mujtama* and *al-'alam*. That also means bringing more to the table than words and protests (both of which they like to take the leading positions in in *Black* movements), it means a willingness to bleed for the cause, to lose a little blood.

Accordingly, however, I must now answer an important question that will undoubtedly arise from the Black feminist concerning my suggestion that Black men and women practice light exhibitionism: what about the pornographic gaze that women have been fighting against for decades? In answer to this question I must unfortunately say Black erotica will not prevent our Black women from receiving the pornographic gaze: but that is a problem inherent in any pro-sex female movement. Due to the libidinally charged nature of all organic beings sex is inexorably going to be projected into any movement that involves sexuality. Nonetheless, this is not necessarily a bad thing. Firstly, we need to remember that there is a pure gaze that can also come from men with a more refined palette. Secondly, the pornographic gaze is not limited to men, but women also have a tendency to view their male constituents with the same pornographic gaze. Basically, any sexism feared by the Black woman will also be encountered by the Black man, and she must remember that Black men are just as exoticised by White women as they are by White men.

Again, when we deconstruct the pornographic gaze we find that it is not so much the problem at all but the misogyny attached to it. When White women use the pornographic gaze on Black men it is hardly problematised due, firstly, to the oppressed (*mazlum*) situation women occupy, and, secondly, to the dominant images of Black men being the hypersexual stud. The Black woman, on the other hand, if viewed through pornographic lenses usually comes across as the dominatrix or the exotic. Her femininity is quite the opposite, in the dominant parlance, to White femininity, which usually conjures images of innocence and timidity. We are not here suggesting that Black women either try to change these stereotypes or that they should seek to avoid getting viewed with the pornographic gaze. *In fact, the point is to be viewed with this gaze yet remain unavailable, detached, and inaccessible.* The pornographic gaze therefore, gets politically charged and demystified through methods in which protests and speeches would invariably fail.

Of course, I must also make the request that any Black person who choose to practice erotic bodily discourses, including light exhibitionism, as both a weapon to fight White supremacy and as a means of inspiring the *dhikr* Allah in those Black people they interact with, not look with an evil eye on those Black people, or even on those Gods or Goddesses, who do not also join us. Though it is a powerful form of inspiring the *dhikr* Allah – far more powerful than any form of transcendental meditation – on a practical level these are very controversial strategies and it must be respected how difficult it will be for some people to be involved with them, whether out of fear, inertia, or out of respect. The transition will especially be difficult for women; for which cause we men must be their rock.

In all, our struggle takes on a different dimension to the struggle of Algeria, although there will be some levels of similarity, as Fanon explained: "The relations of wife and husband have … become modified in the course of the war of liberation" (Fanon 1965: 111). Indeed, the God and his Goddess will become immersed in the Black struggle through the bodily aesthetic and discursive of Black erotica. The God, at the same time, must also be ready to adopt more overt forms of resistance, he must become the revolutionary *par excellence* very much like the Algerian. "A militant of long-standing, the husband would frequently vanish, and sometimes [his wife] would find a revolver under his pillow. As the searches multiplied, the woman would demand of her husband that he keep her informed. She would insist on being given certain names and addresses of militants to warn in case the husband should be arrested" (Fanon 1965: 112).

In these sorts of instances the God and the Goddess both represent revolutionaries, they are both the extreme antithesis to social norms and realities: here again the godbody represents a movement in similitude to the FLN. Women who join must immediately be armed and trained in physical combat; therefore, though she will, firstly, be called upon for sensual support, as she proves her loyalty to the cause she will be given more challenging and expeditious tasks in the struggle. As time goes by a Goddess within the godbody will command more power in the movement, one not too different even from the Algerian, "The struggle for liberation raised woman to such a level of inner renewal that she is even able to call her husband a coward. Rather frequently, by allusions or explicitly, the Algerian woman would upbraid her husband for his inactivity, his refusal to commit himself, his lack of militancy. This was the period when young girls among themselves would vow never to let themselves be married to a man who did not belong to the F.L.N." (Fanon 1965: 111.) Indeed, any Black woman who is willing to join the godbody, or to at least engage in light exhibitionism, has every right to question the courage of any Black man who is unwilling to also do so.

VI

Now it could be said at this point: Black erotica will only end up exacerbating White complexes. True, but that is the point, by giving White people a fight they are unable to win we create a trauma that invariably ruins their discursive articulation. In the long run they will either yield to our sexual presentation or regress to archaic ideations. In either case the discourse of White superiority will no longer be validated. Still, by striking at the root of biological existence, what makes us a part of nature, with Black erotica, we may to some degree appear to also be trying to justify the pornographic gaze and its heteronormative connotations. That is not the case, however; what we are doing is exacerbating White theories of Black exoticness and otherness in order, not to integrate deeper into White society, but to declare our independence from its normative behaviours.

Any gaze we acquire – whether pornographic, colonial, racial, unwanted, or male – must be recognised as an inevitable side-effect of being othered, of being differentiated, and of being stratified by a power structure in which to be Black will always represent being exotic, being different, and unfortunately, being lesser. We cannot, and perhaps should not, try to change these, *per se*, but instead simply live as representatives of a different and unique culture that is threatened by their discourse of White superiority. Even so, many White people are not ready to accept that they have a discourse of White superiority or that they exoticise non-Whites, the only way to show them will be to take the punch; thus begging the question: is Black erotica really a progressive movement? It appears to neither challenge male sexism nor pornographic fantasies so of what use is it to a Black female intellectual?

In the first instance, though Black erotica as a sexual bodily discourse appears to be creating nothing but a heteronormative male fantasy world, most men would, and will still, fight against the actual practice of it due to the freedoms it provides to the women who perform it. Ultimately, it shows the male populous that women have power. On an important terrain they manifest to men that her body, though desired by him, belongs to her. In the second instance, they take sexual power and racialise it, even as White people have taken economic, cultural, and intellectual power and racialised them. If we, as Black people, must be sexualised then it should be on our own terms and not on the terms of the White man.

Also, while erotica and pornography are both exhibitionistic articulations of libidinal energy (*hubbiyya*) there are two fundamental differences between them that must be acknowledged: first, erotica has class, and, second, erotica has narrative substance. Indeed, one of the most expertly explained definitions of erotica comes to us from the eminent philosopher Socrates in Plato's *Symposium*. Though I may disagree with Socrates' categorising Eros as a daemon I cannot fault his systematic delineation.

Consequently, Socrates saw erotic agency as the instigator of five progressive desires: (i) Love for a singular beautiful body: the love object himself or herself succumbing to standards of both the familiar and the sublime. (ii) Love for all beautiful bodies: the lover learns at this stage that scores of people possess as much, if not more, beauty than the original locus and so desire to see as many as possible. (iii) Love for *psychikos* beauty, that is, love for sensual beauty as *psychikos* was originally translated as sensual: at this stage they realise that a beautiful body is not enough as even a physically unattractive person who is sensually beautiful is more beautiful than the person who is beautiful in body only. (iv) Love for *ergetikos, nomikos*, and *epitdeumikos* beauty or the action, regulation, and practice of beauty: at this higher stage they come to narrow in on which sensual activity or practice always applies to beauty and so desire to see only that. (v) The highest stage, love for *epistemikos* beauty or the science of beauty: at this stage they reach the point of seeking that Absolute Beauty which surpasses all these. Conversely, all these stages, according to Socrates, are inspired by erotica.

Nevertheless, these five stages in *Black* erotica could be articulated as: (i) Black beauty, (ii) polyamory, (iii) Afrosensuality, (iv) light exhibitionism, and (v) seductionism. At the first level would be Black beauty. Basically, the perfume, cosmetics, hair, clothing, and body sculpting industries make billions of dollars convincing ordinary women that they can make themselves and others see them as beautiful. Putting aside all the politics of whether there are actually any "ordinary women," or whether they should have to devote themselves to looking beautiful at all, or even care so much about beauty, let us try to remember that Socrates claimed he learned these stages of beauty from Diotima of Mantineia, who he called a *wise woman* with many kinds of knowledge. The fact is, if the products and methods of the beauty industries were ineffective at raising women's beauty, or at least their confidence in their beauty, they would not be generating the multibillions of dollars they currently do. Effectively, perfumes, cosmetics, hairstyling, good clothing, and an incredible body can make a woman beautiful. Black beauty is when these industries are designed specifically for Black women. Those Black women who use them will ultimately inspire first level erotic feelings.

At the second level is polyamory or plural love. If a Black woman, regardless of her physical beauty, even if she despised the beauty industries and vowed never to care about any of them, she can still inspire erotic desire. She even gives herself an edge over all those beautiful and beautified women, by letting it be known that she is not intimidated if a man has sex with other women. Again, putting aside the politics of male societal dominance, and the ethics of cheating, if a woman genuinely lacks jealousy and has confidence in her own abilities and relationship she will be perceived as sexy. Far sexier even than a woman with just a pretty or beautiful face. With that one move she would have not only reached a place where she can inspire second level erotic feelings, but she would have made herself a regular in his life, not simply a one-night stand.

At the third level is Black sensuality or Afrosensuality. Sensuality itself is when someone uses their sexual energy to drive or inspire others to think of sex with them. Thus, they inspire third level erotic feelings. Afrosensuality is when they consistently, devastatingly, and Africanly use sexuality in their words or behaviours. Again, a Black woman can be subtly or overtly sensual: from talking openly about her body or sexual skills to touching his body or her own. However, when a woman is able to use techniques like anchoring, triggering, amplifying, flirting, or word emphasising in an overtly sexual way, whether she is polyamorous or not, whether she is society's standard of beauty or not, she will leap miles ahead of the women who are any one of the two without doing so. Indeed, the libidinal techniques she uses on the first day she meets him will stay in his mind months after they develop a relationship, even if she is a jealous woman.

The fourth level, however, is the money level: light exhibitionism. Any woman, even if she is absolutely ugly by her own standards and the worlds; even if she is not polyamorous but in fact insecure about her chances if there is another woman; even if she never has had or will have any sexiness at all and has no idea how to get it; she can still leap lightyears above whole groups of women who have great beauty, and practice expertly both polyamory and Afrosensuality, and she can do it with just one practice.

There is a story about a fox and a hedgehog. The fox is crafty, cunning, quick, and dangerous, much stronger and more sophisticated than the lowly hedgehog. The hedgehog is dowdy, ugly, and much slower and clumsier than the fox. Usually the hero of most European folk tales, the fox wins every time. However, when the fox, with his multiplicity of moves and tactics, jumps in front of the hedgehog to catch him, the hedgehog just performs one simple move and the fox is defeated every time. Curling up into a ball, with spikes pointing in every direction, the fox stands no chance and has to admit defeat. Even so, that same ugly, jealous, insecure, and unsexy woman can leap lightyears ahead of a group of very beautiful women, who practice, expertly, both polyamory and sensuality with just one activity.

Let us say the man she desires is a rich, handsome, player with a group of beautiful, polyamorous, expert seducers on call, and an even larger group of beautiful and gorgeous women throwing themselves at him regularly. Well, love is love, the heart wants what the heart wants, and her heart wants him to love her and only her. What chance does she really have, remember, she is ugly by her own standards and the worlds. The truth is, all she needs to do to accomplish her goal is buy a ton of dresses, both simple and complex, that reveal when a woman is not wearing any underwear, then she needs to wear one of them, while practicing light exhibitionism, in front of him.

The first time he sees her he will notice her, and as a player he will pursue. That one action would have effectively not only put her in a league with all the beautiful and sexy women he sees on a regular basis, it would have put her ahead of all of them. Whether they have sex that night or not he will want to see her again. If the next time he sees her she is wearing another, different, dress that also reveals that she is not wearing underwear then she will automatically leap to the top of the list of women he desires. Effectively, she would have inspired fourth level erotic feelings in him. If the next time he sees her she is again wearing a different dress that also reveals that she is not wearing any underwear she will from that time become his only standard of beauty (remember, she even used to see her own self as ugly). Not only so, but he will see her as an extremely beautiful woman, more beautiful than all the other women in his life, who will also feel boring and unimpressive to him (again, remember, these are all expert seducers).

If the fourth time he sees her she is again wearing a different dress that, in its own way, also reveals that she is not wearing any underwear, he will fall madly in love with her. Whether he confesses his love or not is of no concern, the act of light exhibitionism and the consistency of the repetition would have anchored in him the idea that this woman always wears beautiful dresses (the dresses themselves may be cheap and ugly, the point is that he will see them as beautiful) and never wears underwear. She would have effectively taught him to fall madly in love with her with the power of anchoring and fanatical consistency.

At this point, he will be ready to tell her he is giving up all other women for her and with all honesty do it, as very few other women really go without underwear with such consistency. Still, she will have to regulate this practice and make it very permanent, otherwise the inconsistency at whatever stage of this process will cause the outcome to vary. Human beings crave consistency and fear loss. By her not wearing underwear the first day the first manifestation of this fear will be that this is a onetime thing never or rarely to be done again. By her not wearing underwear the second time he sees her the fear will now be manifest in the idea that she sees this as an occasional thing but generally she will be just like every other woman. By her not wearing underwear the third time he sees her the fear will be that she will get bored or give up and just wear underwear the next time he sees her. By the fourth time she would have effectively anchored in his mind that she herself equals no underwear, and all the pleasures that entails. Now his fear of loss will be of losing her. That is the power of true light exhibitionism, and why I encourage it as a godbody practice, so long as the Goddess keeps her lower regions clean and smelling good, she will have this power.

At the final level is seductionism. At this level the Black person (but continuing on with our analogy of a Black woman) applies all four methods of inspiring eroticism together with an unoffendable, unapologetic, and unstoppable drive to have sex with the man she wants. Herein, she makes herself beautiful regularly; she is polyamorous and not intimidated by her man having sex with other women; she is Afrosensual in both words and behaviours; she is a light exhibitionist through and through; and she is determined to have sex with this man come what may. This woman will ultimately inspire fifth level erotic feelings from any and all men.

No woman has to be a seductionist, but the Black woman who is a seductionist has mastered the science of beauty. Such a woman is obviously like hen's teeth, if not imaginary, but she will be the desire, love, and obsession of all the men she interacts with, especially on a regular basis. The level of erotic desire this woman will inspire within the men she interacts with will be the greatest amount they could possibly experience in that moment, and as that will be where she gets her pleasure from she will be like an eroto-masochist.

Yes, I am well aware of how controversial the idea of masochism can be for women, particularly Black women, due to our complex history with slavery, segregation, and colonisation and the sufferings and pains we as a people have endured and currently do endure. Such ideas even go beyond the already "problematic" notion of struggle love that many Black women in the upper classes outright reject, and many in the lower classes are desperately seeking to escape from. However, at the risk of promoting concepts that are unacceptable to these types of Black people, many of whom subscribe to the doctrines of Black Prosperity Theology, those who challenge and critique female suffering, masochism, or struggle love may, at the same time, be policing women's right to engage with and even get pleasure from such realities. Believe it or not there are plenty of women who actually like and respect the realities of suffering, masochism, and struggle love, obviously, within limits and with their caveats.

An even more troubling and problematic notion, for some reason, is the men, especially Black men like myself, who are themselves masochists or have masochistic tendencies. Our existence threatens the Black manosphere and the image of hegemonic masculinity many Black males seek to display to the non-Black world. Herein the two dominant identifiers within the Black communities of the world, but particularly in America, are of Black excellence or the Black girl boss. These highly idealised images of Black love and "Black Power," are promoted and encouraged to the Black communities of the world, not only as aspiration goals but as Black authenticity. Challenges to this model, such as consensual masochistic behaviour, can only be based on deception, weakness, confusion, trauma, or coercion.

It seems there is such a determination to vocalise "the real" voice of those in such transgressive relationships that they fail to believe that we may actually like these. For example, I like seductionistic, exhibitionistic, polyamorous, masochistic relationships. These are, in fact, at the top of my list. To be clear, it is not that I enjoy suffering or pain, nor is it that I get large amounts of pleasure from pain (though I am able to); but great amounts of pleasure filled with trace amounts of struggle and suffering to me make life worth living. Think of any novel, movie, or drama that lacks, DRAMA. Such an epic failure would be such a boring, chessy, vanilla, and banal disaster that its only entertainment value would either be as a cautionary tale of what not to do, or simply to read or to watch the spectacles/parade of awfulness for its sheer awfulness.

This is how I see those pristine, perfect, polished, couples on TV, and in magazines, shit, this is how I see most couples. Though admittedly not all, celebrity or manosphere. They are not "couples goals" to me, they are usually a lie or an inhibition. Either way, leave me with my transgressive/slightly problematic relationships. It seems that in seeking so hard to voice the miseries and difficulties/problems of suffering and struggle love a lot of commentators fail to articulate that there are also beauties in struggle love worth maintaining. That is not to down or vilify those who speak against struggle love, everybody has their thing, just to share another side to the story. There are Black men and women that actually like suffering, such men and women that personify Black eroticism or what could also be called hypereroticism, doing so both privately and publicly, not for validation, respect, or a round of applause, but for the pleasure of behaving hypererotically.

Moreover, if these eroto-masochists were to experience rejection, humiliation, or some other form of suffering for behaving hypererotically, they would not be weakened or destroyed but feed off of that suffering using it to go even further and behave even more transgressive, whether in their words (to get women) or in their visuals (to get men). Again, no woman is being forced to do any of these things, or to climb any of these levels. In fact, the example I have been using throughout of a Black woman may have been a little deceptive. It has purely been based on the understanding that there are a lot more complexities to women than simply those that desire power or wealth, many actually desire to practice and inspire hypereroticism, for and in men, women, or both. For those women that have this desire I have used this example. However, any seductionist, whether the seductionist be male or female, is an eroto-masochist. If you desire to be such, whether you are a man or woman, then you will have to climb the ladder. Again, such a ladder may seem somewhat abominable to the anti-sexer crowd but from a pro-sex perspective it manifests nothing less than the crescendo of life.

True, the sexism of Black men towards Black women will still be an issue, however, we will, to a certain degree, be problematising that sexist mentality by the standard of Black women practicing it. For example, when a model or a nympho practices a form of Black eroticism they may be easily baffled by Black sexism, but when a Black Goddess or even a conscious Black woman practices it, then they will be able to take any Black sexist to school and so expunge his sexism with his humiliation. It is time for a higher class of revolutionary, and that is exactly what the bodily discourse of Black eroticism brings. For this cause, it is not only respectable but important that the Goddesses participate in the practices of Black eroticism, as by doing so they expose and confront the Black male exoticising of Black female bodies, while still showing them their level of power in the struggle against White supremacy.

Finally, it is my hope that this second sexual revolution I am calling for with Black (or hyper-) eroticism may broaden into a sensual resurrection (*ba'th*). How I see this is with Black eroticism introduced into our movement, together with training in armed and unarmed combat to keep our women from rape, we would effectively be creating a situation where we as a people will be able to resurrect (*bi'thah*) our transmigrational, transhistorical, transgenerational souls. The Gods and Goddesses will be the centre of this movement but it will spill over into the Black community as a whole, especially if our women are granted the right to dress how they choose to with no limitations but the underwear thing. Yet, while some Gods may look at some of the arguments raised in this chapter as a corruption of 120, it is my hope that the majority will instead see them as a refining of 120.

The Divine Parousia

In an imperial age the idea of multiculturalism is nothing more than a ruse for the cultural, political, social, and economic supremacy of one power over those within its remit. This is evidenced through the fact that the GUSE not only promotes multiculturalism but also enforces it. That is not to say that what they are doing is good either: imperialism has many forms and US neo-colonialism is one of the most in-your-face yet subtle forms of imperialism that has ever been inflicted upon the world. Cultural supremacy, in the form of cultural imperialism (in this case, the imperialism of multiculturalism) allows the US to continue its domination of the world (Daulatzai 2012) under the ruse of promoting ethical, and thereby reasonable, ways of life, that is, cultural (*thaqafi*) practices.

Yet although culture is itself defined by Chiu et alia. (2011: 4) as "a knowledge tradition of ideas and practices," the representations inherent in recognising a culture also play a big part in how the boundaries faced by bicultural individuals between both mainstream and ethnic identification are negotiated. Ethnic traditions in many cases will differ from mainstream traditions, sometimes substantially so; but as No et alia. (2011: 222) found: "Bicultural individuals often find themselves trying to reconcile the presence of the two cultural identities, and [some] individuals vary in how they negotiate" these positions. In their research they isolated three main responses to the bicultural predicament: creolisation, integration, and contextualisation.

No et alia. (2011) considered creolisation a kind of hybridising of cultures even as "Creolization in language happens when groups speaking different languages have extended contact and develop a common language that has its basis in the different languages spoken by the original groups but is distinct from both as an end product. [Even so, cultural creolization] also refers to the formation of a new culture with inputs from the contacting groups' various cultures of origin" (No et alia. 2011: 225).

Conversely, "Integration occurs when a person maintains [their] heritage culture and a good relationship with the host culture, identifying with both cultures at the same time" (No et alia. 2011: 224). Whereas contextualisation is when "Bicultural individuals ... switch between two modes of behavior depending on situational demands. They adopt the language, problem-solving strategy, social behavior, response style, and self-description that are characteristic of one of the two cultures so as to create a context-dependent cultural identity" (No et alia. 2011: 222). Though these three methods of dealing with bicultural identification are the most common, one of the smarter methods of handling this type of situation is to follow the example set by Ashkenaz and practice your culture as counter-culture regardless of mainstream opposition.

There are, at the same time, some obvious differences between the Ashkenazim and the Blacks, as Sartre pointed out, "A Jew, white among white men, can deny that he is a Jew, can declare himself a man among men. The Negro cannot deny that he is Negro nor claim for himself this abstract uncolored humanity" (Sartre 1976; quoted in Mudimbe 1988: 84). That is, the Ashkenazim can always change their name to a more American or Irish sounding name and so blend in with White society, whereas we Blacks are unable to conceal our true identity or racial orientation. The fact is, and it is a controversial fact, the Black race probably subconsciously has a predilection towards suffering that has caused our race to suffer more than most other groupings.

The Ashkenazi, the Irish, the Italians, and the Germans who fled to the United States in the late nineteenth and early twentieth centuries may have had problems, and even the Chinese, the Japanese, and the Arabs had difficulties, but none of these groups were subject to the viciousness and cruelty of European slavery. And even after slavery was abolished in the United States none of them had to deal with mass lynchings, police dogs, fire hoses, mob beatings, or arrests for sitting on buses or eating at cafés; that was endured by Black people simply for being Black, and if they did experience it such was usually the result of their closeness to Blacks racially. True indeed, while it is very easy for a bicultural Ashkenazi to feel uncomfortable, even excluded, when surrounded by Arabs; or for them to feel isolated in a conference attended only by Blacks, particularly when slavery is discussed; it is still easier for them to blend in with White society and find inclusion than it is for those same Arabs or those same Blacks.

(Women may claim a similar exclusion with regard to men as Blacks claim with regard to Whites but they have never had to face the danger of getting locked up for drinking from the same fountain as a man; yet there was a time when my own late father could have been locked up for drinking from a White fountain, and when his contemporaries could have been lynched for whistling at White women. The legacy of those days has not passed simply because we elected a Black President or put up some new national flags. Indeed, women definitely do have difficulties, some even worse than what we Black brothers have, and I could never possibly understand them nor do I deny that, but Blacks face difficulties non-Black women could never possibly understand either and they have to admit that too).

No et alia. in articulating how this societal exclusion affects most bicultural groups explained that, "feelings of exclusion from a cultural group predict lower identification with that group ... Thus, how bicultural individuals negotiate the existence of their two cultural identities could depend on their perceived inclusion in the relevant cultural groups" (No et alia. 2011: 218). The societal exclusion of any cultural group, whether Ashkenazi, Muslim, White, or Black, is equivalent to what Durkheim (though not most of his followers) called *anomie*; and when it is combined with a collective consciousness of exclusion the product will be counter-culturalism, and if enough individuals from that social group or *mujtama* join the counter-culture it will be social crisis. What most White people fail to understand with Blacks and Muslims is that it is our exclusion from mainstream Western cultural identification that creates our rebellion against the dominant culture, thus producing the social crises that Daulatzai elucidated throughout his work.

The fact is, even Ashkenazi sufferings give them no right to be racist towards Black people or to feel superior to us. As a people we Blacks have also suffered and been ostracised very frequently, and, particularly in the United States, where we are currently far more under the heel of the White power structure than they are, who can just blend in and pretend to be a non-Ashkenazi White person. In fact, the only people in the Americas to have historically experienced something similar to the Black experience is the Native Americans (of both North and South America); though in the current global situation they are far more integrated into the mainstream than both Blacks and Muslims. Furthermore, the historical sufferings of Black people still run deep. We were slaves before the rise of Islam, we were slaves in the midst of the Muslim empires, and we were slaves during the rise of the European empires.

Although these aspects of our history are to our shame they are all the more proof, not that we are under Ham's curse, but that we are under Israel's curse, being the true people of Israel, as the prophet Hosea prophesied to the children of Israel in the Scriptures: "Because Ephraim hath made many altars to sin, altars shall be unto him to sin. I have written to him the great things of my law, but they were counted as a strange thing. They sacrifice flesh for the sacrifices of mine offerings, and eat it; but the Lord accepteth them not; now will he remember their iniquity, and visit their sins: they shall return to Egypt" (Hosea 8: 13). It is clear when the prophet Hosea said "they shall return to Egypt" he was not simply speaking of the physical land of Egypt, but he was speaking symbolically of bondage.

Or consider when no less an authority than the prophet Moses himself said,

> *"I will even appoint over you terror, consumption, and the burning ague, that shall consume the eyes, and cause sorrow of heart: and ye shall sow your seed in vain, for your enemies shall eat it. And I will set my face against you, and ye shall be slain before your enemies: they that hate you shall reign over you; and ye shall flee when none pursueth you" (Leviticus 26: 16-17).*

> *"And the Lord shall bring thee into Egypt again with ships, by the way whereof I spake unto thee, Thou shalt see it no more again: and there ye shall be sold onto your enemies for bondmen and bondwomen, and no man shall buy you" (Deuteronomy 28: 68).*

Allah even said, again, "The children also of Judah and the children of Jerusalem have ye sold unto the Grecians, that ye might remove them far from their border. Behold, I will raise them out of the place whither ye have sold them, and will return your recompence upon your own head" (Joel 3: 6, 7). Basically, this was clearly not meant to signify the physical lands of Egypt and Greece he was thus speaking of, but the symbolic. In like manner, as much as I respect all that the Ashkenazim have suffered at the hands of the Nazis, and their being delivered into a land that they can call their own, it is virtually impossible to look at these Scriptures and not at least notice how much closer they resemble Black history and reality than Ashkenazi. Indeed, a return to Egyptian bondage was prophesied by most of the prophets, though the second Egypt was believed to be Greece. Obviously, someone could look at these Scriptures and say they were already fulfilled during the time of the Grecian Empire, but as the law of repetition says, history will keep repeating itself until repentance is made. As our ancestors had not repented their destiny was set.

Still, it is very rare for an Ashkenazi to sow and another reap the benefits, but that constantly happens in the Black community. In fact, the Ashkenazi themselves have a proverb about us, calling us "liquid money" because we are so incapable of holding on to the money we make or sharing it within *our own community*. These Scriptures could be more aligned to the Black situation than the Ashkenazi because the Ashkenazi may not be the real Israel, at least not in Allah's sight, if they were then surely they would have been returned to bondage by ships and not just the Blacks of West Africa – Blacks which surprisingly enough migrated to West Africa from East Africa and the physical Egypt where many of the people of Israel were scattered to after the various exiles from their land.

To be sure, the Ashkenazi may say that these Scriptures are beside the point, the Ashkenazi have, indeed, suffered bondage and were ruled over by those that hated them, the result of which was the death of more than half of the then world's Ashkenazi population at the hands of the Nazis; they were also rounded off into camps and forced to work slave labour during the time of the Nazi regime whereby they sowed and their enemies reaped, thus showing that as a people they have suffered hard and were able to overcome.

While it is true their time of slave labour lasted a good four years during which time the "final solution" of their extermination was already underway; Black chattel slavery lasted 446 years from 1442-1888, and on a global scale; during which time those who died of forced overwork (aside from those who died from lynching) was far in excess of the 6 million Ashkenazi that died in Europe, or the supposed 3-4 million Africans that died in the Trans-Atlantic Middle Passage. And even after slavery in America, the slave codes were only replaced with the black codes to undermine Black future progress, and so segregation was instituted, and on the continent colonisation. Furthermore, today we still have our rights denied us as a result of neo-segregation, neo-colonisation, and neoliberalisation. These are all situations the Ashkenazim avoided after World War II as no structural impediments were instituted to block them from progress: instead they were given their own country and support, both financial and military, from the United States and Europe as a result of their sufferings at the hands of the Nazis and as a compensation for the trauma they experienced.

Furthermore, the Blackness of the original Hebrews was also presented in the Quranic verses, where it says, "And Moses said: O Pharaoh, surely I am a messenger from the Lord of the worlds, Worthy of not saying anything about Allah except the truth. I have come to you indeed with clear proof from your Lord, so let the Children of Israel go with me. He said: If thou hast come with a sign, produce it, if thou art truthful. So, he threw his rod, then lo! it was a serpent manifest. And he drew forth his hand, and lo! it was white to the beholders" (Quran 7: 104-108).

Now for the record, the Prophet did not have access to the true colour of Moses, however, he did have access to the colour of the Judeans of his own day. The Prophet obviously saw the colour of Moses to be the same colour as the Judeans of his own day. If the Judeans of the Prophet's day were White then Moses' hand becoming white "to the beholders" would have been seen as an impotent sign. Not only so but it is also written in the hadiths: "No, by Allah, the Messenger of Allah ... did not say that 'Eesa [Jesus] was red (skinned). Instead, he said, 'While sleeping ... making circuits around the Ka'bah, I came across a man with a brown complexion. His hair was flowing, and from one leg to the other he was taking slow steps. His head was dripping with water or water pouring from it. I said: Who is this? They said: This is Al-Maseeh Ibn Maryam [the Messiah son of Mary]" (Ibn Katheer Dimashqi 2006: 150).

Again, for the record, in those days the racial categories were substantially different so what was translated a brown complexion was most likely meant to be what we would call Black. Basically, the description the Prophet gave of the Messiah is similar to that of a Black Dread or a man of East Africa. Moreover, if the Judeans of his time were not similar to the East Africans then the validity of this hadith would have been questionable, especially considering that one of the largest groups in Madinah at the time of the Prophet was the Judean population. Then again, I personally do not accept this hadith or any of the hadiths to be of any serious value, *per se*; as it is written in the Quran: "These are the messages of Allah, which We recite to thee with truth. In what announcement [hadith] will they then believe after Allah and His signs?" (Quran 45: 6). Basically, what Allah, through his Prophet, was saying was that hadiths are not to be authoritative bodies of knowledge about Allah or his signs.

As a final clincher, some people may argue that many of the Hebrews and biblical characters were painted White during the days of the early messianic movement, claiming, if the original Hebrews were Black then this would not have been seen as credible. To this I will, firstly, say, many Hebrews and biblical characters were also painted Black during the days of the early messianic movement. Secondly, most of the White Hebrews and biblical characters they have painted were usually hundreds of years after the actual person's death. Thirdly, this particular problem was one that they faced throughout the length and breadth of their history as Hebrew people.

It even says in the first book of Maccabees, "Wherefore the Israelites assembled themselves together, and came to Maspha, over against Jerusalem; for in Maspha was the place where they prayed aforetime in Israel. Then they fasted that day, and put on sackcloth, and cast ashes upon their heads, and rent their clothes, And laid open the book of the law, wherein the heathen had sought to paint the likeness of their images" (1Maccabees 3: 46-48). Since the heathen in this case were the Greeks it is clear that the Greeks painted the people of the book of the law (the biblical characters) in the likeness of their own image. Basically, the Greeks (or Whites) have been painting the Hebrews White for centuries.

At this point, some godbodies may, again, question the necessity of this arguing that the original Hebrews were Black instead arguing that the truth of the Original people being Black is far more important. The reason I believe it is actually more important that we see the true Hebrews, those fated to be sold into bondage to the Grecians, as Black people, is because it was later prophesied in those times:

> *"Therefore behold, the days come, saith the Lord, that they shall no more say, The Lord liveth, which brought up the children of Israel out of the land of Egypt; But, The Lord liveth, which brought up and which led the seed of the house of Israel out of the north country, and from all countries whither I had driven them; and they shall dwell in their own land." For, "As I live, saith the Lord God, surely with a mighty hand, and with a stretched out arm, and with fury poured out, will I rule over you: And I will bring you out from the people, and will gather you out of the countries wherein ye are scattered, with a mighty hand, and with a stretched out arm, and with fury poured out. And I will bring you into the wilderness of the people, and there will I plead with you face to face. Like as I pleaded with your fathers in the wilderness of the land of Egypt, so will I plead with you, saith the Lord God" (Jeremiah 23: 7, 8; Ezekiel 20: 33-36).*

Just like the Hebrew bondage in the Global North was prophesied, so the Hebrew deliverance from the Global North has also been prophesied. A prophetic figure will no doubt arise from among us to bring judgment to the West and deliverance to us Blacks in the West (or the North countries). We as Black people thus need to be prepared as this prophetic character precedes *al-Masih*'s revelation. Not that *al-Masih* (the Messiah) flies from the sky to save us, but that we learn the truth about, and come to know the truth about, *al-Masih* only after this prophetic character has delivered us. "And so all Israel shall be saved: as it is written, There shall come out of Sion the Deliverer, and shall turn away ungodliness from Jacob: For this is my covenant unto them, when I shall take away their sins" (Romans 11: 26, 27).

Basically, there is a Muslim tradition that three will remain until the last days: the prophet Idris (Enoch), who would remain in *al-'alam al-khayali* until the *Yaum al-Ba'th* (Day of Resurrection) takes place; the prophet Ilyas (Elijah), who would remain invisible in *al-'alam al-hissi* until the *Yaum al-Adyan* (Time of the Gentiles) is fulfilled; and the Messiah Isa (Jesus), who would also remain invisible in *al-'alam al-hissi* but until the *Fitnah al-Akbar* (Greater Tribulation) is complete. To us Black thearchists the Great *Dajjal* started the *Fitnah al-Akbar* from the time of the beginning of slavery. But the *Yaum al-Adyan* only actually ended in 1914, after that time the prophet Ilyas came in the form of the Elijah Muhammad to spread the message to Black people of our coming freedom. Following the Elijah there have been many liars and pretenders to degrade his name but his truth still remains. Soon there will arise a last *dajjal*: a single-eyed, dogmatic, fanatical Christian, who will practice and master the art of manifesting. He will be defeated at the Divine Parousia, when we all gain knowledge of self and knowledge of truth. Then we shall be liberated from all the *dajjalin* and everything they have taught.

What we see from all this is that the prophet Moses, the Messiah Jesus, and the original Hebrew people were most likely Black people and not the Ashkenazim we have been made to believe them to have been; so that while some people like to say that we Blacks have built nothing and contributed nothing to the civilisations of the world; it is in fact most likely that we built the greatest civilisations of the world: the Hebrew civilisations. Though in Israel itself Black people are treated like the Palestinians, being denied the rights of the White Jewish citizens. In India it is the darker

Indians that are in the lower castes, doing the work while the others give the orders or live in leisure. In the Maghreb Blacks are still being taken as slaves. In the Middle East Blacks are harassed, attacked, and sometimes even lynched by the Arab population. In Latin America Blacks are deemed second class citizens and occupy the poorest and most forgotten regions. Blacks are not even welcome in China and have to endure vicious racism there. And on top of all that Blacks are killed for sport by police and vigilantes in the seat of the Empire.

At the same time, if the real Messiah was a Black man then the false messiah (*al-dajjal*) is the White man we see images of around the world. But how does that relate to the ideas of the Second Coming we spoke about in Chapter 4? It is written: "Let no man deceive you by any means: for that day shall not come, except there come a falling away first, and that man of sin be revealed, the son of perdition; Who opposeth and exalteth himself above all that is called God, or that is worshipped; so that he as God sitteth in the temple of God, shewing himself that he is God" (2Thessalonians 2: 3, 4). There is no idol, whether in heaven or on earth, that fits this description better than Jesus, who is called by his followers God; but if Jesus is the false messiah (Great *Dajjal*), who is the real Messiah (*al-Masih*) if not also Jesus?

There are basically two Jesuses – one real and one false. The false Jesus would be this son of perdition, the man of sin, who leads the world to apostasy. "And then shall that Wicked be revealed, whom the Lord shall consume with the spirit of his mouth, and shall destroy with the brightness of his coming: Even him, whose coming is after the working of Satan with all power and signs and lying wonders, And with all deceivableness of unrighteousness in them that perish; because they received not the love of the truth, that they might be saved" (2Thessalonians 2: 8-10). This counterfeit

(*Dajjal*) preached by modern day prophets was created during the Renaissance to endorse their pan-European narrative; and those who refused to worship this false messiah (who I call the Great *Dajjal*) or believe in the teachings of his false prophets (*anbiya al-za'if*), risk not simply a fiery furnace, but risk eternity in a fiery lake. That said, the miracles and signs performed by these prophets were not of the truth but were deceptions of White people to keep the true Hebrews from coming to the knowledge of truth, therefore they must be exposed. This is also the Second Coming or Divine Parousia.

Obviously, there are those who say there was never even a first coming: that the whole Jesus story was a forgery derived from the Ptolemaic god Sarapis (a Greek amalgam of Osiris and Apis), for the purpose of formalising European world domination. First of all, these conspiracy theorists fail to appreciate that Europe as an entity did not exist until after the Renaissance. Second, that even the Prophet made mention of Jesus in the Quran, saying, "When Allah said: O Jesus, I will cause thee to die and exalt thee in My presence and clear thee of those who disbelieve and make those who follow thee above those who disbelieve to the day of Resurrection. Then to Me is your return, so I shall decide between you concerning that wherein you differ" (Quran 3: 55).

What we see in this is that the current Muslim view that the *Masih* did not die is thereby rendered false. Again, the Prophet was six hundred years after *al-Masih*: so news of this Judean sage having reached as far as Arabia in those days, in spite of such a long amount of time passing – international knowledge of him shows that he must have been of the calibre of Hannibal, or Saladin, or Siddhartha Gautama or he would have been forgotten. To say any of these figures were fictional in that they all eventually led up to European domination is to take anti-imperialism to the point of absurdity, what next? Was the Prophet also fictional or was he deceived?

At this point, they would very likely say *al-Masih* was transformed into an historical character at the Council of Nicaea in the early fourth century for the purpose of creating the spiritual enslavement of the world. But even that is a ridiculous argument, as, for the Roman Emperor Constantine to call for a Council of all the Christian Bishops of his empire to make a hero out of a fictional character who died unjustly at the hands of a Roman imperial governor – and as a back story to say that all the Roman Emperors from Nero to Diocletian (his immediate predecessor) murdered his followers for their belief in him – and all during a time when his own imperial position was still under threat, that makes so much sense (!). In fact, it is the pan-Europeanism created during the Renaissance that did more to corrupt the story of *al-Masih* than the Council of Nicaea, a pan-Europeanism whose offspring is the multiculturalism of the GUSE.

Indeed, even the Roman Empire was multicultural: while all citizens of Rome deemed themselves superior to the other races of the planet – labelling them as barbarians – even so the US extols multiculturalism as the height of ethical distinction, while condemning other cultural variations as closed off. US imperialism is a far less tolerant and far more insidious form of multiculturalism than Roman imperialism was due mostly to the discourse of White superiority and the existence of racial stratification. Daulatzai remarked on how, "With the United States embodying the West, its renewed and redefined multicultural identity has echoed and edified American exceptionalist ideas about the country's role and position in the world. As the United States has sought to protect the world from the supposed threat of Islam … the new multicultural and cosmopolitan nationalism has positioned the United States as a representative embodiment of the world" (Daulatzai 2012: 158). Effectively, its sham multiculturalism justifies its racially stratified and plutocratic practices.

I

If we are genuine in our desire to overcome the imperialism and chicanery of the GUSE we must first expose the inherently White supremacist logic of its multiculturalism. To this end there arose in the 1970s a challenge to the univocal chorus of US multiculturalism hailing from the urban ghettos of America: the counter-cultural aesthetic of hip-hop. In order to explain some of the ethnologisms of the hip-hop counter-culture I shall be using as the archetypal hip-hop ambassador of the 1990s: the rapper Nas. Nas being, at least by association, both a godbody and a street lifer, represents one of the most intelligent and yet thoroughbred examples of street culture to arise in the mid-1990s. Hailing from the Desert of Queens, Nas effectively took "rappers to a new plateau through rap slow" (Nas 1994). For the purpose of fully articulating the mythical status Nas had in the counter-culture of hip-hop I shall hermeneutically examine a few lyrics from his vast anthology, comparing them to those of other 1990s hip-hop artists. I shall start by considering the style of cultural transmission Nas undertook in his delivery.

For artists like AZ, a member of Nas' rap crew *The Firm*, spreading lessons was about dropping dope lyrics: in "Life's a Bitch", which he co-performed with Nas, the jewels dropped were instantaneously, "Visualizing the realism of life in actuality/fuck whose the baddest a person's status depends on salary/And my mentality is money-orientated/I'm destined to live the dream for all my peeps who never made it/'cause yeah, we were beginners in the hood as Five Percenters/but something musta got in us 'cause all of us turned to sinners" (AZ 1994). Here AZ outlined a mentality in the New York City streets that was concurrent throughout, that of the hustler. New York was not known for its murder rate or its violent crimes but for its hustlers. AZ, being himself a hustler, provided the prototypical variant that composed the New York City streets. In a way he here provided a manifesto of the ghetto mentality: survival by any means necessary.

In like manner, Nas also spewed jewels galore in virtually every line of his song "Silent Murder": "It's sorta like the conclusion to *Color Purple*: N!gg@s is losing/confusion when One Time on pursuit moves in/Grabbing N!gg@s up in this movement to rule shit/Cop versus the block, shorties is schooled quick/Lesson number one if you arrested and hung/where N!gg@s is from gotta keep a lid on your tongue/It's like silent murder" (Nas 1996). In fact, the amount and level of jewels to be acquired from this assortment of bars is immediately quite profound and instantly recognisable. First, there is the reminiscent tale of *The Color Purple*. By plugging this particular novel by Alice Walker Nas showed his solidarity with the struggle of Black women in the Jim Crow South; he also interestingly enough created somewhat of a bridge unifying the situation in the urban New York City streets with that of the rural Georgia planes. The racism there may not be as obvious as that experienced by the strong Black women in *The Color Purple*, particularly Sofia Johnson, but it was still there. What Nas was saying was the same cultural racism those Blacks experienced in the Jim Crow South was the same cultural racism Black people were still experiencing in the late modern North.

Furthermore, as Frantz Fanon (1969) predicted, culture today has only become a pan-European euphemism for race. It is by using this race neutral term that they are able to be as racist as they desire without the consequence of public outrage. Yet, there is still a hierarchy within the rhetoric: "the cultures supposed implicitly superior are those which appreciate and promote 'individual' enterprise, social and political individualism, as against those which inhibit these things" (Balibar 1991: 25). With individualism being a purely European and Eurocentric conception, and with the desire of the European and American to promote this concept to all nations as a "global ethic," the West propagates the so-called "cultural handicaps" of the non-West in order to decelerate their cultural reproduction. Invariably, "This latent presence of the hierarchic theme … finds its chief expression in the priority accorded to the individualistic model" (Balibar 1991: 25); thereby depreciating all competitors: or at least that has been the hope.

Indeed, by replacing racially charged messages and ideologies with more race neutral and deracialised discourses on cultural illegitimacy there has been a camouflaging of racism under the guise of the "global ethic" of individualism which has made the White power structure far more ubiquitous. But where did these tendencies initially come from? From the discourse of White superiority and the narrative of pan-European distinction. The fact that these two devices were never effectively transcended, neither at the abolition of colonisation nor of segregation, has meant that the racism inherent in both these systems has been able to revive as neo-racism.

In showing the relation between theory and racism Balibar stated, "The neo-racism hypothesis … has been formulated essentially on the basis of an internal critique of theories, of discourses tending to legitimate policies of exclusion in terms of anthropology or the philosophy of history" (Balibar 1991: 17). Neo-racism is thereby explicated as a theoretical racism, a racism of theory. Moreover, these "racist theories are indispensable in the formulation of the racist community. There is in fact no racism without theory (theories)" (Balibar 1991: 18). So, what distinguishes racism from neo-racism? Neo-racism is a "racism without race" a racism of the post-colonial/post-apartheid, indeed, the post-racial epoch. It is a racism that uses cultural distinction to justify White Negrophobia and Islamophobia, and uses multicultural phraseologies to justify White megalomanical and superiority discourses.

Insofar as full assimilation can only be just that, a simulation, the Black and Muslim will never really be accepted as fully integrated nationals. Within neo-racist theoretics the truth of our cultural distinction forever differentiates us. Still, the underlying premise of these theories is that culturally there is a hierarchy, even as classical racism was based largely on a biological hierarchy: "behind this situation [lies] barely reworked variants of the idea that the historical cultures of humanity can be divided into two main groups, the one assumed to be universalistic and progressive, the other supposed irremediably particularistic and primitive" (Balibar 1991: 25). This hierarchical structure of the current discourse on culture, reveals the fact that multiculturalism is only a neo-racism in disguise, a disguise that the United States police departments, "One Time on pursuit", are definitely aware of. That Fanon was able to see through the discourse of multiculturalism even back at its conceptual inception shows that these tendencies were always inherent within it.

Nas, being the archetypal hip-hop artist, showed the ways in which the street counter-culture is opposed by, and has been opposed by, this power structure, and particularly those forces that police it, not only through the enforcing of "global ethics" but also through pursuit and arrest; being in those days justified by the rhetoric of the War on Crime. The so-called "Black criminal" is represented in his verse as "the block," seeing as how most ghetto youths were on the block regularly. "Cultural deviance", however, is the rhetoric used to cover over the barely hidden fact that the targets for police harassment are predominantly Black. The problem is no longer our race but our cultural practices (Balibar 1991), we are effectively told that if we stop behaving like criminals the police would stop harassing us (?).

The mysterious "shorties" Nas spoke of in the verse were Black women who were taught by the Black men, or in this case, very likely, Black Gods, in their immediate company (or in their cipher) not to have words with those police: "keep a lid on your tongue". Basically, Nas was showing that the godbody counter-culture he was associated with did not condone working with the police, who had made themselves more or less our enemies. Thus, Nas here represented the thug life and the rules of the game by articulating what went down in the streets and how our culture worked and was yet opposed.

Accordingly, under the current circumstances of US multicultural imperialism, that is, neo-racist imperialism, the public institutionalisation of exploitation that occurred in mid-modernity has been replaced in late modernity by the spatial institutionalisation of neo-racism – and the more relevant acculturation that comes with the alienation of ethnicity. This turn of events is not due to an overt discursive as such but is based on a theoretical premise inherent within social institutions. "Étienne Balibar calls [this] new racism ... a racism without race, or more precisely a racism that does not rest on a biological concept of race. Although biology is abandoned as the foundation and support, he says, culture is [now] made to fill the role that biology had played" (Hardt & Negri 2000: 192). Hence, in Balibar's view, the current form of racism is an eidetic correlate of late modernity that occurred to silence the anti-racists while still maintaining the structures and mechanisms of the former racist system. The end result of all this neo-racist theorising is then a justification for cultural racism, for cultural imperialism, and for cultural genocide.

What is also interesting about neo-racism is that it is propagated as a mechanism for integration, even primarily so. This is even to the point that any opposition to its dominance is heavily discouraged, even penalised. Thereby turning society into an amorphous homogeneity without identity or distinction, on the one hand, and so fragmented and individualistic, so immersed in one's own distinction, that they are of non-effect in bringing about substantial change to the system, on the other hand. Indeed, the languages of hybridisation, integration, and assimilation are currently tools of neo-racism in an effort to homogenise Western society. As all non-Whites in Western societies are of necessity bicultural their personal negotiation of the two cultures plays a major role in their psychological and sociological development and can produce either positive or negative long-term effects.

Notwithstanding, it is currently the policy of most Western countries to try to force non-White natives, migrants, refugees, and expats to integrate with the Western standard, believing this to be the maximum of toleration and identification on their part, and the minimum of duty and obligation on the part of the non-White (Farris 2016). Such a view is based on an idealising and vulgarising of Dr. King's struggle for integration in the 1950s and 1960s. But a Western state enforcing Dr. King's ideal is merely the fox dressing like a hen, walking like a hen, and clucking like a hen yet still thinking and behaving like a fox.

Far from freeing itself from its colonial legacy it has metamorphosed colonialism into ghettoism. The ethnic communities, usually segregated by race, are ghettos in the midst of the Western metropoles, and the poverty ridden shanty towns of the so-called Third World are the ghettos of the Southern city centres. In both cases the duty of the neo-colony is to follow the Western cultural rules as dictated by the Western government or by the multilateral lender. The Western culture is dominant, the non-Western culture is expendable, even criminalised. For the legislating of hybridisation, integration, or assimilation, no matter how it is done or how the West tries to moralise it, will inevitably prove disempowering and humiliating to the non-West.

II

But the hip-hop counter-culture presented more than simply a challenge to the existing power structures and neo-racist hegemonies of the 1990s, it also presented a case for atypical relationships. Method Man and Mary J. Blige were the culmination of a 1990s Black sexual revolution in which the Black woman was dressing and acting far more sexual than in times past, yet to godbodies like Method Man she was still held as a Queen:

> Method Man – *"Back when I was nothing, you made a brother feel like he was something/ that's why I'm with you to this day boo, no fronting/ Even when the skies were gray/ you would rub me on my back and say baby it'a be okay/ Now that's real to a brotha like me baby/ never ever give my pussy away, and keep it tight a'ight/ And Imma walk these dogs so we can live/ in a phat ass crib with thousands of kids/ Word*

life, you don't need a ring to be my wife/ just be there for me and Imma make sure we/ be livin' in the fuckin' lap of luxury/ I'm realizing that you didn't have to fuck with me/ but 'cha did, now I'm going all-out kid/ and I got mad love to give, you my N!gg@ " Mary J. – *"Like sweet morning dew/ I took one look at you/ and it was plain to see you were my destiny/ You're all/ I need/ to get by-y" (Method Man & Mary J. Blige 1995).*

Nas, on the other hand, showed the paranoid side of ghetto relationships and how the godbody taboo of marriage could present a dilemma to the Black woman:

Nas – *"I'm never free, always on the move, business oriented/ lifestyle expensive, attract women/ You wanna search my pockets and act all foul/ say I hurt your heart, ask how can I smile/ When I call back all my numbers *69 me/ Check my car for rubbers but quit tryin'/ before you find what you looking for and get to cryin'/ You always say what 'chu gone do if you catch me a lyin'"* Aaliyah – *"You won't see me tonight/ you won't see me tomorrow/ I'll be gone by daylight/ and you'll be so full of sorrow/ You'll go tell all your friends/ how you hopin' I follow/ but you won't see me to-night/ you won't see me tomorrow" (Nas & Aaliyah 1999).*

The infidelity of the street life, and even of the godbody, is no mystery; however, it was not limited to just men cheating on women, the women cheated just as much on the men. Nas here may have been glorifying himself so as to boost street cred points, but sleeping around was so common in the streets that to be loyal was actually anomalous. Even so, when Meth made statements like "you don't need a ring to be my wife" so as to articulate the godbody taboo of marriage, he did so recognising the popularity of "creepin'" in ghetto culture. Yet there are many within the White community who consider a Black woman who has sex with multiple partners a "gang-rape victim"; and many within the Black community who just consider her a "hoe." On the one hand, the White community fails to appreciate that monogamy has not been internalised in certain sections of the Black community like it has been in most of the White. On the other hand, the Black community fails to appreciate that the sexual appetite of a horny Black woman can actually benefit the Black community in many ways beyond the actual act of having sex.

It seems that the monitoring of Black and Muslim bodies, and the mystifying of them through sexualised signification and moralised articulation further compounds the so-called criminal perceptions of the street life. While Black erotica and "deviant" sexual behaviour re-appropriate the Black body demystifying it for non-Black people, and light exhibitionism transforms the same Black body into the sexual object *par excellence*, thereby exposing the primal force of society's sexual drive; the performative of social deviance – what James (2015) called the performance of nihilism – extends the confrontation to society's most normative behaviours and practices, thereby undoing the neoliberal, neo-racist implications of multiculturalism.

That said, the godbody counter-culture's form of marriage without marriage, and of deviance from the normative of social conditioning makes us a distinctly oppositional culture disaffected by society and to society. We seek not to fit-in to social normativity but to revolutionise it starting with societal opinions of sexuality and relationships and continuing on to considerations concerning law enforcement. If Black people are publicly denoted as deviant and criminal, hip-hop culture – rather than wasting their time trying to undo these stereotypes – chose instead to run with them and expunge them of the more negative connotations implied within the public discourse. The social transformative of deviant symbols, spaces, and positionings, within hip-hop particularly, and the godbody culture more generally, helped to erase many of the stigmas that seemed inherent in the Black community (but were only manifestations of White fears concerning us).

On a completely different note the 1990s hip-hop culture, or counter-culture, was also a product of its time, a time immersed in eschatological discourses. As an example, Tek from Smif-N-Wessun said in "P.N.C.": "See, my forefront of soldiers ready to blow ya/leave ya back broken, ya body slumped over/The war is on and the stakes is gettin' high/You kill a man dead if him shit where him lie/It's the code of the streets/when ya out wid ya peeps/bumpin' on da beat/be on point fa da sweets/Pigs, harass dat ass for da drug cash/Armageddon soon come keep da guns stashed" (Smif-N-Wessun 1995). Here we see Tek (himself also a godbody) basically showing how eschatological visions of a future war affected ghetto culture in the 1990s. We all lived with an understanding of the potential for a Second American Civil War, one which would invariably lead to martial law and the rounding off of American citizens into concentration camps.

When Tek said things like "Armageddon soon come keep da guns stashed" he was speaking based on a real fear during those days that Blacks would be the victims of Gestapo style internment and the targets of an American police round up. Again, the "forefront of soldiers" were those who in the 1990s wore army fatigues and carried semi-automatic or fully automatic weapons to fight back. The war was on and we were all soldiers. Though such an eschatological vision has since faded, we will inevitably need to return to that sort of militarism. There seems to be a feeling among certain sections of the Black community that the state and the White supremacists are better armed and better prepared than us so why bother going down the "self-destructive path of violence." However, that is the very reason we need to militarise. We need to train, prepare, and arm ourselves better because one thing is for certain, whether we see them as our enemies or not, they see us as their enemy and they are training and arming up in preparation for us.

Still, if we continue on in the eschatological tone of the 1990s, Nas said in "Eye for an Eye (Your Beef Is Mine)": "What's up to all my N!gg@s warring in New York Metropolis/the Bridge brings apocalypse/shoot at the clouds feels like the holy Beast is watching us/Madman my sanity is going like an hourglass/Gun inside my bad hand I sliced tryna bag grams/I got hoes that used to milk you/N!gg@s who could of kill't you, is down with my ill crew of psychos/Nas Escobar's movin' on your weak production/pumping corruption in the Third World we just bussin'" (Nas 1995). Interestingly, Nas here gave a description of the godbody counter-culture that was even more fine-tuned than what Smif-N-Wessun gave: Firstly, Nas took the standard White dehumanisations of the non-White – ill, psycho, violent, madman – and while de-euphemising them he somehow also glamorises them, particularly by juxtaposing them with the signifier "New York Metropolis".

Following that, Nas articulated his *Tales from the Hood* concerning a gun inside a hand that he had sliced trying to bag up grams of what we only can assume to have been cocaine; thus showing again that he strove for the same thug points in the thug life as most of his hip-hop contemporaries, even if that statement is preceded by the patently deep "the Bridge brings apocalypse, shoot at the clouds feels like the holy Beast is watching us". A line which itself showed three essential truths: (i) the Armageddon War Tek prophesied was believed by Nas to start in Queensbridge; (ii) while "Beast" is usually street slang for the police and could very well mean police in this case, it could also have another more nuanced meaning too; and (iii) if Nas was using Beast here to symbolise something other than the police then the apocalypse he spoke of or the Armageddon War Tek spoke of was the overthrowing of a global force more sinister even than the police.

Then again, there was a significantly unifying quality in Nas speaking on the streets of New York as part of the so-called Third World; the solidarity he expressed here was, however, deeper than mere rhetorics. Although it is hard to believe or appreciate that the so-called richest country in the world could have had slums back in the 1990s that rivalled slums in the so-called Third World but the New York City ghettos were immensely impoverished. Having myself grown up there I can say that the metaphor was not far from the mark. The reality of "cop versus the block" when seen from the perspective of eschatological revolution presents the dilemma of late modern America as poor Blacks made up the urbanised streets of Ghetto America. National security, in this sense, meant protecting the true citizens of the US national-state from the pseudo-citizens, who in this case were the non-White Americans.

To be an American national was more than applying for citizenship – though legally having the documentation to prove citizenship carried weight – one could never be a true national of the United States without being European by descent. Nas in this respect critiqued American domestic policy and measures of national security showing how Black people in the United States represented a de-territorialised community at war as a nation within a nation. And by calling his community a part of the so-called Third World he demonstrated the realistic situations experienced by those within the spatial variations of that nation, whether they be public or semipublic. Though most 1990s hip-hop artists showed no significant political affiliations and articulated no obvious ideological positions there was undeniably a kind of ideological struggle that they recognised going on between the system, defended by the police and FBI, and the brotherhood experienced within the ghetto counter-culture, which the artists themselves belonged to.

The opposition between these two worlds (what I call the neocosmos and the palacosmos: neocosmos meaning new world, palacosmos meaning present world) usually involved the exile, arrest, or the death of the street lifer at the hands of the enforcer class (the police, FBI, or DEA); hip-hop was not slow to recognise this dilemma as the late Prodigy was not shy to delineate in "Temperature's Rising": speaking here to one of his homeboys on the run for a murder, "What up, Black! hold ya head wherever you at/on the flow from the cops with wings on ya back/That snitch N!gg@ gave police your location/We'll chop his body up in six degrees of separation/Killah listen, shit ain't the same without you at home/Phony N!gg@s walk around tryna be your clone/They really fear you, when you wasn't home they was pale/That's why they wanna see you either dead or in jail/By the time he hear this rhyme he'll probably be locked up/tried to hide somewhere along the lines ya plan slipped up" (Mobb Deep 1995).

What is also clear is how influential Nas was in the writing of the rhyme itself, which was inspired hugely by his "One Love", a rhyme written to his homies locked up: "What up, kid! I know shit is rough doing your bid/when the cops came you shoulda slid to my crib/Fuck it, Black, no time for looking back it's done/Plus congratulations, you know you got a son/I heard he looks like ya, why don't ya lady write ya/told ha' she should visit, that's when she got hypa'/flippin', talkin' 'bout he acts to rough/he didn't listen he be riffin' while I'm tellin' him stuff/I was like yeah, shortie don't care, she a snake too/fuckin' with them N!gg@s from that fake crew that hate you" (Nas 1994).

In both instances the life of crime is the motivation for the dialogue, based heavily on opposition from the national-state to the ghetto culture and the godbody counter-culture. The GUSE with its prison industrial-complex and its neo-racist War on Crime represented an antagonistic force antithetical to the street life. Therefore, though in the technical sense there may be said to be three kinds of Black prisoner in the United States: the inherently wicked, the illegitimate capitalists, and the political prisoners; in actuality they are all political prisoners rebelling against the system the best way they know how.

Even with no substantial political ideology of their own street lifers recognise that they are still political prisoners, as, in spite of not possessing an actual ideology the national-state that wars against them most definitely does have an ideology (Alexander 2011), one that is contained in its discourse of White superiority and its ideology of White supremacy (Daulatzai 2012). Conversely, it is the performative of crime – the counter-cultural act of breaking the law – that represents the means of challenging an inherently unjust system such as what exists in the United States and those countries under the remit of the GUSE. In both cases it is not what is said that represents either a challenge or an inspiration, it is the fact that what is being said is being spoken directly to the Black criminal, real or imagined, thereby discrediting completely the value tied in to the American legal justifications.

III

In contrast to the ideas just mentioned Fredrick Engels' theory – that "The state is … the admission that society has become entangled in an insoluble contradiction with itself, that it has split into irreconcilable antagonisms which it is powerless to [dispel; and] in order that these antagonisms, these classes with conflicting economic interests, might not consume themselves and society in fruitless struggle" (Engels 1884; quoted in Lenin 2014: 42); the state was formulated – if one looks at the most ancient form of social organisation one understands, first of all, that people originally existed in tribal federations (that were the ancient nations), each tribe being itself a federation of clans. (The most popular of the ancient tribes being that of Shabazz). There are very few things we know about the most ancient societies, but one thing we can know for sure is that they had sexual intercourse. The second thing we can know for sure about the ancient tribes is that without a government or legislature to legitimate it, neither a monogamous nor a polygamous family would have existed in these most ancient forms of social organisation.

Though neither I nor anybody else can present substantial evidence for it, we can make a fair estimation based on existing pre-modern societies that there were classes in the earliest societies; but they would not have been Marx's economic classes, they would have more likely been generational classes (Ferguson 2014). The then existing power relations these Original people instituted would have had elders (both male and female) as the central powers, young adults as the intermediates, and youths as the subordinates. The elders' power over the young adults would have derived from their monopoly on the traditions, culture, and education. The young adults' power over the youths would have derived from the fact that they gave birth to them, and from their personal strength, training, and energy. The elders would not have needed a state to maintain power so these were most likely stateless communities, even as contemporary tribal communities are (Ferguson 2014).

From here we see the state could have only arisen from these tribal relations as a result of two developments: these Original people must have first created a law and then developed an enforcer class to enforce that law. Any enforcer class includes an active militia to enforce the law not only for the tribe or federation of tribes, but also for any non-federated tribe that sought to impose its own law on them. The modern state is distinguished from the tribal state in that it has added to the legal and enforcer aspects of the state a bureaucratic administration, a judiciary, penal institutions, and a class of hypocritical politicians that blind the masses to the ineptitude of the system. The enforcer class still exists but has become more refined and more compartmentalised. In the United States, for example, there are correction officers, police officers, the SWAT division, the FBI, the National Guard, the NSA, the CIA, the DIA, the USIB, the armed forces (which includes the Army, Marines, Navy, Seals, Air Force, et cetera.), the Pentagon, and at the top the President; not to mention the individual departments and ranks within all these groups individually.

Within the state bureaucratisation and the division of labour are the marks of an advanced modern systemic construction, however, the refinement of the enforcer class is the significant area in which the modern state has distinguished itself. The main purpose of the bureaucracy is as administrators and publishers of the law, yet as Hardt and Negri explained, both "Domestic and supranational law are … defined by their exceptionality." And thus "is born, in the name of the exceptionality of … intervention, a form of right that is really a *right of the police*" (Hardt & Negri 2000: 16, 17). The law effectively creates the necessity of a class to enforce it based on the exceptional responsibility of the state to maintain safety, security, and order.

So while a transition from statism to statelessness may at first sight appear hard and complicated, and Marx further complicated it with his two phases of communism theory; the fact is that it is actually not as intense or immensely difficult as it at first sight appears. If a revolution was to occur in which the state was overthrown it would not need to be replaced by another state but by a decentralised planning system of syndicalist parliaments, each including a division of labour, but in which bureaucracy is either abolished or substantially reduced. The division of labour will be a necessity in any modernist or futurist society, though neither bureaucracy nor the state will be necessary once we have abolished all law: whether criminal, constitutional, familial, business, or military.

The enforcer class will not be necessary to police the people and Congress/Parliament will no longer need to institute new laws. After the *smashing* of the machinery of the state, and with it the smashing of the law as the basis for its justification (together with all the government institutions presupposed within the law: courts, prisons, corporations, families) the central necessity will be to immediately place power in the hands of the people through a people's militia (not to be confused with a militia class), to ensure that neither an enforcer class nor any other hostile power rises up seeking to impose on us another form of state – whether it be a proletarian state, a fascist state, an Islamic state, a Zionist state, a pluralist state, or a bourgeois state.

This people's militia, by Engels' definition, constitutes a state in and of itself, but that is based on his misguided definition of the state being an instrument of class rule created to justify and protect private property. This quasi-Lockean definition of the state is projecting onto past civilisations a modernist interpretation of existence – something I must also admit is unavoidable as I have undoubtedly done so myself – a technique that can be substantially diminished through empathic anthropological research.

Engels lacked anthropological training and was therefore hugely weakened; and even if he had been trained, in those days, he would have still been weakened to judging things by the colonial standard and not by empathic interaction. Here godbody sociology has the advantage over Marxism, which, as a result of the colonial positioning of its founders, not only projected modern ideas and interpretations onto pre-modern societies, but also projects Eurocentric standards and arrogance onto non-European peoples and cultures. Like colonialism it dehistoricises them by, firstly, erasing their actual history, then, as Fanon (1965) would say, it reconstructs a demoralised pseudo-history for them.

Through a godbody analysis we can see that the actual victory over statism is a lot easier than the Marxists and postmodernists have made it seem. In practical expression Lenin's socialism (which was the actualisation of Marx's first phase of communism) was realised in the proletarian state instituted in Russia. It was the armed workers fighting back against a greedy and reactionary bourgeoisie (who were helped, financed, and armed by several Western countries) during a bloody civil war. Lenin overthrew the bourgeoisie twice: once through a revolution, and again through a civil war – as well as overthrowing the Soviets and all political rivals afterward.

The proletarian state did not fall apart because Stalin took control of it, although that may not have helped, it fell because it was based on several false premises: in particular, that by abolishing the capitalist class-relations the state would eventually just "wither away," and that by taking control of the means of production the proletarians would become the ruling class. Lenin successfully or semi-successfully instituted Marx's first phase of communism, and as Marx anticipated bourgeois rebellion in the first phase of communism, the civil war is not an effective counter-argument in defence of its ultimate failure. Marx even drew from the failure of the Paris Commune so he knew the price of revolution in psychic, economic, and human costs. The problem was not so much Stalin, I say that not to justify Stalin or his crimes, the problem was always Marx, but I discuss this in greater detail in Chapter 4.

As we can see, every state apparatus exists on its own terms and due to legal implementations; therefore every kind of state formation, even a proletarian state (whether genuine or nominal), will seek to perpetuate itself. The state is not intertwined with economic classes, or the economy in general, it is intertwined with the law; when the law creates institutions that inhere to White privilege and discursively promote their superiority then it is a White supremacist state. That is not to say we should overthrow it with a Black supremacist state, or any other form of state for that matter, but that we should seek to abolish the state altogether.

Accordingly, if we wish to return to a stateless society we must employ better methods than simply superseding private property. It will only be by superseding legal articulation, which includes a justification of private property, and the discourses which are used as their own justification, that we will overcome the state; and such an act would be by definition revolutionary. Incidentally, Lenin made a point about most revolutionary movements that is quite pertinent: he said that their opportunist section have a tendency, at the height of their public acceptability, of denying the more utopian elements of their initial programme, even "as Christians, after their religion had been given the status of state religion, 'forgot' the 'naiveté' of primitive Christianity with its democratic, revolutionary spirit" (Lenin 2014: 81).

Yet, in our current day and time most Western scholars love to brag about democracy and how it creates the need for a minimal state. But what were the circumstances under which our democracy was itself created? Modern democracy and republicanism came about in England due to the tyranny of King Charles I towards the Puritans. Charles I seized many peasant lands for the Crown and had numerous ideological opponents put through secret trials where guilt was determined beforehand and they were sentenced to death by these no jury, no trial, no witness, kangaroo courts, sometimes after having been tortured for months.

The first modern republic was founded in England when Charles I wanted to invade Scotland and organised parliament to fund the expedition. When parliament wanted justice for the murder of countless Puritans he ended parliament. Parliament, however, refused to end so he used his army to target parliament instead of Scotland. This forced parliament to decide that Charles I was no longer worthy to rule the people. It was neither justice nor intelligence that brought about the desire for a republic, it was tyranny and necessity. The American revolutionaries simply repeated what Britain did but in America.

As for secularism. America only dreamed that up after the many years of Catholic persecutions and denominational persecutions took their toll. The West's history of intolerance towards different denominations and sects spurred on their newfound tolerance. Again, it was necessity. We should not forget that immediately preceding the then current idea of freedom of religion was the Salem Witch

Trials in which the so tolerant and feminist West (?) murdered countless women for no reason at all other than an accusation. That is nothing for the West to brag about. In fact, the current tolerance of the modern West was not inevitable due to the inevitable tolerance of White people. It was fought for and won by numerous historical martyrs from both the West and the non-West.

At the same time, many White people look at their position in the world today and say, "If we are the dominant race in the world today it is because we earned it. Our ancestors worked hard to build technologies and sciences that would benefit the world and that is why we are in this position of power in the world right now." They fail to appreciate that White people were only able to develop those technologies and those sciences because they had enslaved millions of Africans, which provided them with funding for other projects. Many of the great philosophers and scientists of the 18th and 19th centuries were either slave-owners or at least racists encouraged by slavery. Then, after slavery was abolished those same ancestors White people glorify were in the process of colonising the world, thereby holding non-Western countries in a political and cultural time-warp. Basically, the non-West became the tail-end of the West, if that, after the West held back their progress.

Europe now claims that they progressed Africa and the Middle East with their sciences and technology. Indeed, far more than they could have done on their own, but Africa and the Middle East on their own developed great sciences and technologies during Europe's Dark Ages. In fact, many European scientists of the 16th and 17th centuries owed their great knowledge to lessons they had learned from Muslim books and scholars. In all, democracy and secularism are superior to tyranny, but the West has no real reason to brag about how great they are for developing them when the truth is they actually benefited from circumstances that were rather spurious.

IV

An important question to ask at this time would be, what happens to society during the transitional phase between modern statism and the stateless society? Will we need a new kind of state, like a proletarian state, to ease the transition? Firstly, the central *raison d'etat* is not to protect citizens from crime or abuses, but to perpetuate itself (Foucault 2009). Secondly, even Lenin's proletarian state in Russia showed that any state will seek to perpetuate itself and must therefore be overthrown to be abolished. A proletarian state does not "wither away" (Lenin 2014) it in fact becomes more refined, more specialised, and more complex.

But society has already become quite complex and a leap into statelessness, whether thearchic or anarchic, may end up producing chaos, or at least that is the fear. Therefore, in order to explain the circumstances that could potentially lead to the abolition of the state, we must first explore the central realities of the state and its key functions. See, the state currently exists as the only body that holds a legitimate monopoly on violence; and the most prominent symbol of state violence, in our time, is the penitentiary. Prior to the founding of the penitentiary in the 18th century the symbols of state violence were the whip and the chain.

Prisons, at that time, were merely holding facilities before trial; and punishments were usually state orchestrated corporal punishments such as beatings, amputations, mutilations, placement in the stocks, or being drawn. Having a monopoly on all legitimate violence meant, back then, that these acts of violence were public spectacles that would leave a flesh wound on the body, hence, the name corporal. However, around the 1750s many reformists believed that a more civilised form of punishment would be the carceral form, where people could be put in a quiet location to think about what they had done and the harm they had caused. This, it was believed, would lead to penitence and thereby reform the convicted into an upstanding citizen.

Since those days carceral punishment has become not only legitimised but normalised. Even to the point that society is unable and unwilling to think of non-carceral measures of dealing with deviance. The strongest case for carceral punishment comes from the carceral feminists who say that men who abuse or rape women must be locked away and kept from harming others in the future. This legitimation of carceral punishment fails to see passed the societal gendering of prisons as male or to appreciate the nightmare of female incarceration. True, there is a far greater quantity of males incarcerated. Still, those women that do get locked up face many problematic scenarios as a result of their sentencing.

Even before their sentencing women have to face the sexual abuse of the strip search, in which officers and nurses search every cavity of their bodies: vagina, anus, and mouth, with their fingers. Male officers have even been known to grope vaginas, chests, and buttocks in sexually suggestive ways while on duty; and these are regular occurrences for women in jails and prisons (Shakur 1987). On top of that, there are the numerous reports of sexual harassment and vaginal, anal, and oral rape from correction officers. More importantly, they are unable to escape from their abusers being imprisoned by them. I can attest from my own experience on Rikers, correction officers were well known for taking advantage of inmates' vulnerable position to acquire sexual favours from them. This is due to public unawareness and officer vilification of the inmates, hypersexualising and fetishising them.

But we still have not addressed the fear of the carceral feminists. What do we do with all the rapists and paedophiles? This is a loaded question, but it is also a misconception of the situation. These labels used to dehumanise and demonise these people allow us to forget that everybody has a shadow side, and we are all capable of untold atrocities given the right circumstances. By demonising these people as inherently evil and not the victims of circumstances that occurred in their lives to corrupt them, we fail to notice or deal with what creates rapists and paedophiles. Herein, the problem is not the individual (as in them being inherent evil), the problem is in the current system of modernity.

The very popular copaganda circulating throughout society is that prisons are to protect "good people" from the "bad people," usually coded as Black people. This creates the idea that prison is only filled with those who deserve punishment. The police, therefore, like your typical Marvel superhero, save innocent people from these "evil villain" ghetto people. This black and white way of thinking couples the idea of the Black criminal with that of the supervillain and not with that of the misled or misguided human being, capable just as much of good as they have been of negativity. Thereby it also justifies the state's and the law enforcer class' monopoly on violence as ordinary people are potentially too evil to be allowed to use violence at their own discretion.

In all, to envision a world without the state we must first envision a world without the traumatising and distorting realities of carceral punishment. To do this we must now understand, with Angela Davis (2003), that prisons will not be replaced by one all-encompassing solution but with several interconnected solutions. These solutions are: (i) decriminalising all currently illegal drugs and substances. To go with this the allowing of all users that wish to quit easy access to the best programmes and counselling, including Narcotics Anonymous, with which to do so. The example here would be American prohibition. By legalising all forms of alcohol, they put an end to those lucrative criminal enterprises and the mob violence they entailed.

(ii) Decriminalising all forms of consensual sexual performances, including: all forms of public nudity, all forms of public consensual sexual performances, and all forms of media consensual sexual performances. If a woman or a man chooses to provide any form of sexual favours with their own body as a compensation for a given product or service, such is their prerogative. Along with this, teaching, training, and guidance on sexual preferences, performances, and potentials should be provided to all young people as they mature, as well as guidance in sexual safety and contraceptives all for precoital, coital, and postcoital experiences. Finally, the institutions of marriage and divorce should also be abolished in the possess, thereby allowing for new forms of relational and intimate interaction to be developed. All this will go a long way in eliminating the need or desire to rape or molest anybody.

(iii) Organising and establishing meeting grounds that are based on livelihood or employment within all neighbourhoods, workplaces, and universities to create social accountability, and to determine service capability. All this will go a long way in eliminating the need or desire to resort to deviant behaviours. (iv) Abolishing all forms of monetary compensation and monetary valuing. Compensation should thereby be through products and services, but the system itself should determine actual compensation through form of employment. All this will go a long way in eliminating the need or desire to steal anything. (v) Establishing a fighting ring as the new form of punitive justice, the rules of which can be decided by the community.

Now, the question: what about rapists and murderers seems somewhat moot. With the abolition of money and decriminalisation of all drugs there will be no reason to kill anybody. Also, with the decriminalisation of all forms of consensual sexual performative there will be no need to rape or molest anybody. With no monetary means of valuing products and persons no individual or group will feel their work is of higher or lower value than others. With punitive justice turned to a more humane form of corporal punishment than tortures, whippings, amputations, and mutilations the psychological trauma of internment and the hyperincarceration complex of the United States can be abolished. Again, prison and state abolition in our time is as unimaginable as slave trade and slave labour abolition were in their time, but it can definitely happen if we are willing to fight for it. Hereby, without a law there can be no crime and therefore no criminalisation, only unjust or uncivilised actions. This is the key.

By abolishing the law we also bring about the abolition of law enforcement, and the hyperincarceration complex. The abolition of the state, and the state monopoly on violence. The abolition of exploitation, as our work will be done for self-fulfilment. The abolition of scarcity, as we will get everything we desire through our employment. The abolition of markets, and the commodification of all objects. The abolition of money, and the commodification of all subjects. The abolition of marriage, and all forms of female subjugation. The abolition of underwear, and all forms of sexual subjugation. The abolition of genders, and all forms of queer subjugation. And the abolition of secularism, and all forms of religious subjugation.

Still, that is not to say that religion cannot also be corrupted, "Look at the Magis. Look at the priests in Europe. Look at the rabbis of the Israeli tribes and types like

Balaam. Look at tribes, idolatrous tribes. Look at Africa and Australia, the religion of witchdoctors, those who spoke of the unseen, the astrologers, those who claimed to be the preservers of the existing religion. They all held hands and moved alongside with the rulers or else they dominated over them" (Shari'ati 2003: 39). What we can be sure of is that religion (*din*) and culture (*thaqafah*) can be used as much for harm as they can be for good; thereby justifying the current turn towards secularism among most intellectuals: "the judgment of intellectuals in relation to religion – that religion opposes civilization, progress, people and liberty or that it is inattentive to them – is a judgment which came into being based upon objective and precise scholarly studies of the realities and continuous historical experiences" (Shari'ati 2003: 25).

Yet it will have to be culture, and some might even say "religion," that reorganises and restabilises society after the removal of a state, if the state is to be removed at all. This circumstance is inevitable, something most Marxists, anarchists, and utopians have failed to appreciate; under real circumstances the state will not wither away but it can be abolished so long as the people have the law written on their hearts (consciences) and abide by the laws faithfully without the need for compulsion. This situation is possible but is only possible with a people who are versed in the truth and not self-deceived. So, what is the truth? The truth is *tawhid*. As Shari'ati (2003: 30, 31) continued, "As I have said, the unity of God, of necessity, brings about the unity of the universe and the unity of [the] human being"; and "a belief in the unity of humanity [is a belief in] the unity of all races, all classes, all families and all individuals, the unity of rights and the unity of honor."

But if such is *tawhid*, then *shirk* would produce the opposite, the belief in the hierarchical separation of humanity: through races, classes, cultures, sexualities, genders, rights, honours, prestige, and personality; and would have a vested interest in maintaining this hierarchical structure for as long as it can. According to Shari'ati (2003) it is the central objective of *shirk* to perpetuate division not only among *al-nas* but also between *al-nas* and *al-ma'nawi*, *al-nas* and *al-ijtima*, *al-nas* and *al-kulliyya*, *al-nas* and Allah, by having them *believe* that the existing order is all part of the will of Allah and that their duty is to just be content with their place in life and with humanity's corruption of nature.

By Shari'ati's definition *shirk* is a religion: the religion of multitheism, and it was *tawhid* and the representatives of *tawhid* that in every generation or paradigmatic shift fought to bring *al-nas* back to the knowledge of truth (*al-'ilm al-haqiqa*). It is through the knowledge of *al-haqiqa* that *al-nas* will be able to see through the corruptions of the current Empire and all its avowed *shirk*. The representatives of *shirk*, the *Mushriks*, only call "humanity to rebel against [the] great Beloved of Existence ... Who is the meaning of all of existence and the eternal goal of all life, and ... [they subjugate them] automatically in surrender and slavery to hundreds of other powers, to hundreds of other polarizations and forces, where each pole, each power, each class and each group has a god" (Shari'ati 2003: 34).

The *Mushriks* come in many shapes and forms but ultimately they are those who rebel against *al-haqq*. They are the 95 percent, the vast majority of the population – the 10 percent and the 85 percent. The rulers and the ruled – if the Five Percenters are to be placed among the ruled it is only by the coercion of the system, not by blindness or corruption – both 10 percent and 85 percent are blind, for if either of them knew the full truth they would not rebel against Allah's laws, the laws of existence; or Allah's power, the power of creation; or, most importantly, Allah's monism, the theocentric monism.

Like the *anbiya* (prophets) of old we Five Percenters exist within a powerful empire: the prophet Moses dwelt within the Egyptian Empire, the next batch of *anbiya* dwelt within the Philistine Empire, the next within the Syrian Empire, the next the Neo-Assyrian, the next the Neo-Babylonian, the next the Neo-Persian, then the Grecian, then the Roman, then the Byzantine. The *anbiya* have always spoken within an empire, whether that empire is righteous or unrighteous has depended on their acceptance of the message of *tawhid*; but all the prophets (*anbiya*) had the same message and spoke it to global forces and their personifications in their own time: forces and people that sought to legitimate the status quo and the oppression (*zulm*) of the poor and powerless.

Shari'ati (2003: 34) said concerning the message of *tawhid* that it "was announced to stand before the worship of the arrogant ruler who rules against God's Commands, the *taghut*[;] to stand before this movement which invited humanity to submit before [the] great Beloved of Existence, this great secret of Creation, this great goal of Creation which ended and terminated in God." Basically, the *anbiya*, being the preachers of *tawhid*, were compelled by the revelation of the mystery of *tawhid*, by discovering *al-haqiqa al-tawhid*, to speak, in the midst of their respective empires, against the rebellious emperors (the *taghuti*) who were self-deceived while also deceiving the people into *shirk*. Though *ishrik* could be any religion, ideology, or meta-discourse that is false: thereby subjecting the followers of it to all manner of oppressive forces, it is better termed a false metanarrative, any metanarrative that does not come from, and thus lead to, *tawhid*.

In a technical sense there are many throughout the Scriptures that could be identified as *taghuti*, however, the two most prominent are Iblis and the Pharaoh of Moses. It is written in the Scriptures: "And We indeed created you, then We fashioned you, then We said to the angels: Make submission to Adam. So, they submitted, except Iblis; he was not of those who submitted. He said: What hindered thee that thou didst not submit when I commanded thee? He said: I am better then he; Thou hast created me of fire, while him Thou didst create of dust" (Quran 7: 11, 12). Iblis (the devil) refused to submit to man (in this case man), because he thought himself better than him, that is, he had a superiority complex.

It is clear that the word translated here as fire (*nar*), bearing similarities to the Hebrew word *ur*, actually means light and could more readily in our day be translated as electromagnetism. If Allah was really Mind before he took on a body of flesh, and thought is nothing more than electrical signals being transmitted throughout our brain, then Allah, Mind, or Intelligence must have existed in *al-'alam* as electromagnetism before he took on a body of flesh. The Quranic origin of the devil would be with a section of electromagnetism rebelling when Allah took on that body, the body of the Original man, for why would Allah ask the angels to submit to any being lower than himself? But if the Original people are the embodiment of Allah and, as we said in Chapter 1, White people could be called the embodiment of the devil, then the lessons of the godbody ultimately demystify the spiritual doctrines of the Scripture.

That said, in the story the Quran presents about the Pharaoh the case remains the same: "And Pharaoh said: O chiefs, I know no God for you besides myself; so kindle a fire for me, O Haman, on (bricks of) clay, then prepare for me a lofty building, so that I may obtain knowledge of Moses' God, and surely I think him a liar" (Quran 28: 38). Any oppressor (*zalim*) who has a segment of truth will exalt himself beyond measure, and though, as an Original man it could be said that the Pharaoh technically was a God, like a vampyre he sucked the blood of the masses through giving them a message of *shirk* and was therefore of the 10 percent. The Pharaoh, though of the Original nations, was of the *Mushriks* and thus had the mind of a devil. The *taghuti*, whether they be of the devils or of the vampyres, use *shirk* to deceive and dominate the masses; but it is the godbodies' destiny to free all the Original nations of the world from the dominion of the devil's world system and bring them into the glorious liberty of the Nation of Gods and Earths.

Indeed, while it could be said that "Moses' movement was a struggle against racial discrimination which was the superiority of the Coptics over the Sebtians, a struggle against the social situation, which was the domination of one race over another race, or the enslavement of a race" (Shari'ati 2003: 36); when Shari'ati (2003) said Coptics he was most likely speaking of the Original Egyptian race, and as for the Sebtians they were most likely the Ta Setians (the Original Aethiop race), in which case they were both of the Original nations. It is therefore, contrary to Shari'ati's conclusion, more likely that the Moses movement was primarily not a racial movement but was an ideological movement – though their races were separate the distinguishing characteristics were that the Hebrews were an impoverished people whereas the Egyptians were a wealthy and powerful state. Furthermore, in the eternal struggle for liberation, "God and the deprived people form one front in the Pentateuch and the Gospels … [and] the Holy Quran and everywhere without exception. [On the other side are the *Mushrik*] worshippers of an arrogant leader who rebels against the Commands of God, the *taghuti*" (Shari'ati 2003: 46).

The deepest lesson we gain from *tawhid* is that the *taghuti* are impostor leaders and usurpers of the position of Allah who have some knowledge of truth but corrupt it into trick knowledge. These *taghuti* could either be of the devils (that race that, in pride, seeks to dominate and oppress anything or anyone other to themselves) or be of the vampyres (those Original people who, following the example of the devils, use lies to dominate and oppress other Original people). It is our devotion to *tawhid*, and above all to Allah, that causes us to oppose these *taghuti* and their *Mushrik* religion, and as Shari'ati noted: "Whenever a prophet was sent … to stand and confront the [*Mushrik*] religion, human beings were invited to follow the laws of nature which rule the universe in the universal, revolutionary journey of creation which is the theophany of the Divine Will" (Shari'ati 2003: 46). The mission of a prophetic people is not a rendezvous it is aggressive, polemical, and confrontational. The *anbiya* (prophets) were never trying to create a new *Mushrik* religion or another manifestation of *shirk*, they were out to destroy the then existing systems of their time by exposing all their *shirk*.

V

Now while the idea of using prophets, Scriptures, and "forces" as the basis of academic enquiry may make most intellectuals cough; and though late modern scholarship tends to be of the opinion that certain truth is unattainable, that just shows the embedded primacy of *shirk*. And though it could be said that the current atheism that exists in the world is a reaction against *shirk*, if we judge that assessment critically we find it more problematic. Atheism has its roots in the Western tradition which is heavily Christianised; atheism borrows from a scientific tradition that was massively influenced by Christian scholarship, medieval and modern, and therefore is subject to Christian biases.

The Christian tradition was corrupted at the Council of Nicaea when it began the process of becoming the state religion of the Roman Empire – that is not to say that Islam itself was not also corrupted through the *Khalifah* empires too. When a *tawhidic* movement goes to bed with the state, no matter how righteous the state leader, then its leaders become opponents to that very *tawhid* they claim to represent, they effectively become the practitioners of *shirk* (multitheism, multiculturalism, and multiplicity) and although such may be unavoidable, it is still in itself very problematic. Herein, late modern atheism, with its emphasis on multiculturalism and multiplicity, by its going to bed with US imperialism, has most definitely become *Mushrik*.

Yet the corruption of *tawhid* into multiplicity does not end in simply an absence of *al-haqiqa*, it goes deeper, into a hatred for *al-haqiqa* and desire only for comfortability; and to be sure, even if these practitioners of *shirk* are overcome, due to the socio-elasticity of *al-mujtama*, they are able to revive, even if only as *jinni*: "when Balaam, who stood before Moses, is removed from the way as a result of the movement of Moses, he takes the form of the rabbi of the religion of Moses and the form of the Pharisees who murdered Jesus. It is this group which destroys Jesus and stands alongside the idolatrous Caesar of Rome against the defenders of [*tawhid*]." "It is these very Pharisees who have now taken the form of priests so that they can turn Jesus' religion from within, towards [*shirk*] and they ended up doing so." In fact, "it has been this religion [the *Mushrik* religion] which has continuously legitimated the status quo" (Shari'ati 2003: 41, 42, 40). Indeed, religion (*din*) has been, and will be, used to pacify the people, but the answer is not in atheism it is in theocentric monism.

The GUSE is the current seat of the *taghuti*, those who oppose the Muslims, on the one hand, and the Five Percent, on the other hand, for our being the representatives of *tawhid*. The GUSE is able to run its plutocratic Empire based on the ignorance and illiteracy of the people, and through the self-deception and chicanery of the scholars. The neoliberal intellectuals, the current representatives of *shirk*, also have a part to play here too as the neoliberal intellectuals, regardless of how much they speak against neoliberalism only perpetuate neoliberalism, offering no means or inspiration to fight against non-truth with truth (*haqiqa*), they simply qualify their inactivity by saying there is a multiplicity of truths and we have no right to deny another person or group their truth.

With this definition of *tawhid* it may appear that Allah has a complete relation to the universe (*al-'alam*), that there has therefore been no reason to look outside of yourself for Allah historically. Yet what that can also mean is the falsehood of all the historical *anbiya* who have looked beyond the self for help and guidance. While such may be the appearance, it is not the truth of the matter. Firstly, all the prophets believed in the *tawhid* (oneness) of Allah, that Allah was one with everything in *al-'alam* and that the whole universe was in perfect Islam. Secondly, all the prophets (*anbiya*) believed in the *tanzih* (uniqueness) of Allah, that though Allah was internal and everywhere Allah also had and has an essence which is beyond *al-'alam*: the *Dhatullah*. When one speaks of the *tawhid* they speak of the monism of all things, when one speaks of the *tanzih* they speak of the incomparability of Allah's essence, his *Dhatullah*.

While I agree to an extent that all are entitled to cultural truth (*al-haqiqa al-thaqafi*), that does not negate the existence of actual facts (*al-haqiqat*), which must also be taught to the ignorant so that they can raise self-awareness to the rest of the 85 percent, and give them awareness of the tricks of the *taghuti*, as Shari'ati explicated, "Similar to the prophets … enlightened souls … neither belong to the community of scientists nor to the camp of unaware and stagnant masses. They are aware and responsible individuals whose most important objective and responsibility is to bestow the great God-given gift of 'self-awareness' to the general public" (Shari'ati 2002: 11).

Even so, it also becomes perceptible that the biopolitic of late modernity is towards a plutocracy, which is protected by the neo-colonialism of the GUSE, which promulgates the ideology of multiculturalism as a ruse for White supremacy and neo-racism, both being ideologies that are justified by the discourse of White superiority. Moreover, we godbodies, as enlightened souls in the tradition of the Prophet and of the Five Percent Nation, and as opposed to the neoliberal intellectuals, represent a movement within the GUSE that counters its domination and chicanery, it is therefore our only responsibility to not be corrupted by *shirk*.

In this light the revolution or Armageddon War announced and prophesied by hip-hop – again, in contradistinction to the protest and boycott stance of the Black Lives Matter activists – was not merely a fantasy but a counter-narrative to rebel against the systematic *shirk* prevalent in *al-mujtama*. And if the godbody culture is really a rebellious counter-culture with a counter-narrative of deviant Black revolutionism, a counter-programme of participatory Black syndicalism, and a counter-discourse of embodied Black eroticism then the master narrative of pan-European distinction, the totalitarian programme of resurrected White liberalism, and the grand discourse of contemporary White superiority, all three being forms of *ishrik*, will thereby face a significant threat. Ultimately, we concede not to invert the grand discourse of Black criminality but to subvert its meaning, to blur its Westernised interpretation.

What we therefore find is that in an ethnographic narrative of the street life there are certain correlates that must be immanently presented. For such narratives to be honest (as opposed to being objective) they must have intersubjective intentionality. To fully understand the streets the ethnographer must stop looking on the players as victims of the system or as passive alteregos being acted upon, but as revolutionary deviants fighting against the system the best way they know how. True, a perceptive anthropologist takes into consideration all underlying political and economic factors to their current condition; but an intersubjective anthropologist also recognises that they do not see themselves as victims or behave as victims but like with Paul Willis (2015) as willing participants in their current circumstances. Accordingly, where Said (2003) felt that the Orient was misrepresented as sensual, erotic, violent, irrational, and childish; the same cannot be said of the ghetto, which is, indeed, *very* sexual, *very* erotic, *very* violent, *very* irrational, and *very* exciting, though not without its banality – a fact underplayed by most movies and criminal dramas.

There is perhaps (and I am speaking autobiographically here) nothing more boring than waiting outside a building at 4:00 in the morning hoping somebody will come by to buy drugs from you. The low-level drug dealer sees no excitement in this they merely do it to survive. Even violence, when it is done to the extent that it is done on the streets, becomes ordinary, normative, even banal. Thus, showing that the question of criminality is not so clear cut, the choices these individuals make to break the law is usually for survival not for thrills, kicks, or incorrigibility.

But on an even deeper level, it is not as though that choice was forced upon them either; they could easily choose to live an honest life and rise within their chosen profession over time. Granted many, like myself, may not have graduated from high school and thereby would be unqualified for fulfilling work so that their options would be severely limited, but the choice of living the street life is itself a rebellion, a form of resistance to the social superstructures in places that have limited their options and have made it so that to be Black is to be in a racially underprivileged position.

Nas, as the archetypal street lifer, godbody, and hip-hop artist, rationalised these "performances of nihilism" (James 2015), by articulating "through rap slow" the implicit cultural value of deviation. The anti-sociability he and his contemporaries glorified was a rebellion against the marginalisations and reconfigurations inherent in neoliberal assimilation. With urban centres like the "New York Metropolis" being the home of rapid globalisation and multicultural disintegration, the godbody performances of nihilism represented a counter-narrative of the similitude to the counter-discursive of Black eroticism and counter-performative of Black syndicalism. Effectively, the performative of the destruction of social theoretics, the tearing down of societal legitimation, was the methodology of choice for opposing the master narrative of pan-European distinction.

Hip-hop, as a ghetto counter-culture, underscores the incompatibility of the urban centre with the suburban periphery – or in contradistinction, the centres of power from the margins of society. The godbody, as the Black culture that spawned hip-hop, is an interesting movement. The basis of the godbody culture is the 18th degree of the 1-40: "What is the duty of a civilized person? To teach the uncivilized people – who are savage – civilization, righteousness, the knowledge of himself, and the science of everything in life, which is love, peace, and happiness." Thereby we have an injunction to educate: "Each one should teach one," as we say. Our teachings, however, go deeper into our counter-culture revealing practices and phenomena that occur uniquely within godbody communities. However, it may seem at this point that some of the solutions I have presented here and throughout this book may be more likely to exacerbate racism and White supremacy than extinguish them; I must therefore remind the reader of the bigger picture.

The main differentiation between defiant revolutionism and violent criminality is a matter of perspective: just like "one man's terrorist is another man's freedom fighter." Distinction is also perceptible through that based on what could be called consciousness, or to better clarify, the central disparity between a criminal and a freedom fighter is their level of consciousness. Yet one could also say that the distinguishing quality between a freedom fighter and a divine is that based on what could be called a love-triad: agape, empathy, and eroticism, which all, in this definition, make up the essence of libido. This I believe will ultimately prove to be the most effective weapon against White supremacy and the abolition of it.

In presenting here my case that White supremacy has not died but has instead become inherent and commonsensical through its discourse of White superiority and its institutions of the plutocratic Empire, I hope to have proven that racism, and its current neo-racist manifestation, will not disappear through the currently adopted academic strategy of deracialisation. I hope to have also shown that due to socio-elasticity even abolished institutions can revive in a more insidious, or even in a *jinn*, kind of way, thereby making them harder to exorcise. Moreover, it seems to be the tendency of human beings to forget atrocities when the heat of them cools down a little. In this, while Black Lives Matter was important from 2013-2020 its novelty seems to have worn off.

We should now therefore try to keep from wasting our time fighting to stop White people from killing Black people as such would be a futile effort. Nor should it be the determination of our people to simply have White people leave us alone – as two generations down the line they will only return to their ways in a more subtle and unconscious manifestation. What the second election of Donald Trump has shown, is, no longer must it be the determination of our people to extinguish the symptoms of White fear, hatred, and racism towards us; but to extinguish the source, which is White supremacy. The current form of White supremacy itself has its basis in the concatenation of neo-racism, neo-statism, neoliberalism, and neo-colonialism (each needing to be opposed and abolished in the order provided here). For this cause, I recommend that you re-read this book a few times to fully capture the general principles of what each of these systems represents as we mount our opposition throughout this potentially centuries long late modern epoch. True indeed, it must be a counter-cultural opposition, but it is the only thing short of all-out race war that can redirect our frustration toward the goal of freedom, justice, and equality for the Black diaspora.

Conclusion

The social science that has been provided throughout this book was a case of what has been called *observant participation* (Wacquant 2008) and was based primarily on personal discussions and debates I had in the 1990s with my friend from Brooklyn. It is now up to those who have read it – being admittedly more apologia than ethnographa – to articulate and disseminate this counter-narrative of deviant Black revolutionism, thereby showing to both the street lifers and the mainstream the revolutionary significance of the Black counter-culture. Basically, and speaking in a very generalised fashion, just as White supremacy has become inherent within White society, even so, opposition to White supremacy has become inherent within the psychology of Black street lifers.

I have therefore also tried throughout to promote godbodyism as a form of anarcho-Islamism in its fight against the evils of White supremacy and White neo-colonialism. It is engraved on the tombstone of Karl Marx: "philosophers have only interpreted the world in various ways, the point however is to change it" (Marx; quoted in Giddens & Sutton 2021; 75). This quote was taken from his Theses on Feuerbach, yet the same could also be said of us theologians if we are not careful to fight for definite changes in the world. In our current world of neo-colonialism various groups may comment or speak out, but it is only four groups that are actively fighting. These four groups are: the post-colonialists, the anti-imperialists, the Islamists, and the godbodies.

Post-colonialism uses anti-colonialism, anti-racism, and pro-representationalism for people of colour. According to Homi Bhabha one of the chief spokesmen on the subject, post-colonialism: "introduces a temporal dimension … that the future of the colonized world – 'The Third World must start over a new history of Man …' – is imaginable, or achievable, only in the process of resisting the peremptory and polarizing choices that the superpowers impose[d] on their 'client' states" (Bhabha 2004: xxi). Herein, the post-colonial discourse is about separating the so-called Third World from the domination and influence of the superpowers. However, the main method used by post-colonialists is still the discourse and discursive reasoning.

Anti-imperialism is a form of post-colonialism that also uses anti-capitalism, anti-communism, and pro-justice ideas for both local and global communities. According to Susan George, one of the leading lights of this movement: "My own basket of global campaigning priorities … include debt cancellation, international taxation with democratic redistribution in order to move towards welfare states everywhere, global warming and ecological destruction, food security and sovereignty, the protection and improvement of public services … total overhaul of the international financial institutions and the establishment of an International Trade Organisation along the lines proposed by John Maynard Keynes" (George 2004: 49). The anti-imperialism struggle is mainly fought non-violently through protests, strikes, and occupations. Though they have won some gains, they, however, have had major losses, particularly since the 2008-09 recession.

Islamism is a form of anti-imperialism that also uses anti-secular, anti-democratic, and pro-Muslim ideas so as to inspire global solidarity. To be sure, not all Islamists are terrorists as represented by bin Laden and his ilk. However, all Islamists have a problem with modernity and modernisation. According to Ali Shari'ati, a prominent Islamist, "Modernity was the best method of diverting the non-European world, from whatever form and mold of thinking, from their own mold ... [of] thought and personality. It became the sole task of Europeans to place the temptation of 'modernization' before the non-European societies of any complexion. The Europeans realized that by tempting the inhabitants of the East with a compulsive desire for modernization, [they] would cooperate with them to deny [their] own past and desecrate and destroy with [their] own hands the constituents of [their] unique culture, religion and personality" (Shari'ati 2006: 27). As secularism, democracy, capitalism, communism, and imperialism are all aspects of modernism the Islamists view modernity itself with suspicion and fight to bring these institutions to an end.

Finally, godbodyism is a form of Islamism that also uses anti-state, anti-tricknology, and pro-sex ideas to prove that all people of colour are a divine people. We are Islamist inasmuch as we love and believe in the Quran, and in that we say, "Islam is a natural way of life, not a religion." Though we are a form of Islamism, we are non-religious, or, at least, supra-religious. Again, our anti-imperialism, anti-racism, and anti-statism are mainly due to our desire to remove all oppression, but being pro-sex we believe in the sexual liberation of all women in their struggles against the Victorian standards of sexuality. Also, though cultural

Muslims, we say Allah is manifested in all people of colour and that those people of colour who otherwise behave or have behaved other than divine have only done so due to the aftereffects of slavery, colonialism, racism, and orientalism. Thereby we go beyond anti-racism and seek to empower the various races of the world by delineating and personalising their divinity providing historical and social proofs of such divinity and potential.

The second purpose of this book has been to articulate the anarchism of the godbody theory. Hereby, due to the current illegalism of some of our members, and our own aggressive hatred of the police, most of us are already anti-state seeing the state as a means of oppression against the people that corrupts nations. While some of us may be willing to work with the government to fight for social change, for the most part the government is deemed just as corrupted as the state it directs. Ultimately, we godbodies seek the overthrow of the state and its replacement with ghetto parliaments and ciphers. This is a second area where the godbodies agree with anarchism: we have a syndicalist structure. Our parliaments operate similar to labour councils and would be very effective as labour councils if put into practice as such.

A third area where the godbodies are similar to anarchists is with the use of social revolutionism, predominantly illegalism. Though most anarchists are ideologically social revolutionaries we godbodies have thus far had no ideological training. But our righteousness is an even higher righteousness than that of the state, whose laws we do not recognise, therefore there is some serious significance to our illegalism. Finally, our prohibition of marriage according to the government means that we also advocate for free love, and some even go so far as practicing plural love. In these ways we have much in common with anarchism, so it is my hope that through introducing these truths to us godbody I may help us to achieve the goal of becoming a world class Black ideology in the near future.

Obviously, there are other areas of this theory that still need tweaking, however, as a form of Black ideology this could take godbodyism very far. Ultimately, the Black thearchy developed throughout is a kind of countercultural, hypersexual, theocentric, postsecular, supra-religious, neo-libertine, trans-utilitarian, quasi-Freudian, socio-Newtonian, ultra-Darwinian, eroto-masochist, proto-seductionist, light-exhibitionist, semi-essentialist, anti-racist, beta-militarist, pan-eternalist, bio-monist, inter-subjectivist, and Négro-theist perspective and lifestyle. Though this variation in itself may not be the common version of godbodyism it is the Shahidian version I myself have chosen to adopt and encourage for those willing to join me and the rest of the Black thearchists in our struggle to overcome all the ills of the modern status quo. It has also allowed me to apply the methodologies of supreme mathematics, mechanical analysis, and *observant participation* (Wacquant 2008) to various correspondences I had with my enlightener God Born Supreme Allah for the spreading of his GBSA-ideology thereby popularising our movement.

Lastly, this has been a very joyful project to write about and I am so glad you made it all the way to the end. If you are willing I have one final request: if you have gained or learned anything you feel to be of value please remember to leave a review on the platform that you purchased this book from. It is little things like that that allow authors like myself to gain a wider readership and validation for our efforts. I would also love to hear some of the stories from those who have been touched by this work. Thank you so much for your love and support, and to you my people: all the love in the world. Peace.

Afterward

In unifying all the desultory ideas of this book – late modernism, neoliberalism, neo-colonialism, post-Marxism, cultural Islamism, Black revolutionism, pseudo-multiculturalism, and defiance against the GUSE – I would like to end with a section from a poem by Aimé Césaire:

> *"THE REBEL (harshly): My name – an offence; my Christian name – humiliation; my status – a rebel; my age – the stone age.*
>
> *THE MOTHER: My race – the human race. My religion – brotherhood.*
>
> *THE REBEL: My race: that of the fallen. My religion … but it's not you that will show it to me with your disarmament …*
>
> *'tis I myself, with my rebellion and my poor fists clenched and my woolly head … (Very calm) I remember one November day; it was hardly six months ago … The master came into the cabin in a cloud of smoke like an April moon. He was flexing his short muscular arms – he was a very good master – and he was rubbing his little dimpled*

face with his fat fingers. His blue eyes were smiling and he couldn't get the honeyed words out of his mouth quick enough. 'The kid will be a decent fellow,' he said looking at me, and he said other pleasant things too, the master — that you had to start very early, that twenty years was not too much to make a good Christian and a good slave, a steady, devoted boy, a good commander's chain-gang captain, sharp-eyed and strong-armed. And all that man saw of my son's cradle was that it was the cradle of a chain-gang captain.

We crept in knife in hand ...

THE MOTHER: *Alas, you'll die for it.*

THE REBEL: *Killed ... I killed him with my own hands ...*

Yes, 'twas a fruitful death, a copious death ...

It was night. We crept among the sugar canes.

The knives sang to the stars, but we did not heed the stars.

The sugar canes scarred our faces with streams of green blades.

THE MOTHER: *And I had dreamed of a son to close his mother's eyes.*

THE REBEL: *But I chose to open my son's eyes upon another sun.*

AFTERWARD

THE MOTHER: *O my son, son of evil and unlucky death –*

THE REBEL: *Mother of living and splendid death,*

THE MOTHER: *Because he has hated too much,*

THE REBEL: *Because he has too much loved.*

THE MOTHER: *Spare me, I am choking in your bonds. I bleed from your wounds.*

THE REBEL: *And the world does not spare me … There is not anywhere in the world a poor creature who's been lynched or tortured in whom I am not murdered and humiliated …*

THE MOTHER: *God of Heaven, deliver him!*

THE REBEL: *My heart, thou wilt not deliver me from all that I remember …*

It was an evening in November …

And suddenly shouts lit up the silence;

We had attacked, we the slaves; we, the dung underfoot, we the animals with patient hooves,

We were running like madmen; shots rang out … We were striking. Blood and sweat cooled and refreshed us. We were striking where the shouts came from, and the shouts became more strident and a great clamour rose from the east: it was the outhouses burning and the flames flickered sweetly on our cheeks.

Then was the assault made on the master's house.

They were firing from the windows.

We broke in the doors.

The master's room was wide open. The master's room was brilliantly lighted, and the master was there, very calm ... and our people stopped dead ... it was the master ... I went in. 'It's you,' he said, very calm.

It was I, even I, and I told him so, the good slave, the faithful slave, the slave of slaves, and suddenly his eyes were like two cockroaches, frightened in the rainy season ... I struck, and the blood spurted; that is the only baptism that I remember today" (Césaire 1946; quoted in Fanon 1969: 68).

Attention African American Theologians!!!
Introducing the Revolutionary New Way of Understanding Black Theology

Black Divinity: A Ghetto Theology for the Black Community [Remastered] is the first instalment in Shahidi Islam's Shahidi Collection revealing the depths of street spirituality and the theological genius of Black thearchic principles.

Black Divinity

Bibliography

Various Authors (2008); *The Bible Authorized King James Version with Apocrypha*; Oxford University Press.

Ali, M. M. (2002); *The Holy Qur'an with English Translation and Commentary*; Ahmadiyya Anjuman Isha'at Islam Lahore Inc,. U.S.A.

Abu-Lughod, L (1991); "Writing Against Culture." In R. G. Fox (Eds), *Recapturing Anthropology, Working in the Present*; School Of American Research Press.

Adler, A (1964); *The Individual Psychology of Alfred Adler: A Systematic Presentation in Selections From His Writings*; Harper & Row, Publishing, Inc.

Ahmad, A (2008); *In Theory: Classes, Nations, Literatures*; Verso.

Alexander, M (2011); *The New Jim Crow: Mass Incarceration in the Age of Colorblindness*; The New Press.

Allah, G. B. S. (2015); *Letter From God Born Supreme Allah to Shahidi Islam*.

Arnold, G (2006); *Africa: A Modern History*; Atlantic Books.

AZ (1994); "Life's A Bitch." In: *Illmatic* [CD]. Columbia, Sony Music Group.

Bakunin, M (2005); *Statism and Anarchy*; Cambridge University Press.

BIBLIOGRAPHY

Balibar, E, Wallerstein, I (1991); *Race, Nation, Class: Ambiguous Identities*; Verso.

Bauman, Z (2016); *Liquid Modernity*; Polity Press.

Bauman, Z (2003); *Identity Conversations with Benedetto Vecchi*; Polity Press.

De Beauvoir, S (2009); *The Second Sex*; Vintage Classics.

Behrent, M, C (2016); "Liberalism without Humanism: Michel Foucault and the Free-Market Creed." In D. Zamora & M. C. Behrent (Eds), *Foucault and Neoliberalism*; Polity Press.

Berman, E (2010); "Domestic Intelligence: New Powers, New Risks." Brennan Center for Justice at NYU School of Law.

Bernasconi, R (2011); "The Great White Error and the Great Black Mirage: Frantz Fanon's Critical Philosophy of Race." In N. Gibson (Ed), *Living Fanon: Global Perspectives*; Palgrave Macmillan.

Bhabha, H (2004); 'Forward: Framing Fanon', in F. Fanon *The Wretched of the Earth*; Grove Press.

Bruder, E (2012); *The Black Jews of Africa History, Religion, Identity*; Oxford University Press.

Callinicos, A. T. (2003); *An Anti-Capitalist Manifesto*; Polity Press.

Castells, M, Portes, A (1989); "World Underneath: The Origins, Dynamics, and Effects of the Informal Economy." In A. Portes (Ed), *The Informal Economy*; John Hopkins University Press.

Chittick, W (1989); *The Sufi Path of Knowledge*; State University of New York Press.

Chittick, W. C (2013); *Sufism: A Beginner's Guide*; Oneworld Publication.

Chomsky, N (1999); *Profit Over People: Neoliberalism and Global Order*; Seven Stories Press.

Chomsky, N (2003); *Understanding Power: The Indispensable Chomsky*; Vintage Books.
Chomsky, N, Foucault, M (2006); *The Chomsky-Foucault Debate On Human Nature*; The New Press.
Chomsky, N, Achcar, G (2007); *Perilous Power: The Middle East and US Foreign Policy Dialogues on Terror, Democracy, War and Justice*; Penguin Books.
Chiu, C-y, Leung, A, K-y, Hong, Y-y (2011); "Cultural Processes: An Overiew." In A. K-Y. Leung, C-Y Chiu & Y-Y Hong (Eds), *Cultural Processes: A Social Psychological Perspective*; Cambridge University Press.
Christofferson, M, S (2016); "Foucault and New Philosophy: Why Foucault Endorsed André Glucksmann's *The Master Thinkers*." In D. Zamora & M. C. Behrent (Eds), *Foucault and Neoliberalism*; Polity Press.
Clifford, J (1986); "Introduction: Partial Truths." In J. Clifford & G. E. Marcus (Eds), *Writing Culture: The Poetics and Politics of Ethnography*; University of California Press.
Comte, A (1986); *The Positive Philosophy of Auguste Comte*; Bell & Sons.
Daulatzai, S (2012); *Black Star, Crescent Moon: The Muslim International and Black Freedom Beyond America*; University of Minnesota Press.
Davis, A (2003); *Are Prisons Obsolete?*; Seven Stories Press.
Degnbol-Martinussen, J, Engberg-Pedersen, P (2005); *Aid: Understanding International Development Cooperation*; Zed Book Ltd.
Descartes, R (2003); *Meditations and Other Metaphysical Writings*; Penguin Classics.
Derrida, J (2006); *Specters of Marx*; Routledge Classics.
Douglas, M (2002); *Purity and Danger: An Analysis of Concepts of Pollution and Taboo*; Routledge Classics Edition.
Houston, D. D. (2007); *Wonderful Ethiopians of the Ancient Cushite Empire*; NuVision Publications, LLC.

Durkheim, E (2013); *The Rules of Sociological Method: And Selected Texts on Sociology and its Method*; Free Press.

Durkheim, E, Mauss, M (2009); *Primitive Classification*; Taylor & Francis.

Engberg-Pedersen, P, Gibbon, P, Raikes, P, Udsholt, L (1996); *Limits of Adjustment in Africa: The Effects of Economic Liberalization, 1986-94*; James Curry Ltd., Heinemann, Reed Publishing.

En Vogue (1992); *En Vogue – My Lovin' (You're Never Gonna Get It)*. [ONLINE] Available at: https://www.youtube.com/watch?v=JIuYQ_4TcXg. [Accessed 27 August 2016].

En Vogue (1996); *En Vogue - Don't let go (Love) Version 2*. [ONLINE] Available at: https://www.youtube.com/watch?v=Uyu7Oq7qApo. [Accessed 27 August 2016].

Fanon, F (1965); *A Dying Colonialism*; Grove Press.

Fanon, F (1969); *The Wretched of the Earth*; Penguin Books.

Fanon, F (2008); *Black Skin, White Masks*; Pluto Press.

Farrakhan, L (1989); *The Announcement: A Final Warning to the U.S. Government*; The Final Call Inc.; (1996); "Day of Atonement." In H. R. Madhubuti & M. Karenga (Eds), *Million Man March Day of Absence: A Commemorative Anthology Speeches commentary, Photography, Poetry, Illustrations, Documents*; Third World Press, University of Sankore Press.

Farris, S, R (2016); *Dispossessing the private sphere? Civic integration policies and colonial Legacies*. [ONLINE] Available at: http://www.darkmatter101.org/site/ [Accessed 5 September 2016].

Ferguson, J (2014); *The Anti-Politics Machine: "Development," Depoliticiation and Bureaucratic Power in Lesotho*; University of Minnesota Press.

Feuer, L. S., McLennan, D. T. (2015); "Marx, Karl." Encyclopæpia Britannica; *Standard Edition*; Encyclopæpia Britannica.
Ficek, D (2011); "Reflections on Fanon and Petrification." In N. Gibson (Ed), *Living Fanon: Global Perspectives*; Palgrave Macmillan.
Foucault, M (1989); *Madness and Civilization*; Routledge Classics.
Foucault, M (2006); *The Chomsky-Foucault Debate On Human Nature*; The New Press.
Foucault, M (2009); *Michel Foucault Security, Territory, Population Lectures at the Collège de France 1977-1978*; Palgrave Macmillan.
Foucault, M (2010); *Michel Foucault The Birth of Biopolitics Lectures at the Collège de France 1978-1979*; Palgrave Macmillan.
Fukuyama, F (2012); *The End of History: And the Last Man*; Penguin Books.
George, S (2001); "Corporate Globalisation." In E. Bircham & J. Charlton (Eds), *Anti-Capitalism A Guide to the Movement*; Bookmarks Publications Ltd.
George, S (2004); "Taking the Movement Forward." In T. Behan & A. Brown (Eds), *Anti-Capitalism: Where Now?*; Bookmarks Publications Ltd.
Gholson, W (1996); "One Million Men." In H. R. Madhubuti & M. Karenga (Eds), *Million Man March Day of Absence: A Commemorative Anthology Speeches commentary, Photography, Poetry, Illustrations, Documents*; Third World Press, University of Sankore Press.
Giddens, A, Sutton, P. W (2021); *Sociology 9th Edition*; Polity Press.
Gleick, J (1998); *Chaos: The Amazing Science of the Unpredictable*; Vintage Books.
Goldman, R, Papson, S (1996); *Sign Wars: The Cluttered Landscape of Advertising*; The Guilford Press.

Greenberg, I (2014); *Surveillance in America: Critical Analysis of the FBI, 1920 to the Present*; Lexington Books.
Hardt, M, Negri, A (2000); *Empire*; Harvard University Press.
Harvey, D (2011); *A Brief History of Neoliberalism*; Oxford University Press.
Hoover, J. E. (2016); *COINTELPRO Long-Range Goals and Prevention of a Black "Messiah"*. [ONLINE] Available at: http://genius.com/Federal-bureau-of-investigation-cointelpro-long-range-goals-and-prevention-of-a-black-messiah-annotated. [Accessed 22 December 2016].
Hudson, M (2021); *Super Imperialism: The Economic Strategy of American Empire Third Edition*; ISLET-Verlag.
Huntington, S. P. (1996); *The Clash of Civilizations and the Remaking of World Order*; Simon & Schuster, Inc.
Husserl, E (1999); *The Essential Husserl Basic Writings in Transcendental Phenomenology*; Indiana University Press.
Ibn Katheer Dimashqi, H (2006); *Book of the End: Great Trials and Tribulations*; Maktaba Dar-us-Salam.
Islam, S (2023); *Demystifying God: Redefining Black Theology in the Age of iGod*; Draft2Digital.
Jackson, S. A. (2005); *Islam and the Blackamerican Looking Toward the Third Resurrection*; Oxford University Press.
Jade (1994); *Mind, Body & Soul - Every Day of the Week*. [ONLINE] Available at: https://www.youtube.com/watch?v=SNmGFx0c-ck. [Accessed 27 August 2016].
James, M (2015); "Nihilism and urban multiculture in outer East London." *The Sociological Review* 63 (August 2015): 699-719.
Klein, N (2010); *No Logo: Taking Aim at the Brand Bullies*; Picador.
Jowett, B (2016); *Symposium by Plato*; Enhanced Media Publishing.

Knight, M. M. (2011); *Why I Am a Five Percenter*; Penguin Group.
Lear, J (1998); *Love and Its Place in Nature: A Philosophical Interpretation of Freudian Psychoanalysis*; Yale University Press.
Lenin, V (2014); *State and Revolution*; Haymarket Books.
Lévi-Strauss, C (1972); *The Savage Mind*; World University, Weidenfeld and Nicolson Ltd.
Madhubuti, H. R. (1996); "Took Back Our Tears, Laughter, Love and Left a Big Dent in the Earth." In H. R. Madhubuti & M. Karenga (Eds), *Million Man March Day of Absence: A Commemorative Anthology Speeches commentary, Photography, Poetry, Illustrations, Documents*; Third World Press, University of Sankore Press.
Majavu, M (2008); "Africa: Life After Colonialism." In C. Spannos (Ed), *Real Utopia: Participatory Society for the 21st Century*; AK Press.
Malcioln, J. V. (1996); *The African Origins of Modern Judaism: From Hebrews to Jews*; Africa World Press, Inc.
Marx, K (1978); *The Marx-Engels Reader*; W. W. Norton & Company, Inc.
Marx, K, Engels, F (2012); *The Communist Manifesto*; Verso.
McChesney, R. W. (1998); *Profit Over People: Neoliberalism and Global Order*. Seven Stories Press.
Mellino, M (2011); "Notes from the Underground, Fanon, Africa, and the Poetics of the Real." In N. Gibson (Ed), *Living Fanon: Global Perspectives*; Palgrave Macmillan.
Mendelssohn, S (1920); *The Jews of Africa: Especially in the Sixteenth and Seventeenth Centuries (1920)*; Kissinger Legacy Reprints.
Method Man, Blige, M, J (1995); "I'll Be There for You/You're All I Need to Get By." In: *I'll Be There for You/You're All I Need to Get By* [EP]. Def Jam Recordings, Universal Music Group.

Mobb Deep (1995); "Temperature's Rising." In: *The Infamous* [CD]. Loud, RCA, Bertelsmann Music Group Company.
Morel, E. D. (1902); *Affairs of West Africa*; William Heinemann.
Mudimbe, V. Y. (1988); *The Invention of Africa Gnosis, Philosophy, and the Order of Knowledge*; Indiana University Press.
Muhammad, E (1965); *Message to the Blackman in America*; Muhammad's Temple No. 2, The Final Call Inc.
Muhammad, E (1973); *The Fall of America*; Muhammad's Temple No. 2, The Final Call Inc.
Muhammad, E (2004); *The Theology of Time: The God Science of Time*; Secertarius Publications.
Muller, G (2013); Eden: *The Biblical Garden Discovered In East Africa*; Pomegranate Publishing London.
Nas (1994); "One Love." In: *Illmatic* [CD]. Columbia, Sony Music Group.
Nas (1995); "Eye for an Eye (Your Beef Is Mine)." In: *The Infamous* [CD]. Loud, RCA, Bertelsmann Music Group Company.
Nas (1996); "Silent Murder." In: *It Was Written* [CD]. Columbia, Sony Music Entertainment Inc.
Nas, Aaliyah (1999); "You Won't See Me Tonight." In: *I Am...* [CD]. Columbia, Sony Music Entertainment Inc.
Neocosmos, M (2011); "The Nation and Its Politics: Fanon, Emanicipatory Nationalism, and Political Sequences." In N. Gibson (Ed), *Living Fanon: Global Perspectives*; Palgrave Macmillan.
Newton, H. P. (2002); *The Huey P. Newton Reader*; Seven Stories Press.
Nkrumah, K (2009); *Consciencism: Philosophy and Ideology for De-Colonization*; Monthly Review Press.
No, S, Wan, C, Chao, M. M., Rosner, J. L., Hong, Y-y (2011); "Bicultural Identity Negotiation." In A. K-Y. Leung, C-Y

Chiu & Y-Y Hong (Eds), *Cultural Processes: A Social Psychological Perspective*; Cambridge University Press.

Ortner, S. B. (1974); "Is female to male as nature is to culture?" In M. Z. Rosaldo & L. Lamphere (Eds), *Woman, Culture, and Society*; Stanford University Press.

Perkins, J (2006); *Confessions of an Economic Hitman: The Shocking Inside Story of How America Really Took Over the World*; Ebury Publishing, Random House Group.

Philips, A (1991); *Engendering Democracy*; Polity Press.

Pinker, S (2003); *The Blank Slate: The Modern Denial of Human Nature*; Penguin Books.

Rehmann, J (2016); "The Unfulfilled Promises of the Late Foucault and Foucauldian 'Governmentality Studies'." In D. Zamora & M. C. Behrent (Eds), *Foucault and Neoliberalism*; Polity Press.

Ross, R (2014); *A Concise History of South Africa*; Cambridge University Press.

Said, E (2003); *Orientalism*; Penguin Books.

Shakur, A (1987); *Asata: An Autobiography*; Lawrence Hill and Co.

Shari'ati, A (1979); *On the Sociology of Islam: Lectures by Ali Shari'ati*; Mizan Press.

Shari'ati, A (1980); *Marxism and Other Western Fallacies*; Mizan Press.

Shari'ati, A (1981); *Man & Islam*; Islamic Publications International. [ONLINE] Available at: https://www.amazon.co.uk. [Accessed 01/03/2023].

Shari'ati, A (2002); *Where Shall We Begin? Enlightened Thinkers and the Revolutionary Society*; Citizens International.

Shari'ati, A (2003); *Religion vs. Religion*; ABC International Group.

Shari'ati, A (2006); *Civilization and Modernization: What's the Difference*; Citizens International.

Shari'ati, A (2011); *The Islamic Renaissance Series: Capitalism Wakes Up!*; [Kindle App Edition]; ABJAD Book Designers and Builders. [ONLINE] Available at: https://www.amazon.co.uk. [Accessed 19/11/2022].
Sheller, M (2012); *Citizenship From Below: Erotic Agency and Caribbean Freedom*; Duke University Press.
Skousen, M (2017); *The Big Three in Economics: Adam Smith, Karl Marx, and John Maynard Keynes*; Routledge.
Smif-N-Wessun (1995); "Home Sweet Home." In: *Dah Shinin'* [CD]. Wreck Records, Nervous, Inc.
Stenning, D, J (1959); *Savannah Nomads: A Study of the Wodabe Pastoral Fulani of Western Bornu Province Northern Region, Nigeria*; Oxford University Press.
Stoller, P (2002); *Money Has No Smell: The Africanization of New York City*; The University of Chicago Press, Ltd.
Strong, J (1990); *The New Strong's Exhaustive Concordance of the Bible*; Thomas Nelson Publishers.
SWV (1996); *SWV - Use Your Heart*. [ONLINE] Available at: https://www.youtube.com/watch?v=7H_o5whdCQA. [Accessed 27 August 2016].
Tyldesley, J (2011); *The Penguin Book of Myths & Legends of Ancient Egypt*; Penguin Books.
Wacquant, L (2008); *The Body, the Ghetto and the Penal State*. [ONLINE] Available at: http://loicwacquant.net/assets/Papers/BODYGHETTOPENALSTATE.pdf. [Accessed 16 November 2016].
Wacquant, L (2016); "Bourdieu, Foucault, and the Penal State in the Neoliberal Era." In D. Zamora & M. C. Behrent (Eds), *Foucault and Neoliberalism*; Polity Press.
Walker, A (1982); *The Color Purple*; Harcourt Brace Jovanovich.
Williams, J (1928); *Hebrewisms of West Africa: From the Nile to the Niger with the Jews*; Africa Tree Press.

Willis, P (2015); *Learning to Labour: How Working Class Kids Get Working Class Jobs*; Ashgate Publishing Limited.

Windsor, R. R. (2003); *From Babylon to Timbuktu A History of Ancient Black Races Including the Black Hebrews*; Windsor Golden Series.

Worrill, C. W. (1996); "Beyond the Million Man March." In H. R. Madhubuti & M. Karenga (Eds), *Million Man March Day of Absence: A Commemorative Anthology Speeches commentary, Photography, Poetry, Illustrations, Documents*; Third World Press, University of Sankore Press.

Xscape (1995); *Off the Hook - Feels So Good*. [ONLINE] Available at: https://www.youtube.com/watch?v=7H_o5whdCQA. [Accessed 27 August 2016].

Zamora, D (2016); "Foucault, the Excluded, and the Neoliberal Erosion of the State." In D. Zamora & M. C. Behrent (Eds), *Foucault and Neoliberalism*; Polity Press.

www.ingramcontent.com/pod-product-compliance
Lightning Source LLC
Chambersburg PA
CBHW071732150426
43191CB00010B/1552